UML Applied:
A .NET Perspective

MARTIN L. SHOEMAKER

Apress™

UML Applied: A .NET Perspective
Copyright ©2004 by Martin L. Shoemaker

ISBN (pbk): 1-59059-087-2

Printed and bound in the United States of America 10987654321

Contributor: Victoria Hudgson

Technical Reviewers: Gary Evans, Victoria Hudgson

Editorial Board: Steve Anglin, Dan Appleman, Ewan Buckingham, Gary Cornell, James Cox, Tony Davis, John Franklin, Chris Mills, Steve Rycroft, Dominic Shakeshaft, Jim Sumser, Karen Watterson, Gavin Wray, John Zukowski

Assistant Publisher and Project Manager: Grace Wong

Senior Copy Editor: Ami Knox

Production Manager: Kari Brooks

Production Editor: Janet Vail

Proofreader: Elizabeth Berry

Compositor: Susan Glinert Stevens

Indexer: Valerie Haynes Perry

Artist: April Milne

Cover Designer: Kurt Krames

Manufacturing Manager: Tom Debolski

Distributed to the book trade in the United States by Springer-Verlag New York, Inc., 175 Fifth Avenue, New York, NY, 10010 and outside the United States by Springer-Verlag GmbH & Co. KG, Tiergartenstr. 17, 69112 Heidelberg, Germany.

In the United States: phone 1-800-SPRINGER, email orders@springer-ny.com, or visit http://www.springer-ny.com. Outside the United States: fax +49 6221 345229, email orders@springer.de, or visit http://www.springer.de.

For information on translations, please contact Apress directly at 2560 Ninth Street, Suite 219, Berkeley, CA 94710. Phone 510-549-5930, fax 510-549-5939, email info@apress.com, or visit http://www.apress.com.

For Dad . . . for teaching me how to work
For Mother. . . for teaching me how to think
For Sandy . . . for teaching me how to be me

Contents at a Glance

Contents

Foreword

I WANT TO TELL YOU about three things: 1) myself, 2) my view of UML, process, and .NET and 3) Martin L. Shoemaker. From these three things, I hope to give you a perspective on the value this book offers me—and most likely you, too.

About Me

As a developer, I've been "introduced" to several development processes and methodologies. The documentation for these processes literally covered feet of shelf space. I've also encountered a number of diagramming systems. To me, most of the latter come across as a boatload of funny symbols with a bunch of nuanced meanings dreamed up by their inventors and proponents. In both cases, I could easily see a half year of my life dedicated to understanding these systems.

What would I gain from investing so much time in learning how someone *else* thinks about building software? And, if I do invest the time to learn a new vocabulary to discuss software systems, with whom will I communicate?

Let's face it, irrespective of the part of the software lifecycle you're involved in, you're expected to produce something that looks or behaves in a specific, predictable manner. Note that I didn't say we always know what form that behavior will take! What I'm getting at here is that we have to have a mental model of what we're creating, and that model must be communicated and understood. To be successful, that model must also be complete and internally consistent. Complete, not in every detail, but complete end to end. If you aren't a control freak at some level, you're ill equipped to navigate the myriad process paths—and spirals and dead ends—that characterize today's projects.

For me, I must have that mental model and then I can get something working that takes me from point A to point B or at least from point A.1 to A.2. Then I go back and refine what I have created.

About UML, Process, and .NET

UML is a large, complete system for modeling and describing software systems. Rest assured, however, that UML (Unified Modeling Language) is both an industry standard, meaning people actually use it, and standardized, meaning that there is some precision and formal acceptance of its definition. When you speak UML, you aren't just talking to yourself!

When I attended Martin L Shoemaker's UML Bootcamp class, I suppose you could say I was both skeptical and jaded. But I learned two, deeply interrelated things in this class that changed my perspective. I learned about modeling software in the context of a process, in a way that helped me get from point A to point B. For me, this is the most important thing I want to tell you, so I'll say it another way just to underscore my point. I learned that process and modeling could be mutually reinforcing and beneficial for me in building software.

What was the magic bullet? If you read about software development these days, you can't have missed the message that modeling and process are vital to your success. Even before attending Martin's class, I knew that—or at least I knew it intellectually. So how did I get modeling religion? Well, for starters, Martin didn't make us learn diagramming separately from process. He didn't lay out a big project and a complex process for the week as a means of learning UML. Instead, he told us that UML basically is about *pictures in a process*. He taught us a couple of simple diagrams and a simple process called Five-Step UML and helped us get from point A to point B using both. And best of all, Step 2 of Five-Step UML is "Refine" and Step 5 is "Repeat". Hey, that's the way I work!

As a programmer, I know that .NET is a complete abstraction. The CLR is a virtual machine. Developing with .NET is also immediate and results based. Look at how the "code-behind" model brings together namespaces and assemblies on a Web page to deliver applications on the Internet. In the same way, UML is a complete abstraction. With UML you operate in a virtual world in which you design an application. Yet, with Five-Step UML, Martin has made UML very real, very concrete, and very results based.

In addition, because .NET development is largely about creating components and using components (objects, classes, ADTs...choose your *mot du jour*), the ability to model and treat these components as black boxes is a natural fit. Again, with Five-Step UML, it doesn't take 3 forms, 6 approvals, and 2 weeks to take a component, an abstraction, to the next level of detail. I can see it I can use it, and, yes, I can get my head around it.

About Martin

The thing about Martin is that he has a special mix of attributes. Most important for me is that he's a practitioner; he has developed real software for pay in a number of roles. (In other words, he's not just an academician or writer.) That said, Martin is a gifted teacher; he actually cares whether his students have learned something. He's not just someone who delivers *x* hours of content. Nor is Martin pedantic; he wants to use UML to communicate. As Martin says, if it communicates, it's a good diagram. Last, you'll find Martin has an interesting, well-organized mind. Not only will you learn and understand UML at a useful level, you'll have fun in the process.

—Karl Gunderson
Software Design Engineer, Microsoft Business Solutions
Fargo, ND

About the Author

Martin L. Shoemaker is a software developer with seventeen years experience in the industry. He has worked in the fields of color science, online shopping, databases, material handling, medical imaging, and customer relations management. Martin is also an accomplished speaker, having presented to the Detroit Colour Council, the Ann Arbor Computer Society, the Ann Arbor IT Zone, Rubi-Con Security Conference, VS Live!, UML World Conference, Software Development Conference, and Web Services Edge. His most popular presentation is Richard  Hale Shaw's UML BootCamp. He has presented this course both in public settings and for individual clients including: Microsoft, Microsoft Great Plains Business Solutions, Intermec, Siemens Dematic-Rapistan Division, Arthur Andersen Consulting, University of Michigan, Target, Syngenta, Silicon Energy, Tyco International, and more.

Acknowledgments

I WOULD LIKE TO gratefully acknowledge the following inspirations, colleagues, friends, and family for everything they did to inspire or support me in the years that led up to this book. What is good herein has been shaped by what I learned from them; any mistakes herein are all mine.

- My mother and father, for encouraging me to dream and teaching me how to make the dreams come true.

- Richard A. Mulholland and Dr. Charlene Waggoner: best friends, spare brains, consciences, and more.

- The Three Amigos, for creating a communication tool that continues to be better than I think. Every day, I find new power in what they created.

- Richard Hale Shaw, for launching UML Bootcamp and making it grow.

- Bill and Mary Heitzeg, for launching UML for Everyone, for all the work on UML Bootcamp, and for all the chances to play with Gunther.

- Josh Holmes, for great XDE feedback, lots of .NET information, and XML support.

- The managers who encouraged me to learn and apply UML: John Olsen, Steve Stark, and Phil Newsted.

- The friends who have tried to kill me for a fifth of a century: Anita and Mark Buckowing, Rich and Amy Fowler, Brett and Nancy Emaus, Dana and Mary Beth Jack, Aaron Zichterman, John Nash, Lisa Nash, Mark Emaus, Paul Troost, Jim Troost, Gus Lukow, Dale Begley, Brian Ladd, Tim Marvin, Ray Lowrey, Ted Shaw, and Jerry Wyrick. After handling you folks, a room full of students is no challenge at all. Trust me . . .

- Samir Emdanat and Gurusami Sarathy: great roommates who also taught me to appreciate new cultures, new foods, and design patterns.

- Grieg Pedersen, for teaching me that two egos *can* fit in a cubicle and still come out friends.

- The developers at Rapistan who had to suffer through my UML ranting more times than anyone should have to: Mike Kelley, Rob Entingh, John Schroeder, Brian Ruhoff, Jason Hill, Keith Carman, Dale A. Moore, Dave Gritter, Tim Lindgren, Tom Cruttenden, John Williams, Greg King, Lisa Skalecki, Tom Lenartz, Kimberly Sager, Kragh Hertel, Tom Cruttenden, and Jim Terpstra.

- The Ann Arbor Computer Society, for letting me try out material on them.

- My editor, Karen Watterson, for teaching me just how much work a book really is; and all the other fine folks at Apress, for being patient as I learned.

- And always, Sandra M. Shoemaker: partner, teacher, confidante, best and longest friend, favorite artist, and my reason for missing home when I'm teaching. "Wife" hardly seems good enough to describe all you do for me.

Introduction

 TIP **For those who are impatient . . .** If you have no time for philosophy and you just want to start learning the UML notation right away, skip ahead to Chapter 2.

UML for Everybody

ONE OF THE GREAT ironies I see in UML—in any new topic in software technology, but UML is the example I know best—is the incredible mystique it develops, and how that mystique becomes a brick wall between the folks in-the-know who put the technology to use and those who could really benefit from it but don't have time to conquer that mystique. This is ironic and a bit depressing, because often those are exactly the folks with exactly the problems the technology was designed to help. The new technology is supposed to enable them to work faster and more productively. The very fact that they're too busy dooms them to being too busy. And the mystique—with the new buzzwords and a whole new vocabulary—far exceeds the actual learning curve for the technology itself.

And now there's .NET, the newest Microsoft strategy to build a common development platform for the Net-enabled world. As I write this, it's far too soon to tell how successful this strategy will be in the long term. But looking at past paradigm shifts, I can safely predict what the immediate impact will be: even more pressure to *just write code!* We all know that pressure is there. We all know that we succumb to it when we're weak. And we all know the disastrous consequences when we do: the wrong system gets built in the wrong way on the wrong schedule; and all the benefits we hoped to gain instead slowly slip through our fingers. With pressure like that, we feel even less able to explore a new topic like UML. But if you want to lead the pack in the coming world of .NET development, the key is to get to market early *with a well-designed product that meets well-defined user needs.*

The key to UML (with or without .NET) is to ignore the mystique and tackle the learning curve head on. Those who approach UML without fear can usually understand it quickly, with just a little guidance. This is the Unified Modeling *Language*, after all, so it's intentionally designed for communication. The Three Amigos (Grady Booch, James Rumbaugh, and Ivar Jacobson) and the OO community put a lot of thought into making the diagrams communicate if used well. But the mystique and the perceived complexity are huge—I have over 6000 pages of

UML books on my bookshelf right now, and there are a lot I haven't seen yet—and so busy developers and designers keep struggling with problems that Object-Oriented Analysis and Design with UML has already solved. The Unified Modeling Language is many things: a notation for expressing the requirements, architecture, and implementation of a system; a synthesis of ideas from Booch, Rumbaugh, and Jacobson; and a standard adopted by the Object Management Group, just to name a few. But above all, UML is a tool for communication. That's the lesson I want readers to come away with, the key that will unlock the mystique and make sense of it all: if you're communicating, you're using UML well.

So what are you going to communicate? *Models:* high-level, abstract, focused pictures of what a completed system ought to look like in broad strokes. There should be enough detailed information so the developers can see what they have to build, but not so much detail that stakeholders can't see the forest for the trees. These are pictures and descriptions of the system at a sufficient level of abstraction to allow useful feedback from users, analysts, architects, and domain experts. But remember: the point isn't the pictures, but the model. You should never be simply editing a diagram; you should always be editing an underlying model, of which the diagram is just a partial representation. Modeling will let you catch your most costly bugs early, and early detection and correction can save you a factor of 50 to 200 on the cost and schedule of a bug fix.[1]

That leads us to the *U* in UML: *Unified.* Really smart people have been thinking about the problems of OOAD and design in general for over 30 years, and have come up with a wide range of approaches to the problems. Some of these ideas were good, some were brilliant, and some overlapped—a lot. And a lot of effort was wasted in petty little wars over clouds vs. rectangles; while the deep thinkers behind these ideas kept trying to get us beyond petty differences and into larger processes. So the Three Amigos merged the best of their respective ideas and then shamelessly adopted the best ideas from anywhere in the field. "Not Invented Here" wasn't in their vocabulary: if somebody had a good solution to a design problem, they adopted it and folded it into the UML. The result is a rich modeling language that lets you explore design ideas from very simple to very complex, all fitting into the underlying model in well-defined ways. This helps you build solutions faster for two reasons: the language is rich enough to address most common design problems without having to invent or learn a new design approach; and the language is understood by a wide audience, meaning you'll be able to communicate more quickly and effectively.

---

1. Steve McConnell, *Software Project Survival Guide*, p. 29.

Model-Driven Development

As students of my UML Bootcamp can attest, I'm very much a proponent of Object-Oriented Analysis and Design using the Unified Modeling Language, or UML. In my consulting work and in my instruction, I've advocated a process I call *Model-Driven Development,* or MDD:

- You have a number of interrelated models of the problem domain, the requirements, the architecture of your solution, and the individual components of your solution.

- All specification docs reference and are referenced by the models.

- All design and code derives from the models.

- All estimates and schedules are based on the elements of the models.

- All test plans and test cases derive from the models.

- All end-user documentation is shaped by the models.

- All status of all project artifacts is reflected in the models.

So the models become the central artifacts of the process, the central repository of all that is known about the system. I've found that Model-Driven Development with UML consistently helps developers to build better systems by enabling better communication about requirements and designs and concerns and solutions and estimates and schedules, *if* . . .

And that's a big "if": first everyone has to be up to speed and using UML consistently; and *then* your development process must be built around UML. I've developed a discipline that, with practice and patience, will let me base every development activity off the models. But it's not easy, and it can be hard to master. Many teams look at the effort involved and say, "That's great, but we're too busy to learn all that right now." So in this book and in my classes, I start out with Five-Step UML, a lightweight process that's just enough process to help you use UML, but not so much that you can't find the UML among all the process steps.

UML, MDD, and .NET

.NET is more than just a common development platform for networked systems. From the UML perspective, the key feature of .NET is that it's component based, meaning it's inherently easy to reuse and extend—more so even than earlier technologies like COM or COM+. And effective component reuse is best done with component modeling as part of OOAD. Again, you want to get to market early with a well-designed product that meets well-defined user needs. OOAD with UML can help you reach that goal.

Is UML a silver bullet? Of course not. We all know there's no such animal. Good code will still require blood, sweat, tears, pizza, and ingenuity. Good analysis and design will still require well-managed interviews and meetings with customers and domain experts. Good planning will still require realistic, attainable schedule estimates based on analysis, not on trade show schedules—and managers willing to stand up for the estimates. But UML can feed into these activities with better information: better designs for programmers to implement, better communication to get better feedback from the customer during analysis, and better inputs to your schedule estimates. Then you just have to do the rest of the hard work. And I know this will save you time and development costs, because I've seen it on my own projects. By doing detailed OOAD with UML and feeding the results into an estimating tool, I was able to tell the customer exactly what I would deliver when; and though it still took some long nights and a lot of pizza, I delivered the first release of a major subsystem early, under budget, with no major defects, and with more features than originally requested—the sort of results I had never experienced before on any big project. Now that I know that UML can help me do that, I never want to develop any other way. And I hope I can help you to get the same sort of results.

That's the purpose of this book: to cut through the mystique and introduce you to the powerful elements of an Object-Oriented Analysis and Design process (Model-Driven Development) closely centered on the Unified Modeling Language; and then to show how OOAD with UML can help you to master the complexities of .NET development. Some of the material herein was inspired by lessons learned in writing and teaching Richard Hale Shaw's UML Bootcamp seminars (http://www.umlbootcamp.com): not the lessons in the course, but the lessons I learned as I taught the course. Although this book is entirely new material, it builds upon those lessons, the lessons I learned as I taught the course to students from around the world. As I learned what messages got through to the students and what messages fell short, I envisioned a simpler way to convey the principles of UML. I hope that the result is a lightweight, straightforward introduction to UML that will short-circuit the learning curve I experienced. I'm fully convinced that an OOAD process with UML will save you far more than the cost of the learning curve; but if I can slice 6 months off that learning curve for you, I'll have accomplished my goal, reducing the complexity of software development beyond the reach of my own individual projects.

Who Should Read This Book

When I read a statement like that—"Who should read this book"—I imagine the author proclaiming, "Everyone! Everyone should buy *two* copies, in fact, just in case they lose one." The author's responsibility to identify the right audience is in conflict with their pride and their desire to share their work with the world (and their desire to sell lots of copies).

Nevertheless, I'll try to keep my focus on four core audiences:

- *.NET developers:* The most fundamental principle of UML in regard to .NET is simply this: far too few developers know anything about the Unified Modeling Language or how to apply it to .NET development. The first section of this book is thus designed as a tutorial to introduce UML to .NET developers. "Developer" has been my own role throughout most of my career; and this is clearly where my perspectives originate. As I'll point out often throughout this book, if I can keep one developer from being stranded in a warehouse at 3 a.m., I'll have succeeded. Under "developers" I include the following roles: analysts, architects, designers, coders, and maintenance coders. At the same time, I recognize that these roles overlap to a lesser or greater degree in most organizations. If that's the case in your organization, I encourage you to still think of the separate roles as a way to focus on getting the right tasks done at the right time. It's a mistake to get into coding issues during analysis . . . a mistake that is repeated in project after project, in organization after organization.

- *Managers:* I confess: I've made as many manager jokes as anyone this side of Scott Adams.[2] But underlying the jokes is a basic truth: good, effective software management is the key tool in letting developers succeed. Furthermore, managers have a harder job than developers, as a rule, and often the hardest job in all of software development. They're caught in the middle between frustrated developers and frustrated executives and frustrated customers; and somehow, they have to mediate a process that is always in flux. Making their jobs easier will make *everyone's* jobs easier, and I hope I can help in that regard.

---

2. As I'm sure most readers of a book like this know, Scott Adams is the author of the *Dilbert* comic strip, where utterly clueless management is a staple feature. See *The Dilbert Principle* for all the manager jokes anyone should ever need.

- *Testers:* Beleaguered testers who get no respect from developers should be happy to know that *this* developer believes their role to be key to the success of the OOAD process; if they don't provide constant assessment of the process, then *there is no process.* Every bug they find is one less bug that a customer finds and one less developer stranded in a warehouse at 3 a.m. I hope to help their developers and managers to share this perspective and to integrate testing both earlier and more thoroughly.

- *Documenters:* Anyone who writes a book of this length has to have a renewed sympathy for documenters: it's usually easy to tell when you've produced functioning code; but the most thorough reviews and the most careful rewriting will not guarantee successful written communication. And when they have to translate complex technical concepts into useful end-user instruction, their job only gets harder. As I'll emphasize throughout this book, communication is the goal of UML, and that includes communication in the technical and user documents. I hope that an OOAD process that involves documentation both earlier and more thoroughly will make the documenters' jobs easier and thus also make easier the jobs of their end users.

This book provides only minimal introductions to common OO concepts: objects, classes, instances, methods, properties, relations, interfaces, and related topics. Readers who seek further OO instruction should consult one of the OO books listed in the bibliography in Appendix C.

About the Case Study

Selecting an example for teaching UML is no easy task: the subject covers such a wide range of activities; and the potential audience comes from such a wide range of backgrounds. My goal in designing exercises for UML Bootcamp was to find "universal" examples that would be familiar to all of the students; yet I found these to be not universal so much as generic. They were useful for explaining broad concepts, but less useful when I needed to explain rich detail either in the process or in the notation. For those topics, I drew specific examples from my own experience or from projects where I had consulted. The resulting exercises had varying degrees of success: students understood some better than others (based on their own past experience); but the most common feedback I received was that the most useful exercises were the ones that tied together into a larger framework. When the students saw how their decisions in one exercise led into further work in another, they saw the process, not just individual pieces. Their feedback was clear: *carry one project through from start to finish.* This approach isn't without risk: a single project as an example means a single perspective, familiar to some and foreign to others.

I might find that some readers can't get their minds inside a particular novel problem domain and thus can't learn from the examples.

But my main message is that UML is about—say it with me, class—*communication.* If you can't understand the problems, then I've failed to communicate. And while a UML Bootcamp gives me only 5 brief days to communicate ideas to as many as 30 students (and virtually no time to revisit a topic if it remains unclear after a couple of explanations), here I have the luxury of an entire book; and the reader has the luxury to go back and reread the explanations.

So I've defined a hypothetical project for a hypothetical client to use as a case study throughout the book. This case study is the Kennel Management System, as described in the specification in Appendix A. I encourage you to read the vision statement if you need clarification on any of the examples.

 NOTE While I've included some exercises for you to do yourself, these are mostly open-ended, and I leave the choice of project to you. For most of the exercises, you'll need only lots of paper and pencils. You may also find some Post-it notes handy, since you can draw a diagram with them and then rearrange it.[3] If you have a favorite UML tool, I encourage you to use it; but don't let the lack of a tool get in the way of learning UML.

Because UML is about communication, you'll get only limited benefit from performing the exercises in isolation. UML solo is powerful, make no mistake; but the real power of UML comes into play when you share your designs with others and get their feedback. I encourage you to review your solutions with either a partner or an entire team. Good design requires review from other sets of eyes.

I strongly *discourage* you from accepting my solutions for the Kennel Management System herein as "correct" in some absolute sense. You learn as much from flawed designs as from good ones—maybe even more, as you must apply what you learn in order to recognize and correct the flaws. In the process of recognizing my mistakes, you learn to use UML. Mistakes happen, and it's foolish to pretend they won't. It's smart to review for them and correct them.

—Martin L. Shoemaker
Hopkins, MI

---

3. Some authors prefer the generic term *sticky notes;* but I find that generic notes often aren't sticky, falling off after you rearrange them once or twice. Real Post-it notes can be rearranged multiple times, and they just keep on sticking!

A Digression (the First of Many)

As any of my UML Bootcamp students will attest, I'm prone to digressions when I speak. Lots of them. In fact, it's something of a signature in my presentations. (I blame my Dad for this trait, personally. No matter the topic you name, it reminds him of another story . . . which reminds him of another story. . . . Along with his work ethic, I appear to have inherited his penchant for anecdotes. And yes, I know this is a digression within a digression.) I pride myself on eventually tying the digression back to the point I'm trying to make, either directly or through analogy; but I'll admit that the path through the underbrush gets a mite difficult to see at times.

Furthermore, I allow my students to push me into these digressions with no real resistance. I'm there to answer their questions, not simply to blurt out a canned spiel. If they ask a question that points toward arcane questions of programming minutiae—or even off the track from programming entirely—I'll follow the question wherever it leads. Somewhere out there is a relevant point to be made, if we just look hard enough.

I've re-created the best and most relevant of these digressions in this book (and, no doubt, added more). My hope is that these little metaphors will shed light on the development process, helping you to think about it from a different point of view. I think real design is a messy process that can only be structured to a limited degree. Thinking outside the structure is often the key to the hardest problems. I want to encourage that sort of metaphorical thinking.

But to protect those of you who just want the raw material without the metaphorical flavor, I've carefully boxed up these digressions as shown here. A digression like this is a side issue from the main text: a philosophical perspective, a related issue, or an idea for further thought. Feel free to ignore these boxes if you feel the message is clear enough without them.

Part One
UML and Five-Step UML: It's All About Communication

In this first part of the book, I'll introduce you to Object-Oriented Analysis and Design, and the role that UML serves in OOAD. Now that's a bit easier to say than it is to do. A modeling process isn't much use without a modeling language, and a modeling language is only a theoretical abstraction without a process in which to use it. For this reason, we're going to look at both together.

In Chapter 1, I'll focus on some of the basic concepts, moving on in Chapter 2 to look in more detail at Five-Step UML, a light-weight, iterative model-centered process, and at those essential parts of the UML language that will get your development underway. You'll be introduced to different UML diagrams as we use them, so that you can understand their purpose and how to use them in a practical context.

Rules about language and process are all very well in theory, but you'll also need some common sense and some solid practical advice to help you along the modeling road, and that's what we'll focus on in Chapter 3. The guidelines presented in this chapter will improve the communication level in your diagrams.

Finally, because the focus of this book is on learning how to apply UML OOAD to .NET projects, the final chapter of this part of the book will look at the representation of some core .NET concepts in UML. This will facilitate your understanding of the diagrams in the case study that we'll go on to look at in detail in Part Two.

CHAPTER 1

Introducing UML: Object-Oriented Analysis and Design

 TIP   For those who are impatient... If you already understand objects, you don't need convincing that UML is a great thing, and you just want to start learning the UML notation right away, skip ahead to Chapter 2.

IN **UML**, the L is for language, one of the definitions of which is "any means of communicating," according to the *Merriam-Webster Dictionary*. That is the single overriding purpose of UML, or the Unified Modeling Language: to provide a comprehensive notation for communicating the requirements, architecture, implementation, deployment, and states of a system.

UML communicates these aspects from the particular perspective of Object Orientation (OO), in which everything is described in terms of objects: the actions that objects take, the relationships between the objects, the deployment of the objects, and the way the states of the objects change in response to external events.

The starting point in this chapter will be an overview of Object-Oriented Analysis and Design (OOAD), focusing in on the three most important concepts it encompasses—objects, analysis, design—because to understand UML, you first must understand these broader concepts. If you've programmed with any OO language, then you're probably already familiar with a lot of these ideas, so I'll keep this discussion brief. Besides, a full discussion of OOAD is beyond the scope of this book. If you want to explore OOAD further, you should read Booch's *Object-Oriented Analysis and Design with Applications*.[1]

Next, I'll discuss the results of the OOAD process, namely, a model. I'll take a bit of a diversion to discuss the nature of models, how you use them, and why they're important.

---

1.   Grady Booch, *Object-Oriented Analysis and Design with Applications, Second Edition* (Addison-Wesley, 1994). This is the classic work on OOAD, and a must-read.

For the rest of the chapter, I'll be focusing on UML, looking at what it is, and—perhaps more importantly—what it isn't. But before I get started into the nitty gritty of all the different UML elements and diagrams and what the notation looks like (I'll save that for the next chapter!), I'll be showing you some UML diagrams from the case study that I'll be developing in detail in the next part of the book. Now these diagrams aren't there to scare you off: quite the contrary. When you start to look at some real-world UML, you'll see how intuitive it is, and how you can understand much of it without any formal teaching.

Objects

Many modern programming languages depend largely or exclusively on the concept of *objects:* a close syntactic binding of data to the operations that can be performed upon that data. In these Object-Oriented languages—C++, C#, Java, Eiffel, Smalltalk, Visual Basic .NET, Perl, and many others—programmers create classes, each of which defines the behavior and structure of a number of similar objects. Then they write code that creates and manipulates objects that are instances of those classes.

One reason why objects are a powerful programming technique—the reason most often touted in the early literature on Object-Oriented Programming—is that programmatic objects map naturally to real-world objects. Suppose, for example, that your company has to deal with orders. These orders would probably have an ID number and contain information on products. You could create **Order** objects, which would map to these real-world objects, and which would have properties such as **ID** and **ProductList**. You'd probably want to be able to add a product to the order and to submit the order, so you could write **AddProduct** and **SubmitOrder** methods. This mapping between objects in the real world and more abstract code objects encourages programmers to think in the problem domain, rather than in computer science terms. This benefit has perhaps been overstated, however; unless you're building a simulator of a real-world process, such surrogate "real-world" objects form just the surface of your system. The complexity of your design lies underneath that surface, in code that reflects business rules, resource allocation, algorithms, and other computer science concerns. If you only use objects to reflect the real world, you leave yourself with a lot of work.

A more important benefit of classes and objects is that they form a nice syntactic mechanism for achieving some classic aspects of well-designed code:[2]

Encapsulation. The goal of encapsulation is to expose only enough of a module or subsystem to allow other modules to make use of it. Object-Oriented Programming allows you to specify the degree of visibility of elements of your code, so that client code is restricted in what it can access. Thus, you can syntactically seal off implementation details, leading to more flexibility and maintainability in your system.

Loose coupling. *Coupling* refers to the ways in which and degrees to which one part of the system relies on the details of another part. The tighter the coupling, the more changes in one part of the system will ripple throughout the system. With loose coupling, the interfaces between subsystems are well defined and restricted. What lies beyond those interfaces can change without any changes needed in the client subsystems. Object-Oriented Programming supports loose coupling by allowing you to define and publish a class's methods without publishing how those methods are carried out. This principle goes even further in OO languages that support interfaces (described later in this section).

Strong cohesion. *Cohesion* refers to the degree in which elements within a subsystem form a single, unified concept, with no excess elements. Where there is high cohesion, there is easier comprehension and thus more reliable code. Object-Oriented Programming supports strong cohesion by allowing you to design classes in which the data and the functions that operate on them are tightly bound together.

Does OO force you to have these quality attributes in your code? I wish! No matter the language, you can write shoddy code with no encapsulation, pathological coupling, and no cohesion. Furthermore, some OO languages are less rigid than others in how much they require you to design around objects. But OO languages certainly support these quality attributes if you take the time to pursue them.

The key concepts in Object-Oriented Programming are these:

Classes. A class is the definition of the behavior and properties of one or more objects within your system. A class binds the data (attributes) of an object to the behavior (operations) that it can perform.

---

2. Steve McConnell, *Code Complete: A Practical Handbook of Software Construction* (Microsoft Press, 1993), pp. 81–93, 116–130, 150. McConnell provides far more information on code design than I can cover here.

Attributes. An attribute is a data value or state that describes an object and helps you to tell one object from another of the same class. It seems that every new OO language author feels the need to distinguish their language by coming up with new terminology. In some OO languages, these data values are called *properties* or *member variables* or *member data;* but in UML, the proper term is *attributes.*

Operations. An operation is a behavior or function that an object can perform. Depending on the OO language, these might be called *methods* or *member functions* or even *messages.* The last term, *messages,* comes from Smalltalk, one of the earliest OO languages, in which all objects communicated by sending messages to each other. You'll see a similar use of the term *message* when we study Sequence Diagrams.

Objects. An object is an instance or specific example of a class. If Dog is the class, then Betsy, Ladi, Patches, Jake, Radar, and Frosty are specific instances of the class found in my house. The attributes of the class have specific values within an object of that class; and the operations of a class operate on the attributes of individual objects.

Inheritance. This concept indicates that one class (the superclass) provides some common or general behavior inherited by one or more specific classes (the subclasses). The subclasses then provide more or different behavior beyond that defined in the superclass. For example, besides the Dogs, I have Cat objects and Horse objects that live on my property. Each class has unique behaviors: Dogs must be walked, Cats use the litter box, and Horses drop manure that must be scooped up and thrown in the manure pile. Yet all classes have some common behavior: they must be fed, and they must have vet visits. So I can define a super-class, Pet, and have my subclasses, Dog, Cat, and Horse, derive their shared behavior from the Pet class. In UML, this concept is known under the slightly different term of *generalization,* in which a superclass provides the generalized behavior of the subclasses. It's really the same concept, but just looking at it the other way up.

Components. A component is a collection of related classes that together provide a larger set of services. Components in your system might include applications, libraries, ActiveX controls, JavaBeans, daemons, and services. In the .NET environment, *most* of your projects will require component development.

Interfaces. An interface is a definition of a set of services provided by a component or by a class. This allows further encapsulation: the author of a component can publish just the interfaces to the component, completely hiding any implementation details.

Each of these concepts will be explored in more detail as I discuss the UML diagrams that represent them.

Analysis

In software development, *analysis* is the process of studying and defining the problem to be resolved. (We all define the problem before we start solving it, right? Right? Oh, please, *somebody* say "Right!" We can't *all* be that screwed up, can we?) It involves discovering the requirements that the system must perform, the underlying assumptions with which it must fit, and the criteria by which it will be judged a success or failure.

Object-Oriented Analysis (OOA), then, is the process of defining the problem in terms of objects: real-world objects with which the system must interact, and candidate software objects used to explore various solution alternatives. The natural fit of programming objects to real-world objects has a big impact here: you can define all of your real-world objects in terms of their classes, attributes, and operations.

Design

If analysis means defining the problem, then *design* is the process of defining the solution. It involves defining the ways in which the system satisfies each of the requirements identified during analysis.

Object-Oriented Design (OOD), then, is the process of defining the components, interfaces, objects, classes, attributes, and operations that will satisfy the requirements. You typically start with the candidate objects defined during analysis, but add much more rigor to their definitions. Then you add or change objects as needed to refine a solution. In large systems, design usually occurs at two scales: architectural design, defining the components from which the system is composed; and component design, defining the classes and interfaces within a component.

Models

Did you ever build a model ship? When I was young, my mom and I built a model of the famous clipper ship *Cutty Sark*.[3] I've always been fascinated by the tall ships of old; but I really learned about how they work when we built that model. All of the strange nautical terminology from the old pirate movies—forecastle, capstan, main mast, and especially belaying pins ("You mean they're not just there so somebody can pull one out and swing it as a club?")—gained concrete meaning when I assembled them and saw them in the context of the entire system.

Well, that's a central goal of using UML in OOAD: to let you study and understand a system via a model of that system. Like aerodynamic engineers, construction architects, and others in the physical engineering world, you'll build models of systems yet to be built, not just models of existing systems. Your models will let you explore design alternatives and test your understanding of the system at a much faster rate and much lower cost than the rate and cost associated with actually building the system.

"But wait a minute!" the skeptic in the crowd shouts. "I can see the *Cutty Sark*, if I travel to London. And I can see the model *Cutty Sark*, if I visit your home. I can look at the two, and see how the model relates to the real thing. But I can't 'look at' software, except at its user interface. So your model looks like the UI? Isn't that just a prototype?" That's the problem with the usual engineering model analogy as applied to software models: there's no direct physical correspondence between the model and the final product. A better analogy is to models in less tangible scientific disciplines. Quantum physics is a good example of a field in which models help you to understand things you can't see: no one can see quarks or leptons or hadrons or any of the many subatomic particles; and attributes like charm and strangeness have only metaphorical meaning. The models of quantum physics aren't literally true, yet they're very useful in understanding physical phenomena. Software models are like that: useful metaphors and abstractions to help you think about a problem and a solution, not literal depictions of the code itself.

In the case of OOAD with UML, your models consist primarily of diagrams: static diagrams that depict the structure of the system, and dynamic diagrams that depict the behavior of the system. With the dynamic diagrams, you can trace through the behavior and analyze how various scenarios play out. With the static diagrams, you can ensure that each component or class has access to the interfaces and information that it needs to carry out its responsibilities. And it's very easy to make changes in these models: adding or moving or deleting a line takes moments; and reviewing the change in a diagram takes minutes. Contrast that with actually building the code: hours to implement the change, hours more to test and review it.

---

3. See http://www.cuttysark.org.uk/ for pictures and the history of this vessel.

But remember **The Model Rule**:

To use UML effectively, you should never be simply drawing pretty pictures; you should always be editing an underlying model, using the pretty pictures as your user interface.

Your core artifact of the OOAD process is the model. In fact, you will likely have multiple models:

- **Analysis Model.** This is a model of the existing system, the end user's requirements, and a high-level understanding of a *possible* solution to those requirements.

- **Architecture Model.** This is an evolving model of the structure of the solution to the requirements defined in the Analysis Model. Its primary focus is on the architecture: the components, interfaces, and structure of the solution; the deployment of that structure across nodes; and the trade-offs and decisions that led up to that structure.

- **Component (Design) Models.** This is a number of models (roughly, one per component) that depict the internal structure of the pieces of the Architecture Model. Each Component Model focuses on the detailed class structure of its component, and allows the design team to precisely specify the attributes, operations, dependencies, and behaviors of its classes.

Depending on your development process, you may have even more models: a Business Model, a Domain Model, possibly others. The major benefit of models is that you can make *model* changes far earlier in the development cycle than you can make *code* changes, and far easier. And because you can make changes early, you can make your mistakes early. And that's a good thing, because early detection and correction is cheap detection and correction. Modeling will let you catch your most costly bugs early; and early detection and correction can save you a factor of 50 to 200 on the cost and schedule of a bug fix.[4]

---

4. Steve McConnell, *Software Project Survival Guide* (Microsoft Press, 1997), p. 29

Equal Time for an Extreme Perspective

Although software engineering literature is rife with research that demonstrates that the cost to fix a defect rises catastrophically over time, those in the Extreme Programming camp disagree. They argue that all such research is dated, and that modern development tools and techniques allow a maximum limit to the cost of change.[5] They see not an exponential growth, but an asymptotic approach, as shown in Figure 1-1.

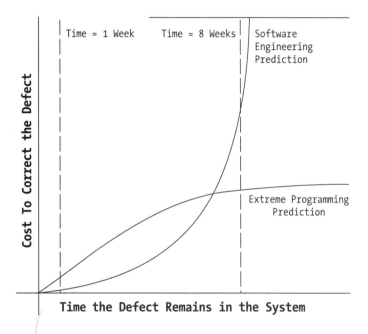

Figure 1-1. Cost to correct defects over time

5. Kent Beck, *Extreme Programming Explained: Embrace Change* (Addison Wesley, 1999), pp. 21–25

To which theory I can only reply, "So?"

- First, their theory is a prediction, not a guarantee: *if* you apply the techniques they advocate and *if* you do everything correctly and *if* you are working in the right sort of environment on the right sort of project, *then* the lessons of 30 years of software engineering will allow you to attain the asymptotic curve. Good for you, if you can do that; but the exponential curve is the default behavior. (Furthermore, I would argue that modeling is a useful tool for attaining that asymptotic curve.)

- Second, look at those curves. Do you want to argue over which curve is "right" at the 8-weeks mark? Or would you rather just fix the problem at the 1-week mark? (Beck argues that there is benefit in waiting for the latest possible time, so that you have the maximum information when you make the fix and also so that you don't waste time fixing problems that never really arise; but his actual example shows the benefits of making a change as soon as you are aware of it. These concerns aren't incompatible.)

Modeling has another benefit, one I call **The Outline Effect**. Back in high school, I never needed study habits: I liked to read, and I liked to learn, so school came easy to me at my small rural high school. Then I went to a Big Ten university, and reality came crashing in on me. I didn't understand that learning at that level was supposed to be *work*, a job you tackled in a systematic fashion with specific goals and strategies. My "strategy" was sort of like code-and-fix: just tackle whatever came along, and hope it all worked out. It didn't, and I didn't understand why. Every night, I sat in my room, reading the textbooks . . . until something distracted me, which happened far too often. Meanwhile, every night, a friend sat in his room across the hall, *outlining* the textbooks. And surprise—he had a much better GPA than I did.

It took me years to appreciate my friend's study skills. The process of outlining the text forced him to focus: he had a concrete goal in mind, and wouldn't allow distractions until he finished it. Furthermore, the outlining involved more of his brain: in order to produce an outline of the textbook, he first had to *comprehend* the textbook; and then to actually write the outline in his own words, he had to involve yet more areas of his brain, as he had to formulate what he wanted to write. Heck, he even had to involve his tactile and motor areas of his brain in order to write the words. He had a much more fully involved brain, and thus he much more fully understood the material.

This is a benefit you can gain from modeling: by listening and talking and reading and by then translating what you learn into a model, you learn it more thoroughly. This is even more important in system design than in studying from a textbook: in a textbook, you *expect* that the text will be more or less consistent, and that any seeming inconsistency is most likely a sign of something you misunderstood; but in requirements gathering, contradiction and inconsistency are inevitable parts of the process. By modeling the requirements, you may highlight the inconsistencies, particularly when you gather details from many different parts of a specification and put them together in the same diagram.

And there's one more modeling benefit, one I believe I may have mentioned earlier: *communication*. It's easier to communicate with models than with text, or even with code; and you can communicate with a wider audience with models than with other forms of expression. Once you've created a diagram "in your own words," I can more easily comprehend how *you* comprehend things by comparing your diagram with what *I* comprehend.

UML

UML, the Unified Modeling Language, is a graphical language designed to capture the artifacts of an OOAD process. It provides a comprehensive notation for communicating the requirements, behavior, architecture, and realization of an Object-Oriented design. As you saw in the last section, UML provides you with a way to create and document a model of a system.

What Makes the UML Unified?

To answer that, you need to jump in the WayBack Machine and travel back to the ancient history of OOAD—say, 1995. At that time, Object-Oriented Programming had proven its worth as a way of building applications and systems; and the hot new topics in the OO world were OOA and OOD. Since these topics were larger in scope than mere programming, the practitioners needed a way of displaying large, complex concepts in a simple graphical fashion. A number of competing OO notations emerged, chief among them being the Booch Notation designed by Grady Booch and the Object Modeling Technique (OMT) designed by James Rumbaugh (and others). And then began the religious wars: fanatical adherents of the competing notations fought petty little battles over clouds (Booch's symbol for a class) versus rectangles (OMT's symbol for a class).

Booch and Rumbaugh looked on this confusion with dismay: they saw the differences between their notations as minor, unworthy of so much rancor. And worse, they saw the religious wars detracting from what they felt should be the new focus: the OOAD process itself, particularly as a means for capturing requirements and behavior. They were very impressed by some of Ivar Jacobson's work on Sequence Diagrams and his Objectory methodology; but with all the shouting about notation, no one was talking about process. So Booch and Rumbaugh and Jacobson (the Three Amigos) went on retreat to hammer out differences in their notations in private, and to adopt other useful notations as well (chief among these being David Harel's State Diagram notation). They emerged with the Unified Modeling Language 0.8, a response to the Object Management Group's call for a standard object modeling notation; and Booch's company, Rational[6] (which had hired Rumbaugh and Jacobson) incorporated UML into Rational ROSE, their OOAD tool. The UML then went through a few cycles of response and revision by the OO community; and UML 1.1 was adopted as a standard by the OMG in 1997. UML has been further refined, and is currently at version 1.4, with version 2.0 on the near horizon.

What UML Isn't

With so much in UML, it's worth mentioning what's not UML. The following sections describe some related concepts that are often confused with UML itself.

A Process

Remember the goal of the Three Amigos: to focus attention on the OOAD process, not on the notation. Their notation isn't a process in itself; rather, it's designed to support a wide range of OO processes. There are a number of UML-based OOAD processes, including Fowler's outline process,[7] controlled iteration,[8] Texel and Williams's complete OO process,[9] and, of course, the Unified Process (formerly Objectory) from the Three Amigos.[10] A full list would be much longer, but would have a lot in common with these prominent examples. These processes differ somewhat in the degree of formality and the order of operations; but all involve using UML to identify and refine requirements, allocate those requirements to

---

6. In December 2002, Rational became a division of IBM Corporation.

7. Martin Fowler and Kendall Scott, *UML Distilled, Second Edition* (Addison-Wesley, 1999), pp. 13–38

8. Murray R. Cantor, *Object-Oriented Project Management with UML* (John Wiley & Sons, 1998), pp. 98–103

9. Putnam P. Texel and Charles B. Williams, *Use Cases Combined with Booch/OMT/UML: Process and Products* (Prentice Hall, 1997), pp. 3–9ff.

10. Ivar Jacoboson, Grady Booch, and James Rumbaugh, *The Unified Software Development Process* (Addison-Wesley, 1999)

functional modules, and refine those modules. Without a process, new UML students are often adrift in a sea of concepts, with nothing to guide their course.

In this book, you'll learn UML within the framework of Five-Step UML, which I find to be a "just enough" process: just enough process to help you understand the purpose of UML, but not so much as to bury you in paperwork and obscure the benefits of UML. Five-Step UML isn't a large, full-featured OOAD process, falling somewhere between an academic exercise and Ambler's Agile Modeling.[11] Still, I find that some particularly process-averse teams that tend to reject a more formal process will accept Five-Step UML.

In the next chapter, I'll show you how the Five-Step process works, and along the way, you should pick up a broad working knowledge of UML. In Chapter 3, I'll talk about some pragmatic rules I like to apply to the Five-Step (and indeed any other) modeling process. Throughout the core chapters of this book (Part Two), we'll work through each of the five steps in more detail, applying it to a real-world case study. Although the focus of this book is on Five-Step UML, we will look in more detail at some other processes and how they work in Chapter 12.

Rational XDE (or Any Other Tool)

Many UML practitioners—and of course, many UML tool vendors—tend to blur the line between UML and a given tool. I myself am prone to equating "what XDE can do" with "what UML can do," since I do most of my UML work with Rational's XDE tool. This habit isn't inherently bad, since it's usually easier to work with your tools than against them; but it's important to realize that the features and capabilities of any given tool—even the market-leading UML tool from the people who gave us UML—may differ from the features and capabilities of UML itself. If UML is a language, then every tool speaks with a unique accent.

You can find a list of available UML tools in Appendix B.

A Silver Bullet

Good code will still require blood, sweat, tears, pizza, good management, and lots of thought. UML will help you to organize these factors (except the pizza), but you won't be able to avoid them.

---

11. Scott W. Ambler, *Agile Modeling: Effective Practices for eXtreme Programming and the Unified Process* (John Wiley & Sons, 2002)

UML Diagrams

UML consists of nine different diagram types, each focused on a different way to analyze and define the system. These diagrams are summarized briefly here:

- **Use Case Diagrams** show the externally visible behavior of the system. You'll see these in the next chapter (Chapter 2) and later on when we look at Step 1 of Five-Step UML in Chapter 6.

- **Activity Diagrams** show an elaboration of the behavior of the system. You'll see these in the next chapter, and use them during Step 2 of Five-Step UML in Chapter 7. A recent addition to UML is the division of Activity Diagrams into swimlanes, which you'll see in the next chapter, and we'll use during Step 3 of Five-Step UML in Chapter 8.

- **Component Diagrams** show architecture of the system. You'll see these in the next chapter, and we'll use them during Step 4 of Five-Step UML in Chapter 9.

- **Sequence Diagrams** show object interactions over time. We don't use these diagrams as part of Five-Step UML, but we'll look at them in Chapter 13.

- **Collaboration Diagrams** show object interactions with emphasis on relations between objects. We don't use this type of diagram as part of Five-Step UML, but we'll look at them in Chapter 13.

- **Class Diagrams** show class definition and relations. You'll see these in the next chapter, and we'll use them during Step 5 of Five-Step UML in Chapter 10.

- **Statechart Diagrams** show state changes in response to events. We don't use these diagrams as part of Five-Step UML, but we'll talk about them in Chapter 13.

- **Deployment Diagrams** show physical architecture of the system. We'll use these in Chapter 11.

- **Package Diagrams** show the hierarchical structure of your design. These can be useful for organizing many different types of elements and you'll be seeing this type of diagram often throughout the book.

I have a secret. You know those different UML diagram types? Does it annoy you just a bit, having to learn so many new notations to use UML? Does it make you feel like skipping OOAD and just jumping into code?

Well, it's true that making good UML diagrams takes some skill and some practice; but reading well-crafted diagrams is a very different matter. Just between you and me, I'll bet you already know how to read UML diagrams, and you don't even know it. For the rest of this chapter, I'm going to show you some examples of the different UML diagrams, and ask you a few simple questions about what it is they are saying. Don't worry if you can't follow all of the notation at this stage—or indeed if you find the questions too simplistic—the point of the following exercises is simply to show you how straightforward it is to read UML diagrams, and how you'll be able to answer questions about them right away. You won't be an expert by any measure—that comes in later chapters—but you'll be able to understand the information contained in the diagrams.

Because, see, here's the secret: UML—it's all about communication . . .

An Introduction to the Kennel Management System

The exercises and examples in this book all derive from the Kennel Management System (KMS) for Sandy's Pets, a high-tech kennel providing temporary and long-term care for cats, dogs, birds, and exotic pets. The Kennel Management System must provide familiar features tailored to the pet care domain:

- **Reservations and occupancy.** Like a good hotel, the KMS must allow pet owners to reserve kennel space (i.e., "pens") and to check pets in and out. Unlike a hotel, a significant fraction of the occupants reside in the kennel long term or even full time.

- **Exercise and grooming schedule.** Like a good physical therapy clinic, the KMS must support and maintain exercise and grooming schedules for each resident. Unlike a clinic, these schedules are dictated by the pet owner rather than by a physician or therapist.

- **Nutrition and dietetics.** Like a good health spa, the KMS must support both standard and customized diets for each resident. Unlike a health spa, some of the residents only eat live food.

- **Inventory and ordering.** Like a good restaurant, the KMS must keep food (and other supplies) on hand to meet the needs of a varied clientele. Unlike most restaurants (and as noted previously), some of the food must be stored live.

- **Surveillance and tracking.** Like a good day care center, the KMS must ensure that its residents are safe and secure, including allowing the pet owners to view their pets via Web cams. Unlike day care centers, each resident will be equipped with a computerized collar or tag, which will allow sensors in the kennel to locate and check the status of each pet.

- **Health care and medication.** Like a good health care management system, the KMS must schedule regular and emergency medical visits, maintain a medical history, and manage dispensing of medications. Unlike typical health care systems, the residents come from a wide variety of species and thus need species-specific medications and treatment programs.

- **Customer relations and pedigrees.** Like a good contact management system, the KMS must track information about residents past, present, and possibly future. Unlike typical contact management systems, the KMS must maintain information about both a pet's parentage and future breeding plans.

The KMS must also provide basic human resources, accounting, and administration functions. For a more detailed specification of the Kennel Management System, see Appendix A.

Use Case Diagrams

A Use Case Diagram depicts actions by people and systems outside your system, along with what your system does in response. It's useful for depicting the functional requirements of your system. Figure 1-2 shows an example of a simple Use Case Diagram for the Kennel Management System.

Care Giver Use Cases

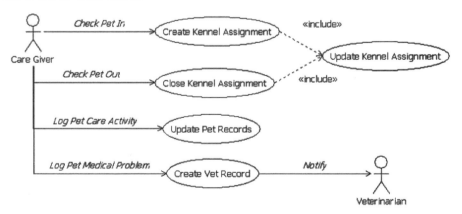

Figure 1-2. Use Case Diagram for care giver requirements

Exercise 101: Reading a Use Case Diagram

Answer the following questions about the diagram:

1. What does the KMS do when the care giver checks a pet in?

2. What does the KMS do when the care giver checks a pet out?

3. What action or actions by the care giver will cause the KMS to update a kennel assignment?

4. What action or actions by the **Care Giver** will involve the **Veterinarian**?

NOTE The answers to this exercise and the exercises that follow can be found at the end of the chapter.

Activity Diagrams

An Activity Diagram depicts the detailed behavior inside a single functional requirement, including a primary scenario and a number of alternate scenarios. It's useful for ensuring that you thoroughly understand a given functionality. Figure 1-3 presents an Activity Diagram for the one functional requirement of the Kennel Management System for Sandy's Pets.

Create Pen Assignment

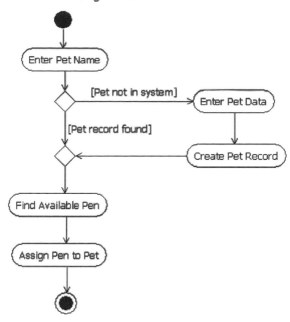

Figure 1-3. Activity Diagram for assigning a pen to a pet

Exercise 102: Reading an Activity Diagram

Answer the following questions about the diagram:

1. What is the sequence of steps the system performs when assigning a pen to a pet that has visited previously?

2. What additional steps are performed for a pet that is new to the kennel?

Component Diagrams

A Component Diagram depicts the deployable units of your system—executables, components, data stores, among others—and the interfaces through which they interact. It's useful for exploring the architecture of your system. Figure 1-4 presents an example of a Component Diagram for the Kennel Management System.

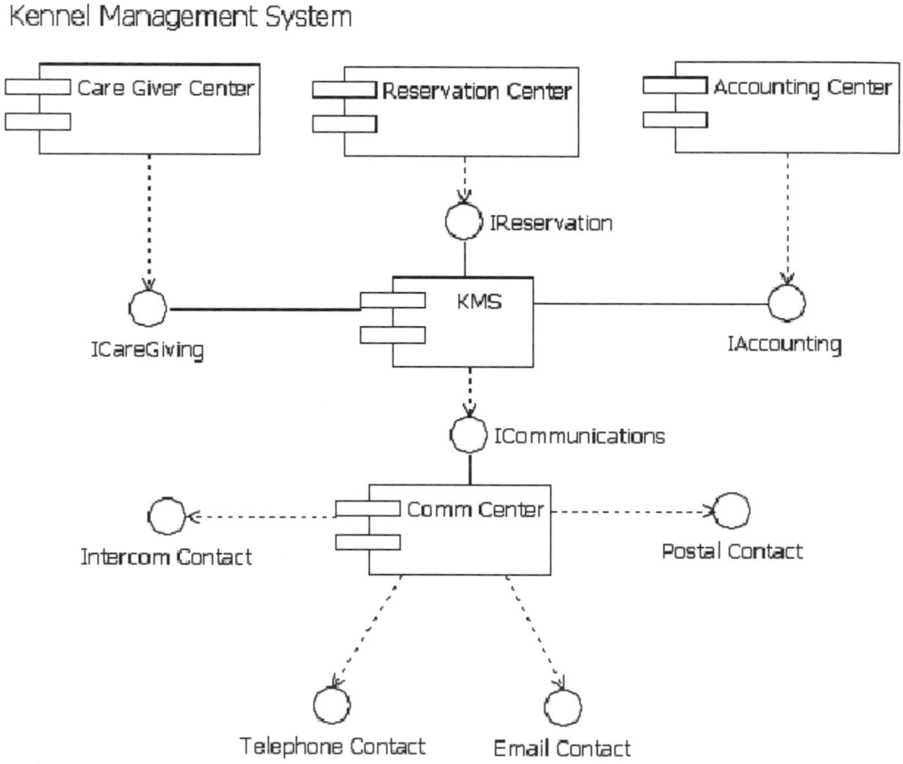

Figure 1-4. Component Diagram of the Kennel Management System

Exercise 103: Reading a Component Diagram

Answer the following questions about the diagram:

1. The **Care Giver Center** is the Web page that the care giver uses to enter information about a pet. What interface does it use to provide data to the KMS?

2. What other components provide data to the KMS, and through what interfaces?

3. What types of contacts can be made through the **Comm Center** component?

Sequence Diagrams

A Sequence Diagram depicts the detailed behavior over time within one path or scenario of a single functional requirement. It's useful for understanding the flow of messages between elements of your system. Figure 1-5 presents an example of a Sequence Diagram for the Kennel Management System.

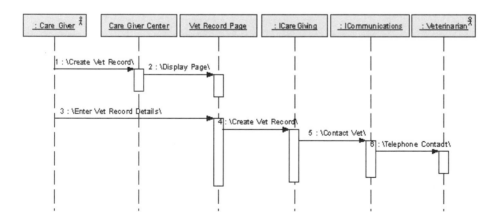

Figure 1-5. Sequence Diagram for creating a vet record.

Exercise 104: Reading a Sequence Diagram

Answer the following questions about the diagram:

1. Which objects in the system are involved in creating a vet record?

2. Which actors outside the system are involved in creating a vet record?

3. What interface does the **Vet Record Page** use for creating a vet record?

4. How does the system contact the veterinarian?

Class Diagrams

A Class Diagram depicts the classes and interfaces within the design of your system, as well as the relations between them. It's useful for defining the internal, Object-Oriented structure of your code. Figure 1-6 presents an example Class Diagram from the Kennel Management System.

Pen Assignment Classes

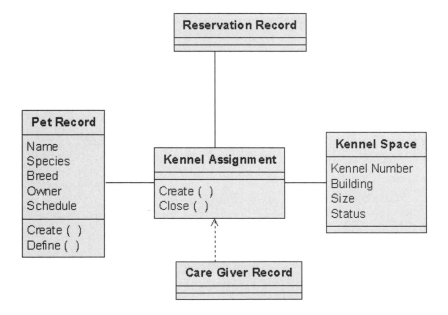

Figure 1-6. Class Diagram for kennel assignment

NOTE   You'll probably notice here the two different sorts of connection between the classes. Here, the solid lines depict an association, whereas the dashed line depicts a dependency. I'll discuss what this means in detail in the next chapter.

Exercise 105: Reading a Class Diagram

Answer the following questions about the diagram:

1. What three classes are associated with the **Kennel Assignment** class?

2. What operations can objects of the **Kennel Assignment** class perform?

3. What attributes describe an object of the **Pet Record** class?

4. What attributes describe an object of the **Kennel Space** class?

Statechart Diagrams

A Statechart Diagram depicts how the state of your system changes in response to internal and external events. It's useful for ensuring that each event is handled properly no matter what state your system may be in. Figure 1-7 presents an example of a Statechart Diagram from the Kennel Management System. This diagram illustrates events involving the availability of kennel spaces.

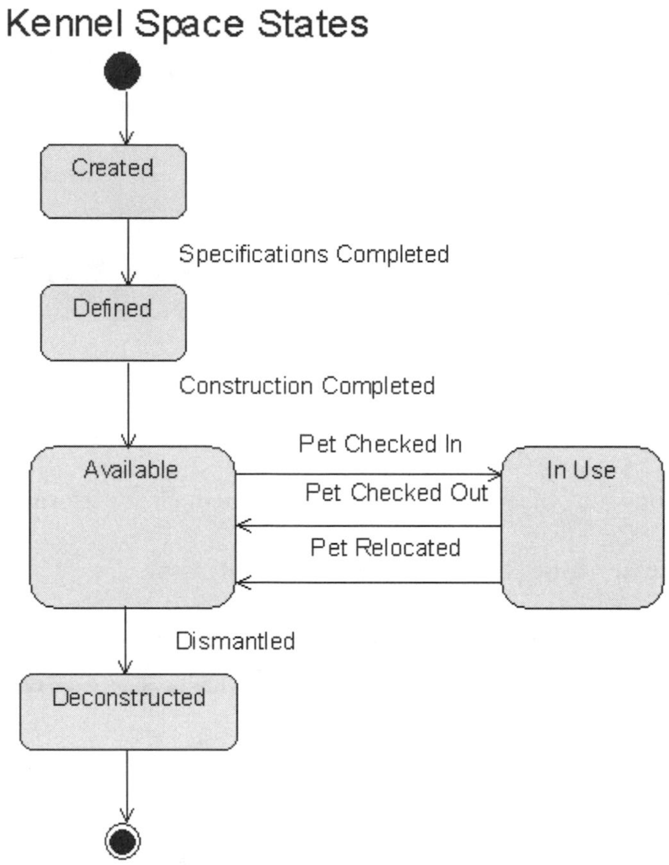

Kennel Space States

Figure 1-7. Statechart Diagram for kennel spaces

Exercise 106: Reading a Statechart Diagram

Answer the following questions about the diagram:

1. What event causes a kennel space, or pen, to enter the **Defined** state?

2. What events (from which states) cause a pen to enter the **Available** state?

3. What state does a pen enter when it's currently in the **Available** state, and a **Dismantled** event occurs?

4. How can a pen go from the **In Use** state to the **Deconstructed** state?

Deployment Diagrams

A Deployment Diagram depicts how the deployable units of your system—applications, components, data stores, etc.—are assigned to various nodes, as well as how the nodes communicate with each other and with devices. It's useful both as a map of your system and as a means for studying the load across your system. Figure 1-8 presents a simple example of a Deployment Diagram for the Kennel Management System.

KMS System Architecture

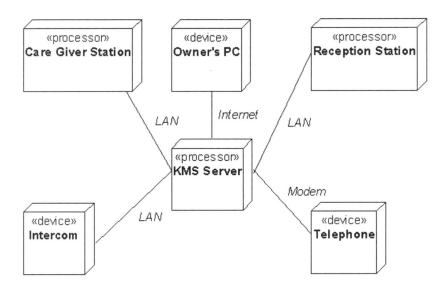

Figure 1-8. Deployment Diagram for the Kennel Management System

Exercise 107: Reading a Deployment Diagram

Answer the following questions about the diagram:

1. Which processes are running on the reception station?

2. How is the KMS server connected to the telephone?

3. How does the owner's PC access pet information on the KMS server?

4. How does information go from the care giver station to the reception station?

Package Diagrams

A Package Diagram depicts how related elements of your design are grouped together, as well as how the groups depend upon each other. It's useful for dividing a complex design into multiple, more manageable smaller designs. Figure 1-9 presents an example of a Package Diagram from the Kennel Management System.

Kennel Management Packages

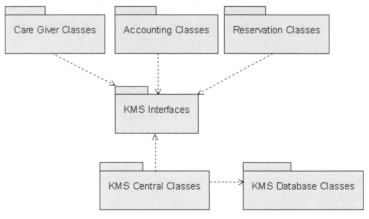

Figure 1-9. Package Diagram of the Kennel Management System

Exercise 108: Reading a Package Diagram

Answer the following questions about the diagram:

1. Which packages make use of information from the **KMS Interfaces** package?

2. Which packages does the **KMS Central Classes** package make use of?

"Wait a Minute! Those Arrows Are Pointing in the Wrong Direction!"

An Apology to Database Modelers and Data Flow Diagrammers

If you come from the database-modeling world and are used to entity relationship diagrams (ERDs), you probably got Exercise 108 exactly wrong. The same is probably true if you come from the world of data flow diagrams (DFDs). In both of those diagramming techniques, the arrows on a diagram indicate the direction of data flow. In UML, the dependency arrows (- - - - >) indicate the direction of knowledge and control. To those people familiar with ERDs and DFDs, this seems exactly backwards. Their instinct is to interpret Figure 1-9 as meaning that KMS Interfaces make use of Care Giver Classes, Accounting Classes, Reservation Classes, and KMS Central Classes.

The UML convention isn't quite as backwards as it seems. How would a class in Care Giver Classes make use of an interface in KMS Interfaces? By calling its methods, of course. And very likely, the class would pass data to the interface as well. So control and even some data do indeed flow in the direction of the dependency arrow.

And if that doesn't help you to keep the meaning of the arrows straight, I can only apologize, and claim innocence: I didn't write the UML (though its convention seems "correct" in my biased perspective). I do know that this is a source of confusion for ERD and DFD practitioners; and I hope that this warning will help to minimize your confusion.

It's All About Communication

I hope that the exercises in this chapter have eliminated any mystique about UML in your mind; but even more, I hope that I have set an example of how UML can be used to communicate ideas. The underlying point for this section and the whole book is this: UML is about communication.

Don't worry about being perfect all at once (or ever!). If you're communicating, you're using UML effectively. There's always room for improvement; but don't let imperfection stop you from progress. That's a key point in learning and applying UML and in applying UML as part of a process. Your designs won't be perfect; but as your team reviews them and you refine them, they will become good enough: good enough to build the system, good enough to guide the testing and the documentation, good enough to drive the management of the process. A team that waits for perfection is just as bad as a team that is wedded to code-and-fix: neither team produces an *effective* design that leads to a successful system. Remember: *code-and-fix bad; design-and-fix good.*

Letting Go of Perfection: A Lesson from the Graphic Arts

If I haven't persuaded you yet to let go of perfection, it won't surprise me. It's easy for me to *say* that you can make imperfect diagrams and improve them later; but how do you do it? How do you just sit down and start drawing diagrams when there's nothing you know? I hear this most often from students who are drawing Sequence or Activity Diagrams: "How can I draw this diagram until I know which objects are in the system?" And they have it exactly backwards: they'll use the diagrams to discover objects that solve the problem. But they want to draw the *right* picture. Maybe they're afraid to look foolish in reviews. (Reviews can be intimidating even to a strong ego like mine!) Maybe they're just hypersensitive to the risks in the wrong design. Maybe they have embraced the idea that the design is supposed to help them get things right, and therefore are reluctant to risk getting things wrong. But whatever the reason, they just can't seem to let go.

So I try a different approach. My students who have seen me sketch diagrams at the flip chart are very aware that one thing I'm not is an artist. But borrowing a technique from the graphic arts,[12] I draw the images shown in Figure 1-10, one on top of another.

---

12. Klutz Press Editors, *Draw the Marvel Comics Super Heroes* (Klutz Press, 1995), pp. 20–32

Figure 1-10. Refining from imperfect to communication

The technique is simple: put down some detail—even if it's wrong, such as the sizing circles in the first image —to serve as a basis for further development; then add and erase detail as needed to refine the picture. I'm still not an artist (I draw fencers because the hard parts are hidden behind a mask and a weapon); but by applying some simple techniques and refining, I end up with a much more recognizable picture than I would have if I sat down and tried to draw a perfect fencer from scratch. Imperfection and refinement produces better (and faster!) results than does a foolish insistence on perfection.

Scott Adams tells us, "Creativity is allowing yourself to make mistakes. Art is knowing which ones to keep."[13] Take this attitude to heart in your analysis and design process.

---

13. Scott Adams, *The Dilbert Principle* (HarperBusiness, 1997), p. 324

Summary

I began this chapter with a quick overview of some of the main concepts under-pinning Object-Oriented development and seeing how these apply to the process of Analysis and Design. Next, I discussed how modeling can help you not only design a better system, but also develop a better understanding of that system and how it should work.

In the second half of this chapter, we dipped our toes in the waters of UML—taking a quick look at some of the different types of diagram—but it'll be time to jump right in during the next chapter.

Exercise Solutions

Solutions to Exercise 101

1. The system creates a kennel assignment, a mapping of a pet to a specific pen.

2. The system closes the kennel assignment.

3. Checking a pet in or checking a pet out.

4. Logging a medical problem.

Solutions to Exercise 102

1. Enter the pet's name. Find available kennel space. Assign the kennel to the pet.

2. Enter the pet's personal data. Create a new record for the pet.

Solutions to Exercise 103

1. **ICareGiving**.

2. Reservation Center through the **IReservations** interface. Accounting Center through the **IAccounting** interface.

3. Intercom, telephone, email, and postal.

Solutions to Exercise 104

1. Care Giver Center, Vet Record Page, **ICareGiving** interface, and **ICommunications** interface.

2. **Care Giver** and **Veterinarian**.

3. **ICareGiving**.

4. Via a telephone contact.

Solutions to Exercise 105

1. **Pet Record**, **Reservation Record**, and **Kennel Space**.

2. **Create** and **Close**.

3. **Name**, **Species**, **Breed**, **Owner**, and **Schedule**.

4. **Kennel Number**, **Building**, **Size**, and **Status**.

Solutions to Exercise 106

1. **Specifications Completed**.

2. **Construction Completed** (from **Defined**), **Pet Checked Out** (from **In Use**), and **Pet Relocated** (also from **In Use**).

3. **Deconstructed**.

4. Via a **Pet Checked Out** event *or* a **Pet Relocated** event, followed by a **Dismantled** event. This prevents the system from having a pet with no defined pen. (Can't have the dogs running loose!)

Solutions to Exercise 107

1. Accounting center and reception center.

2. Via the modem.

3. Via the Internet.

4. According to this diagram, the only path possible is through the KMS server. Although the diagram doesn't explicitly state this, the likely approach is that the care giver station updates information in the central database, and the reception center reads this updated data.

Solutions to Exercise 108

1. **Care Giver Classes, Accounting Classes, Reservation Classes,** and **KMS Central Classes.**

2. **KMS Interfaces** and **KMS Database Classes.**

CHAPTER 2

Five-Step UML: OOAD for Short Attention Spans

IN THIS CHAPTER, I'll introduce you to Five-Step UML. We'll work through the whole process from beginning to end, and along the way, I'll be introducing all the UML notation that you'll need to understand the relevant diagrams. I'll also show you how the whole thing works from the point of view of .NET development.

By way of examples, I'll be using lots of diagrams from the Kennel Management System case study, which was introduced at the end of the last chapter. I'm not going to show you everything in exhaustive detail at this stage, however, because we'll be examining that case study more slowly throughout Part Two of the book. The aim of this chapter is simply to give you an overview of the whole process, a feel for how it all fits together, and a chance to get started with some modeling yourself.

So, I'll begin this chapter with an overview of Five-Step UML to give you the big picture. Next we'll focus in on the various steps. With each step, I'll start by showing you the relevant UML notation that you'll need, then walk through the process, and then we'll look at some examples from the KMS.

Using a Process

OOAD and UML form a chicken-and-egg paradox: a good OOAD process requires a good notation; but when you study the notation, the most common question is, "Why would I do *that*?" where *that* means drawing a particular diagram to show a particular piece of your model. Often, the answer is, "Because we need it for this stage of the process." The best way to teach UML effectively is to teach a software development process. And that's when the groaning begins: *Oh, no, not another process!*

What's Wrong with Process?

Why is it that programmers and process don't mix well? Here are some of the common perceptions:

- **We're too busy.** Process means steps to follow, things to do. Well, we're all overworked already. Who wants yet more work? We've got code to crank out!

- **It's too much hassle.** There are too many steps in a process. They just get in our way. The steps are too difficult or too poorly explained. We spent a lot of time learning to write code; now we have to learn all this other stuff, too? This is just make-work imposed on us by "the suits." Let's just crank out code!

- **It's too complex.** Look, we all know how to write code. Why are we making it all so complicated? Let's just start cranking out the code.

- **It never works.** Every so often, some pointy-haired manager type comes along with a "brilliant" plan that will "fix" everything. Then next year, there's another plan, and another after that. And nothing ever really changes around here. So why waste time trying? We're better off just cranking out code.

- **It's too boring.** Hey, code is fun! Process is work. Which would *you* rather do?

Whether these perceptions are true or not—and there's some element of truth in each of them—they certainly make it harder to teach or learn process.

The Answer: Five-Step UML

In order to learn UML, then, we'll start with Five-Step UML, a lightweight OOAD process that specifically addresses the common perceptions about process:

- **You're not too busy.** Five-Step UML is an aid to thinking about the problem and will give you focus and actually save you time. This isn't about extra steps for you to follow; it's about saving you steps by getting the design right in advance, so you spend less time rewriting code you've done wrong.

- **It's not a lot of hassle.** Although you *can* use a modeling tool, Five-Step UML can be performed with paper, Post-it notes, and a pencil. It doesn't get in your way; it helps you to talk about the problem.

- **It's not too complex.** Five steps. Four diagram types (five, if you need Deployment Diagrams). Paper, Post-it notes, and pencil. How complex can it be?

- It *will* work. Trust me. Or don't trust me, and prove me wrong. But give it a try. Five-Step UML should be just enough process to show the benefits of UML, but not so much process as to drag you down.

- It's not boring, it's fun! Well, that's what I think anyway, and I have a lot of student feedback to support me. But you be the judge.

Now I don't want to mislead you: Five-Step UML isn't a full-featured OOAD process suitable for the development of complex systems. It has none of the management, testing, documentation, and review features that you expect from a complete process. It's only a learning tool, a skeletal process suitable for learning UML, and not much more.

Or Is It ...?

I'm a fan of processes for complex system development. I think you should encourage your team to adopt more than Five-Step UML. But perhaps your team is particularly averse to process. Perhaps after looking at Five-Step UML, they may see it as the maximum process they're willing to implement.

Is that bad? Not necessarily. According to Scott W. Ambler, "Agile Modeling (AM) is a chaordic, practice-based methodology for effective modeling and documentation of software-based systems." [1] Ambler's book describes lightweight modeling practices that might be characterized as "just enough": just enough modeling and just enough process to get the job done. Five-Step UML is compatible with many of the Core Practices of Agile Modeling:

- Apply the Right Artifacts
- Create Several Models in Parallel
- Iterate to Another Artifact
- Model in Small Increments
- Model with Others
- Active Stakeholder Participation
- Collective Ownership
- Display Models Publicly
- Create Simple Content
- Depict Models Simply
- Use the Simplest Tools

1. Scott W. Ambler, *Agile Modeling: Effective Practices for eXtreme Programming and the Unified Process* (John Wiley & Sons, 2002)

As Ambler says, "AM is not a prescriptive process. In other words, it doesn't define detailed procedures for how to create a given type of model; instead it provides advice for how to be effective as a modeler." Similarly, you might apply Five-Step UML as a modeling strategy inside of a larger process, whether it be a prescriptive process like the Unified Process or an agile process like Extreme Programming or Scrum.

Overview of Five-Step UML

Five-Step UML is also an example of what I call *Model-Driven Development*, in which the models become the central artifacts of the process, the central repository of all that is known about the system.

In this chapter, I'll walk you through the complete process of Five-Step UML, but I won't go into a lot of detail or tie together all the tasks outside of modeling, architecture, design, and coding. Later in the book, in Chapters 6 through 11, we'll go though each step in more detail and see how you can tie the models to management, testing, and documentation tasks.

The Five Steps are as follows:

1. **Define.** Identify the requirements of your system via Use Case Diagrams. Add other diagrams where they shed light on the use cases.

2. **Refine.** Detail the steps in each requirement via scenarios captured in Activity Diagrams. Add other diagrams where they shed light on the activities.

3. **Assign.** Use the Activity Diagrams to assign the steps to elements of your system.

4. **Design.** Show the relations among the elements with Component Diagrams. Add other diagrams where they shed light on the components.

5. **Repeat/iterate/drill down/divide and conquer.** Narrow the scope of your process to individual elements (designed with Class Diagrams); or expand it out to whole systems (designed with Deployment Diagrams). Add other diagrams wherever they help you understand the system. Repeat Steps 1 through 4 as appropriate for the current scope. Like Boehm's Spiral development process, Evolutionary Development, and many other modern processes, Five-Step UML is an incremental, recursive approach.

"But What I Know Doesn't Fit These Steps ..."

What happens when you learn something or know something that doesn't "fit" your current step in Five-Step UML? Suppose your requirements tell you beyond a doubt that you'll need a Web server, a DB server, and a firewall box? You can't model that as a set of use cases.

In that case, read the first guideline in Chapter 3, **Do What Works**. These steps and the order they are in form a useful set of guidelines, *not* a rigid set of rules. You can either read ahead in Five-Step UML to find the right way to handle the information; or you can simply write it down and set it aside, then revisit it until you find a step where you learn how to model the information.

Do What Works usually implies "update the model and draw the diagrams that fit what you know." But right now, you're just learning UML, so you can't be expected to know how to model every piece of information. Just write it down and move along.

I'll talk about this idea in more detail in the next chapter, along with a whole bunch of pragmatic guidelines to help you find your way through the modeling maze.

Do-It-Yourself UML

If you quickly flick through the rest of this chapter, it won't take you long to figure out it's a long one; and just sitting reading it from beginning to end could get a little tough, even with a big cup of coffee there to keep you going. And because we all know that the way to learn anything is to do it, not just to read about it, I recommend that you follow along with the exercises listed in this chapter, so you can start using UML right away.

Throughout this chapter, I'll be examining each step in Five-Step UML; but before getting started, you should think about what kind of project you can use to get some practical UML experience.

Look for a Problem

You'll need to select a problem domain which you'll analyze and a solution which you'll design with Five-Step UML. If you're working by yourself, pick a domain in which you're comfortable serving as customer, analyst, architect, and designer, but *not* one you know too well. If you're working as a team, *don't* pick a domain familiar to your team. Why shouldn't you choose a familiar domain? Because experience shows that with a familiar domain, you'll jump straight into designing *the system as it is* when you should be analyzing *the system as it should be.* If you have no problem domain in mind, try one of these suggestions:

- Hotel room scheduling and reservations

- Flight scheduling and reservations

- Rental car scheduling and reservations

- Online travel service, including flight reservations, room reservations, car rental, and travel information (this will be less detailed than the preceding domains, but broader in scope).

- University course scheduling and enrollment

- Online banking

- Online pizza ordering service (a popular choice with many programmers)

- Package shipping and tracking

- A calculator

- A video game

- An electronic diary

Select one person to serve as the customer (and final arbiter of what the customer wants). Call this person the customer rep. The rest of the team will act as analysts and designers.

With a Little Help from Your Friends

Five-Step UML is much more effective as a team exercise than as an individual exercise. The only student who has told me he didn't learn from it was a conference attendee who chose to work by himself rather than join a group. UML is about communication, remember? Well, Five-Step UML is an exercise in team communication using UML. You'll start to see the benefit when you draw the "perfect" picture, and your team members start tearing it apart, showing you what's unclear, what you overlooked, and what you got wrong. And then, to make their points, they'll have to produce even better pictures. I hate to use a management buzzword, but the *synergism* will astound you and sweep you up. Once you've done Five-Step UML with a good team, you may never want to design alone again. (This is the point of the Agile Modeling Core Practice, Model with Others.)

So I recommend you do the exercises in this chapter (and throughout the book) with a team of three to five people. Two is too few to generate enough disagreement; six or more can work, but some might have trouble getting at the paper. They don't all have to have copies of this book (though it won't break my heart if they do). They don't even all have to be developers: managers, analysts, and end users should get a lot out of Steps 1 and 2; documenters and testers should get a lot out of Steps 1 through 4; and anyone who wants to learn more about the development process should learn something from all five steps. So rope in some coworkers, or friends, or relatives, or in-laws, or strangers off the street. For a team, these exercises should take about a day, if you try to do at least two of every diagram. Two diagrams make a good target. With the first diagram, you're learning the process; with the second diagram, you're practicing the process. If you try to analyze and design a whole system, this will take a lot longer.

Step 1: Define

Identify the requirements of your system via Use Case Diagrams. Add other diagrams where they shed light on the use cases.

In this step, you'll describe what your system will do for each external user of the system, as well as what it will require from the users. These requirements shall be captured in Use Case Diagrams.

A Use Case Diagram is a way of depicting the interaction between your system and the outside world: your users, other systems, devices, etc. It's a picture of the things your system will do—and more important, why it does them. At its core, a Use Case Diagram consists of three elements: actors, use cases, and communications.

First, I'll make a quick tour of the UML notation that you need for these three elements, and show you how they fit together to form UML diagrams. After that, I'll describe in more detail what needs to be done as part of this first step of Five-Step UML.

Isn't That Just a Feature?

More than likely, you've used the use case concept in designing systems all along—perhaps even without recognizing it. As I discuss later, a Use Case Diagram is a way of discussing requirements in context. It's that context—the actors and communications that relate to the use cases—that make them an expressive way of explaining and understanding a system.

Actors and use cases are one example of how UML is unified. These concepts were formalized in Jacobson's work on the Objectory process, and were adopted in UML because they filled a great need for a way to model requirements, not just structure and behavior.

UML Notation

In this section, we'll look at the definitions and UML notation for actors, communications, use cases, and domain objects, and see how they all work together in Use Case Diagrams.

Actors

An *actor* represents any outside entity that interacts with your system. It may request services from your system; and it may perform services for your system. An actor can be a person; but it may also be another system, or perhaps a device such as a printer. An actor may even be a signal or event to which you must respond. From a component design perspective, you might model the clients of your component as actors, even though those are "the system" from the perspective of the designers of those components. (And conversely, of course, your component is an actor from their perspectives.)

Actor

In a Use Case Diagram, an actor usually appears as a stick figure icon (whether it represents a person or not). Other icons are allowed if they communicate the point of a diagram more clearly.

Actors: A .NET Perspective

If an actor is "any outside entity that interacts with your system," then in .NET, that covers a lot of territory:

- For a console or WinForms app, the actors include the user of the application, along with any services or controls from which the application gets information.

- For an ASP.NET Web site, the actors include any viewers of the pages in the sites, as well as any servers from which the site gets information.

- For a Web service, the actors include any other components that call the service, as well as any servers from which the site gets information.

Any person or system that requests that your .NET solution perform a task or does work as requested by your solution is an actor to your solution.

Communications

No, this isn't the "communication" that I've been harping on since the start of this book. In this usage, a *communication* is a request or other sort of message between your system and your actors. While you are in the definition phase (Step 1), you don't usually specify the mechanism by which the communication is transferred: it is enough to know that the transfer occurs. During design (Step 4), you should specify the mechanism in detail, either in the Use Case Diagram or in a Scenario Diagram. As you add detail, you may also describe what information (expressed as parameters) is included in the communication.

Communication(Parameters)
————————————————→

In a Use Case Diagram, a communication appears as a line or an arrow connecting an actor and a use case. The arrow is used to indicate the direction of a request for service: from an actor to the system, or from the system to an actor. Use a simple line to indicate an actor collaborating with the system without specifying where the request originates.

Communications: A .NET Perspective

Given the actors described earlier, some communications for .NET solutions include the following:

- **For a console or WinForms app,** the user inputs—typing, button presses, mouse movements—which are all represented as events, any other events to which the app must respond, and any HTML or .NET Remoting calls that the app makes to other components

- **For an ASP.NET Web site or a Web Service,** the HTML requests to the site, and (again) any HTML or .NET Remoting calls that the app makes to other components

Any message or event to which your .NET solution responds or which it sends can be represented as a communication.

Use Cases

A *use case* represents what your system does in response to a communication from an actor, and represents how your system carries out a requirement of that actor. It appears in a diagram as a simple descriptive phrase (an action, not an object); but within your model, it's a placeholder to which you'll attach additional documentation, more detailed diagrams, and anything you learn about the required behavior.

In a Use Case Diagram, a use case appears as an ellipse with a name inside or underneath. (Underneath is usually easier when you're drawing diagrams by hand, because you don't have to fit the ellipse to the name.)

Use Case Diagrams

Given these elements, then, a *Use Case Diagram* depicts the relationships between one or more actors and one or more use cases through one or more communications. Figure 2-1 is a Use Case Diagram that depicts the use cases required by the **Pet Owner** actor, from the Kennel Management System, introduced in the last chapter.

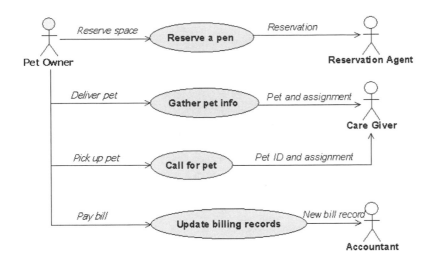

Figure 2-1. Pet Owner use cases

In this example, the actors are the **Pet Owner**, the **Reservation Agent**, the **Care Giver**, and the **Accountant**. They interact with the KMS in the following ways:

- When the **Pet Owner** makes a reservation, the KMS will reserve a pen for the pet and then send the reservation to the **Reservation Agent**.

- When the **Pet Owner** delivers the pet, the KMS will gather all information on the pet and then deliver the pet information and the pen assignment to the **Care Giver**.

- When the **Pet Owner** arrives to pick up the pet, the KMS will call for the pet, sending the pet's ID and pen assignment to the **Care Giver**.

- When the **Pet Owner** pays the bill, the KMS will update the owner's billing records and then send the new billing record to the **Accountant**.

Notice how, in analyzing the requirements of the **Pet Owner** actor, we've identified a number of other actors. You can thus use Use Case Diagrams as a means to discover additional actors that will use the system.

Who Needs Use Cases?

The first time you sit down to draw Use Case Diagrams, you may find yourself—how can I say this?—unimpressed. "Stick figures and bubbles. So what?" I know that was my reaction. It takes a little practice and experience to appreciate the benefit of use cases. After all, you might look at Figure 2-1 and feel that the same information could be conveyed in a simple functional spec, perhaps in bullet-list fashion:

- The system shall reserve pens.

- The system shall gather pet info.

- The system shall fetch pets when called for.

- The system shall update billing records when bills are paid.

So what do use cases tell you that you couldn't get from a functional spec? Well, I found two great quotes that, together, really convey the benefit of use cases:

A functional specification can be said to answer the question, What is the system supposed to do? The use case strategy can be characterized by adding three words to the end of this question: for each user?

—The Three Amigos[2]

The focus on what the users *need to do with the system is much more powerful than the traditional elicitation approach of asking users what they want the* system *to do.*

—Karl E. Wiegers[3]

Who needs use cases? The end users! This is why I feel no Use Case Diagram is complete unless for every use case on it, the actor that initiates it is shown on the diagram and shown to be initiating it. The benefit of use cases is that they tie your model to well-defined user needs.

Does that mean I don't believe in functional specs? Not at all! I like functional specs, for a very simple reason: text isn't pictures. Not the most stunning of observations, but it's important. The brain processes text through different channels and in different ways from pictures. That means that text *and* pictures will involve more brain cells than either would alone. More brain cells is a good thing. Furthermore, different reviewers and different stake-holders have different ways of thinking: some are more verbally oriented,

---

2. Ivar Jacobson, Grady Booch, James Rumbaugh, *The Unified Software Development Process* (Addison-Wesley, 1999), p. 5

3. Karl E. Wiegers, *Software Requirements, Second Edition* (Microsoft Press, 2003), p. 128

while others are more visually oriented. So by having both text (functional spec) and pictures (Use Case Diagrams), you can more fully involve more brains. More brains is also a good thing.

In fact, use cases are more than just a pictorial strategy. Many use case practitioners document their use cases in very structured, very detailed text documents. This subject is beyond the scope of this book (for more information, see Wiegers,[4] the Three Amigos,[5] Schneider and Winters,[6] and Cockburn[7]); but you could easily structure a functional spec not around bullet lists, but around use case documents. And depending on your UML tool, you might even be able to tie use case documents directly to use cases in the diagrams.

But if time is short and you can only have diagrams or text, but not both, which one should you choose? I would go with Use Case Diagrams pretty much every time.

Domain Objects

Often as you model requirements, you'll discover things that your system must maintain or represent: bills, schedules, reports, inventories, contacts, etc. You may want to indicate when and how these *domain objects*—objects within the problem domain—are modified or accessed by your system. You can do this by defining *domain classes* for these things, and then by adding the classes to existing Use Case Diagrams or by creating new Use Case Diagrams that focus on these classes. A class represents the operations and attributes of one or more objects within your system. An *attribute* is a characteristic that describes objects of the class, while an *operation* describes something an object of the class can do.

In UML, a class appears as a rectangle broken into three sections. The top section identifies the name of the class, the middle section lists the attributes of the class, and the bottom section lists the operations of the class.

4. Ibid., pp. 127–139

5. Ivar Jacobson, Grady Booch, James Rumbaugh, *The Unified Software Development Process* (Addison-Wesley, 1999), p. 155–159

6. Geri Schneider and Jason P. Winters, *Applying Use Cases: A Practical Guide, Second Edition* (Addison-Wesley, 2001), p. 27–66

7. Alistair Cockburn, *Writing Effective Use Cases* (Addison-Wesley, 2000)

In Use Case Diagrams, you can add communications from use cases to the classes they affect, indicating how the system interacts with the objects, such as in Figure 2-2.

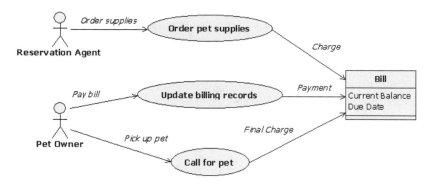

Figure 2-2. Bill-related use cases

By adding Use Case Diagrams with classes, you can see how the actor requirements affect domain objects. This can help you to understand and prioritize requirements related to these domain objects.

Analyzing vs. Designing

When I begin adding classes to a Use Case Diagram, some students start getting nervous. "Wait a minute!" they say. "We're gathering requirements, not designing the system. It's too early to start talking about classes."

And they're absolutely right that it's too soon to talk about design; but classes are *not* just a design issue: they're a way of categorizing the things around us, whether in the code or in the real world. Real-world things can be categorized. Real-world things can be described. Real-world things can do things. From the perspective of a model, real-world things and software things are very similar in nature, and can be modeled with a very similar notation.

So here, you're using classes and objects to represent the problem domain, not the code. At design and implementation time, you'll decide which of these real-world classes must become classes in the software, as well as which additional classes are needed to support the system operations.

If you're still troubled by classes on a Use Case Diagram, consider that actors were originally modeled in UML as a special sort of class. After all, actors have attributes (names, IDs, etc.) and can perform operations (authorize actions, acknowledge tasks, etc.). So in essence, when there's an actor on a Use Case Diagram, there's a type of class on the diagram. Domain object classes are just another way of describing the interaction of the system with the problem domain.

And if you're still unconvinced, read the first guideline in Chapter 3, **Do What Works**. If classes help you to understand the point of a Use Case Diagram, then classes are a good thing; and if *not* having classes makes the diagram less clear, then classes are a must.

Exercise 201: Define Your System with Use Case Diagrams

Taking the problem domain you've chosen, work with your team through each of the processes described next for Step 1 of Five-Step UML. Identify all the actors and domain objects in your problem domain, and use these to uncover and document your requirements as Use Case Diagrams.

Step 1: Process in Detail

You should begin Step 1 by identifying your actors and domain objects (this list doesn't have to be perfect—you can always come back to amend it later on). Next, for each actor you've identified, you should list all the use cases initiated by that actor, and check whether any other actors are involved in those use cases. You can then look at your collection of use cases and see which domain objects are necessary for them.

Let's look at this process in more detail.

Identify Actors

When modeling a complex system, you can identify actors for your system in many ways: end-user interviews, marketing studies, requirements documents, etc. This is discussed in more detail in Chapter 6.

If you and your team are working through Step 1 as an exercise, then you're going to have to rely on yourselves to define all of your requirements, which you can do by brainstorming together to identify useful actors. Think about what actors might either request behavior from your system or provide services to your system.

Don't worry if you can't think of every possible actor: you can use your known actors to identify unknown actors. Also, don't worry if you may have extraneous actors: you can use your Use Case Diagrams to identify the relevant actors. These are candidate actors: you'll revise the list as you go along. Put all actors you identify into an Actor List.

Remember, if the search for actors gets hung up on any question, your customer rep is always the final arbiter.

Brainstorming 101

In case you've never been in a brainstorming session, here are the basics of "formal" brainstorming that you'll need for the exercises in this chapter:

1. The goal of brainstorming is to gather a large number of potentially significant ideas upon which you'll build.

2. One person must act in the role of recorder, ensuring that all ideas are captured. No other formal roles are defined. Everyone is equal in a brainstorming session.

3. **No idea can be rejected!** During brainstorming, no idea is impossible, outrageous, irrelevant, or impractical. Brainstorming is about spanning the range of ideas, not about defining the problem. Filtering and refinement will come later.

Identify Domain Objects

In Chapter 6, we'll look in more detail about techniques you can use to identify your domain objects, but for now you can brainstorm to identify candidate domain objects, just as you did for actors. A good place to start is to think about the sort of information that is important to your candidate actors.

Some useful categories of domain objects are

- Reports

- Schedules

- Appointments

- Tasks

- Purchase Orders

- Work Orders

- Invoices

- Calendars

- Customer Records

- Employee Records

- Tax Records

- Memos

- Assignments

- Contracts

- Inventories

- Inventory Items

- Requisitions

- Messages

Again, these domain objects should depict the real-world entities, not their software representations. Don't worry if you can't think of every possible domain object: you can use your actors and Use Case Diagrams to identify more domain objects. Put all the objects you identify into a Domain Object List.

Remember, if the search for domain objects gets hung up on any question, your customer rep is always the final arbiter.

Pick an Actor

Select the actor that is most likely to use your system. When in doubt, then **Customer** is usually a good bet, because most systems have some sort of customer, who is the ultimate end user of the services provided.

"That's Not What We Call It..."

Your customer rep may tell you that customers are referred to as "clients" (or "patrons," or "guests," etc.). That's great! Learn to speak the customer's language. We all know (or are supposed to know) that code-and-fix is a bad thing; but *design-and-fix* is a good thing. Never be afraid to put something on a page that someone may dispute. The sooner the dispute is out in the open, the sooner you'll resolve it.

You have to be careful, in fact, of the opposite problem: customers who are afraid to tell you that you're wrong. Whether in an exercise or in real requirements gathering, keep the tone loose and comfortable. All participants have to feel free to speak their minds and raise their concerns.

Identify Requirements for the Actor

Document the actor's requirements as use cases in a Use Case Diagram for the chosen actor.

Note that if you're using paper and pencil (rather than a modeling tool), you may find it *extremely* helpful to draw your actors and use cases and even the communications on Post-it notes, so that you may rearrange the diagrams as you refine your ideas. Add each use case to a Use Case List.

Examine the use cases in the diagram. Do any of them affect domain objects? If the diagram isn't too complex, add the domain objects affected, along with any communications to those objects. *Do not* add the objects if the diagram is harder to read as a result. You'll have a chance to address domain objects later.

Identify Participating Actors

For each use case for the chosen actor, identify any new or existing actors that also participate in the use case. Add any new actors to the Actor List.

Repeat for Each Remaining Actor

Check off the chosen actor in the Actor List. Then pick another actor, and draw the Use Case Diagram for that actor. Repeat until all requirements have been diagrammed for all actors. If you find an actor that neither requires any behavior from the system nor provides any services to the system, cross that actor off the Actor List.

If you're working through this process as an exercise, I recommend that you do at least two actor-centered Use Case Diagrams for practice, and more if you wish.

Pick a Domain Object

Select a domain object from your Domain Object List, and start a new Use Case Diagram centered on that object.

Identify Requirements That Relate to the Domain Object

Determine which use cases affect that domain object, and add them to the diagram. Then add the communications from the use cases to the object, and label the communications to describe the changes made by the use cases. Then add the actors that initiate each use case. (Don't add other participating actors, because the diagram will likely become too cluttered.)

Repeat for Each Remaining Domain Object

Check off the chosen domain object in the Domain Object List. Then pick another domain object, and draw the Use Case Diagram for that object. Repeat until all modifications have been diagrammed for all domain objects. If you find a domain object that is never modified by any known use case, cross that object off the Domain Object List.

If you're working through this process as an exercise, I recommend that you do at least two object-centered Use Case Diagrams for practice, and more if you wish.

Example

I won't run through this first step of the process in full detail for my Kennel Management System here, because we'll be looking at that in Chapter 6. But let's look at a couple of diagrams from this, just to get a feel for how it all works.

For example, one of the actors identified for the Kennel Management System is the **Reservation Agent** and Figure 2-3 shows the Use Case Diagram for this particular actor.

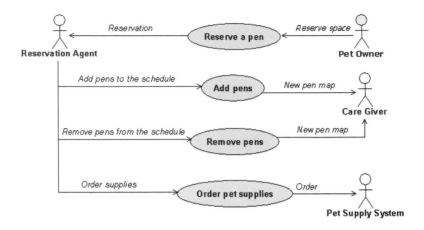

Figure 2-3. Reservation Agent use cases

Note how, for the sake of completeness, I showed the **Reserve a Pen** use case in which the **Reservation Agent** participates, rather than initiates.

If you find that including all the use cases in which an actor participates makes your diagram too cluttered, then you could opt to only show the use cases initiated by a given actor.

Figure 2-4 is another Use Case Diagram from the Kennel Management System, but this time we're focusing on one of the domain objects that has been identified, **Pen**.

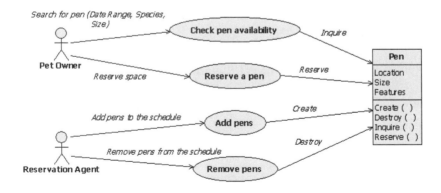

Figure 2-4. Pen use cases

TIP Don't worry if any of this still seems confusing. I'll be walking through this first step of Five-Step UML in a lot more detail in Chapter 6, where you can see how I go about defining all of the requirements of the Kennel Management System.

So that's it! By the time you've finished this first step, you should have a complete set of Use Case Diagrams. You may need to modify these later as you discover more about your model, but for now it's time to move on to Step 2 of the process.

Step 2: Refine

Detail the steps in each requirement via scenarios captured in Activity Diagrams. Add other diagrams where they shed light on the activities.

In this step, you'll describe in more detail what your system will do within each use case. Any given use case will have at least one scenario that describes a particular way the use case may be carried out. This is the Primary Scenario (or less formally, the Happy Path), and reflects what happens in the normal, expected case. If there are decisions or exceptions or errors that must be handled within the use case, these will dictate Alternate Scenarios (or Exception Paths). The Primary and Alternate Scenarios shall be captured in an Activity Diagram.

An Activity Diagram is a way of depicting a set of steps of operation within your system, and is often attached to a use case (as you'll do in Five-Step UML). It has much in common with old-fashioned flowcharts—in essence, the Activity Diagram notation is a simplification of the flowchart notation—and thus should be comprehensible to a very wide audience. I like to call Activity Diagrams "the revenge of the flowchart"; in my more cynical moments, I wonder if teaching UML is a penance I must serve for having such disdain for flowcharts as a younger developer. But in fact, Activity Diagrams both supplement and simplify the old-fashioned flowchart notation, allowing for more useful diagrams than anything I saw in my youth.

UML Notation

At its core, a simple Activity Diagram consists of eight elements: initial states, terminal states, activities, transitions, branches, merges, forks, and joins.

Initial States

An *initial state* denotes where the scenarios in your Activity Diagram begin. Think of it as the entry point to your diagram. There should be exactly one initial state in a well-formed Activity Diagram: if there were no initial state or multiple initial states, readers of your diagram would not know where to look first.

● Initial State

In an Activity Diagram, an initial state appears as a solid black dot.

Terminal States

A *terminal state* denotes the completion of the scenarios in your Activity Diagram. This is the point to which the diagram leads. There should be zero or one in a well-formed Activity Diagram: one if the scenarios have a definite end, zero if the scenarios cycle repeatedly with no defined termination. This rule is often broken, because it can be far less cluttered to have multiple terminal states in a diagram than to have arrows that snake all over the page to reach a single terminal state.

◉ Terminal State

In an Activity Diagram, a terminal state appears as a solid black dot in a larger circle. (Think of it as the "target" of the diagram, to which all paths lead.)

Activities

An *activity* (or more formally, an *activity state*) depicts an action taken by your system. It's a brief description that often represents more detailed actions underneath. (Later, as you refine your design further, you'll create more detailed activities that approach the level of code.)

In an Activity Diagram, an activity appears as a rectangle with semicircular ends. (I call this the "capsule shape," because it resembles a cold capsule. Others call it the "hotdog shape" for similar reasons.)

Why "States"?

Why are activities also called "activity states"? Why "initial states" and "terminal states"? Well, it's time for a little history lesson.

Activity Diagrams are a fairly recent addition to UML; but before there were Activity Diagrams, there were Statechart Diagrams. A Statechart Diagram depicts states of the system or part of the system, along with how events cause changes in those states. They're a very powerful tool, especially in modeling real-time systems and mechanical interfaces.

Now hard-core state modelers are a strange bunch, at first. They will get quite adamant that **Print Invoice** isn't a state, but **Print*ing* Invoice** is. While they can get a bit pedantic about this, their point is fundamentally correct: a state isn't something a system *does*; it is a *description* of a system, and may include a description of what the system *is doing*. States are also (potentially) interruptible by events. If you don't keep these ideas in mind, you may create Statechart Diagrams that are more confusing than helpful.

But less hard-core state modelers—and especially people who had never seen Statechart Diagrams before, and didn't get the point—sat down and used Statechart Diagrams to build glorified flowcharts. UML already had Sequence Diagrams, which could be used like flowcharts in some ways; but it was clear that a flowchart-like diagram was needed by many modelers.

So Activity Diagrams were added to UML; but they were first introduced as a modification of the Statechart Diagram. You still see some of this legacy in the nomenclature.

Expect to see some minor changes to Activity Diagrams in UML 2.0. One of these changes will be to formally separate Activity Diagrams from Statechart Diagrams. There will also be changes to better support business modeling using Activity Diagrams.

Transitions

A *transition* represents the flow of control in your system from one activity to another. You may also create transitions from an initial state to an activity or from an activity to a terminal state; and (as you'll see later) you may also create transitions to and from branches, merges, forks, and joins. The transitions form the "flow" of your scenarios in terms of steps being carried out. They may also indicate events that cause the system to stop one activity and begin another. For example, an activity of **Poll for Input** may end when an **Input Received** transition transfers control to a **Process Input** activity.

Transition
————————→

In an Activity Diagram, a transition appears as an arrow indicating the flow of control. It may optionally include a label that denotes the event that causes the transition; and (as you'll see in the next section) it may also include a guard condition enclosed in square brackets.

Branches

A *branch* represents a decision in your system, a point where you must select exactly one of multiple possible transitions to follow. Each transition leading from the branch must have a guard condition, an expression which evaluates to true or false; and in a well-formed Activity Diagram, exactly one guard condition may evaluate to true each time control reaches a particular branch.

[True]

[False]

In an Activity Diagram, a branch appears as a diamond with one or more transitions entering it and two or more transitions leaving it (each with a guard condition).

Merges

A *merge* is the opposite of a branch: a place where two or more alternate flows of control rejoin and continue as a single flow. You may see diagrams in which a merge is also a branch. For example, the start of a loop is often modeled as a branch (because flow either enters the loop body or skips it) and as a merge (because you can enter the loop start from before the loop or by returning to the start of the loop).

In an Activity Diagram, a merge appears as a diamond with two or more transitions entering it and one or more transitions leaving it.

Forks

A *fork* is a way to show multiple activities that can occur in any order, or even simultaneously. It represents a single flow that splits into multiple flows, such as multithreaded programs or multiple processes.

In an Activity Diagram, a fork appears as a thick horizontal or vertical line with one transition entering it and two or more transitions leaving it. The outgoing transitions from a fork are commonly called *threads*.

Threads vs. Threads

If you come to UML from a parallel processing background, "threads" may imply "multithreaded programming" to you, since that's a common technology for implementing parallel behavior. This is one example of code you might model with UML threads; but threads in UML are more general than that. A thread simply indicates a subflow of control that begins at a fork, ends at a join, and may occur before, after, or simultaneously with other threads of control.

During Step 2 of Five-Step UML, the refining stage, you'll seldom need to think about forks (or about joins, as described next). Unless the requirements specifically state that certain activities must occur simultaneously, forking is more of an implementation issue that may only confuse the gathering of requirements. During design (Step 4), forks and joins will be useful ways to depict simultaneous activities.

Joins

A *join* is the opposite of a fork: a place where two or more threads rejoin to form a single flow. It represents the completion of all activities within each of the threads.

In an Activity Diagram, a join appears as a thick horizontal or vertical line with two or more threads entering it and one transition leaving it.

Activity Diagrams

Given these elements, then, an *Activity Diagram* depicts the transitions between activities, branches, merges, forks, and joins that collectively depict the playing out of one or more scenarios. Figure 2-5 is an Activity Diagram that depicts the scenarios within the **Gather Pet Info** use case from the KMS case study.

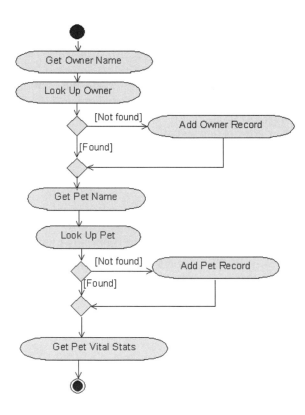

Figure 2-5. Activity Diagram for Get Pet Info use case

In this example, you can see four scenarios:

1. The pet owner and the pet both have records in the system. In this scenario (the Primary Scenario), you get the owner's name, look up the owner's record, get the pet's name, look up the pet's record, and then get the pet's vital stats.

2. The pet owner has a new pet with no record in the system. In this Alternate Scenario, you get the owner's name, look up the owner's record, get the pet's name, look up the pet's record, fail to find a record for the pet, add a new record for the pet, and then get the pet's vital stats.

3. The pet has a new pet owner with no record in the system. In this Alternate Scenario, you get the owner's name, look up the owner's record, fail to find a record for the pet owner, add a new record for the pet owner, get the pet's name, look up the pet's record, and then get the pet's vital stats.

4. A new pet owner brings in a new pet. In this Alternate Scenario, you get the owner's name, look up the owner's record, fail to find a record for the pet owner, add a new record for the pet owner, get the pet's name, look up the pet's record, fail to find a record for the pet, add a new record for the pet, and then get the pet's vital stats.

Subactivity States

So far, I've only identified three Alternate Scenarios in Figure 2-5, and already it is quite complex. Imagine how much worse it could get with many more Alternate Scenarios. If you want to communicate with this diagram, you *might* want to simplify it. (Note the emphasis on *might*: this is an example, not necessarily the only solution.)

You can simplify the diagram by using subactivity states. In an Activity Diagram, a *subactivity state* is an activity that contains a more detailed Activity Diagram. This contained diagram can be depicted on the main diagram (though that seldom simplifies the picture), or it can be shown on a separate page (for a paper model), or it can be placed inside the activity (for an electronic model).

So Figure 2-5 might be simplified as in Figure 2-6, where the new states, **Get Pet** and **Get Owner**, are subactivity states.

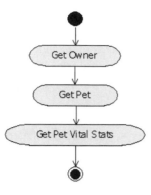

Figure 2-6. Activity Diagram for Get Pet Info use case (with subactivity states)

Then the Activity Diagrams for the **Get Owner** and **Get Pet** subactivity states might be depicted as in Figures 2-7 and 2-8.

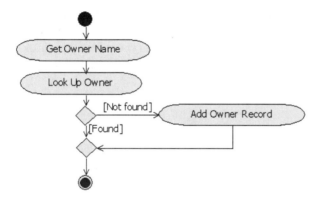

Figure 2-7. Activity Diagram for Get Owner

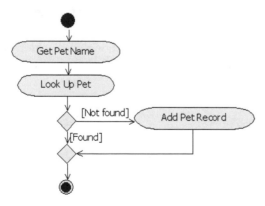

Figure 2-8. Activity Diagram for Get Pet

Note how each contained Activity Diagram has its own initial and terminal state, just as the primary diagram does.

In later examples in this chapter, we'll work from Figure 2-5, *not* from Figures 2-6 to 2-8. Figure 2-5 makes a better example to build upon. But I think you can make a good case that the latter diagrams are easier to comprehend.

A Better Approach?

As a rule, it's better to identify the subactivity states in advance, rather than defining them after the fact. It's often easier to draw the diagrams this way (especially with some UML tools), and you do less rework. So I encourage you: if you foresee a need for subactivity states, add them in from the start. If you can do that, more power to you. You're a "big picture" thinker with a lot of foresight. Me? I'm a detail thinker, and I almost never can foresee the need for subactivity states. Sometimes, I wish I could.

There is one exception to my lack of foresight: I have learned from hard experience that it's pretty much *always* easier to understand forks and joins and threads if the body of each thread is a single activity. That usually means it's a subactivity state.

Exercise 202: Refine Your System Definition with Activity Diagrams

Now that you have an idea of how Activity Diagrams are put together, you can work with your team through Step 2 of Five-Step UML. Taking the use cases you created in the previous exercise (201) as a starting point, follow through the process described next to create your Activity Diagrams.

Step 2: Process in Detail

In Step 2 of Five-Step UML, you need to step through all of the use cases that you documented in Step 1, and examine them to determine the various scenarios of each one. You can then define these scenarios using Activity Diagrams, showing what happens at each stage and how different paths may be found through the use case. If diagrams become too large, complex detail can be hidden in subactivity states.

Let's look at this process in more detail.

Pick a Use Case

To get started, just select any use case from the Use Case List. There's no particular order you need to follow, since you'll analyze every use case eventually.

Find the Scenarios

To work out your scenarios, you can use interviews with the end users, requirements documents, and brainstorming techniques. Ask yourself what should happen in the use case, and what else could occur. Make a Scenario List with some likely scenarios for the chosen use case. When you have finished, select one scenario as the most common or most trouble free or most desirable. This will be your Primary Scenario for the chosen use case.

Draw the Happy Path

Create an Activity Diagram that depicts the Primary Scenario. Break the scenario down into the business rule steps that you understand at this stage. You're not trying to completely design the solution for this use case yet; rather, you're trying to verify that you understand the steps that will satisfy the requirements of the actors. If you feel like you're practically writing code, you're getting too detailed!

Draw the Exception Paths

For each activity in the diagram, think about what could go wrong. At this stage, don't worry about implementation exceptions (e.g., "What happens if the hard drive fills up?"). Instead, worry about exceptions within the problem domain and the business rules (e.g., "What happens if the user isn't authorized to use the system?") Add a branch after each activity that might result in an exception; then add transitions, guard conditions, and activities to handle each exception. Also add merges to reflect the flow rejoining where appropriate.

At about this point, you should be very grateful if you're using a modeling tool or Post-it notes, and very sorry if you're using only paper and pencil. Rearranging hand-drawn diagrams is hard work, and it's only going to get worse in Step 3.

Check off each scenario in the Scenario List for the chosen use case as you add it to the Activity Diagram. Repeat until you're comfortable that you have addressed the major issues and scenarios in the chosen use case. (Don't cross off unrealized scenarios: they may be too detailed for this scope, and you may still have to handle them when you get into implementation design.)

Look for Parallel Behavior

Examine the Activity Diagram. Are there any activities that *must* occur simultaneously? If so, add forks and joins and threads that encompass these activities as appropriate. Don't add threads gratuitously—especially not during analysis!—but be sure that you have them where parallel behavior is required.

Consider Subactivity States and Additional Diagrams

If your diagram is getting complex, consider adding some subactivity states and some contained diagrams. In particular, if you have forks and joins and threads, consider moving the entire contents of each thread into a subactivity state that represents that thread. Like threads, don't add subactivity states gratuitously: multiple diagrams add a comprehension burden that may be worse than one *slightly* complex diagram. Only add subactivity states where they simplify the message.

Repeat for Each Remaining Use Case

Check off the chosen use case in the Use Case List. Then pick another use case, and draw the Activity Diagram for that use case. Repeat until all major scenarios have been diagrammed for all use cases.

If you're working through this process as an exercise, I recommend that you do at least two Activity Diagrams for practice, and more if you wish.

Example

As an example, Figure 2-9 is another Activity Diagram from the Kennel Management System, based on the **Locate Pet** use case discovered in Step 1.

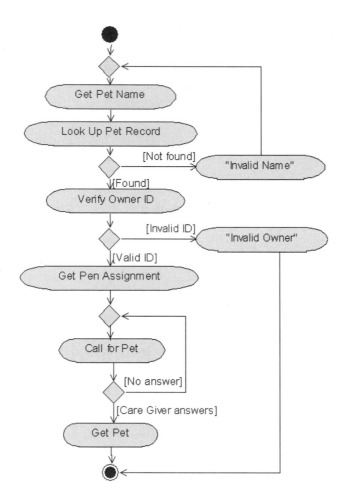

Figure 2-9. Activity Diagram for Locate Pet use case

 TIP   To learn more about developing Activity Diagrams, see Chapter 7.

Step 3: Assign

Use the Activity Diagrams to assign the steps to elements of your system.

In this step, you'll assign your activities (from the previous step) to elements of your system. Because most development today is component-based in some fashion (particularly in the .NET environment), assume that the elements in this case shall be components, interfaces exposed by those components, and user interfaces provided by those components. (In Step 5, you'll zoom in to elements that are classes within a component, or out to elements that are nodes in a distributed architecture.) This step forms the bridge between requirements and architecture, as defined by interfaces, user interfaces, and components. You'll express the activity assignments by adding one new concept to Activity Diagrams: swimlanes.

Swimlanes are so new, in fact, that not all UML tools support them, and there is a wide range of opinions on "correct" and "incorrect" ways to use them. As always, my opinion is if you're communicating, you're using UML correctly.

UML Notation: Swimlanes

Swimlanes are an extension to Activity Diagrams to depict which elements of your system are responsible for which behavior. You simply divide an Activity Diagram into vertical swimlanes, each labeled with the name of the interface or user interface it represents; and then you drag each activity into the swimlane for the interface or user interface that will be responsible for it. Also drag branches, merges, forks, and joins into swimlanes as appropriate, and maintain the transitions between elements. The activities assigned to a given interface may become operations of that interface as the design progresses.

For example, Figure 2-10 is basically the diagram in Figure 2-5 with swimlanes added.

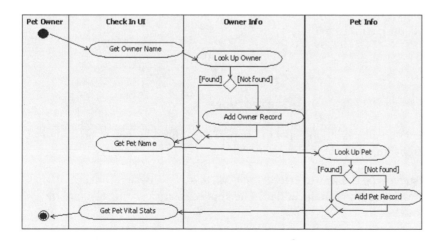

Figure 2-10. Activity Diagram for Get Pet Info use case (with swimlanes)

Here, I've added four swimlanes:

1. **Pet Owner.** This swimlane represents the **Pet Owner** actor that initiates the use case for this Activity Diagram. In this example, the **Pet Owner** is only kicking off the use case. In other diagrams, the initiating actor may take actions within the use case. (See the sidebar "But the Owner Database Is Calling the Check In UI" for an example of this.)

2. **Check In UI.** This swimlane represents the user interface with which the **Pet Owner** interacts.

3. **Owner Info.** This swimlane represents an interface for storing information about **Pet Owners**.

4. **Pet Info**. This swimlane represents an interface for storing information about **Pets**.

The Activity Diagram in Figure 2-10 may look confusing to you. The **Check In UI** calls (i.e., transfers control to) the **Owner Info** swimlane, which makes sense; but then the **Owner Info** swimlane appears to call the Check In UI, which makes no sense at all. The flow of steps made sense before you added swimlanes, and is still correct; but with swimlanes added, the implications may be puzzling.

The confusion arises because transitions in an Activity Diagram aren't really "calls" in the sense of calling a function: they include any way in which control flows from one activity to another: jumps, calls, returns, interrupts, event handlers, etc. A transition usually connotes a simple jump, with no knowledge of from whence the jump came.

Stereotypes

Stereotypes are discussed in detail in Chapter 3; but for now, you only need to know three things:

1. A stereotype is a way to extend the UML to express design concepts it doesn't already contain, and may be applied to any existing element of a model.

2. A stereotype can appear in a diagram inside guillemets (« ») or double angle brackets.

3. UML uses some predefined stereotypes, but you can also create your own custom stereotypes.

We can change this, however, by adding some custom stereotypes of transition (see the sidebar "Stereotypes" for more information on stereotypes). So we'll add three custom stereotypes for transitions:

1. **«invoke».** This stereotype on a transition indicates that, in the normal course of activity A, flow transfers to activity B via a function call or similar mechanism. Then, when activity B is complete, flow returns to activity A, without the need of a return transition.

2. **«interrupt».** This stereotype on a transition indicates that, without regard to the normal course of activity A, flow may transfer to activity B via an interrupt or event or similar mechanism. Then, when activity B is complete, flow returns to activity A as if it had never been interrupted.

3. **«UI».** This stereotype on a transition indicates that a user performs an operation via a user interface.

It may also be useful to use terminal states to indicate the end of a call or interrupt, with a stereotype of «**return**». (Does this make an Activity Diagram not well formed, since it has multiple terminal states? Absolutely! But if my choices are a poorly formed diagram that communicates and a well-formed diagram that doesn't, which do you expect me to choose?)

So examining this use case again, it seems likely that the actual flow will be driven by the **Pet Owner**. We can add new activities and transitions to reflect this, as shown in Figure 2-11.

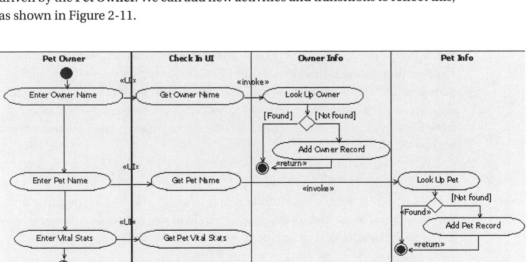

Figure 2-11. Activity Diagram for Get Pet Info use case (with «UI» and «invoke» transitions)

Now the **Pet Owner** takes three actions, and the KMS responds to each.

The Activity Diagram in Figure 2-11 reveals a missing step in the original business rules (as expressed in Figure 2-5): the pet's vital stats are never *explicitly* stored. In the original diagram, we simply assumed that if we gather the vital stats, we store them. But in Figure 2-11, where we explicitly create the owner and pet records, it looks more jarring that we don't store the vital stats.

This should not surprise you. As you try to define an architecture to fit the requirements, you inevitably discover "implied" requirements; and you likely have to add implied activities *and* implied swimlanes to support these implied requirements. These implied elements weren't in the original use cases and business rules because of what Joel Spolsky calls "The Iceberg Secret":

> *You know how an iceberg is 90% underwater? Well, most software is like that too—there's a pretty user interface that takes about 10% of the work, and then 90% of the programming work is under the covers. And if you take into account the fact that about half of your time is spent fixing bugs, the UI only takes 5% of the work. And if you limit yourself to the visual part of the UI, the pixels, what you would see in PowerPoint, now we're talking less than 1%.*
>
> *That's not the secret. The secret is that People Who Aren't Programmers Do Not Understand This.*[8]

Feel lucky if your users give you concise, logical business rules that get you started on defining Primary and Alternate Scenarios. Many can't go far beyond describing the user interface, because that "surface layer" is *all* they interact with. The whole rich structure that underlies that surface is beyond invisible to them: for the most part, it just doesn't exist. So you should expect to find implicit requirements in the business rules; and you should expect to find back-end activities and interfaces that are necessary to support both explicit and implicit requirements. In general, you should expect this architectural assignment stage to be a complex process that raises a lot of questions. Learn to expect these holes in the business rules.

When you find these holes, you patch them, right? *Not a chance!* Oh, if you're doing Five-Step UML as an exercise, patch away! But if you're following a process for fitting architecture to requirements and you find a hole in the requirements, you *have to* go back to the source of your requirements to find out the *correct* way to patch the hole. Take nothing for granted, even something as obvious as "If we're gathering data, we want to store it. Duh!"

---

8. Joel Spolsky, "The Iceberg Secret, Revealed," from the Joel on Software Web log (http://www.joelonsoftware.com/articles/fog0000000356.html). Besides maintaining a popular Web log on software development issues, Joel is the author of *User Interface Design for Programmers* (Apress, 2001), a great book to get you thinking like the user of your application.

Architects and developers aren't the source of requirements, and our instincts aren't to be trusted when it comes to requirements, for multiple reasons:

- You don't know the problem domain. OK, in rare cases, you know the problem well enough, but don't trust your judgment in this respect.

- You're weird. I'm sorry to have to break this to you, but you're weird. Oh, not in the purple-hair-pierced-eyebrow sense, nor in the never-wear-shoes-and-it's-all-we-can-do-to-get-you-to-wear-clothes sense (though I've known developers of both kinds, and they've been fine members of the team). No, you're weird in the brighter-than-average-and-better-at-abstraction sense. It's an inevitable consequence of our profession: we select for those traits; and if you don't have those traits, you don't last long as a developer. All high-skill jobs select for weird people, different people from the norm; and then the jobs usually give those people a chance to practice skills that the average person never practices. Selecting for weird is why most NBA stars are much taller than the population average; and practicing niche skills is why they can make long-distance shots and complex defenses look easy. If you're a developer, you likely can manage more complex abstractions and keep more details straight in your head; and you likely have practiced studying and implementing abstractions far more complex than your average user ever experiences. So you are *not* the best judge of what is simple and comprehensible and practical.

- Your users are weird, often for similar reasons: they work in a specialized domain that selects for certain mentalities. One of my recent clients was an organization that does postmortem studies on brain physiology and genetic traits for studies of mental illness. These people were no dummies! They learned my field far faster than I learned theirs. Don't assume your users are "average."

So if you're not going to patch holes, what should you do? *Suggest* patches. Analyze your suggestions, and prepare descriptions of the implications of and trade-offs from particular patches. Draw the diagrams of how you understand things now *and* of how you think things *might* work. You may not know what the users need, but you're good at knowing the implications of particular architectures and implementations. So go to your users with an explanation of what the hole is, along with one or more suggested patches. Explain the problem, and show them the pictures. The *worst* thing that could happen is they'll accept one of your suggestions, and you'll look like a genius for foreseeing their needs. The *best* thing that could happen is that they'll reject your suggestions and explain why. You and they can then work out a more useful patch; and in the process of suggesting the wrong patches, you learned something new about the requirements. That's *always* a good thing.

In the case of our swimlaned Activity Diagram (Figure 2-11), the obvious patch is to have the **Get Pet Vital Stats** activity write this to some sort of vital stat storage system; but let's assume for now our architecture team want to hide the vital stat details behind the **Pet Info** mechanism, since vital stats are associated with pets. So we'll add an activity to the **Pet Info** interface, **Write Vital Stats**, but we won't worry too much about how that activity manages the process of writing out the data. The result is shown in Figure 2-12.

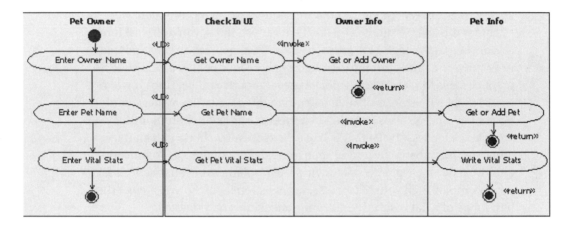

Figure 2-12. Activity Diagram for Get Pet Info use case (architectural view)

Note the other change that we've made to the diagram here: we've simplified it as discussed in the last section (Step 2) by adding subactivity states for **Get or Add Owner** and **Get or Add Pet**. I'll not bother including the separate Activity Diagrams for these two subactivity states here, as the logic is essentially the same as that for the subactivity states we examined in the last section.

But to discuss the architecture with end users, I might retain the more complex diagram, rather than hide details inside subactivity states, so that I can demonstrate to them that their business rules are covered by the system. This is one of many reasons to maintain separate models and separate diagrams. It's also a good reason to not change or throw away old diagrams. (And if the new diagram is *really* difficult to comprehend, maybe you've gone too far. This is why I appreciate a good undo feature in a UML tool.)

Another variation on this diagram is shown in Figure 2-13. Here, we explicitly show how the **Write Vital Stats** activity uses another interface, **Vital Stats Info**, to perform its task.

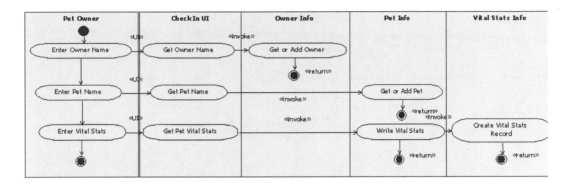

Figure 2-13. Activity Diagram for Get Pet Info use case (alternate architectural view)

Is this the best solution? That depends largely on your perspective, for example, on whether you consider the **Vital Stats Info** interface an implementation detail not needed at this stage. Similarly, we can ask ourselves whether we should explicitly show all of the activity states.

My students have learned that if you ask me *"A or B?"* my answer is usually "Yes" or *"C."* This is a case where my answer is "Yes": the diagrams are all correct, but have different purposes. I believe a model may contain multiple diagrams of a given issue, reflecting different stakeholder perspectives and concerns.

Swimlaned Activity Diagrams vs. Sequence Diagrams

If you've studied or worked with UML before, you may find that Activity Diagrams with swimlanes bear a strong resemblance to UML Sequence Diagrams—especially when I add in the **«invoke»** stereotype. For instance, Figure 2-13 could be redrawn as a Sequence Diagram, as shown in Figure 2-14.

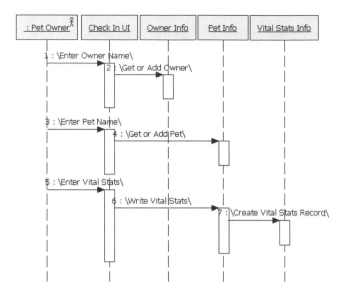

Figure 2-14. Sequence Diagram for Get Pet Info use case

This is the traditional way to model this sort of interaction in UML; but in practice, Sequence Diagrams aren't very effective for showing complex logic. They're really a rather linear form of a diagram, and complex logic isn't linear: it has branches and loops, and it has drill-down into more detailed behavior. This logic is difficult to convey with Sequence Diagrams.

Activity Diagrams, meanwhile, are explicitly designed for showing complex logic, and for showing drill-down with subactivity states; and with the addition of swimlanes, they show interactions very much as you can show them in Sequence Diagrams.

So though some practitioners frown on using Activity Diagrams with swim-lanes where you "ought to" use Sequence Diagrams—arguing that these diagrams should be reserved strictly for business logic—I'll stick with a pragmatic approach: the Activity Diagrams work, *and* it's easy with a tool like XDE to go from business rules expressed as Activity Diagrams to interaction diagrams expressed as Activity Diagrams with swimlanes. If you find it practical to use Sequence Diagrams instead, feel free to do so.

Activity and Sequence Diagrams in UML 2.0, Redux

Perhaps one of the larger changes to Activity Diagrams in UML 2.0 isn't a change to Activity Diagrams at all: it's a change to Sequence Diagrams. The standards committee is adding the concept of *frames*, which are roughly equivalent to subactivity states in Activity Diagrams, and which can also be conditional and iterated. With frames, most of the problems with complex logic in Sequence Diagrams have been resolved.

So there may be a lot less reason to use Activity Diagrams in place of Sequence Diagrams, as I commonly do. Some concepts (like «**invoke**») are modeled directly in Sequence Diagrams, but for these you must create stereotypes in Activity Diagrams. Plus there's a nostalgia factor: Sequence Diagrams were the first UML diagrams in which I really saw a benefit of drawing them. So I'm hopeful that frames will allow me to model a lot more concepts in Sequence Diagrams in situations where I currently use Activity Diagrams. I may still find, though, that the tools make it easier to use Activity Diagrams for these purposes.

Swimlanes: A .NET Perspective

Looking ahead, you can start to think of these swimlanes in terms of the .NET technologies they represent. A user interface swimlane such as the **Check In UI** should represent one of the common .NET user interface technologies:

- **Console I/O.** .NET supports a rich console API, far better than in any version of Windows. In a console app, the system prints messages, and the user types responses.

- **ASP.NET.** Active Server Pages are a Windows technology for dynamically generating Web pages via code and scripts and controls. ASP.NET takes that technology much farther, allowing a wide range of client-side and server-side validation, with rich interaction on advanced browsers and graceful degradation of function on less powerful browsers.

- **Web controls.** These are custom controls that may be hosted in ASP.NET pages, and that are designed to maintain data or state information and render it as HTML code.

- **WinForms (aka GDI+).** The Windows Graphical Device Interface has provided device-independent windowing and graphical user interfaces for more than a decade. WinForms is the latest generation of this technology, allowing faster, safer, and more powerful desktop applications.

- **.NET controls.** These are custom controls that may be hosted in WinForms, and that are designed to maintain data or state information and render it using GDI+.

Since console apps are as dead as the dodo (and painful, too), I recommend against this choice. I would recommend a WinForm if you want this UI to run as a stand-alone desktop application; but since *some* of the user interface will be Web based, an ASP.NET page might make more sense if you want a consistent browser-based UI across the system.

Other swimlanes might represent a number of .NET technologies:

- **Internal classes.** A WinForms app can contain any number of classes, and the swimlanes might represent the classes. More interestingly, because ASP.NET is a true OO technology (as opposed to a simple scripting environment), an ASP.NET app can also contain multiple classes. I don't recommend this approach, however, because you're working at an external, architectural level at this point. Classes are an internal issue.

- **Class libraries.** A class library is a stand-alone component that provides classes for use by other components. Unlike internal classes, a class library is appropriate to discuss during an architectural overview.

- **Interfaces.** As discussed previously in this chapter and in Chapter 1 (and again in Chapter 4), an interface is a set of services provided by some component. .NET supports the interface concept as a fundamental part of the environment.

- **Web services.** A Web service is a program that resides on some Web server and that may be accessed through XML messages. .NET is one of many platforms that supports Web services. Because these platforms all conform to some standard XML message formats (a protocol known as SOAP), clients written for one may be able to work with another. Thus, Web services provide interoperability between environments (and sometimes a performance penalty, of course, since XML is a text-based format and thus not as compact as binary).

- **.NET Remoting.** If the client and server environments are both .NET, you have an alternative to Web services: .NET Remoting, a powerful binary standard for remote components.

- **ADO.NET.** Active Data Objects is a Windows technology for COM access to databases (and data sources that behave much like databases). ADO.NET extends that technology into .NET, and adds a lot more power. If the server is primarily a database, an ADO.NET interface will let clients easily access the data.

- **Native code.** .NET provides wrapper classes and mechanisms for wrapping native Windows DLLs inside well-behaved .NET components. This can be extremely useful when integrating legacy code into your new designs.

- **COM Interop.** .NET provides powerful mechanisms for .NET components to interoperate with COM components, making your .NET designs immediately binary compatible with a very large range of existing Windows code.

The best decision will depend on your chosen architecture, which we'll discuss in Step 4.

Exercise 203: Assign Responsibility to Swimlanes in Your Activity Diagrams

In this exercise, you'll take the Activity Diagrams you created in Exercise 202, identify swimlanes for them, and reorganize activities and update items accordingly. You can do this by following in detail the process described in the next section, adjusting your own model at each stage.

Step 3: Process in Detail

The Activity Diagrams that you created in Step 2 serve as your starting point. In Step 3 of Five-Step UML, you need to work through these diagrams, adding swimlanes to each of them. The best place to start is with the actor that initiates the use case, and then you can look at every activity in turn and think about what part of your system should be responsible for it.

Let's have a look at this process in more detail.

Pick an Activity Diagram

You need to start somewhere, so pick an Activity Diagram. Go for a simple one first off, particularly if you're trying to get some practice. You can work on more complicated diagrams later.

Look at the Initial State

Add a swimlane for the actor that requested the corresponding use case. Drag the initial and terminal states into that swimlane. (Here is where you'll *really* appreciate a modeling tool or Post-it notes.) Or perhaps you'll want to preserve the original diagram and re-create it with swimlanes.

Look at the First Activity

Look at the first activity and try to figure out which existing actor or interface should be responsible for that activity. If it's an activity performed by an actor, the actor is responsible. If it's an activity performed directly in response to an actor (such as processing user input or responding to a timer or receiving a message), an interface for the corresponding actor is responsible. If it's a query to a database, a database interface is responsible. If it's a call to an existing interface, that interface is responsible. And if the activity doesn't seem to "belong" to any existing actor or interface, add a new interface that is responsible for it, as described in the next part of this exercise.

When adding interfaces, think in terms of high-level groups of services that together form a useful set of services.

For a New Actor or Interface or User Interface, Add a Swimlane

If the actor or interface has not been used in the current Activity Diagram before, add a swimlane for it. If the new element is a heretofore-undiscovered actor, add it to the Actor List. If the new element is a heretofore-undiscovered interface, add it to an Interface List. (You may find it convenient to maintain this Interface List as an evolving Component Diagram. We'll see more about Component Diagrams later on in this chapter.) Brainstorm about the purpose of the new interface and what sort of other operations it might support.

Drag the Activity into the Swimlane

Now that you have identified the correct swimlane, drag the activity into it. If the swimlane represents an interface, add the activity to the interface (in the Interface List) as a required operation. If the swimlane represents a user interface, add the activity to the user interface (in the User Interface List) as a required operation.

Update All Transitions to Keep the Activity Diagram Intact

If you're drawing the diagrams by hand, you'll have to correct the transitions to and from the activity that you moved. Consider adding new activities and using the **«invoke»** and **«interrupt»** transitions where appropriate.

Repeat for All Branches, Merges, Activities, Forks, and Joins in the Diagram

Continue revising and adding swimlanes until each element of the diagram has been assigned to a swimlane. Rearrange the swimlanes and activities until you're comfortable with the assignment of responsibilities. Make sure you keep all interface icons, class icons, and node icons up to date with these changes.

Search for Implicit Requirements and Back-End Activities

Look at your architectural assignments, and see what's missing. Have implicit requirements been revealed? Have you found back-end activities that are needed? Add the new activities, along with swimlanes for interfaces to support them.

Consider Subactivity States and Additional Diagrams

As in Step 2, consider adding subactivity states and contained diagrams where they simplify the message.

Repeat for Each Activity Diagram

Add swimlanes to each of the remaining Activity Diagrams. Reuse interfaces where appropriate, but try to keep each interface cohesive. Don't assign an activity to a given interface unless it fits the overall purpose of the interface.

If you're working through this process as an exercise, then I recommend that you add swimlanes to at least two Activity Diagrams for practice, and more if you wish.

Example

As an example, Figure 2-15 is the Activity Diagram for the **Locate Pet** use case (shown in Figure 2-9), with an initial swimlane for the actor added.

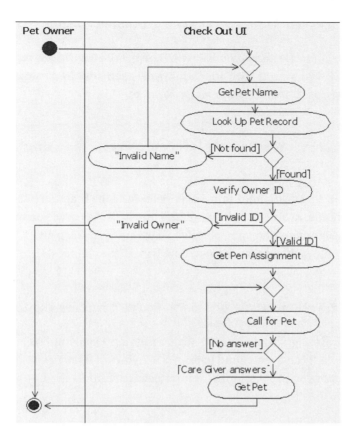

Figure 2-15. Activity Diagram for Locate Pet use case (with swimlanes)

To add further structure to this, we can add activities that reflect the **Pet Owner** controlling the process, and we can add support interfaces to carry out back-end services. This is shown in Figure 2-16.

There are a few interesting things to note on this diagram:

I rearranged some of the flow, so that if the pet name is wrong, we simply display an error message. It's up to the pet owner to reenter the name. Nothing in the application forces the pet owner to do so.

Note that the **Call for Pet** activity uses the **Fetch Pet** activity of the **Care Giver** swimlane (corresponding to the **Care Giver** actor). It does so via an «**invoke**» transition to the **Call for Pet** activity of the **Care Giver UI**, which then instructs the **Care Giver** to fetch the pet. This diagram doesn't indicate the mechanism behind this asynchronous UI request. It might be a pager, it might be a pop-up message, it might be electrodes implanted in the care giver's brain, but you can't tell from this diagram. That is an implementation issue for the **Care Giver UI**.

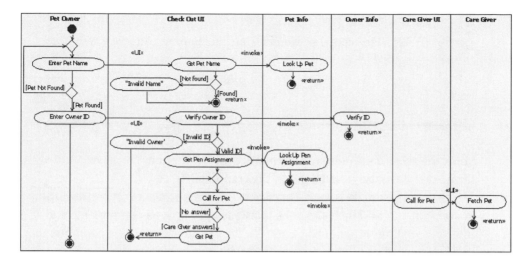

Figure 2-16. Activity Diagram for Locate Pet use case (interfaces added)

Next, let's turn the preceding diagram into an architectural diagram by wrapping the business rules in subactivity states, as shown in Figure 2-17.

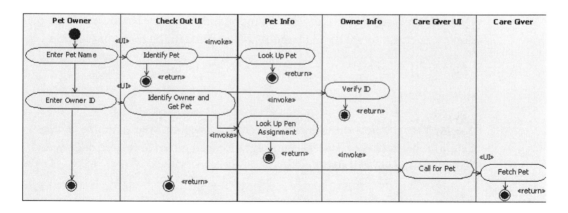

Figure 2-17. Activity Diagram for Locate Pet use case (architectural view)

TIP For more on swimlanes, architecture, and interface design, see Chapter 8.

Step 4: Design

Show the relations among the elements with Component Diagrams. Add other diagrams where they shed light on the components.

In this step, you'll assign the interfaces and user interfaces discovered in Step 3 to components, and then show the relationships between components and interfaces in Component Diagrams. You'll try to identify existing components and interfaces that can be reused, along with new components that will support the new interfaces.

UML Notation

A Component Diagram is a way of depicting the executables and other components that form the logical architecture of your system. At its core, a simple Component Diagram consists of four elements: components, interfaces, realizations, and dependencies. Each of these elements is described in the following sections.

Components

A *component* depicts a deployable part of your system: an executable, a library, a data store, etc. It's a physical representation of a group of related classes and objects within your design.

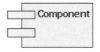

In a Component Diagram, a component icon appears as a rectangle with two rectangular "attachment points" (which are purely decorative; nothing actually attaches to them).

Components: A .NET Perspective

In a .NET solution, a component is any chunk of code or data that you deploy and maintain. Some examples include

- An EXE that represents a console app, a WinForms app, or a Windows service

- A DLL that represents a code library, a WinForms custom control library, or an ASP.NET control library

- The ASPX files that define the Web pages in an ASP.NET site

Some UML practices and tools go even farther, modeling components for the source files that make up your solution as well.

Interfaces

An *interface* represents one or more related services realized (i.e., provided or implemented) by a component. One component may realize multiple interfaces; and multiple components may realize a given interface.

 Interface

In a Component Diagram, an interface icon appears as a circle. An interface should also include documentation of its attributes and operations. These might be depicted in a Class Diagram, using the standard class notation with the UML «**interface**» stereotype; or you might simply list them.

«interface» Interface
+ Attribute
+ Operation ( )

Interfaces: A .NET Perspective

It is important to remember that UML is conceptual, not technological: it isn't tied to a particular technology; rather, its concepts can be used to represent a range of technologies. When people name things, unfortunately, they have a tendency to reuse and overload terms; and thus, the names are potentially confusing when different speakers come from different backgrounds.

So from a UML perspective, *any* mechanism that two components use to communicate is an interface: socket messages, HTTP messages, .NET Remoting calls, SQL calls, etc. But in .NET, "interface" has a very specific meaning: a precise protocol by which you can specify a set of operations and attributes that may be used by multiple client classes and provided by multiple server classes. A .NET interface may certainly be modeled as an interface in UML; but not every UML interface is a .NET interface. (You may find it useful to use stereotypes to distinguish various kinds of interfaces.)

Realizations

A *realization* indicates that a component realizes a given interface. It's indicated via a solid line connecting the component to the interface.

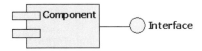

Dependencies

In general, a *dependency* in your model indicates that one element makes use of or depends upon another; and thus changes in the source element will necessitate changes in the dependent element.

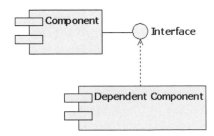

In Component Diagrams specifically, dependencies are drawn from components to the interfaces they make use of. A dependency appears as a dashed arrow.

Component Diagrams

Given these elements, then, a *Component Diagram* depicts components, interfaces realized by them, and dependencies from components to interfaces. Figure 2-18 is a Component Diagram that depicts the interfaces and components discovered in the Kennel Management System so far.

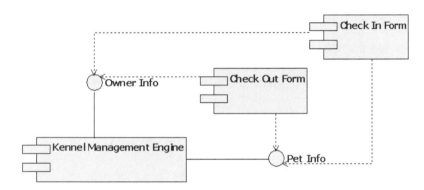

Figure 2-18. Component Diagram for the Kennel Management System

So how do you arrive at this diagram? I'll discuss that shortly, in the section "Step 4: Process in Detail," where you'll also see how to extend the diagram to more completely reflect your architecture; but first let's take a quick look at .NET components.

Components: A (Further) .NET Perspective

Now the .NET developers have to make some specific technology choices, based on the interface technology choices from Step 3. ASP.NET pages and Web services have to be assigned to URLs and deployed to one or more Web sites. Each WinForm needs to be assigned to a component. Does one component provide all forms, or do you have forms distributed among multiple components? If you're using interfaces or .NET Remoting, which components provide these services? If you're using ADO.NET, which databases and tables and queries and views will you access? These and many more questions are part of designing a .NET architecture.

Exercise 204: Assign Interfaces to Components with Component Diagrams

Build Component Diagrams based on the work you've already completed in previous exercises. Work with your team to pick out the interfaces from your swimlaned Activity Diagrams from the last step, define components, and create dependencies between them. The next section explains the process in detail.

Step 4: Process in Detail

Your starting point for this step is—naturally enough—the swimlanes that we created in the last step.

Pick an Interface

Your swimlanes from Step 3 reflect actors, interfaces, and user interfaces, so you need to select one of these as a starting point. Put an icon for it in a Component Diagram. Also, you should put the interface on a Class Diagram as a class icon with an «**interface**» stereotype, or you could just list it in a document. In either case, go through your swimlaned Activity Diagrams and find each place where the interface appears. Find each activity in the swimlane that is called from another swimlane, and add that activity to the interface as an operation. (If the activity has been converted so that it is now part of a subactivity state and is no longer called from outside, then you should only list the subactivity state as an operation, not its constituent activity states.)

Assign the Interface to a Component

Brainstorm and describe the component that might realize the interface. Perhaps you have a preexisting interface provided by a known, existing component. Here are some common preexisting interfaces:

- **ODBC (Open Database Connectivity).** A common SQL mechanism supported by many databases. It might be realized by Oracle, Microsoft SQL Server, Microsoft Access, or a number of other SQL databases.

- **ADO.NET.** The .NET answer to common database access.

- **MAPI (Messaging API).** A common mechanism for accessing mail services. It might be realized by Microsoft Outlook or a number of other mail servers.

- **HTTP (Hypertext Transfer Protocol).** A common mechanism for document transfer on the Internet. It might be realized by Microsoft Internet Information Server (IIS), the Apache Web Server, or other Web servers.

- **FTP (File Transfer Protocol).** A common mechanism for file transfer on the Internet. It might be realized by Microsoft Internet Information Server (IIS) or other file servers.

- **SQL (Structured Query Language).** A common mechanism for storing and querying data. It might be realized by Microsoft SQL Server, Oracle DBMS, or other database servers.

Or perhaps you have already defined a new component, and believe it should provide a newly identified interface. Or perhaps your new interface will require a freshly discovered new component.

If the component (preexisting or new) isn't already on your Component Diagram, add it as a component icon. Then connect the component to the interface via a realization line.

Repeat for Each Interface

Add all additional interfaces to the Component Diagram, and indicate which component or components realize each interface.

From the Activity Diagrams, Identify Dependencies

For each interface, examine its corresponding swimlanes in the Activity Diagrams. Look at the other swimlanes that have transitions into those swimlanes. Those transitions define dependencies: the component that realizes a "calling" swimlane is dependent upon the interface for the "called" swimlane. Add the dependencies indicated. (See the later example for more details on how to do this.)

Rearrange to Make a Legible Diagram

Consider ways to make the Component Diagram more legible:

- Try to avoid crossing lines whenever possible.

- Consider whether you may need to break the Component Diagram into multiple diagrams to show various interactions.

- Hide extraneous details in the diagrams.

Consider also that some rearrangements are worse than others. Save your work, and be ready to undo and try other approaches. Aesthetics and readability can involve a lot of trial and error.

Repeat and rearrange until you're comfortable that you have an architecture that can fulfill the scenarios as depicted in the Activity Diagrams.

That all sounds straightforward enough, doesn't it? Still, there's a lot going on here, so let's see how this all works in an example.

Example

Let's start of with an interface for the **Owner Info** swimlane (which appeared on many of the diagrams we examined in Step 3).

Owner Info Interface

We'll put a corresponding interface on the (currently trivial) Component Diagram, depicted in Figure 2-19.

◯ Owner Info

Figure 2-19. Initial Component Diagram for the Kennel Management System

At the same time, we'll add the interface to a Class Diagram. Then, looking at the swimlaned Activity Diagrams shown earlier in this chapter, we can pick out the operations of **Owner Info.** You'll find that we need two operations: **Get or Add Owner** and **Validate ID.** (Some other *possible* operations are **Look Up Owner** and **Add Owner Record**; but because these have been converted to activities inside **Get or Add Owner** and are no longer called from other swimlanes, we can skip these as operations. We could *choose* to make them operations, giving us flexibility in the future; but so far, nothing in our architecture *requires* them to be operations.) So our initial Class Diagram for our interfaces looks like Figure 2-20.

Figure 2-20. Initial interface Class Diagram for the Kennel Management System

Kennel Management Engine Component

Let's assume that the **Owner Info** interface will be provided by the **Kennel Management Engine**, which we've just defined. The **Kennel Management Engine** shall provide a wide range of data management and validation services. It is essentially the middle tier between presentation and storage. We'll add this as a component to our Component Diagram, which should now look like Figure 2-21.

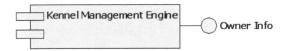

Figure 2-21. Revised Component Diagram for the Kennel Management System

Other interfaces we can define from our swimlanes (in the earlier Activity Diagrams) are **Pet Info** and **Vital Stats Info**. Adding these, our interface Class Diagram looks like Figure 2-22.

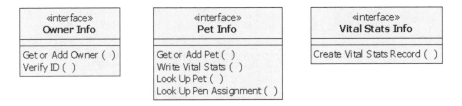

Figure 2-22. Revised interface Class Diagram for the Kennel Management System

Both of the new services really belong in our middle tier, and thus belong to the **Kennel Management Engine**. So our revised Component Diagram looks like Figure 2-23.

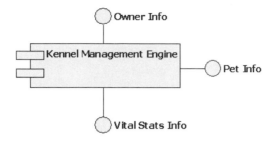

*Figure 2-23. Component Diagram for the Kennel Management System,
second revision*

Hmmm . . . not very informative yet, is it? Well, it is, a little: it tells us three
sets of things that we can ask the **Kennel Management Engine** to do. But it will
tell us a lot more when we add dependencies.

When we look at our swimlaned Activity Diagrams, however, we see that
almost all of our "calls" to our interfaces come from user interface swimlanes,
not interface swimlanes. The only exception, as shown in Figure 2-13, is that the
Pet Info swimlane has a transition to the **Vital Stats Info** swimlane. The provider
of the **Pet Info** interface is the **Kennel Management Engine**; so this implies that
the **Kennel Management Engine** is dependent on the **Vital Stats Info** interface,
as shown in Figure 2-24.

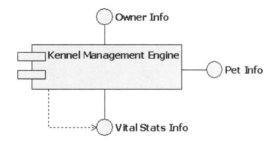

*Figure 2-24. Component Diagram for the Kennel Management System,
third revision*

Although this is *legal* UML, is it *meaningful*? Perhaps.

Perhaps we believe that components yet to be defined will need the **Vital
Stats Info** interface, so we need it in our architecture; and then Figure 2-23 would
indicate both that the interface exists *and* that the **Kennel Management Engine**
accesses vital stats through the interface, *not* through its internal mechanisms.
(We might choose this approach so that we may change the architecture to add

a separate vital stats component without having to significantly rewrite the **Kennel Management Engine**.)

On the other hand, we could decide that vital stats will only ever be accessed by the **Kennel Management Engine**. In that case, we can "collapse" the **Vital Stats Info** interface, demoting it to a mere class within the **Kennel Management Engine**. Don't be afraid to collapse interfaces: discovering superfluous interfaces is a natural part of an evolving architecture. Similarly, don't be afraid to preserve a seemingly superfluous interface: modularizing and exposing your "internal" services gives you a wide range of architectural choices down the road. You have to select your own balance between simplicity and flexibility; and whichever choice you make, you can always change your mind later. It just may entail some work—maybe a lot of work . . .

In this example, we'll collapse the interface to yield the diagram shown in Figure 2-25.

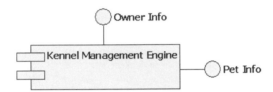

Figure 2-25. Component Diagram for the Kennel Management System, fourth revision

OK, so we've resolved the vital stats issue; but in the process, we're back to a pretty simplistic Component Diagram. Looking at our Activity Diagrams, we can see some dependencies that are pretty clearly implied: our user interface swimlanes have transitions to our interface swimlanes, so *some* sort of user interface components must lie behind those swimlanes. We just need to define them. Looking at the swimlanes, it appears we need some sort of **Check In Form** and some sort of **Check Out Form**. We can add these to the Component Diagram as components, add the dependencies implied by the Activity Diagrams, and *voilà!* We have the Component Diagram shown earlier in Figure 2-18.

Working with User Interfaces

Did that last step bother you? It bothers me: some of the swimlanes correspond to interfaces, but others correspond to actual components. Now this is legal UML. (In fact, it's irrelevant UML: UML doesn't require any mapping from interfaces or components to swimlanes, though the mapping is allowed. We use the mapping here as a useful convention of the Five-Step UML process.) But it's inconsistent UML.

That *bugs* me. I had a nice, linear process: look at a swimlane; make it into an interface; assign it to a component; look at a component and its swimlanes; draw the dependencies. Now there's a bump in my process.

In fact, there are *two* bumps: we also have swimlanes that correspond to users of the system, and those don't show up on the Component Diagram at all. Even worse, those end users are represented in the model as actors; and so are other computer systems with which our system must interact. Yet we interact with those systems via interfaces, which *do* appear on the Component Diagrams. So we have two kinds of actors and two kinds of swimlanes that are similar in nature (within our model, anyway); but one is represented on the Component Diagram, and one isn't. Traditional architecture diagrams don't actually represent the end user; but if architecture is about " . . .the selection of structural elements and the interfaces through which they are connected, the large-scale organization of structural elements and the topology of their connection, [and] their behavior as specified in the collaborations among their elements . . .",[9] then I believe it is a mistake *not* to include the end user in relevant architectural diagrams. Users are "connected" to the system through user interfaces; the topology of elements is shaped in part by the users with which it must be "connected"; and users collaborate with the system to do work (witness the fact that actors can appear as collaborators in Sequence Diagrams).

We can smooth out both of these bumps by adopting a new stereotype, «**user interface**», which may be applied to interfaces. The attributes of a «**user interface**» element represent the data fields displayed by the UI; and the operations of a «**user interface**» element represent the actions a user may take through the UI. Besides defining this stereotype, I find it useful to define a custom icon that looks somewhat like a computer monitor. Its square shape makes it easy to distinguish from regular interfaces.

User Interface

Then we can add «**user interface**» elements to the Component Diagram the same way we added regular interfaces: look at a swimlane that represents a user interface, and add the corresponding «**user interface**» element. Then document the «**user interface**» element in a Class Diagram to depict its data fields and actions.

So, for our example, the user interfaces we have defined so far could be modeled in a Class Diagram as shown in Figure 2-26.

---

9.   James Rumbaugh, Ivar Jacobson, and Grady Booch. *The Unified Modeling Language Reference Manual* (Addison-Wesley, 1999), p. 151

Check In UI

Owner Name
Pet Name
Vital Stats

Get Owner Name ( )
Get Pet Name ( )
Get Vital Stats ( )

Check Out UI

Pet Name
Owner ID

Identify Pet ( )
Identify Owner and Get Pet ( )

Care Giver UI

Figure 2-26. User Interfaces for the Kennel Management System

And then we can select or define a user interface component to realize the **«user interface»** element. Following this procedure (and ignoring that whole vital stats controversy—what *was* I thinking when I put that in the architecture?), the diagram in Figure 2-23 would now look like the one in Figure 2-27.

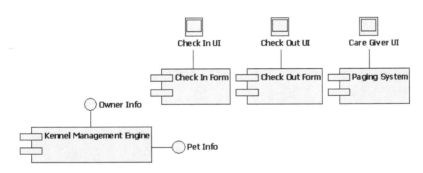

Figure 2-27. Component Diagram for the Kennel Management System, fifth revision

Note how we assign one component for each user interface. This is a common practice for modeling ASPX pages: each page is a component in its own right. In this sense, we can think of the user interface as the HTML delivered to the user's browser, and the component as the code-behind component that creates the HTML and processes the response. Although this approach can be useful, it can also be cumbersome, as you'll see in Chapter 9.

Note also how, by adding **«user interface»** elements and corresponding components, we pick up something we had missed in our architecture earlier: the **Paging System** to notify the **Care Giver** when the pet needs to be retrieved. This is certainly an improvement in our architecture; but it also reveals another problem. In Figure 2-17, we have one user interface swimlane (**Check Out UI**) calling another (**Care Giver UI**). Now this is legal, because a form can certainly launch another form; but it's clearly not what we meant: we wanted an interprocess communication

that would cause the **Care Giver UI** to notify the **Care Giver**. Interprocess communication implies a new interface, one we didn't capture correctly in Figure 2-17.
We'll call it **Care Giver Notify**, and add the corresponding swimlane to the
diagram in Figure 2-17, producing the one shown in Figure 2-28.

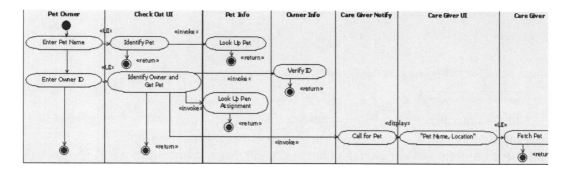

Figure 2-28. Activity Diagram for Locate Pet use case (architectural view, revised)

Note the use here of a new stereotype, **«display»**, applied to a transition to a
user interface to indicate that it must display information for the user's response.
From this diagram, we can add the **Care Giver Notify** interface to the diagram in
Figure 2-27, producing the one in Figure 2-29.

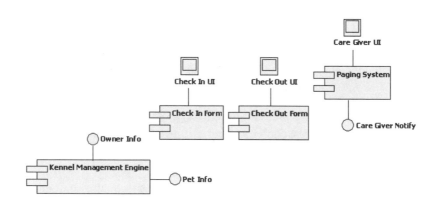

*Figure 2-29. Component Diagram for the Kennel Management System,
sixth revision*

Next we can add dependencies the same way we did before. Recall that in order
to add dependencies, we examine each swimlane, and look at the swimlanes that
have transitions into it, converting those into dependencies. By following this
procedure and rearranging for legibility, we get the diagram in Figure 2-30.

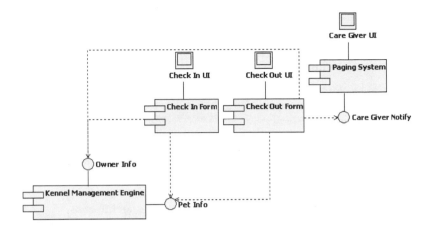

Figure 2-30. Component Diagram for the Kennel Management System, eighth grevision

Now that we've gone this far, we might as well go all the way: adding the actors corresponding to swimlanes, and adding dependencies from the actors to the user interfaces they use. This will give us a complete picture of the roles that users play within the architecture, as shown in Figure 2-31.

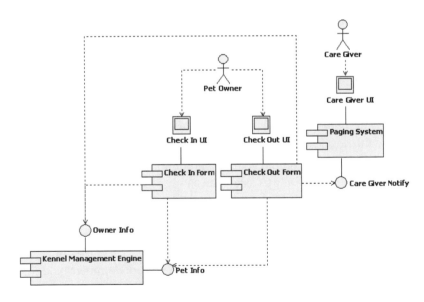

Figure 2-31. Component Diagram for the Kennel Management System, eighth revision

If you would rather stick with formally correct UML notation, you could define a new stereotype for components: «**user**». You could then add a new component with that stereotype wherever you want to show a user interacting with a user interface. But even though it's not standard UML, I find it easier and clearer to just put the actors on the Component Diagrams, as shown above. And again, if it helps you to communicate, it's useful UML, even if it's not perfect.

So What About Those Names?

Here in Step 4, we're stepping out of analysis and into design (architectural design, to be precise). That means the programmers in the crowd are starting to think about implementation (because we programmers have a nasty habit of running ahead of where we're supposed to be). And that means that some of you reading this right now are saying, "Hey, those names aren't legal identifiers in my implementation language. What's up with that?" And you're right, of course: **Kernel Management Engine**, **Owner Info**, and **Get or Add Owner** aren't legal identifiers in any programming language I know. And if you start talking corporate naming standards and coding conventions, the situation only gets worse.

So what *is* up with that? Well, in my practice, I usually try to share my architecture with my stakeholders as it evolves, so that they can give me an outside perspective. (OK, I *really* only share selected, simplified views. I don't want to bury them in technical details.) So I prefer human-readable names. andIfYouThinkThisIsHumanReadable, youHaveBeenProgrammingTooLong, and youNeedToGetOutIntoTheRealWorld. So how do I deal with this disconnection between readable names in my model and legal identifiers in my code? I have three suggestions:

1. If you're not generating code from your model automatically, you have to translate your model into code by hand. While you're doing so, translate the names into legal identifiers.

2. If you *are* generating code from your model automatically, most modeling tools will automatically translate the names into legal identifiers. Some will even let you define the translation rules, such as "Convert all spaces to underscores" or just "Remove all spaces." You can even specify common conventions such as "All class names begin with 'C'" and "All interface names begin with 'I'."

3. If you're not worried about communicating with nonprogrammers (and why not, eh?), follow your naming rules and conventions in the model.

Of these approaches, I personally prefer the second choice.

TIP   To learn more about Component Diagrams and architecture, see Chapter 8.

Step 5: Repeat

Narrow the scope of your process to individual elements (designed with Class Diagrams). Add other diagrams where they help you understand the system. Repeat Steps 1 through 4 as appropriate for the current scope.

In this step, you'll narrow your scope to look at a single component (as identified in Step 4). By zooming in to the scope of the component, you can apply the same analysis and design processes to determine the structure of the component.

You'll begin by playing "Interface Hangman": treating the interfaces to a component as actors from the perspective of the component, as shown in Figure 2-32.

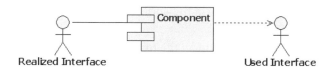

Figure 2-32. Interface Hangman

If you're confused about this step, consider this definition of an actor:

An actor *represents any outside entity that interacts with your system. It may request services from your system; and it may perform services for your system.*

Well, in this step, you narrow your scope so that the only "system" of interest is one particular component (at a time). And "outside" that component lie any actors that interact with it *and* any other components that interact with it. These all meet the definition of "actors" now that you've narrowed your scope; however, one rule for interfaces is that they define everything that is known about the connections between components, both for the source component and for the client component. Thus, from the perspective of the current component, the interfaces and user interfaces that it realizes are all that you know about the actors that make requests of it; and the interfaces on which it depends are all that you know about the actors that provide services to it. So it will have actors that represent the users of any user interfaces it provides; but you'll also create "component actors" that represent the interfaces related to the current component. (Despite Figure 2-32—which is drawn *only* to convey the idea of interfaces as actors, *not* as an example you should follow—you may want to use interface icons to represent these component actors, rather than actor icons. This will emphasize that these are interfaces, not people.)

If the interfaces are component actors, then the methods of interfaces realized by the current component may be treated as component use cases. Again, consider this definition of a use case:

> *A* use case *represents what your system does in response to a communication from an actor, and represents how your system carries out a requirement of that actor. It appears in a diagram as a simple descriptive phrase (an action, not an object); but within your model, it's a placeholder to which you'll attach additional documentation, more detailed diagrams, and anything you learn about the required behavior.*

So if a use case represents behavior required by an actor, then a component actor's requirements—and thus its component use cases—are defined by the operations of the interface it represents. No other requirements are possible, because the interface completely defines how the component and its client may interact. The only other requirements are those of the end user actors who make use of the component's user interfaces.

So in this step of Five-Step UML, you'll perform the following substeps:

- **Define** the component's behavior with component Use Case Diagrams, one or more for each interface of the current component, and one or more for each user interface of the current component.

- **Refine** the behavior by producing a component Activity Diagram for each component use case.

- **Assign** the activities in the component Activity Diagrams to classes, using swimlanes.

- **Design** your internal architecture of the component with Class Diagrams (described in the next section).

UML Notation

The only particularly new elements in this step are those related to Class Diagrams: classes, associations, and dependencies.

Classes

A *class* represents the operations and attributes of one or more objects within your system. It binds attributes and operations to completely define the behavior of the objects. Thus a class definition serves the same purpose for an object that an interface definition serves for a component: it describes the ways in which client elements may use the given element.

In a Class Diagram, a class appears as a rectangle broken into three sections. The top section identifies the name of the class, the middle lists the attributes of the class, and the bottom section lists the operations of the class.

If it makes the diagram less cluttered and thus more clear, you may hide the attributes or operations for any class in the diagram. You may even hide *some* of the attributes and operations, while showing others. But I usually discourage this—unless the class definition is really large and overwhelms the rest of the diagram—because readers tend to assume that a partial list is a full list.

Classes: A .NET Perspective

Now you're moving from domain classes to code classes. You need to consider the precise .NET mechanisms for implementing each class. What is its base class? What are its attributes, including types and initial values? What are its operations, including parameters and return types? What kind of class is it: a class, a structure, an enumeration, a delegate?

Associations

An *association* represents an object of one class making use of an object of another class. It is indicated simply by a solid line connecting the two class icons. An association indicates a persistent, identifiable connection between two classes. If class A is associated with class B, that means that given an object of class A, you can always find an object of class B, *or* you can find that no B object has been assigned to the association yet. But in either case, there is always an identifiable path from A to B. Class A uses the services of class B or vice versa.

Associations: A .NET Perspective

In .NET code, an association is most probably implemented as one class containing another—or to be more precise, containing a reference to the other, since all .NET classes other than structures are always contained by reference. For some designs, each class might contain a reference to the other. These concepts are discussed further in Chapter 4.

Dependence

In Class Diagrams, a *dependence* represents an object of one class making use of or somehow "knowing about" an object of another class; but unlike association, dependence is a transitory relationship. If class X is dependent on class Y, then there is no *particular* Y object associated with an X object; but if the X object "finds" a Y object—perhaps it is passed as a parameter, or it receives one as the return from an operation that it calls, or it accesses some globally accessible Y object, or it creates one when it needs one—then it knows what it can do with the Y object. Object X is potentially affected by a change in Object Y.

As in other diagrams, dependence is indicated by a dashed arrow connecting the two class icons.

Dependence: A. NET Perspective

In .NET code, dependence has become almost a nonentity. In old C++ code, for example, dependence could be implemented as one class **#include**'ing the header file for another class. That **#include** statement indicated that the first class knew what to do with the second class. But in .NET, most classes are visible to other classes. The closest things to dependence in .NET are

- The **using** directive, indicating that all code in a file can use all classes in a particular namespace

- Assembly references, indicating that a project can use all classes in a particular assembly

But both of these uses are package specific, or perhaps component specific. You may choose to avoid dependence for this reason; but I still prefer to model dependence among classes, because it indicates that one class may create or otherwise manipulate objects of another class.

Class Diagrams

Given these elements, then, a *Class Diagram* depicts classes and associations between them. Figure 2-33 is a Class Diagram that depicts the classes and associations that may be useful in the Kennel Management System.

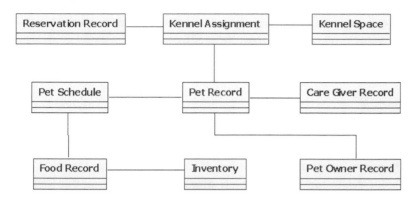

Figure 2-33. Class Diagram for the Kennel Management System

Classes: A (Further) .NET Perspective

The .NET Framework contains over 3,300 classes for common infrastructure operations. Before you design your own classes, you might save time to see if .NET gives you classes that provide the functionality you need, or at least a large chunk of it.

TIP   To learn more about Class Diagrams and design, see Chapters 4 and 9.

Exercise 205: Define, Refine, Assign, and Design Within Your Components

Pick a component to design. (You'll design all of them eventually.) Then walk through the following procedures to build a design model for that specific component.

Step 5: Process in Detail

In this step, you simply take each component identified in the last step, and repeat the whole process from beginning to end, as if the component were a system in its own right. For each interface of the component, you break out the detail into Activity Diagrams and then, by adding swimlanes, identify the classes that are responsible for each action. By examining how calls are made between swimlanes, you can work out the associations and dependencies between classes.

Let's see how this process works in more detail.

Define

Collect together all of your components by adding a component to your model for each interface to your component. Treat your component like an actor and repeat the requirements definition process, as if each method of an interface were a use case for the (component) actor. If an earlier diagram indicates that a method uses another interface from some component, add that other interface as a collaborating actor, and label the communication to that actor with the name of the requested method.

If you're working through this process as an exercise, then I recommend that you do at least two component Use Case Diagrams for practice, and more if you wish.

You should also think about user interfaces at this stage. If your component provides any user interfaces, add the actors that use those interfaces to your model; and add the actions supported by that user interface as use cases for that actor. If an earlier diagram indicates that an action uses another interface from some component, add that other interface as a collaborating actor, and label the communication to that actor with the name of the requested method.

Refine

Take each component use case, and repeat the requirements refinement process by creating a thorough component Activity Diagram for the use case. (If you're working through this as an exercise, do at least two component Activity Diagrams for practice, and more if you wish.) Define your Primary Scenario for each Activity Diagram, and then define your Exception Scenarios.

Recall that during analysis, you were supposed to concentrate on business rule exceptions (e.g., "What happens if the user isn't authorized to use the system?"). *Now* is the time to concentrate on implementation exceptions (e.g., "What happens if the hard drive fills up?"). These component Activity Diagrams aid you in pre-planning how to detect and handle exceptions.

Note that, if you used subactivity states in Step 2 or Step 3 to simplify your requirements Activity Diagrams, you may have given yourself a head start in designing your component Activity Diagrams. If a subactivity state represents one method of an interface or one action of a user interface, then its constituent activities capture some important business rules that must be implemented.

Finally, examine your Activity Diagrams to see whether subactivity states might simplify any complex logic.

Assign

Add swimlanes to each component Activity Diagram. Within a component Activity Diagram, the swimlanes will represent component actors (either true actors or interfaces related to the class) and objects of classes. As you add swimlanes for new objects, add the corresponding class icons on a separate Class Diagram. As you assign activities to each object, make them into operations documented in the class icon.

It is common to have some sort of "gateway class" that serves as the entry to the component for the interface. For a user interface, the gateway class will be the form or dialog box that provides the user input. For a component interface, the gateway class will be a class that realizes the interface, providing the same attributes and operations as the interface (plus others as needed). The gateway provides the surface implementation of the responsibilities specified in the interface. (This isn't the only way to implement an interface, but it is a very natural approach in any OO language.) You depict a class realizing an interface much as you show a component realizing an interface: a circle for the interface, connected to the class via a solid line.

Design

Now revise the component Class Diagram to depict the associations required by the component Activity Diagrams. Your swimlanes in this step reflect interfaces, user interfaces, and classes. Select one of the interfaces from the swimlanes, and put an icon for it in a Class Diagram. Then, if the interface is realized by one of your classes, add that class, with the realization line connecting them. (If the interface is external to your component, just show the interface.) Repeat for each interface swimlane. (Don't add «**user interface**» elements, because they're entirely described by the classes that provide them.)

Next add classes for the remaining swimlanes. Also add classes for the object flow states in your Activity Diagrams. Think about what attributes each class will need to support its operations. Add these to its class icon.

Needless to say, all of this takes a lot longer to do than it does to say. Let's see how all this works out in an example.

Example

As part of our example in Step 4, we saw that the **Kennel Management Engine** component will realize two interfaces: **Pet Info** (the interface for manipulating Pet information) and **Owner Info** (the interface for manipulating **Pet Owner** information). **Pet Info** and **Owner Info** both require simple edit and query methods.

Pet Info and Owner Info Interfaces

For the **Pet Info** interface, this results in the component Use Case Diagram shown in Figure 2-34.

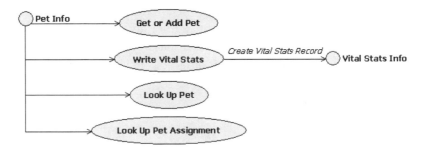

Figure 2-34. Component Use Case Diagram for the Pet Info interface

Note the communication from the **Write Vital Stats** use case to the **Vital Stats Info** interface, with a **Create Vital Stats Record** label. This corresponds to the information in our earlier swimlaned Activity Diagram shown in Figure 2-13, and tells the designers and implementers of **Write Vital Stats** how they are expected to carry out this responsibility.

Now, I know I told you to design one component at a time (on a real project, you might have one team designing each component simultaneously); but for the sake of this example, I'd like to turn to another component, one that has a user interface. We'll choose **Check In Form** because it's most interesting. Because they provide complementary examples, we'll look at both **Kennel Management Engine** and **Check In Form** for the rest of this example.

So looking at **Check In Form**, what was the next step again? Ah, yes:

If your component provides any user interfaces, add the actors that use those interfaces to your model; and add the actions supported by that user interface as use cases for that actor. If an earlier diagram indicates that an action uses another interface from some component, add that other interface as a collaborating actor, and label the communication to that actor with the name of the requested method.

Well, by examining the **Check In Form** component that we diagrammed in the last step, we can see that it provides a user interface, **Check In UI**; and that it has three actions, as indicated in Figure 2-26: **Get Owner Name**, **Get Pet Name**, and **Get Vital Stats**. These become component use cases for **Check In Form**; and the actor interacting with those use cases is the **Pet Owner**, as indicated by Figure 2-30. Combining this information, we end up with Figure 2-35.

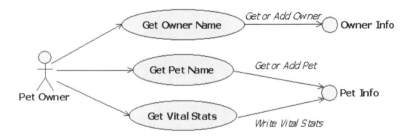

Figure 2-35. Component Use Case Diagram for the Check In UI

Note how, based on our swimlaned Activity Diagram for the **Get Pet Info** use case shown in Figure 2-12, we add one communication to the **Owner Info** interface and two to the **Pet Info** interface.

Creating Activity Diagrams

Figure 2-36 shows the Activity Diagrams for **Get or Add Owner**, with logic added to handle implementation exceptions.

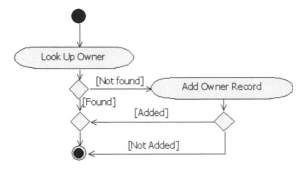

Figure 2-36. Component Activity Diagram for the Get or Add Owner use case

Looking at Figure 2-36, you may think, "Hmmm, that doesn't tell me much. How can the caller tell the difference between found or added and not added?"

Good question! There's no UML convention for this, so instead, I'm going to break a UML rule to make this clearer—the rule that says a well-formed Activity Diagram should have only one terminal state. In component Activity Diagrams like these, I like to indicate different possible return values via different terminal states, as in Figure 2-37.

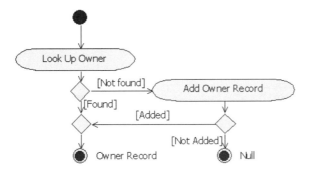

Figure 2-37. Component Activity Diagram for the Get or Add Owner use case, revised

Now, in the **Check In Form**, we have an action, **Get Owner Name**, but we have no specifics on how that name is to be entered: first and last names as one string, first and last names as separate strings, first and middle and last names, etc. So how are we going to handle that?

"How Did I Miss That?"

You may find that, as you try to refine a component use case, there are business rules implied but not specified within your requirements model, for example, our confusion over how to correctly enter information for the **Get Owner Name** action.

Now you could argue that I just didn't do a very good job of gathering and documenting and modeling the requirements for this project. And since this is simply an example project with an example model created to instruct you readers, you might even be right; but that would miss the point.

The point is simply this: *Requirements work is never done.* Period. For that matter, neither is architecture work, nor design work, nor coding work, nor testing work, nor documentation work, nor maintenance work (and *certainly* not management work). But the reason why the other tasks are never done is that, until the project is gone and no longer supported, new requirements keep trickling in.

You don't believe me? Good! Skepticism is healthy for a developer. But let me try to persuade you by bringing in some outside help.

Both of these attitudes fail to acknowledge the reality that it is impossible to know all the requirements early in the project and that requirements will undoubtedly change over time.

—Karl E. Wiegers[10]

With rare exceptions, the requirements must change as the software job progresses. Just by writing a program, we change our perceptions of the task. The ripple of change starts with the requirements and continues through implementation, initial use, and even through later enhancement. Even if we could plan for all this development learning, the computer implementation of human tasks changes the applications themselves. Requirements by their very nature cannot be firm because we cannot anticipate the ways the tasks will change when they are automated.

—Watts S. Humphrey[11]

While each iteration is a sweep through requirements, analysis, design, implementation, and test workflows, the iterations have different emphases in different phases. . . . During the inception and elaboration phases, most of the effort is directed toward capturing requirements and preliminary analysis and design. During construction, emphasis shifts to detailed design, implementation, and testing.

—The Three Amigos[12]

---

10. Karl E. Wiegers, *Software Requirements, Second Edition* (Microsoft Press, 2003), p. 35

11. Watts S. Humphrey, *Managing the Software Process* (Addison-Wesley, 1989), p. 25

12. Ivar Jacobson, Grady Booch, James Rumbaugh, *The Unified Software Development Process* (Addison-Wesley, 1999), p. 104

For many years, the holy grail of requirements management has been to collect a set of requirements—scrubbed, minimally specified, or otherwise—encase them in permafrost, and then build a complete product design, implementation, documentation, and quality assurance atop them. Unfortunately for developers and their ulcers, projects that have successfully frozen their requirements have proven to be almost as hard to find as the Holy Grail itself.

—Steve McConnell[13]

Give up yet? If not, I can just keep pulling books off my shelf and citing experts who all agree: the Waterfall Model is dead. (I'll discuss this further, along with different development models, in Chapter 12.) As McConnell said, requirements freeze was an unattainable holy grail, and teams that didn't accept this up front and plan to deal with it were in for a rude awakening. Modern software processes and methodologies are all predicated on a recognition that requirements *will* evolve, so you had better have a means to deal with the changes.

In Model-Driven Development (Five-Step UML being a simple example), the means to deal with requirements changes are twofold.

First, there is a place in your model for the newly discovered requirements, and the model has to be the central artifact. When you discover a new requirement during design (or implementation, or whenever), make sure you incorporate it back into the requirements model and trace through its implications just as you did during analysis. You have a process that works; don't give up on it late in the game, because that's when you need it most!

The second way you handle change in Model-Driven Development is the common way found in many modern processes: iteration through the same core activities, over many parts of the problem and at many scales of abstraction. In Model-Driven Development, of course, those core activities are the Five Steps.

In this case, we could decide that the process of **Get Owner Name** consists of getting a first name, getting a last name, and verifying that neither is blank. This is shown in Figure 2-38.

However, this diagram reveals a basic problem with modeling user interfaces, especially the modern Graphical User Interface (GUI) paradigm: to the extent possible, users are permitted to do work in an order that makes sense to them, not in an order specified by the system. If a form has a **First Name** field and a **Last Name** field, nothing stops the user from filling in the last name first, perhaps because that's what they're given first. The more a system allows users to work the way they wish, the more satisfied the users are.

---

13. Steve McConnell, *Rapid Development: Taming Wild Software Schedules* (Microsoft Press, 1996), p. 331

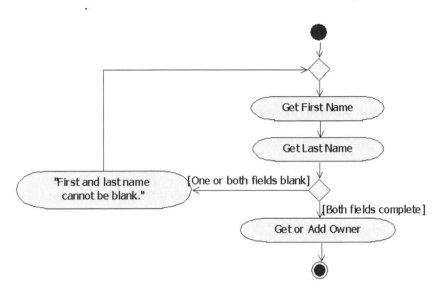

Figure 2-38. Component Activity Diagram for the Get Owner Name use case

Yet a diagram like Figure 2-38 may imply to developers that users *must* enter the first name first; and thus they may implement this constraint, a constraint that will take time and effort and money *and* annoy the users. Talk about a lose-lose proposition!

So how can we convey the freedom we want the users to have? There are a number of legal but less than satisfying approaches.

First, we could model every possible path that users might follow. This pretty much never works: there's too much redundancy and too much clutter, as in Figure 2-39.

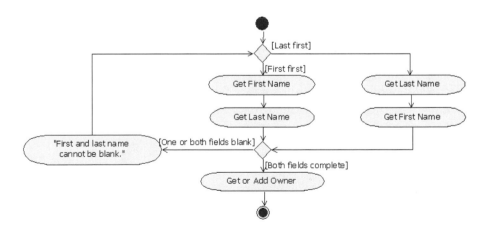

Figure 2-39. Component Activity Diagram for the Get Owner Name use case: a redundant revision

As an alternative to this, we could model the user selection with forks and joins and threads. Recall that a *fork* is a way to show multiple activities that can occur in any order, or even simultaneously. Although a very common usage is for simultaneous activities, don't overlook the "in any order" clause. You can use forks and joins and threads to show that all the activities can be performed in whatever order the user chooses, as in Figure 2-40.

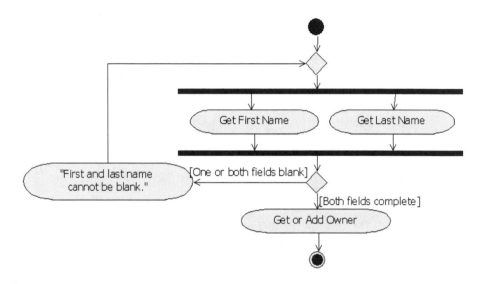

Figure 2-40. Component Activity Diagram for the Get Owner Name use case: a confusing revision

Although this is technically correct, I find it makes matters worse, because forks and joins are a hard concept for nondevelopers. So to solve a simple problem, we introduce a hard notation and have to explain it every time it appears. Plus, I really do prefer to reserve forks and joins for simultaneous activities.

Another alternative is simply to go with the diagram that we had to start with, but this time we'll add a note to explain, as in Figure 2-41. This is pretty clear, as long as no one misses the note.

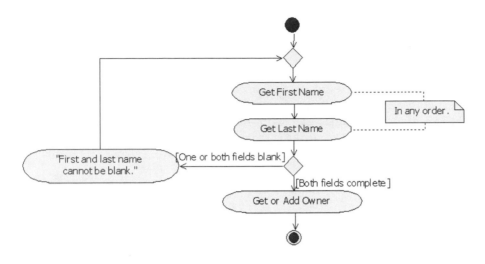

Figure 2-41. Component Activity Diagram for the Get Owner Name use case: a not-too-bad revision

But the best approach I believe is to use a note *and* a not-so-revolutionary technique called a *screen shot*. Really, is there any developer working in a modern GUI who will be confused by Figure 2-42?

Figure 2-42. Screen shot for the Get Owner Name use case

As Ambler says in *Agile Modeling*, "The UML Is Not Sufficient."[14] There are things that UML expresses well; and there are things that are more easily expressed with other forms of diagrams, with pictures, or with words. I may disagree with Ambler in degree—I think UML may be applied in a lot of places where he thinks it's insufficient—but I think he's fundamentally correct. As always, our job is to communicate, not to be "correct."

---

14. Scott W. Ambler, *Agile Modeling: Effective Practices for eXtreme Programming and the Unified Process* (John Wiley & Sons, 2002), pp. 169–171

But What If the User Clicks Cancel?

There's another problem with modeling the modern GUI: users can cancel what they're doing in a wide variety of circumstances, often at any point along an Activity Diagram. (Curse those users! Always doing what they want, rather than what we tell them to do.) Just imagine trying to modify Figure 2-40 to add a branch at every point where the user *might* cancel the procedure. (And if that doesn't scare you, imagine trying to modify Figure 2-38 or Figure 2-39.) Flexibility is hard to model.

So how would you model this flexible ability to cancel? You could simply train your people to expect cancellation at any time, regardless of whether it's shown in the diagram or not, or make sure that you add a note to your diagrams that explicitly declares that the user may cancel.

Another option would be to add a subactivity state that contains all the activities that may be cancelled. Unlike my earlier advice on subactivity states, when I use a subactivity state for common event handling, I like to show the subactivity state and its constituent activities on the same diagram, as in Figure 2-43.

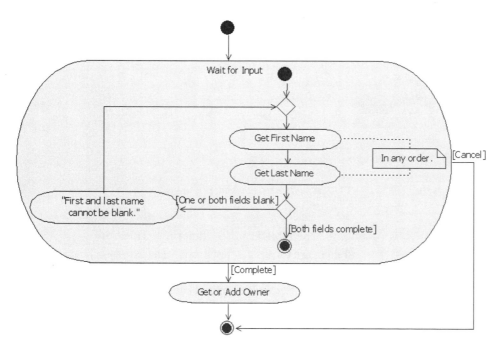

Figure 2-43. Component Activity Diagram for the Get Owner Name use case, with Cancel

This picture may seem a bit like overkill, so you might want to stick with Figure 2-41 and add another note. But this diagram *does* convey that the user *can't* cancel during the **Get or Add Owner** activity.

A Note on Notes

UML isn't perfect. Nothing is, and the creators of UML knew better than to try for perfection. That's why they included stereotypes as an extension mechanism. (See Chapter 3 for more on stereotypes.) And that's also why they included notes. A *note* is a block of text that appears in a diagram and describes some aspect or detail of the diagram that might be unclear, or that might be difficult to convey pictorially.

A note appears in an icon that looks like a page with a corner turned down. It may also be attached with a dashed line to the diagram elements it describes.

You should be sure to add notes wherever they provide useful clarification to a diagram. But don't get carried away: if you have a three-page note with three little diagram icons in the lower-left corner, you're writing a functional spec, not building a UML model; and most UML tools make lousy word processors.

Adding Swimlanes

Adding swimlanes to our Component Activity Diagram for the **Get or Add Owner** use case (Figure 2-37), we get the Activity Diagram shown in Figure 2-44, where the **Owner Info** interface is realized in a gateway class, **COwnerInfo**, which carries out the assigned method.

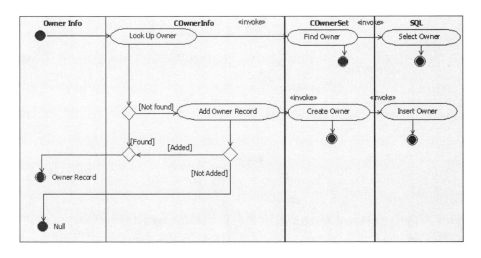

Figure 2-44. Activity Diagram for the Get or Add Owner use case, with swimlanes

Usually, a gateway class relies upon deeper classes and interfaces to carry out its responsibilities; here, that's **COwnerSet**, which does the work of calling into the SQL database.

Although we *could* have had **COwnerInfo** call directly into a SQL database to work with owners, that's not the wisest implementation. I like to isolate the SQL handling inside wrapper classes, because SQL itself isn't inherently object-oriented. Mixing SQL's relational behavior into the design may make matters more confusing.

Furthermore, I usually have a wrapper class that represents a table or result set, and another class that represents one record in the set. The set class supports lookup, creation, and deletion. The record class supports editing and (perhaps) deleting. Both classes make use of a SQL interface to the database.

Note how the **SQL** interface wasn't previously reflected in our architecture. Depending on our organization rules, this might be a decision that a component team can make on its own, because other teams don't need to know how the team implements its responsibilities; or it might require the architecture team to add the interface, select a SQL engine, and update the architecture, as shown in Figure 2-45.

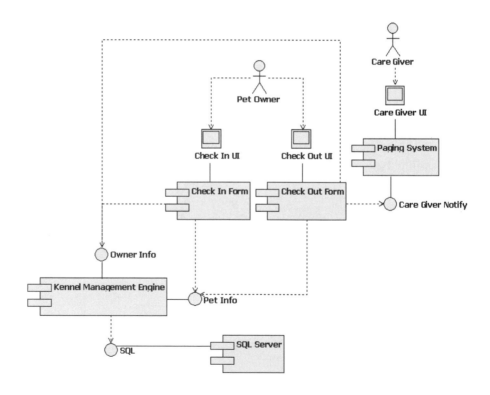

Figure 2-45. Component Diagram for the Kennel Management System, ninth revision

Again, the real design process is sloppy and iterative, with a lot of feedback and retracing of steps. Just as architecture influenced requirements, design will influence architecture.

SQL Code or Stored Procedures?

Notice the two activities assigned to the **SQL** interface: **Select Owner** and **Insert Owner**. These might correspond to actual SQL Select and Insert and Update statements; or you might make SQL stored procedures to carry out those tasks. A stored procedure is a canned set of SQL statements—Select, Insert, Update, and a number of other commands—that may be called with parameters and that look from outside the database as a single SQL call. (Depending on your database engine, a stored procedure may also be compiled and optimized for better performance.)

I prefer to consider these activities as stored procedures (it lets me think of SQL more like an interface to a service than like a complex language), but this diagram doesn't actually reflect that. So to make my SQL intentions clearer, I like to use two new custom stereotypes for transitions: «**SQL**» for hard-coded SQL calls, and «**stored proc**» for SQL stored procedure calls. So the diagram in Figure 2-44 can be revised as shown in Figure 2-46.

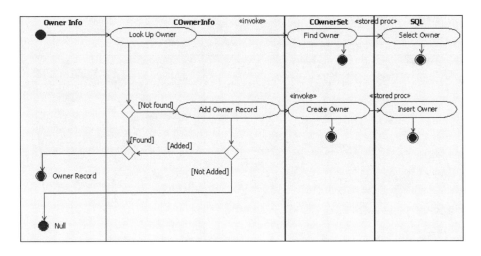

Figure 2-46. Activity Diagram for the Get or Add Owner use case, with swimlanes, second revision

Object Flow States

Earlier, I said that I preferred a separate class to represent individual records in the set of items from the database; but that class doesn't appear in Figure 2-44 or Figure 2-46. Why is that?

Well, I *could* have added a separate swimlane to represent that class (**COwnerRecord**); and then I could have shown transitions from **COwnerSet** to that swimlane to indicate when a record object was created. That would be entirely legal UML; but would it communicate? I don't think so: in the context of this diagram, that swimlane would have no other responsibilities. So it would take up space and add detail without really adding information.

Instead, I prefer to use a more advanced part of the Activity Diagram notation: *object flow states.* These are icons you add to the Activity Diagram, not to represent activities the system will perform, but simply to represent objects that are manipulated by the activities. An object flow state (or more simply, an object) appears as a rectangle with the name and the class of the object, separated by a colon, both underlined. (If you haven't selected both a name and a class yet, just list the one you have selected.) You can show an activity creating or modifying an object by a dashed arrow from the activity to the object; and you can show an activity reading information from an object by a dashed arrow from the object to the activity.

For example, we could add the **COwnerRecord** to the diagram in Figure 2-46 as shown in Figure 2-47.

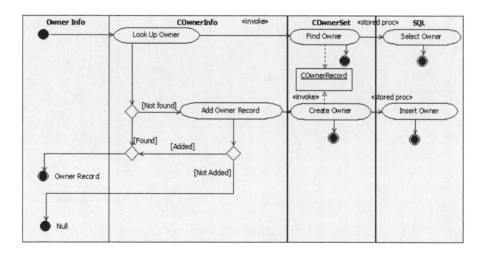

Figure 2-47. Activity Diagram for the Get or Add Owner use case, with swimlanes and object flow state

There are three situations in which I find object flow states to be particularly useful. One is when I need to demonstrate creating an object that's a return value, as in Figure 2-47. I find that it helps to see where the return object comes from.

The second is when I want to show some sort of cumulative results from within a loop, which are then used by an activity outside the loop. The object flow state can represent the cumulative results, as shown in Figure 2-48.

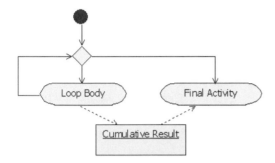

Figure 2-48. Activity Diagram for a loop with object flow state

The third situation in which I find object flow states to be particularly useful is when I want to show an object through which two threads communicate and share information. This object can then hold any synchronization mechanism used to prevent contention between the two threads. If the two threads both write to the object (such as, perhaps, a logger object), then both threads would have outgoing transitions to the object, such as those shown in Figure 2-49.

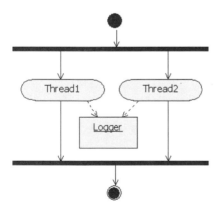

Figure 2-49. Activity Diagram for threads writing to a common object flow state

But if one thread is using the object to signal or control the other thread, then one transition should go in, and one should go out, as shown in Figure 2-50.

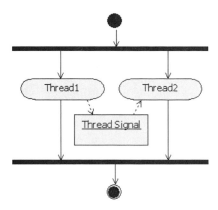

Figure 2-50. Activity Diagram for a threads communicating via an object flow state

A common practice when working with object flow states in this way is described by the Three Amigos:

The control flow (solid) may be omitted when the object flow (dashed) arrows supply a redundant constraint.[15]

In other words, if an object flow state and a transition connect the same two activities, as shown in Figure 2-51, then you may omit the transition, as shown in Figure 2-52.

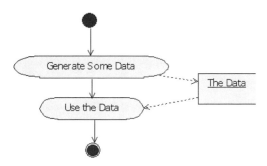

Figure 2-51. Activity Diagram with an object flow state and a redundant transition

---

15. James Rumbaugh, Ivar Jacobson, and Grady Booch, *The Unified Modeling Language Reference Manual* (Addison-Wesley, 1999), p. 139

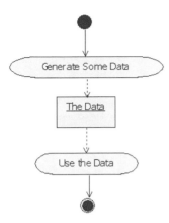

Figure 2-52. Activity Diagram with an object flow state (redundant transition omitted)

This is legal UML, but *I strongly discourage it*. Now usually, I'm very flexible in the use of UML: you've seen that already in this chapter. So it surprises my students how strongly I object to this usage. But in my experience, this trains readers to think that dashed arrows *always* indicate control flow, not just data flow; and once they're trained in that wrong habit, other diagrams can really confuse them. Look back at Figure 2-48: suddenly, **Cumulative Result** looks like some sort of "escape hatch," allowing a premature exit from the loop. Even worse, look back at Figure 2-50: suddenly, **Thread Signal** looks like some sort of mechanism for breaking the wall between thread execution contexts, allowing the CPU to "jump the track" from one context to the other. Neither of those misperceptions is a correct reading of the diagram according to the rules of UML; but both misperceptions are encouraged when people are used to seeing the redundant transitions omitted. Thus, this habit leads to miscommunication, which is never our goal with UML.

Don't go overboard with object flow states, because they may add excess detail to the diagram. Consider drawing the diagram with and without the objects, and then deciding which communicates better.

Creating Class Diagrams

Recall that our classes correspond to the swimlanes from the component Activity Diagrams. So for instance, look back to our latest version of the Activity Diagram for the **Get or Add Owner** use case (Figure 2-47). You can see our initial Class Diagram would look like the one in Figure 2-53.

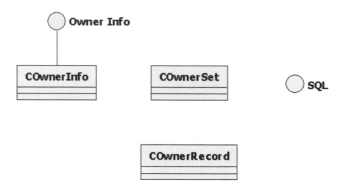

Figure 2-53. Initial Class Diagram for the Kennel Management Engine

Then from the Activity Diagrams, you need to identify associations and dependencies. For each class, examine its corresponding swimlanes in the Activity Diagrams. Look at the other swimlanes that have transitions into those swimlanes. Those transitions define either associations or dependencies. As discussed earlier, if the relation is persistent, draw it as an association (a solid line); but if the relation is transitory (lasting no longer than a single operation, as a rule), draw it as a dependence (a dashed arrow). You can also model return types via dependence. A good convention is to draw a class using an interface as a dependence, because an association (a solid line connecting the class to the interface) would look just like a realization (a solid line connecting the class to the interface).

Thinking about this example. It will make sense for **COwnerInfo** to always have a **COwnerSet** with which it is working, so we'll add that as an association. **COwnerSet** uses the **SQL** interface, so that is a dependence; and because **COwnerSet** creates **COwnerRecord** objects as it needs them, we also model that as a dependence. Finally, because the **Owner Info** interface—and thus the **COwnerInfo** class—return a **COwnerRecord**, those should also be dependent on **COwnerRecord**. Thus, we end up with Figure 2-54.

In this case, however, I feel that the dependence of **Owner Info** on **COwnerRecord** just clutters the diagram with not a lot of benefit. I prefer the diagram in Figure 2-55.

Next we'll look at the swimlane for each class, and convert its activities into operations of the class. Adding these to the class icon, we get the diagram shown in Figure 2-56.

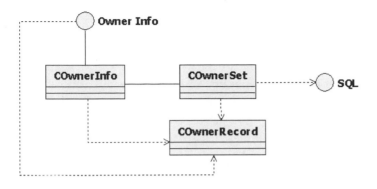

Figure 2-54. Class Diagram for the Kennel Management Engine

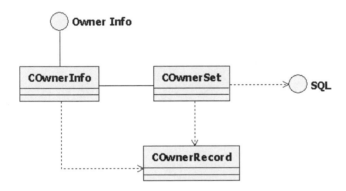

Figure 2-55. Class Diagram for the Kennel Management Engine, revised

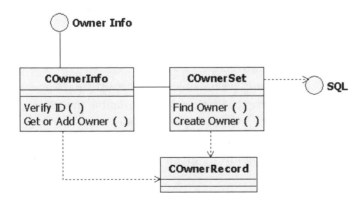

Figure 2-56. Class Diagram for the Kennel Management Engine, with operations

Note I didn't add **Look Up Owner** nor **Add Owner Record** to **COwnerInfo**. Those represented logical steps within **Get or Add Owner**, not separate operations. I could even have hidden these within a **Get or Add Owner** subactivity state in Figure 2-47; but I felt that would complicate the picture, not improve it. Later, I might decide that neither **Look Up Owner** nor **Add Owner Record** are useful operations to have to simplify the code; but for now, I haven't committed to that choice.

Finally, let's add our attributes for these classes. Earlier examples tell us that a **COwnerRecord** needs **First Name** and **Last Name** attributes. We could depict these as shown in Figure 2-57.

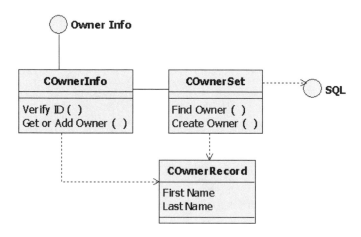

Figure 2-57. Class Diagram for the Kennel Management Engine, with attributes

Step 5(a): Repeat Again

Now narrow the scope of your process to individual classes. Repeat Steps 1 through 4 as appropriate for the current scope.

Once you have your Class Diagrams, it's possible to go through Step 5 again, this time narrowing your scope to look at a single class. By zooming in to the scope of the class, you can apply similar analysis and design processes to elaborate the structure of the class.

So in this step, you'll perform the following substeps:

1. **Define** the class's behavior by specifying the precise parameters and return values for each operation.

2. **Refine** the behavior by producing a class Activity Diagram for each operation.

3. **Assign** the activities in the class Activity Diagrams to attributes, associations, temporary objects, and parameters, using swimlanes.

4. **Design** your class in detail with Class Diagrams.

Now it may be that you find it easy enough to jump straight to code, skipping this step. Great! Do what works for you. But the same strategies that helped you to simplify complexity in requirements and in components may be useful in studying and designing complex classes.

Exercise 206: Define, Refine, Assign, and Design Within Your Classes

---

From one of the Class Diagrams you've developed in the last exercise, pick a class to design. Then walk through the procedures described next to elaborate the design of that class.

Step 5(a): Process in Detail

Again, building on the work we did in the last step, we go through the same cycle again, this time focusing down to the level of the class. The following sections describe the process in detail.

Define

Look at each operation of your class, and determine its proper return value and parameters. Look at how the operation is used in earlier diagrams, and determine what information is provided to it and what is expected from it. Also consider whether any of its parameters should have default values.

You can add more detail to an operation in a Class Diagram by listing its parameters and return value. The parameters are listed inside the parentheses in a comma-separated list of the form **param : type = default value, ...** If a parameter has no default value, none is listed. Also, if there are any language-specific characteristics (such as .NET attributes that identify a parameter as **in**, **out**, or **inout**), these are listed in front of each parameter. The return type is listed after the parentheses, separated by a colon.

Refine

Take each class operation, and create a thorough class Activity Diagram for the use operation. (If you're working through this process as an exercise, then you should do at least two class Activity Diagrams for practice, and more if you wish.) Define your Primary Scenario for each Activity Diagram, and then define your Exception Scenarios. As before, if you used subactivity states in the previous step to simplify your component Activity Diagrams, you may have given yourself a head start in designing your class Activity Diagrams.

Assign

Add swimlanes to each class Activity Diagram. Within a class Activity Diagram, the swimlanes will represent the class itself, along with its attributes, associations, and dependencies; so as you add swimlanes, you may discover that you need new attributes, associations, and dependencies. As you add swimlanes for these, update the class icons on related Class Diagrams. Swimlanes may also represent parameters to the method and return values, *if* these are required to carry out activities in the diagram. Once you've done this, then look for implementation operations required by the original Activity Diagram, and look for object flow states that may help explain how activities collaborate.

Design

Now revise your class definition to depict the new attributes, associations, and dependencies required by the class Activity Diagrams. Examine each swimlane (other than the swimlane for the class).

If a swimlane should be an association and the class doesn't have that association yet, add it. Then, based on how the attribute is used, select an appropriate type for it, and perhaps a default value if one is appropriate. Update the class to reflect these decisions. The attribute type is listed after the attribute name, separated by a colon. If there is a default value, it is listed after the type, separated by an equals sign.

For each class, consider drawing a separate Class Diagram centered on the class, with associated and dependent and realized classes and interfaces arrayed around it. Sometimes this "halo" diagram, depicting a class and everything related to it, can be a useful overview for understanding the class. (Other times, it can be too trivial to be useful.)

Let's see how this process works in practice.

Example

For our example, let's look at the **COwnerSet** class. The **Find Owner** operation of the **COwnerSet** class needs the names of the owner to be found; and for simplicity, these names will be of type **string**. **Create Owner** needs the same information; and both operations may return a **COwnerRecord**. So **COwnerSet** looks like the class depicted in Figure 2-58.

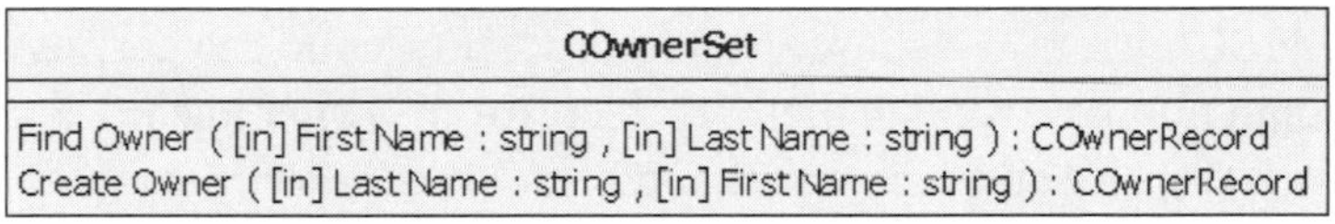

COwnerSet
Find Owner ([in] First Name : string , [in] Last Name : string) : COwnerRecord Create Owner ([in] Last Name : string , [in] First Name : string) : COwnerRecord

Figure 2-58. Class Diagram for COwnerSet

Next, we need to create the Activity Diagrams for these two operations, but here, we'll just focus on **Find Owner**. Figure 2-59 is an Activity Diagram for the **Find Owner** operation.

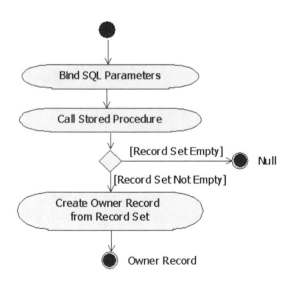

Figure 2-59. Activity Diagram for Find Owner

At this time, we can delve even further into implementation exceptions to aid us in preplanning how to detect and handle exceptions. In the same way that I used subactivity states to demonstrate common cancel handling (Figure 2-43), we could use subactivity states to depict common exception handling such as C#'s **try/catch** mechanism.

For example, in the diagram in Figure 2-59, there are two very likely exception categories. First, any time you call out to another component, exceptions are possible; and in particular, SQL operations are known to propagate exceptions. So we need to handle a range of possible SQL exceptions, which we can do by treating all possible SQL errors as a simple Null return. The second category of error is that we might not have enough memory to create an **Owner Record**. So, as shown in Figure 2-60, we'll add exception handlers for these exceptions.

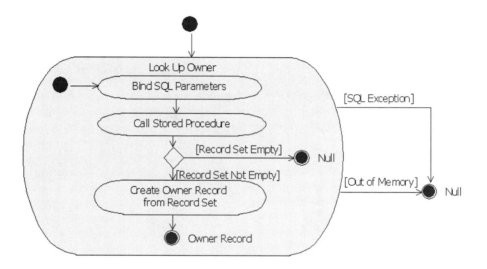

Figure 2-60. Activity Diagram for Find Owner, with exception handling

We might decide that this exception handling is too much detail for the design, and better left to code. Different teams will take different approaches to this technique.

Adding swimlanes and related activities to Figure 2-59, we get the Activity Diagram shown in Figure 2-61.

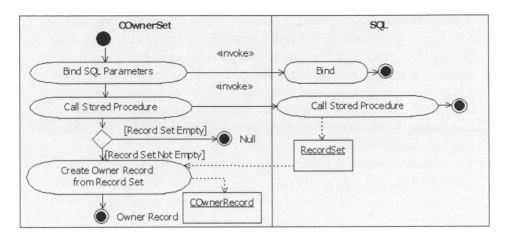

Figure 2-61. Activity Diagram for Find Owner, with swimlanes

Step 5(b): And Again?

Some use case practitioners may take issue with the steps I'm recommending here. "Too detailed!" they'll say. There are business analysts who employ use cases who will argue that the largest of organizations might be modeled with maybe 15 use cases. They will argue—*strongly*—that more than that is a sign that you're thinking in too much detail. They will further tell you that you can't "decompose" a use case into smaller pieces.

But then there are system designers who say, "I was working on a small system last month. It was only around 80 use cases." (I've even heard both perspectives— a few large use cases versus many small use cases—coming from two different people within the same organization.)

So who's right? Remember: if you ask me "*A* or *B*?" my answer is usually "Yes" or "*C*." This is another "Yes" answer. I think business analysts are right: when trying to think of how to organize a business's operations, you have to look at very high-level operations. If you have a large number of operations, you can lose track of everything. Their use cases are often along the lines of **Accounting** and **Facilities** and **Human Resources**.

But I think system designers who have more and more detailed use cases are right in that these use cases are more concrete and more implementable. If I ask ten programmers to implement a use case like **Facilities**, I'll probably get 20 different implementations—or I'll get ten programmers throwing things at me for giving them such a lousy spec. But if I ask ten programmers to implement **Display Available Facilities**, I'll get a lot closer to consensus.

So it's important that, at various stages of software development, you have use cases of varying size and scope, ranging from large and broad to small and

detailed. I think that the same basic strategy embodied in Five-Step UML—
define your system requirements in terms of the use cases needed by something
outside your system; refine each use case into a set of activities; assign those
activities to parts of your system; design the relationships among those parts;
and repeat at the scope of a more detailed part of your system, in an iterative
fashion—is a useful strategy across all the scopes of use cases. (It's also neither
new nor earth-shattering; but I think that when merged with UML, it becomes
very clear and easy to apply.)

The scopes to which I believe this Five-Step strategy may be applied can be
summarized in Table 2-1.

Table 2-1. Five-Step UML at Varying Scopes of Analysis and Design

Scope	Usage
Business	At this scope, you're analyzing the organization and functions of an entire business or organization, with a focus on its interactions with other businesses, governments, etc.
	Actors reflect broad categories of external entities: governments, vendors, suppliers, customers, etc.
	Use cases reflect the basic operations of the organization.
	Structural elements reflect the business units or departments that carry out the operations.
Service	At this scope, you're analyzing the organization and functions related to particular services of the organization. For instance, if the service is Purchasing, then operations might include ordering, tracking, receiving, and returns. (This scope, falling somewhere in between Business and Domain, won't be necessary except for larger organizations.)
	Actors reflect the individuals and systems that require and carry out these operations.
	Use cases reflect the services performed by the business units or departments.
	Structural elements reflect broad categories of domain objects that must be maintained, subunits of departments that carry out particular operations, and facilities where operations take place.
Domain	At this scope, you're analyzing particular domain objects that must be represented or maintained in the system.

Table 2-1. Five-Step UML at Varying Scopes of Analysis and Design (Continued)

Scope	Usage
	Actors reflect the individuals who require the domain objects, along with the individuals who maintain them.
	Use cases reflect the maintenance and transfer of domain objects (documents, schedules, etc.) that support the services of the business units.
	Structural elements reflect the specific domain objects maintained, particular teams that carry out operations, and particular machines or devices used in maintaining or producing domain objects.
System	At this scope, you're analyzing the workflows involved in maintaining particular domain objects, along with the user interfaces and components that support those workflows.
	Actors reflect the individuals who implement the workflow.
	Use cases reflect the steps in the workflow. Use cases may also reflect detailed user interface interactions, when this helps to explain the user interface.
	Structural elements reflect the user interfaces, interfaces to other systems, the components that provide the interfaces and user interfaces, other components, and interfaces between the components.
Implementation	At this scope, you're designing particular components of the system.
	Actors reflect persons and other systems *and* other components that interact with the component.
	Use cases reflect the requests made through interfaces and user interfaces.
	Structural elements represent classes and interfaces within each component.
Class	At this scope, you're designing particular classes.
	No actors.
	No use cases, simply class operations; but these may be analyzed in a fashion similar to use cases.
	Structural elements represent attributes, associations, dependencies, and interfaces of each class.

The strategy is important; it's not just rigid rules about counting use cases. It's a way of thinking about problems and communicating your thoughts and solutions.

Step 5(c): Repeat (In Reverse)

Expand the scope of your process to whole systems (designed with Deployment Diagrams). Repeat Steps 1–4 as appropriate for the current scope.

This optional step is for distributed systems: systems that must be deployed to multiple nodes. In this step, you'll expand your scope to look at an entire system made up of the components identified in Step 4. By zooming out to the scope of the entire system, you can apply a similar Assign-and-Design process to determine the structure of the system.

UML Notation

In UML, the structure of a system is displayed using Deployment Diagrams, which consist primarily of two types of elements: nodes and associations.

Nodes

A *node* represents any hardware system in which your components may be installed or with which your components may interact. It may be thought of as a large component, realizing the interfaces of the components installed on it (though the only significant interfaces for a Deployment Diagram are those accessed by components on other nodes).

In a Deployment Diagram, a node is depicted as a cube with shaded top and right edges.

Nodes: A .NET Perspective

In .NET code, a node is primarily any machine to which you deploy .NET components. At the time of this writing, that means mostly Windows PCs (and soon, I hope, the Pocket PC platform as well). But there are ongoing efforts by third parties to port .NET to other environments and platforms.

And of course, there are other nodes besides Windows machines even in today's .NET apps, including

- The devices—printers, modems, etc.—with which your code interacts

- Other computers that access an ASP.NET site via the Web

- Other computers that access Web services via SOAP

Associations

In a Deployment Diagram, an *association* represents a connection between two nodes through which two components may communicate (via their interfaces). It is depicted on a Deployment Diagram as a solid line connecting the nodes.

Deployment Associations: A .NET Perspective

In .NET code, the associations between nodes will represent concrete mechanisms like Ethernet and R/F, hardware protocols like TCP/IP and 802.11b, and software protocols like SOAP and .NET Remoting.

Deployment Diagrams

Given these elements, then, a *Deployment Diagram* depicts nodes and associations between them. Figure 2-62 is a Deployment Diagram that depicts the nodes and associations that may be useful in the Kennel Management System.

KMS System Architecture

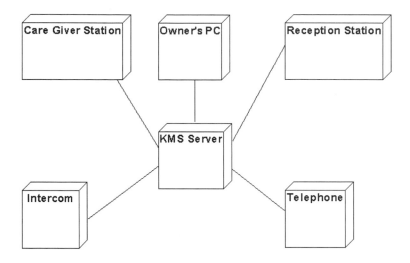

Figure 2-62. Deployment Diagram of the Kennel Management System

In addition, you may choose to list within or under each node the components that are deployed to that node. Such a diagram is illustrated in Figure 2-63.

KMS System Architecture

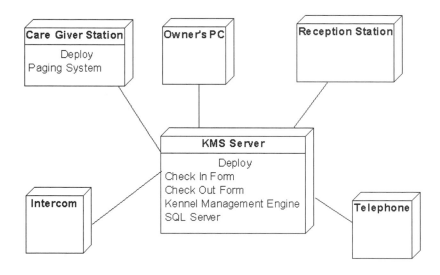

Figure 2-63. Deployment Diagram of the Kennel Management System, with components

Looking at the Deployment Diagram and at earlier Component Diagrams, you can see which interfaces must be remote interfaces. For instance, **Care Giver Notify** is realized by the **Paging System**, which is deployed to the **Care Giver Station**; but it's accessed by the **Check Out Form**, which is deployed to the **KMS Server**. Therefore, **Care Giver Notify** must be a remote interface, and we must define a remoting protocol for it.

Note also that **Check In Form** and **Check Out Form** are deployed to the **KMS Server**, *not* to the **Owner's PC**. This reflects our intention that these should be Web user interfaces: no code is actually delivered to the **Owner's PC**, just HTML pages. The actual components that generate the HTML reside on the **KMS Server**. This also allows us to provide the identical interface to the **Reception Station** to support walk-in reservations.

Logical Deployment vs. Physical Deployment

The diagram in Figure 2-63 is an example of a logical Deployment Diagram: it depicts the components, the nodes to which they are deployed, and the necessary communication between the nodes. You may also wish to produce a physical Deployment Diagram that depicts the *physical* mechanisms by which the nodes are connected (usually without showing the components). This will help you to plan hardware acquisitions and connections.

In a physical Deployment Diagram, it is very common to use custom stereotypes that reflect the type of each node. You may also label the associations to describe how two devices are connected if it isn't clear.

For example, Figure 2-64 is a physical Deployment Diagram for the Kennel Management System.

Exercise 207: Assign Components to Nodes with Deployment Diagrams

In this final exercise of the chapter, you and your team can wrap things up by creating Deployment Diagrams from the components and interface dependencies you've identified in previous exercises. The steps are summarized in the section that follows.

KMS Physical Architecture

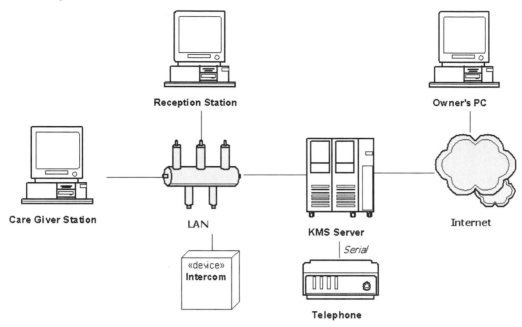

Figure 2-64. Physical architecture of the Kennel Management System

Designing Deployment: A Summary

Start the process by looking through your components and assigning them to an appropriate node.

If you don't have an existing node that should host that component, then you'll need to add a new node icon to the Deployment Diagram. List the component under the appropriate node icon.

Next, based on the interface dependencies identified in the Component Diagrams, add appropriate associations between the nodes.

Finally, redraw the Deployment Diagram, adding appropriate devices and associations to produce a physical Deployment Diagram.

TIP   To learn more about Deployment Diagrams, see Chapter 11.

Summary

In this chapter, we've worked through a complete iteration of each step in Five-Step UML. Along the way, I showed the new UML notation that you've needed at each stage of the process. The UML we've used in this chapter is by no means the complete language, but an exhaustive tutorial in the entirety of UML[16] is not the aim of this book.

The UML notation that we've focused on in this chapter has been

- Use Case Diagrams, with actors, use cases, and domain objects.

- Activity Diagrams, with initial states, activity states, and terminal states, all joined together by transitions, branches, merges, joins, and forks. We also looked at how to assign different activities in an Activity Diagram into swimlanes.

- Component Diagrams, with components, interfaces, realizations, and dependencies.

- Class Diagrams, with classes divided up to include information on attributes and operations, and the connections between classes defined by associations and dependences.

From this point forward, I'll assume you understand UML well enough to understand any diagram that I'll draw, introducing any new notation as we come across it. If you're still not comfortable with UML, I recommend that you do some more Five-Step exercises, and solve problems with your team. Practice with UML won't make you perfect, because "perfect" is an unattainable goal; but practice is certainly the best way to learn. Remember, you don't need to learn everything immediately. Like any language, you'll pick more of it up as you use it, and become proficient more quickly with some parts of the language than others.

As you worked through the exercises in Five-Step UML, you should have got a taste of the power of UML. You've seen how you can apply a straightforward development process of define, refine, assign, and design, repeating it at different scopes in your system. Continue to practice this simple OOAD approach until you feel comfortable deriving classes and components and nodes and ultimately code, all from user requirements. At this stage, you aren't defining these elements in enough detail to lead to implementation. Instead, you're simply learning to think in UML.

---

16. For an exhaustive tutorial, I recommend Martin Fowler and Kendall Scott, *UML Distilled, Second Edition* (Addison-Wesley, 1999), followed by James Rumbaugh, Ivar Jacobson, and Grady Booch, *The Unified Modeling Language Reference Manual* (Addison-Wesley, 1999).

In Part Two, I'll drill down into Five-Step UML in more detail, dedicating a chapter to each step of the process as we work through the design of the KMS in depth. Along the way, you'll see more details of the UML notation that will allow you to very precisely design your system.

Before we delve further into Five-Step UML, however, let's take a break and have a look at some general modeling advice. The set of pragmatic guidelines presented in the next chapter are not only applicable to the Five-Step process described in this book, but also to modeling in general.

CHAPTER 3

Pragmatic Guidelines: Diagrams That Work

IN THE LAST CHAPTER, we spent a long time working through the process of Five-Step UML, and looking at all of the new UML notation which that entailed. But in this chapter, we're going to take a quick break from learning all the formal rules and all the step-by-step instructions on how to use UML as part of a modeling process. Instead, I'm going to present a set of pragmatic guidelines that will help you stay on the right track during your development work.

By this point, you may already be tired of hearing me say that UML is about communication. But that's easy to say, and much harder to do. Listen to any political speech, and you can hear lots of words with no real meaning communicated. Read the telephone book from cover to cover, and you'll find lots of factually accurate information that's too voluminous and too complex to be useful.

The same sorts of things can happen with UML diagrams: you can make a set of diagrams that seem to say something, but that actually fail to communicate. You can pour time and sweat into getting the lines just right and all of the right icons in the right places, only to find that no one else can understand what you drew. You are, quite literally, back to the drawing board.

This frustrating event *is* going to happen to you. Nothing can prevent it, and it's part of the normal, healthy design process: the missteps are merely steps to a better design. The only designers who never design anything poorly are those who never design anything. But there are some common mistakes that you'll see in your own work and in that of others.

The following guidelines are my attempt to warn you away from some of these mistakes. And despite some of the names, they are guidelines, not rules. You can break them, and still communicate. Sometimes you *must* break them in order to communicate. But when you find that one of your diagrams is failing as a communication tool, check these guidelines: chances are, the bridge for your communication gap is here somewhere.

Do What Works

The number one guideline is that simple: **Do What Works.** Not what's right. Not what's "supposed to be done." Not even what I tell you to do. Just what works. At the end of the day, if you don't communicate, if you don't solve a problem, you haven't succeeded. Don't let me or anyone else sell you on "the one true way to produce software." We may be very bright (or think we are), and we may have really good reasons for what we're saying; but maybe those reasons depend on factors that don't apply in your situation.

And this is (unfortunately) a slippery rule: "what works" changes for different purposes, different problems, different audiences, and a range of other variables. I'll look at that in a bit more detail in the next three sections.

Purpose

If your purpose is to document an existing system, you'll probably start with Class and Component Diagrams that reflect its structure, and then add Interaction Diagrams to show how that structure works, and then add Use Case Diagrams to show the externally visible behavior embodied by those interactions. Then, as you extend and maintain the system, you'll update and add to those diagrams. But if your purpose is to design a new system, on the other hand, you'll start with Use Case Diagrams to depict requirements in context, and then work in. If your purpose is to understand a strange bug, you might start with Interaction Diagrams. Your purpose will also determine the level of detail you apply: if you're just trying to understand some existing code, you might apply much less detail than you would in designing new code.

Problem

For a small problem, too much modeling can bury you in paperwork, and you'll suffocate. For a large problem, not enough modeling can mean that your vision isn't abstract enough to encompass the system at varying levels of detail. For a familiar problem, a single stereotype icon on a diagram can convey pages of meaning to the team; and too much detail really doesn't communicate anything *new*, because "We've seen all this before." For a new problem, you'll need much more detail, because people need lots of help learning the new domain.

Audience

For your fellow developers and designers, you'll add lots of detail. These people are basically pre-reviewing your code by reviewing your design; but if you don't include enough detail to demonstrate that you know what you're doing, trust them to call you on that. (And if you can't trust them for that, what good are they?) But for business analysts, customers, and other nontechnical stakeholders, this detail is just clutter: they don't know what it means, they don't want to know what it means, and they'll get it wrong if they *try* to know what it means. For them, you draw less-detailed diagrams, but perhaps try to fit a broader scope into each diagram.

A .NET Perspective

In particular, what works well for me in .NET modeling is reverse engineering. My UML tool of choice, Rational XDE, is one of many that will generate the elements of a model from your source code. So often, after I have gathered requirements and started on a shell of architectural design, I'll use the powerful tools in Visual Studio .NET to generate the basic components of my architecture; and then I'll reverse engineer those components into my models and incorporate the reverse-engineered elements into my UML diagrams and designs. So I'm not a modeling purist: sometimes I start with a model and lead to code, and sometimes I start with code and work towards a model. But either way, my real approach is circular: code leads to models leads to code leads to models leads to . . .

Using a Tool

So though I describe some useful steps for applying UML, my *real* technique is to do whichever step makes most sense next. That's one advantage of a good modeling tool like Rational XDE: no matter what I discover or envision, there's a place for it in the model, and I can put it there quickly, explore it as much as I need to right now, and go back to what I was doing when the topic came up, with only minimal interruption. Then later I can go back through the model and find all these proto-ideas and work on fleshing them out. The model evolves very naturally this way. And that leads us to . . .

The Model Rule

We saw **The Model Rule** in Chapter 1; but it bears repeating. To use UML effectively, you should never be simply drawing pretty pictures; you should always be editing an underlying model, using the pretty pictures as your user interface. Thus, the model should contain more information than is displayed in any one diagram, and information in one diagram shouldn't explicitly contradict information in another diagram. Information that is found in one diagram but not in another shouldn't be considered a contradiction. Rather, this simply indicates that the former diagram displays more detail than the latter. Details may be omitted from any given diagram to make it more comprehensible.

But how do you keep these diagrams consistent with each other? How do you maintain the underlying model? This is where a good modeling tool proves its worth: a good modeling tool will maintain the model as you create and edit your diagrams.

If you aren't using some sort of modeling tool, this very mechanical burden will fall on you, rather than on the machine. That's a poor division of labor: brains should do brain work and machines should do mechanical work. If you do the mechanical work, you'll do it imprecisely and inefficiently, and you'll have no time for brain work. I urge you to investigate and use one of the many UML tools available. A list of UML tools can be found in Appendix B.

"Legible" Does Not Mean "Pretty"

The point of UML is—do I even need to say it?—communication. But there are different kinds of communication, even when the medium is the same. For example, speech is a very common communication medium; but there's a very wide range of speech styles that all manage to communicate. The stops and pauses and half-finished sentences and even grunts of a casual phone conversation between old friends are very different from the formal, scripted, ritualized sentences of a traditional marriage ceremony. Yet each is a successful style of communication.

So which should you prefer? Well, just imagine holding every conversation in your day with the same degree of formality and structure of a marriage rite. It would sound like parody:

"I, Martin, ask thee, Sandra, if thou wouldst enjoy a noon repast with me?"

"I, Sandra, ask thee, Martin, if thou may tarry a brief moment, and that thou might help me to escort our canines into yon field? Else, I fear, they shall do in our abode that which canines should do in fields."

"Yea, verily, shall I assist you in this, as in all endeavors. I shall fetch the Dane."

Compare this with an actual conversation:

"Hey, Sandy, ready for lunch?"

"Just a minute. Help me take the dogs out first."

"Glad to! I'll grab Betsy."

The casual conversation ain't pretty. It ain't even grammatical, in every particular. And it leaves a lot unsaid, requiring the participants to fill in a lot of blanks. But it's real. And it's also economical (20 words versus 72), and it gets the job done. Plus, it's a lot easier to create.

We create casual conversations on the fly, nearly as fast as our thoughts can flow. We create formal conversations by careful planning, thought, rehearsal, revision, and review. That slows down the fundamental process of *thinking* because the thinking is concentrated too much on form and not enough on substance. Now we can't take this too far: we can't casually invent words and usage any time we wish, without also slowing down communication. We do so only when it serves a greater purpose, our ultimate purpose: communication.

That's the approach you should take to communicating with UML: legible over pretty, and standard over creative. Put in as much effort and as much customization as needed to get your point across; put in *no* effort on unnecessary prettification, and customize only when the standard notation fails to communicate efficiently. If you're drawing diagrams by hand, make the lines and shapes as straight and regular as you can, but don't break out the ruler and compass and protractor. (Fine-ruled graph paper helps a lot, though.) If you're drawing diagrams with a UML tool, stick to the easier features of the tool, and use more esoteric features only when necessary.

Maybe Even Ugly?

In case you haven't noticed by now, I see the primary value of UML in its role as a communication tool. But in *Agile Modeling*, Scott Ambler describes another value of UML.[1] He talks of "modeling to communicate" versus "modeling to understand." The latter is another perspective on **The Outline Effect** that I described in Chapter 1: a way of understanding a problem by building a model of the problem, or even of understanding existing code by building a model of it. This is certainly a valuable use for UML; but when you're modeling to understand, like this, you may go even further in the direction of legible versus pretty. In fact, you may very well produce some pretty *ugly* diagrams.

Don't let this worry you, and don't let it slow you down. When you're trying to understand something, "cleaning up" diagrams will only distract you. If *you* can read it, it's good enough. Move on. Keep the momentum going. Making sense of a new problem domain is hard work. Making sense of existing code is even harder. (Robert L. Glass, author of *Facts and Fallacies of Software Engineering,* argues that it's one of the most important *and* least taught skills a programmer can have.) Comprehension is hard, and neatness isn't necessary for it. You can always clean up later, when your brain goes into idle and you're just going through the motions. I've spent many hours rearranging diagrams to make them more legible, while simultaneously listening to the TV or even taking part in a conversation. I don't want to imply that legibility is easy; but it doesn't take the same sort of intense concentration that's required for comprehension.

There's a place for pretty, just as there's a place for formal, ritualized speech. In fact, the places are the same: any occasion of ceremony, of transition. You can and should apply extra polish to diagrams that are to be presented in large, ceremonial settings (sign-off meetings, executive presentations, etc.), because it demonstrates attention to detail that will give participants confidence. No, strike that, they won't notice the detail; rather, if you *don't* apply the polish, they *will* notice the unpolished details, and their confidence will be shaken.

And there's one other place where a little effort on pretty goes a long way: when you have to prepare diagrams that others will read when you won't personally be there to guide them through the rough spots—like, say, when you're writing a book on UML. You *don't* want to see the diagrams in this book the way they looked when I was just getting my thoughts together. I put in a lot of effort to

---

1. Scott W. Ambler, *Agile Modeling: Effective Practices for eXtreme Programming and the Unified Process* (John Wiley & Sons, 2002)

clean them up to help you understand them as best you could. But in your day-to-day work, you should do exactly what I do in *my* day-to-day work: I get the diagram to the point where I think it makes sense; and then I hand it to someone else and ask if it actually does. And that leads us to . . .

The MTB Rule

One of my favorite television programs is The Learning Channel series *Junkyard Wars* (also known as *Scrapheap Challenge* on the BBC). This reality program has a great geeky premise: place two teams of engineers in a junkyard with an assignment to build something, such as a catapult or a submarine; give them a time limit; and when the time is up, pit the contraptions against each other in a contest sure to test them to the limit. In the semifinals for the 2000 season, the NERDS—a team of American programmers—built the winning steam-powered car (proving that yes, programmers *can* do hardware, if we want to). And along the way, they propounded **The MTB Rule:**

> *Design checks (aka MTB: Minimum Two Brains)—When you are about to build some part of your machine and it's not totally trivial, grab some (any) other team member and explain it to them. If they agree that's a good way to do it, do it. If they find a problem with your way, come up with a solution. If it isn't clear, call a Team Design Review and spend five minutes getting it right.*[2]

Communication—you know, that thing that UML is about—requires a Minimum Two Brains: one that proposes the idea, and one that responds to it. And then the magic begins, we hope: the two brains change roles, back and forth over one idea after another, tumbling ideas against each other like rocks in a tumbler, polishing them to a bright shiny finish.

Can you use UML with only one brain? Certainly, just as you can write a novel and never let anyone read it: you can enjoy the craft of writing, and you can practice your skill with words, and you can even use the unpublished novel as a springboard for other projects. The time isn't wasted; but you're only getting

---

2. Jeff Del Papa, and The New England Rubbish Deconstruction Society, "The NERDS Tactical Rules for Scrapheap Challenges (Project Management for 10 Hour Projects)," The New England Rubbish Deconstruction Society Web site (http://www.the-nerds.org/ contestant-advice.html). Along with **The MTB Rule**, this site has some great practical rules for software development and management: "KISS. Keep It Simple, Stupid." "Just remember: If brute force doesn't work, you aren't using enough." "If you break, you lose." "MCF: Mission Critical First." "Test Early, Test Often." "Leave margins." "Identify your hidden assumptions." "The machine shop should be a last resort." "Make time for silliness." "If something isn't right—LET THE DIRECTOR KNOW RIGHT AWAY!!!" These rules are stated in the context of a high-pressure hardware effort; but the spirit of these rules applies to software as well.

a tiny fraction of the benefit you can get when you share your ideas with others. For UML design is an activity very much like writing; and Stephen King tells us:

> **What Writing Is.** *Telepathy, of course. It's amusing when you stop to think about it—for years people have argued about whether or not such a thing exists, folks like J. B. Rhine have busted their brains trying to create a valid testing process to isolate it, and all the time it's been right there, lying out in the open like Mr. Poe's Purloined Letter.*[3]

With a clear UML design, you can pull an idea from your brain and insert it into another brain. Then you can view that idea from a new perspective, that of a brain that didn't conceive the idea originally and thus perceives it from different angles and a different background. This becomes an exercise in statistical coverage: if one defect in ten will slip past a single brain, then one in a hundred will slip past two brains, and one in a thousand will slip past three. There is some number of brains for which the marginal return is less than the overhead cost of adding another brain into the mix; but although I can't tell you what that number is— it varies based on the project, the team, and the organization—I can assure you that the number is always greater than one. We *all* can benefit from an editor or a reviewer.

This review process is often not pretty: one of the brains is very emotionally attached to an idea that springs from deep within that brain; and the other brain is skeptical, having seen far too many good ideas that crumbled to dust in the rock tumbler. These two perspectives will clash, and both brains may be bruised in the impact. Thick-skinned brains are essential; but the impact can be cushioned quite a bit by clear communication. And *that* is what we hope to see in our UML diagrams.

The 7 ± 2 Rule

There's a very simple reason why UML is primarily a diagramming language: a picture is worth 2 kilobytes, after all. That's roughly a thousand words. Oh, all right, if you think like a mainframe programmer, call it 4 kilobytes. (God, I hate having to explain a joke.) Cognitive scientists tell us that the brain processes pictures in a different way and in different paths from those involved in processing text and formulae (i.e., code). So one advantage of diagrams as a design tool is simply that they cause you to think about the problem differently. But there's another, simpler reason why diagrams are useful: the brain processes text one word

---

3. Stephen King, *On Writing* (Pocket Books, 2002), p. 103. King goes on to demonstrate what he means by writing as telepathy; and he makes a compelling (if metaphorical) case.

or phrase or line at a time; but it processes a picture all at once. You can see, as they say, the Big Picture.

But there's a limit to the effectiveness of pictures in this regard: the brain can keep only so much of a picture all in memory at one time. Cognitive scientists (who have a whole lot to teach about problem solving and how we approach it) also tell us that the average human brain can keep in its short-term memory only seven things, plus or minus two.[4] This limit constrains the level of useful detail in a diagram. Beyond that range, details begin to blur; and the brain can only comprehend a part of the picture, focusing on one aspect to the exclusion of others, or focusing on *no* aspects and simply grokking the entirety with no sense of detail.[5] The image becomes the Too Big Picture.

Does that mean I never draw a UML diagram with 10 elements, or 15, or 20? Mea culpa: I understand all too well that sometimes proper communication seems to demand more elements. (Note how I said *seems:* when I find my diagram fails to communicate, I can most often find the cause simply by counting the elements in the diagram. To my chagrin, the answer will be *much* more than 7 ± 2.) Clutter is always a danger in a complex system design. Remember: "comprehensive" does not mean "comprehensible."

There are two common situations in which it makes sense to break
The 7 ± 2 Rule:

1. When you have a large group of related elements—species of animals, for example—and you want to show their relations to each other and to other elements—biological classifications, perhaps. Although it makes sense to draw this sort of diagram, the result can still be a confusing diagram. You can improve the legibility of such a diagram by grouping the related elements physically on the page. The brain will then group them together mentally as well, and will treat the group as a single element related to the nongrouped elements (thus reducing the complexity at the expense of detail). When the brain wants to understand detail *within* the group, it zooms in on the detail at the expense of the larger relations. For an example of this technique in action, study Michelangelo's painting on the Sistine Chapel ceiling: it tells a complex story in many panels that collectively make up the familiar story of Genesis (and related motifs); but within each panel is rich detail worthy of a masterpiece by itself. You can see the story, or the detail; but it's very difficult to see both at once.

---

4. George A. Miller, Ph.D., "The Magical Number Seven, Plus or Minus Two: Some Limits on Our Capacity for Processing Information," (http://www.well.com/user/smalin/miller.html).

5. Robert A. Heinlein, *Stranger in a Strange Land* (Ace Books, 1991), p. 266: "'Grok' means to understand so thoroughly that the observer becomes part of the process being observed—to merge, to blend, to intermarry, to lose personal identity in group experience." In this usage, grokking the whole picture is to see in it something beyond its individual elements.

2. When you want to show the entire sweep of a system, the whole that is larger than its parts. This sort of diagram—what I like to call "The Everything Diagram"—is popular with managers who want to know that there's a place for everything and everything is in its place. The sense of security that gives them is false, I think: the diagram is too complex for anyone to ever really know that it's accurate or to comprehend the roles of individual elements. It becomes a single image made up of many tiny elements, rather than a useful description of the elements themselves. When you look at Van Gogh's *Starry Night*, you see a cypress tree and a little village set against a turbulent night sky, not the individual brush strokes that make up the shapes of the tree and the village and the sky. If you were to concentrate on the brush strokes instead, you would find that they look like nothing whatsoever; but the impression formed by all these nothings is recognizably *Starry Night*. The value of an Everything Diagram is more navigational than communicative: you can use it to trace a path through related elements involved in a scenario. But once you have traced the path, you will *comprehend* the path more fully if you create another diagram consisting solely of those related elements.

What counts as an element for purposes of **The 7 ± 2 Rule**? Primarily, the icons: actors and use cases in Use Case Diagrams, objects and activities and swimlanes in Activity Diagrams, objects and actors in Sequence or Collaboration diagrams, interfaces and components in Component Diagrams, classes and interfaces in Class Diagrams, states in Statechart Diagrams, nodes and devices in Deployment Diagrams, and notes and packages in any diagram. Other features in a diagram are closely associated with a given icon or depict the relationships between icons, and thus can be understood within the context described by the icons themselves.

Learn from the Masters

It's no accident that I chose famous paintings as metaphors in the preceding examples. The great artists have spent generations studying techniques for communicating visually: discovering rules, breaking rules, and testing the results to "see" what they learned about the rules. I'm never ashamed to adopt the lessons learned by others, so that I can focus on the new lessons I must learn. If you want to use UML for better visual communication, it couldn't hurt to spend a day in an art museum.

The Résumé Rule

There's another problem with the Everything Diagram: either it's too darn big, or the font is too darn tiny. You'll be tempted to zoom out to fit everything, and then play games with the font to make it legible. But there are limits to that approach: when the font size is 1 point, it really doesn't matter what the font face is; and if you enlarge the font disproportionately to the icons, the labels can obscure the icons. No one can review a diagram they can't read. Amount of information communicated: zero.

So you'll err in the other direction: larger diagrams at a scale you can read. Beware! That way, madness lies. You might split the diagram across many pages. Then you'll ask me to review it. Unlike you, I don't automatically recognize how the pages fit together. (Let's be honest: you may not, either.) So I take it home to review. First, I have to clear off the kitchen counter so I have space to lay it all out. Then I have to throw the cat off the nice clear spot she's just discovered. Then I have to try to lay out the pages. Then I have to throw the cat off again, because if there's one thing she likes more than a clear counter, it's whatever piece of paper is most important to me at the moment. Then I have to quiet the dog, who has decided that I need help disciplining the cat. Then I have to pick up the sheets that the cat knocked off the counter in her rush to escape the dog. Then I have to figure out if those marks are cat prints, dog slobber, or UML . . .

....

Plotter Horror

Or you'll make the mistake I did: learning the arcane art of using the company plotter. Now I *hope* that plotters are better supported today than they were then; but in 1997, it took me and my boss all day to download the correct drivers and install them on my machine. (We installed a lot of incorrect ones along the way.) Now, truth to tell, I'm a night owl. We had that driver working at 5 p.m., just when my energies were really flowing; so the wasted day didn't bother me. I proudly printed my first UML diagram to the plotter. Then, because of the physical layout of the company offices, I had to go up a flight of stairs, down a hill, around a corner, down another hill, around another corner, down *another* hill, across a busy street, around yet another corner, down *yet another* hill, through a security door, through a building I didn't know, into the plotter room . . . only to discover that *the diagram had printed incorrectly!* So reverse the process (all uphill this way, of course), and repeat. By 11:00 p.m. (what a waste of prime programming time!), I finally had copies of all six diagrams I needed, one copy for each team member. I rolled them up, put them in tubes, and capped the ends. Then I carried all these tubes back up the hill, and put one in each team member's cubicle, along with a handwritten note: "Hi! Martin here! These are the diagrams I promised you for review. I'd like to hold a review meeting Tuesday at 10:00 a.m. I look forward to your feedback. Thanks!" And then, Tuesday at 9:55 a.m., I heard *pop! Pop-pop! Pop-pop-pop!* All over cubeville, tubes were being uncapped for the very first time. Needless to say, that review was not very productive.

Your logistics may not be as bad as mine were. The plotter may be right next to your desk. But the result will be the same: your reviewers will glance at your work, compliment you on how much effort went into it, and *never once review your design.* Amount of information communicated: again, zero.

The best solution is the same rule the guidance counselors taught us all for résumés: one page. If a diagram can't fit legibly on a single 8½×11" page, no one will review it. Although it's true that such a page can get buried in an in-box, it also can easily be carried home in a briefcase, read on the airplane, and photocopied for more reviewers. The standard page size is overwhelmingly more convenient than is a great big plotter sheet or a diagram that must be laid out along an entire kitchen counter.

What if your diagram *won't* fit legibly on a single 8½×11" page? Then, first of all, it's likely that you have broken **The 7 ± 2 Rule**, but more significantly, you probably have too much detail at too many levels of scope. You can usually group many of the elements of such a diagram into fewer, larger elements, each with its own attached diagram on another page. Although it may seem to you like more work to add these additional elements and diagrams, that is from your perspective as the designer and originator of the idea. From an outside perspective, you'll end up with a more comprehensible set of diagrams that convey your intent.

Sorry for My Cultural Centrism

Yes, I realize that in other parts of the world, 8½×11" is not the standard page size. Don't take me too literally here. Use whatever is the standard page size for your locale. (Perhaps in those cultures, this should be called **The Curriculum Vitae Rule.**) But be hesitant of nonstandard sizes, even that of the infamous "yellow legal pad," because they tend either to get lost in piles of larger paper, or they stick out of piles of smaller paper and get smudged, snagged, and ripped. Take a look at your last pointless memo from human resources, and use that size paper.

With both **The 7 ± 2 Rule** and **The Résumé Rule**, remember that you as the designer are not the best judge of what is comprehensible. First, as I discussed in Chapter 2, you're weird: as a software developer, you're better than the average reviewer when it comes to managing abstractions. So when you're sharing your model with nondevelopers, they may be at a disadvantage. But even other developers won't read your diagrams as readily as you will. When you read your diagram, you're reading the *real* picture that's already in your brain; but when reviewers read your diagram, they are reading the diagram and trying to understand what's in your brain. Those reviewers need a lot more help than you do. And that leads us to . . .

"You Just Don't Get It!" Is *Never* an Excuse

As the designer and originator of the idea, it's your responsibility to communicate it, and *no one else's*. As long as the reviewer makes a reasonable effort to understand the idea, it's up to you to make sure that effort pays off. The only measure of successful communication of an idea—in a slippery, circular sense—is when the idea is communicated back with no errors (and preferably in a different form). Until the reviewer understands the idea, you haven't communicated. Keep trying.

But how do you keep trying? Try another approach:

- Add more detail to your diagram, to make a better picture of what you need.

- *Remove* detail as a way to reduce clutter. Every diagram need not display every detail. Remember **The Model Rule:** completeness lies in the model, not in any single diagram.

- Remove the detail—and maybe even some of the major elements—and place them in another diagram.

- Redraw the diagram. If you can't get your point across, maybe a fresh start will inspire you to a better way of presenting the information.

- Ask reviewers to create a diagram of what they *do* understand. Perhaps when you see their interpretation, you'll discover where the miscommunication lies, and you can correct it.

Don't I ever get frustrated? Don't I ever run into people—real, competent developers—who just don't get it, just can't see how superior and brilliant my idea is? Sometimes I think I do; and then I recall the words of Jim McCarthy:

> *The clearest sign that people are thinking is that they listen to other people's ideas and critical feedback. They quiet their initially competitive responses to a possibly superior line of thought. They demand of themselves the intellectual rigor it takes to fairly and properly evaluate the new, potentially valuable information. They can filter out the ego-driven aspects of the communication they've just received because they can bring an understanding of human nature to a distillation of the true spirit of the message from the raw communication of it.*[6]

And then I apply those words, not to the other programmer, but to *myself*. If I can't explain my point to my fellow developers, at least I can listen to their point. It matters not in which brain communication begins; it matters only that it begins.

Every Picture Tells a Story

This is a corollary of the previous guideline and of **The Model Rule:** you draw those diagrams that answer questions or explain points. Every diagram should have a purpose that you want it to communicate to your audience. For each diagram, you should be able to convert the diagram to a PowerPoint slide, project the slide on a screen, and explain the story of that slide within the recommended 2 minutes per slide. The audience should be able to grasp the point of the story with minimal reference to other material. Although some amount of knowledge of the model behind the diagram will be necessary, each diagram should be complete enough to tell its story on its own. Add notes where necessary to fill in gaps in the explanation.

Conversely, examine the detail on each diagram. If a particular detail doesn't add to the story, consider removing it; and if some detail *detracts* from the story, definitely hide it within the current diagram.

Some stories are too large to tell in 2 minutes with one diagram. This is another example of how multiple diagrams at different levels of scope can make your

---

6. Jim McCarthy, *Dynamics of Software Development: "Don't Flip the Bozo Bit" and 53 More Rules for Delivering Great Software on Time* (Microsoft Press, 1995), pp. 30–32. The communication issue is discussed in depth under "Rule #4: Don't Flip the Bozo Bit." McCarthy's point in this rule is that assuming that anyone is a bozo—i.e., they just don't get it—is destructive for that person and for the entire team. If they have the skills to make a contribution to the team, they have a valuable perspective to bring to any problem; and if you cut off the chance for them to make that contribution, you might just as well cut them loose from the team. Never assume your fellow programmers are bozos.

communication more clear. Tell the broad outline of the story in one diagram; then bring the scope down to tell individual stories where they make the design more clear.

The Highway Map Rule

As the number of diagrams and models grows, some people will worry: "How do we keep this up to date as the code evolves?" Those in the Extreme Programming/ Agile Development worlds will answer: "You can't, so don't bother trying. Once you've got the code, throw away the model." Their focus is entirely on functioning code, and maintaining the model past the point of coding is considered extraneous effort. And worse, because they're *not* maintaining the model consistently with the code, the model will eventually be misleading: the model will lead you to believe the code works one way, when it really works another. In their view, the code is the only true design; and once a model helps you produce code, the model is "wrong" after that, so throw it out.

And then, of course, there are those with less discipline: those who use this mismatch between model and code as a justification for never modeling at all.

Well, I understand these concerns (except for those who never model), but I think they're wrong-headed. For an example of why, I point to the highway map in the glove compartment of my car. This is a map of Michigan (the state where I live), which I use to navigate to any part of the state that I don't already know how to find. It's also a useful way to teach someone basic Michigan geography. Without the map, I could set you down outside my front door, and let you start walking. In a few days, you would probably know a lot about the square mile closest to my house; but with the map, you could learn the major cities and highways in Michigan in less than an hour (and you wouldn't have to walk anywhere). So the highway map is pretty useful, except for a couple of problems:

- The map lacks detail. It covers over 160,000 square miles in around 1,100 square inches, a scale of nearly 1,000,000:1. That means that my entire local village of Hopkins—about half a square mile in area—should take up a square 0.04 inches on a side, and that's about the size of the dot that represents Hopkins on the map. But there's just no way to *legibly* draw the 22 streets of Hopkins within that dot. All you see of Hopkins is a dot. This is true for most Michigan cities: they appear as dots or larger geographic areas, but with only major streets drawn in. Only a few of the largest cities are reproduced at a larger scale so that you can see the streets in more detail. (In this way, the map is consistent with my advice to make your model out of multiple diagrams.) So there are many things in the real world that don't appear in the map.

- The map doesn't show the *inevitable* highway construction that takes place on practically every Michigan highway, all summer long. And the map is static, not dynamic, so it also doesn't show the inevitable traffic jams that occur on certain streets at certain times of day.

The map is wrong, in other words. So if I plan a route from my house to the monthly Ann Arbor Computer Society meeting, it's very likely that the map will mislead me. For instance, on one recent trip, the map didn't show the traffic jam that occurred in Jackson during rush hour; and the map didn't show the road construction between Ann Arbor and Jackson that exacerbated the traffic jam; and the map *certainly* didn't show the traffic accident (caused by the traffic jam, perhaps) that brought traffic to a complete standstill; *and* when I got frustrated with the progress and got off the highway onto local Jackson roads, the map didn't show enough detail to guide me, so I had to explore by myself.

So I should throw the map away, right? The only *real* design is the streets themselves, and the pattern of traffic on those streets, right? Yeah, the map *could be* updated to show all those details; but that would take too long to be worth the bother, right?

Of course not! We don't throw away models just because they're inaccurate or incomplete. The problem of keeping models and implementation up to date is not unique to software: building architects have to constantly revise their architectural blueprints to reflect the building as built; car designers have to update designs to reflect last-minute design changes; and map makers must occasionally print new maps to reflect new roads. And in fact, it's far easier for us to maintain software models than for others to maintain their models: automated tools can reverse engineer most of the structural changes, leaving it to us to model the behavioral changes based on those structural changes. (Building architects can only wish for that kind of power.)

As George Box once said, "All models are wrong; some models are useful." Even though our models are wrong, they're useful:

- The requirements model documents the intent of the analysts and the users.

- The architecture model documents the modular breakdown of the system, and thus probably the breakdown of teams and assignments and responsibilities as well.

- The design models are broad-scale maps to what's in the code. To say, "The code *is* the design," is simply impractical: it doesn't scale well. Any given diagram may reflect hundreds or even thousands of lines of code. If you try to comprehend that code a line at a time, you might never be able to understand the system; but if you try to comprehend a model first and then dig into the code for more specifics, your understanding will grow much more quickly.

So if you don't throw out the models (except, perhaps, for temporary models: proof-of-concept sketches that you throw together just as you're playing with ideas), when do you maintain them? It's not possible to be constantly changing your model, updating every single time you make a change to your code. Instead, you should consider one or more of the following approaches:

- **Frequently**

  Every time you start a new phase of development—a new release, a new iteration, a new set of requirements—start by modeling what is new and what has changed.

- **When you inherit code, and nobody ever bothered to create a design for it in the first place**

  A powerful technique for learning existing code is to reverse engineer the existing structure with an automated tool, and then to reverse engineer the behavior of that code by reading the code and reading the structure. As you learn what the code does, capture that understanding as Use Case, Activity, and Sequence Diagrams. This is one example of **The Outline Effect** at work (see Chapter 1).

- **When you see a problem**

  In *Refactoring*, Fowler[7] describes this approach when it comes to code: when you see an opportunity to improve code, you make the change immediately (and then thoroughly test to ensure that you didn't break anything in the process). Essentially, you "polish" the code wherever you see that it's tarnished. Similarly, if you see that the model is incorrect or incomplete in an area where you're working, don't throw the model out, and don't ignore the problem. *Fix* the problem now, when you see it. This way, the model naturally improves precisely in those areas where the most work is being done. This is another way to leverage **The Outline Effect**: by fixing the model, you have to think about the existing code and your new code more thoroughly, and will be thus more likely to make correct changes in both the model *and* the code.

- **When you *can't* see a problem**

  If you're chasing down a bug and you can't find it in the model *or* in the code, make a new model, based on the code. That will be an "as built" model. Then compare the "as built" model to the "as designed" model. The contrast will give you one more way of looking for the bug. Then, when you find it, fix the "as built" model, fix the bug, and replace the "as designed" model with the "as built" model.

---

7. Martin Fowler et al., *Refactoring: Improving the Design of Existing Code* (Addison-Wesley, 1999)

- **When it hurts**

  When you find that the model is consistently wrong and consistently misleading you in understanding the code, take time out to bring it up to date.

Some developers advocate an approach whereby they don't bother updating the model, as long as it still conveys the correct *intent* of the code, even if the two have become inconsistent in places. But if the model and code have diverged to such an extent that the code is unrecognizable with respect to the model, then the team should have a meeting, to figure out whether the model is wrong or the programmer just decided to do his own thing. The value of models in this kind of situation is in their ability to capture intent, more than implementation. As ever, follow rule number one, and **Do What Works**.

So in summary, **The Highway Map Rule** is this: throw away temporary models; keep permanent, official models; update the official models as you get the chance; and don't get overly concerned when the official model and the code aren't quite in step.

Define Your Own UML with Stereotypes

We have seen stereotypes a lot in our models so far. Now it's time to explore them a little more completely.

An important thing to realize is that the *U* in UML means *Unified*, not *Universal* (a common misconception). The UML authors recognized early on that a "universal" notation is an impossible dream: any attempt to make a universal notation was doomed to fall short, but would end up with a large, bloated notation that no one could use.[8]

So instead of striving for universal, the UML authors settled on *extensible*; and the primary extensibility mechanism they defined is stereotypes. A *stereotype* is a label applied to an existing element of UML notation that carries some extra meaning beyond the UML element itself. When you define a stereotype, you may also define a custom icon for that stereotype that replaces the standard icon for the base element. Then, when the stereotyped element appears in a diagram, you may show the stereotype either by using the custom icon (if any) or by listing the stereotype name in guillemets (« ») or double angle brackets.

---

8. In *Agile Modeling* (p. 171), Ambler argues—correctly, I believe—that they still ended up with a notation that is too large and bloated for most developers to use completely. Most modelers use only a fraction of the entire language. A large part of the UML 2.0 effort is to identify the "core" elements of UML.

In essence, stereotypes allow you to define your own "dialect" of UML: particular recurring modeling concepts that you want to express with a shorthand visual or text notation.

To define a new stereotype, first . . . well, first go read the Three Amigos' *The Unified Modeling Language User Guide* and *The Unified Modeling Language Reference Manual*. Although not universal, the UML is *huge*. It contains many obscure notations for special needs. Then go read their *Unified Software Development Process* for some useful stereotypes that they recommend for business and process modeling. Review other sources and see if the stereotype you need already exists. Before you go reinventing the wheel, see if someone will give you one, one that other people may already recognize.

But after you're sure that you need a new stereotype, find the UML element that comes closest to your new concept. Often this will be a class or actor; but it might be a use case, a component, or any other element of a UML model. Then define a stereotype named for the new concept. Document the new stereotype: what it means, why you need it, why it occurs often enough that a simple note won't suffice, and why an existing UML element won't suffice.

After that, you can apply your stereotype throughout your model. When someone asks what the stereotype means, point them to the documentation, and then answer their questions. The purpose of the stereotype is to make a simple way to communicate complex recurring concepts; but before you can use it, you have to make sure people understand the complex concepts.

Don't get carried away with custom stereotypes. You need them occasionally, and they can really increase communication within your team; but there's a risk that they will *decrease* communication with newcomers who do not yet know the stereotypes. For instance, I find that casual readers of Use Case Diagrams can get confused by actors, because they are depicted as stick figures even when they don't represent people. Sometimes a reader will even ask, "Who is this person called 'Mainframe'?" So I usually define the following custom stereotypes and icons in my designs:

Timer   Computer   Printer

These should be familiar concepts that are obvious to anyone who reads the diagrams. If the intent of the diagram is communicated more clearly by using custom icons, use them! But this customization may be carried too far. For instance, this icon may connote a great deal of information to someone who knows the Kennel Management System, but not as much to other readers.

Pet Worker

Pet Worker is anyone who works with pets directly, as opposed to someone who works with the system but not with pets. So **Care Giver** might be a **Pet Worker**, but **Accountant** probably would not be. So this may be a useful stereotype for the **Kennel Management System** problem domain, but it may confuse someone outside that domain.

One final warning in regard to stereotypes: do not use them when you really need a superclass/subclass relationship, i.e., when you want to use inheritance (as described in Chapter 1). Stereotypes are about extending UML itself, not about relationships between classes in the code.

Stereotypes: A .NET Perspective

.NET has a few concepts that are not well represented in UML. For instance, .NET supports properties, which look like attributes to outside client code but behave like operations internally. These and other unique .NET features will be represented with stereotypes, as we'll see in later chapters.

Just Enough Modeling: Analysis, Not Paralysis

The final pragmatic guideline is to avoid analysis paralysis. If every picture must tell a story, then *no* picture should be drawn *unless* it tells a story. Track only the scale and amount of information you need to answer questions. A good design principle, whether for UML or not, is design what you need, and then *shut up!* Don't draw diagrams that don't reveal more about the system than you already know. Eliminate truly trivial diagrams. The principle here is *just enough modeling*: just enough to answer questions, discover new questions, and answer those, but not to create every diagram you possibly could. That's too much.

Is it possible to overlook a valuable diagram this way? Of course. But with a good review process, you'll catch these, when reviewers scratch their heads and look at you funny. They'll tell you that you've missed something, and you'll insist that it's trivial. Fine. Prove that it's trivial; but prove it by drawing the trivial diagram. Either you're right, and you'll prove it trivial through use of the new diagram; or you're wrong, and the new diagram will reveal why. In either case, your communication will improve. But in no case do you say, "It's obvious! You just don't get it!"

This rule does not apply, of course, if you're on a MILSPEC or mission-critical system that demands much more extensive documentation. You have to manage the artifacts of your process, not just the process itself. This rule encourages a focus on artifacts over process. Sometimes, however, the process demands certain artifacts. Part of the review process must include verifying that all legally mandated diagrams are produced.

How Much Can "Too Much" Be?

A student recently asked me, "How many diagrams *could* we draw, if we wanted to be thorough?" I'd never really thought about that problem before, because I always knew in my heart that the answer was "Too many." But I realized that this could be a pretty useful question: if some manager did insist on *every* diagram as part of a "correct" process, how much effort would be involved? So we did some back-of-the-envelope calculations for a small system, based on all the different diagrams that I might draw under certain circumstances. These are necessarily *very* rough estimates, but they give a pretty good feel for how large such a "correct" process can be:

- Within the requirements model, assume a top-level "navigational" diagram. **1 diagram.**

- Assume the system is designed for the requirements of approximately 10 different primary actors. That's enough actors to make me expect that there are at least 2 actor packages—each with a diagram—and a package of actors with a diagram that shows the 2 packages. You'll often find a "common" package of actors as well, with its own diagram. **4 diagrams.**

- For a really thorough understanding of the problem domain and requirements, you might draw a domain Class Diagram for each actor, including all the other actors and all the domain objects with which it interacts. **10 diagrams.**

- For each actor, you'll produce a requirements Use Case Diagram that depicts the use cases required by that actor. **10 diagrams.**

- For each actor, you might also want a requirements Use Case Diagram that depicts the domain objects modified or maintained by its use cases. **10 diagrams.**

- As a rough average, each actor will require approximately 5 use cases; and of those 5, roughly 2 will have complex relations to other use cases, which will require separate diagrams. As another rough average, these complex use cases will each be related to approximately 2 new use cases. **20 diagrams.**

- For each actor, you'll have roughly 3 simple requirements use cases, 2 complex use cases, and 2 related use cases for each complex use case, which gives you a total of 9 requirements use cases per actor. For each requirements use case, you'll draw an Activity Diagram. **90 diagrams.**

- Each requirements Activity Diagram will have roughly 7 activities (action states) in it; and of these, roughly 3 will be complex enough to be subactivity states, each with its own Activity Diagram within it. **270 diagrams.**

- The activities within a subactivity state are usually simpler than the activities in a top-level diagram; but even so, some will have enough complexity to deserve to be subactivity states themselves. Assume this second set of Activity Diagrams have on average around 5 activities, and further assume that 1 out of 10 of these are complex enough to be subactivity states. **135 diagrams.**

- As a rough average, assume each actor is involved with 2 unique domain classes. (Many actors will be involved with more than 2, but there will be some overlap.) This leads to 20 domain classes. That is enough for a domain objects package with approximately four subpackages, along with a diagram for each package. **5 diagrams.**

- To really comprehend each domain class, you can produce a separate diagram to show the class and the classes that are immediately related to it. **20 diagrams.**

- To really understand each domain class and how it changes in response to events, you can produce a Statechart Diagram for the class. **20 diagrams.**

- As a rough average, assume each domain class Statechart Diagram consists of 5 states. Of those, roughly 2 may in fact be composite states, each with its own diagram. **40 diagrams.**

- Within the architectural model, assume a top-level "navigational" diagram. **1 diagram.**

- For each requirements Activity Diagram—including Activity Diagrams nested in subactivity states—you'll draw an architecture Activity Diagram with swimlanes. **495 diagrams.**

- Within the architectural model, assume a package for interfaces and a package for user interfaces, each with a detail diagram. **2 diagrams.**

- As a rough average, assume that for every 10 architectural Activity Diagrams 1 new, unique swimlane is introduced. (Most Activity Diagrams will involve many swimlanes; but there will be lots of overlap, so assume 1 per 10.) This leads to 50 swimlanes, and thus 50 actors, interfaces, and user interfaces. Because you're already assuming 10 actors, that leaves 40 interfaces and user interfaces. Those 40 can be grouped into roughly 8 packages, each with a diagram. **8 diagrams.**

- For each interface or user interface, you can draw a protocol for its use, consisting of an average of possibly 2 Interaction Diagrams each. **80 diagrams.**

- Within the architectural model, assume a package for the architectural view of components. This package should include both an Everything Diagram of the overall architecture, as well as a package diagram that shows the packages for the components within the architecture. **2 diagrams.**

- Assume that, on average, each component provides 5 interfaces or user interfaces. That means that, for our 40 interfaces and user interfaces, you'll need 8 components. For each of these components, you'll make a new design model, including a top-level "navigational" diagram and a diagram that shows the component and those components immediately related to it. **16 diagrams.**

- For each interface or user interface to a component, assume an average of 4 methods, each with 2 Activity Diagrams (with and without swimlanes). **80 diagrams.**

- Within each component, assume an average of 10 classes. These are enough to justify 2 class packages per component (each with Class Diagrams) and a top-level class package with a diagram that shows the subpackages. **24 diagrams.**

- You can understand each class more thoroughly by drawing a Class Diagram specific to it, showing it in the context of other classes. **80 diagrams.**

- To really understand each class and how it changes in response to events, you can produce a Statechart Diagram for the class. **80 diagrams.**

- As a rough average, assume each class Statechart Diagram consists of 5 states. Of those, roughly 2 may in fact be composite states, each with its own diagram. **160 diagrams.**

- As an average, assume each class has 4 operations. For each operation, you can draw 2 Activity Diagrams: 1 with swimlanes and 1 without. **640 diagrams.**

- The 8 components need to be deployed; so you need 1 logical Deployment Diagram and 1 physical Deployment Diagram. **2 diagrams.**

- Assume an average of 4 nodes in the deployment. For context of each node, you'll draw 1 logical Deployment Diagram and 1 physical Deployment Diagram. **8 diagrams.**

So to analyze and design this fairly simple system—only 50 functions, really—you could potentially draw as many as 2,313 diagrams. Assuming that each diagram takes a half man-hour to create and another half man-hour to revise after review feedback, and that a team of four spends a half hour reviewing each diagram, then that's a total of 6,939 man-hours spent on diagramming—or, even more frightening, three-and-a-half man-years.

It ain't gonna happen. This project can't justify that time expenditure. Only if it's mission critical, only if *lives* depend on it, can you justify that much time spent on analysis and design for a system of that size.

So clearly, there's such a thing as analysis paralysis, such a thing as too much modeling. And experience shows that there's also such a thing as not enough modeling: not enough to really understand what you're building. The trick, of course, is just enough modeling.

Summary

In this chapter, I've given you a set of practical "golden rules" to some of the issues that you'll be dealing with as you begin to analyze your problem domain and develop your model. These are summarized here:

- **Do What Works**

  The first rule is self-explanatory. There's no point rigidly obeying the rules if your model fails to communicate itself to others, so do whatever works for you in your particular situation.

- **The Model Rule**

  UML diagrams are like a user interface into your underlying model. Different diagrams illustrate different aspects of the model, and so they will contain different information, but the complete set should present a coherent picture. Completeness lies in the model, not in a single diagram.

- **Legible Does Not Mean Pretty**

  Don't spend an age getting your diagrams perfect: they only need to look good enough to get across the information that they are designed to communicate.

- **The MTB Rule (MTB—Minimum Two Brains)**

  When you're working on a new model or idea, always get another member of the team to look at it. They might spot flaws in a model that you didn't, or help you to correct a diagram. Two or more brains can spark a creative process.

- **The 7 ± 2 Rule**

  The average human brain can only hold 7 ± 2 things in its short-term memory, so cluttered diagrams lead to confusion. Simplifying diagrams and reducing the number of elements often improves communication. When circumstances demand complexity, grouping related elements can aid understanding.

- **The Résumé Rule**

  Each diagram should fit onto one standard-sized sheet of paper.

- **"You Just Don't Get It!" Is *Never* an Excuse**

  It's your responsibility to ensure information is communicated. When there's a problem, listen to the other people, and find out what they understand and where they think the problem lies. Make sure they can communicate the idea back to you.

- **Every Picture Tells a Story**

  Every diagram should tell a story in its own right. All the details on that diagram should contribute to that particular story.

- **The Highway Map Rule**

  Your models are maps to your code, so maintain them alongside your code, even after it has built. Although they might become a little out of step at times, don't throw them away.

- **Define Your Own UML with Stereotypes**

  UML doesn't contain a symbol for everything that you need. Sometimes it's helpful to define your own symbols or add extra information to elements using UML stereotypes, but always check first that there's not already something defined that you can use, or commonly, conventionally used stereotypes.

- **Just Enough Modeling: Analysis, Not Paralysis**

  Your model will never be completely perfect, and sooner or later you need to start coding. Learn to recognize when you have created a "good enough" model. Holes and other problems will show themselves up in review.

We're going to come back to the process of analysis and design again in Chapter 5, when we look at gathering and analyzing requirements, but because I want to focus on how you can apply modeling and UML in a .NET environment, let's take some time out first to see what .NET itself looks like as a UML model. That's going to be the focus of the next chapter.

CHAPTER 4

A UML View of .NET

IN THE NEXT PART of the book, we'll be working though a .NET case study, during which you'll see bits and pieces of the .NET Framework as UML. So that you can more easily follow the diagrams presented during the case study, I'm going to spend a bit of time first looking at how some core .NET concepts are represented in UML. UML can be a useful tool in enabling us to gain a better conceptual model of .NET.

Also in this chapter, I'll be introducing you to more detailed Class Diagram notation than you saw in Chapter 2. Class Diagrams in UML support a lot of rich detail, but I find that sometimes this gets in the way when you're trying to learn UML by doing. Now that you understand the basics of UML, we can discuss some of this more detailed notation.

 NOTE   In the sections that follow, I'm assuming that you already have some experience of .NET.

.NET Fundamentals

In this section, I'll show you how some of the fundamental .NET concepts are represented in UML. In particular, we'll be looking at namespaces, classes, structures, interfaces, enumerations, events and delegates, exceptions, assemblies, and the **System.Object** class.

Namespaces

A *namespace* is a familiar concept for C++ and Java developers (and others, of course). Namespaces form a hierarchy of names, so that two things with the same name can be distinguished by the namespace in which they are found. Namespaces conceptually divide the programming spaces into more comprehensible areas of functionality. They are a way of managing complexity and are essential in the .NET Framework, with classes numbering over 3,300. You can model a .NET namespace as a UML package, with a «**namespace**» stereotype, as shown in Figure 4-1.

Figure 4-1. A .NET namespace

Top-Level Namespaces in .NET

A namespace may contain any element of .NET code—including other namespaces, which is how the hierarchy is constructed. In .NET, there are three common base namespaces:

- **System.** This is the namespace that contains virtually all of the .NET Framework. It defines much of what is .NET.

- **Microsoft.** This namespace defines much of what is Microsoft specific and Windows specific about .NET. The core elements of **System** use elements of **Microsoft**.

- *YourNamespace.* The official .NET coding guidelines strongly recommend that all of your .NET code be grouped into a top-level namespace named for your company.

Figure 4-2 shows an overview of the top-level namespaces in .NET.

 NOTE The darker shaded packages represent those that are out of the scope and intent of the current diagram.

As you can see from Figure 4-2, *YourNamespace* will probably use elements from **System**, and may also use elements from **Microsoft**. The classes in **System** make use of elements from five of its subsidiary namespaces: **System.Security.Policy**, **System.Security.Principal**, **System.Reflection.Emit**, **System.Runtime.Remoting**, and **System.Runtime.Serialization**.

Although it's not mandatory that you show a UML package dependent on packages contained within it, it's a helpful way to show which contained packages are used at the "top" of the package.

Top-level Namespaces

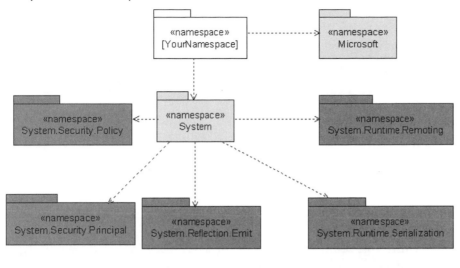

These are the top-level namespaces. The namespaces provide a hierarchy for classes in the .NET Framework, reducing the complexity by grouping related classes into a common namespace.

Figure 4-2. Top-level namespaces

Classes

The concept of a *class* in .NET is very much the same as it is in UML, so you can simply model a .NET class with a UML class. There is a little difference in terminology, though:

- *Method* is the .NET terminology for what UML calls an *operation*.

- *Field* is the .NET terminology for what UML calls an *attribute*.

Structures

In .NET, a *structure* is a special kind of class that is used for simple value types and is only instantiated on the stack. You can model a .NET structure as a UML class, with a «**struct**» stereotype, as shown in Figure 4-3.

Figure 4-3. A .NET structure

Interfaces

An *interface* in .NET means very much what an interface means in UML, so you can simply model a .NET interface as a UML interface.

Enumerations

In .NET, an *enumeration* is a special kind of class that defines a simple value type, has a small number of well-defined legal values, and is derived from the .NET Framework class, **System.Enum**. You can model a .NET enumeration as a UML class, with an **«enum»** stereotype. The attributes of the class will denote the legal values of the enumeration, as shown in Figure 4-4.

Figure 4-4. A .NET enumeration

....

What's with Those Plus Signs?

UML, in common with many OO languages, has the concept of *visibility:* a class, attribute, operation, or association may be restricted in its visibility, allowing only privileged code to access it. This allows more controlled designs in which the designer and implementer of a chunk of code can proscribe what may be done with that code. UML and .NET define four levels of visibility:

- *Public* visibility, indicated with a plus sign (+), means that the item may be accessed by any code, anywhere.

- *Private* visibility, indicated with a minus sign (–), means that the item may be accessed *only* by the operations of the containing class, not by any other code anywhere.

- *Package* visibility, indicated with a tilde (~), means that the item may be accessed by any code *only* if that code is delivered within the same assembly.

- *Protected* visibility, indicated with a pound sign (#), means that the item may be accessed only by the operations of the containing class or of its derived classes.

Events and Delegates

Events and delegates form a .NET mechanism for one chunk of code to asynchronously notify another chunk of code of some occurrence, so that the second chunk of code may respond to it. They are analogous to Windows messages and handlers, COM events and handlers, callback functions, and publish-subscribe communication protocols.

A *delegate* is a special class that represents a signature for a method. You can model a .NET delegate as a UML class, with a «**delegate**» stereotype, as shown in Figure 4-5. The delegate will have an **Invoke** method that defines the signature of the method to which the delegate refers.

Figure 4-5. A .NET delegate

An *event* is a programmatic "signal" that a class can raise. It must have a name, and it must have a delegate that defines the function signature of a function that may respond to the event. You can model a .NET event as a UML association between the containing class and the delegate class, with a role name equal to the event name, and with an «**event**» stereotype, as shown in Figure 4-6.

Figure 4-6. A .NET class with an event

What's with That Arrow? And That Name?

The arrow on the end of the association means that the **MyDelegate** end of the association is *navigable:* **MyForm** can navigate the association to find **MyDelegate**. Because there is no arrow on the other end, however, **MyDelegate** *can't* navigate the association to find **MyForm**. In fact, **MyDelegate** is not even "aware" that the association exists. Now, it's *legal* UML to put arrows on both ends of the association to indicate bidirectional navigability; but it's a more common convention to show bidirectional navigability with *no* arrows, just an association line. When one end of an association is navigable, then a valid way to implement the association is for the nonnavigable end to contain the navigable end as a reference or a value. For instance, **MyForm** contains an event of type **MyDelegate**, called **MyEvent**.

You may choose to give a name to either end of any association (or to both ends). Since the association ends are formally called *roles,* these names are called *role names.* These names allow you to discuss the roles played within the association itself, not just in the context of the classes. For instance, looking at Figure 4-6, I might say, "**MyForm** will fire **MyEvent** whenever the sum becomes negative." Notice how I never had to mention **MyDelegate**. That was implied simply by mentioning **MyEvent**. But without the role name, I would have to rewrite that sentence as: "**MyForm** will fire the event with a signature of **MyDelegate** whenever the sum becomes negative." It may also get confusing if multiple associations exist between two classes. For example, all **System.Windows.Forms.Form** mouse events have the same signature, defined by the **MouseEventHandler** delegate; so you would depict those events as associations between **Form** and **MouseEventHandler**. Without role names, it would be difficult to tell these events apart. When you implement an association in code, a common practice is to use role names to name fields that represent the association.

You may also choose to give a name to an association by itself. This allows you to discuss the association by itself, not just in the context of the classes it associates. An association may have both an association name and one or two role names. For instance, in Figure 4-7, an **Assignment** maps a **Worker** to a **Task**. The **Task** is a **Duty** for the **Worker**, and the **Worker** is **AssignedTo** the **Task**.

Figure 4-7. An association with a name and role names

Exceptions

In .NET, an *exception* is a special kind of class, derived from **System.Exception**, that indicates an extraordinary error (exception) has interrupted normal program flow. You can model a .NET exception as a UML class, with no particular stereotype.

Assemblies

A .NET *assembly* is the unit of distribution of .NET applications and other components. There are two conventions for modeling a .NET assembly: as a UML package, with an «**assembly**» stereotype (this is the convention used by Rational XDE); or as a UML component with an «**assembly**» stereotype. I'll follow the latter convention, as shown in Figure 4-8.

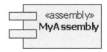

Figure 4-8. A .NET assembly

System.Object

In .NET, **System.Object** is the common base class, which defines the fundamental behavior for all types to share. **System.Object** is depicted in Figure 4-9.

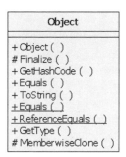

Figure 4-9. System.Object

"How Do I Know That Is a Base Class?"

All right, I can't put it off any longer. I described generalization (aka inheritance) in Chapter 1; and I've discussed many "base" classes and derived classes in this chapter. It's time to show how generalization is depicted in UML: with a closed-headed arrow from the subclass to the superclass, as in Figure 4-10.

Figure 4-10. Generalization

When depicting multiple subclasses, a common practice is to join their generalization arrows, as shown in Figure 4-11.

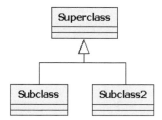

Figure 4-11. Generalization with multiple subclasses

Generalization may also be used to relate actors to each other and to relate interfaces to each other, as shown in Figures 4-12 and 4-13.

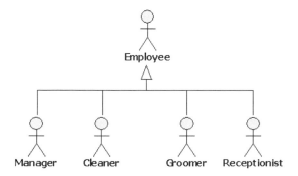

Figure 4-12. Actor generalization

Figure 4-13. Interface generalization

Although UML calls this concept *generalization,* I like to think of it as *specialization:* the subclasses are special kinds or special cases of the superclass. Or I'll call it simply *inheritance,* since that is the common term in many OO languages.

Common .NET Applications

We'll finish this chapter by looking at some common .NET constructs that will occur in many different applications and see how they are represented in UML. In particular, we're going to focus on the following:

- Console applications

- WinForms applications

- WebForms applications

- Web services

Console Application

Console applications are created in .NET using the **Console** class, which has methods for reading and writing, as well as methods for working with the standard console streams (In, Out, and Error). A typical console app is shown in Figure 4-14.

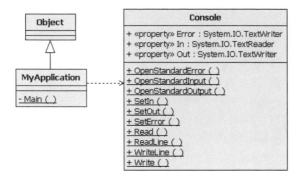

Figure 4-14. A console application

Note that, in C#, when a class has a static operation named **Main**, then that class is an application, and its **Main** operation will be called when the program starts.

WinForms Application

A WinForms application is a desktop program with one or more forms, each containing a number of controls. A typical WinForms app is shown in Figure 4-15.

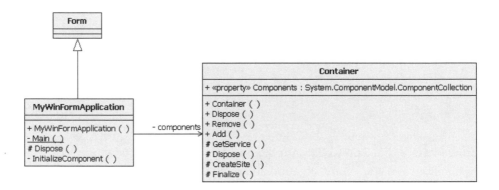

Figure 4-15. A WinForms application

A WinForm class derives from **System.Windows.Forms.Form**, which has far too many events and properties to show here. If a form also has a static **Main** operation, then it's a WinForms application. The **InitializeComponent** operation added to the WinForm class will automatically lay out the controls within a form.

A typical WinForms application also has a **Container** object, a class that tracks .NET components used within the application.

WebForms Application

A WebForms application is a browser-based application designed as a set of forms that automatically convert their contents to browser-sensitive HTML. A typical WebForms app is shown in Figure 4-16.

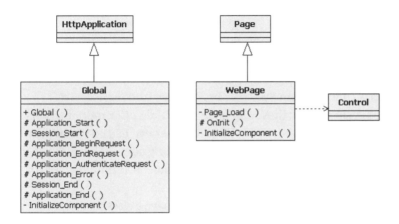

Figure 4-16. A WebForms application

A WebForm class derives from **System.Web.UI.Page**. Like WinForm classes, these can have an **InitializeComponent** operation to automatically lay out the controls within the form, allowing visual editing in VS .NET. A typical WebForm also has one or more attributes or associations derived from **System.Web.UI.Control**, which is the base class for Web controls.

The other major class (commonly called **Global**) in a WebForms app is derived from **System.Web.HttpApplication**, which provides code for HTTP application and session information and operations. The derived class can override some of these operations to provide custom handling for HTTP events.

Web Service

A Web service application is an HTTP-based application that exposes a number of methods for Web access via SOAP. A typical Web service app is shown in Figure 4-17.

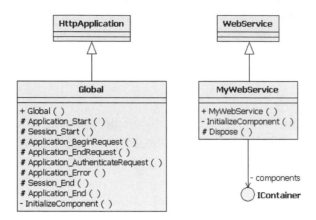

Figure 4-17. A Web service application

A WebForm class derives from **System.Web.Services.WebService**. Like
WinForm and WebForm classes, these can have an **InitializeComponent** operation to allow visual editing in VS .NET. While a Web service has no visual user
interface, VS .NET supports a visual metaphor for adding components for use in
an application. A typical WebForm also has one interface, **IContainer**, used for
tracking such components.

Like WebForms applications, Web services usually have a class, **Global**, derived
from **System.Web.HttpApplication** and used to support HTTP events and session
and application state.

Summary

In this chapter, we've taken a tour around some commonly used elements of
.NET and seen how these can be represented in UML. This will not only be useful
in understanding the diagrams presented later in this book, but also in your own
development work.

Along the way, we also saw some new UML Class Diagram notation, namely
how we represent generalization (inheritance) relationships between classes,
illustrate the visibility of operations, show the navigability of associations, and
add names to associations and roles.

Part Two
Case Study: UML Applied to a .NET Solution

If there's one thing my students have asked for more than anything else in my UML Boot Camp classes, it's more information on how to apply UML. In a 5-day class that teaches Five-Step UML, UML syntax in depth, OOAD fundamentals, and a UML tool (usually Rational ROSE or Rational XDE) with hands-on exercises, there's very little time left for application beyond the examples in the Five-Step UML exercises.

But in this book, we have more leisure to focus on application. I have room to write at length, and you can read at your own pace, so we can explore and apply UML in depth. In this part of the book, which focuses on the Kennel Management System as a case study, you'll learn a little more UML notation, and you'll see more examples of problem solving with UML. We'll also explore other aspects of solution development—management, testing, and documentation—and see how UML can be used to simplify these tasks.

In Chapter 5, the first chapter in Part Two, we'll look at the process of gathering and analyzing requirements. In Chapters 6 and 7, we'll also focus on requirements: defining the requirements in Use Case Diagrams and refining the individual scenarios in Activity Diagrams. We'll use these Activity Diagrams as our starting point for Chapter 8, where we assign responsibilities to different elements of the system using swimlanes. In Chapter 9, we look at the relationships between these different elements in the form of Component Diagrams, drilling down and looking into the structure of the components themselves with Class Diagrams in Chapter 10. Finally, we'll examine designing deployment in Chapter 11.

CHAPTER 5

Requirements: And Here Our Troubles Begin...

 NOTE **For those who are impatient ...** The next three chapters describe requirements gathering with UML. If you want to take requirements as a given and just see how those requirements can be realized in .NET components, skip ahead to Chapters 8 through 10.

IN THIS CHAPTER and the two that follow, we'll analyze the requirements of the Kennel Management System. We'll start in this chapter with an overview of the whole requirements process, which involves gathering, categorizing, diagramming, and reviewing our requirements.

First, we'll take a look at how different organizations go about gathering requirements, and at what kind of sources you can use. Next, we'll examine the different categories you can use to help you organize your requirements and how you should determine dependencies between them. In the final part of the chapter, I'll discuss the importance of an ongoing requirements review process.

Gathering Requirements

If you're very lucky, then your customers will provide clear, comprehensive, complete documents of their precise requirements. More often, however, you'll have to do this work yourself. Depending on the organization, the way this process functions can vary greatly.

In some organizations, skilled analysts review customer documents and interviews and provide detailed analysis and models. Such organizations are still pretty rare; not many organizations value analysis as a skill separate from development. And even among those that do, skilled analysts are a rare find, and are usually overworked.

A more common scenario is that product leads and project leads receive vague, wordy, and even contradictory documents and notes and interviews from end users, and must somehow convert these into a form that means something to their development teams.

Often, the vague, wordy, and contradictory documents and notes and interviews simply go straight to the hapless developers, who have to make sense of information far outside their expertise.

(And in too many organizations, the developers hear, "Why isn't it done yet? I'll tell you what it's supposed to do next week.")

But regardless of how requirements are gathered in your organization, the results of *bad* requirements gathering are always the same, as shown in Figure 5-1.

Figure 5-1. Who's sleeping in that doghouse?

No matter where bad requirements come from, it's the developers—and their friends in testing and documentation—who bear the brunt of the consequences. So those folks—and I'm talking to *you* here, more than likely—have the most interest in improving requirements gathering. If no one else is improving the requirements process, you'll have to take it upon yourself to do so. Notice in Figure 5-1 how the developer decided early on that he knew what to build. Notice what happened when he was proven wrong. Don't let this happen to you!

The subject of requirements gathering and management is much too large for this book—Karl E. Wiegers has an excellent book on this subject[1]—but I would like to discuss just enough about requirements to show how they will relate to your UML modeling.

Requirements Sources

The following are just some of the places where you might find requirements to harvest and analyze:

- **Vision document.** This document describes the business requirements (discussed later in this chapter in the section "Categories of Requirements") and the vision of what would make a successful system.

- **Walkthrough documents.** These are a set of "day in the life" descriptions of how various users will interact with the system. Written as a set of simple verbal narratives, these convey the vision in a tangible fashion.

- **Domain glossary.** This is a guide to the language of the end user, translating user-speak into English, not programmer-ese.

- **Domain expert and end-user interviews.** These are written and spoken conversations between end users (the consumers of the system) or domain experts (consultants and other gurus, either within your organization or brought in from outside, with wide experience in the problem domain) and those who must understand and build the system.

- **Functional specifications and statements of work.** These are detailed descriptions of the problem domain and expected functionality.

I hope that these artifacts—requirements sources, I call them—are provided for you. (Heck, I *hope* that you're provided with completely analyzed and modeled requirements, so that you may just start architecting and designing the system; but I'm not holding my breath.) But if you need to gather and manage these artifacts yourself, check the Wiegers book or another on requirements.

---

1. Karl E. Wiegers, *Software Requirements, Second Edition* (Microsoft Press, 2003)

The Remaining Exercises

The rest of this book is a set of hands-on examples of how I use UML. As such, it doesn't lend itself so well to exercises; but I still hope that it can guide you in practicing hands-on application of UML. So besides giving my own examples, I'll give some suggestions (in the form of exercises) for your hands-on practice. These exercises are suited for a team of four to six working on a project within your area of expertise.

In order to work through these exercises, you should select a current project or subproject on which to practice, and gather your requirements sources for that project. Don't get buried in work: pick a small effort that can be managed and run by four to six people. The ideal project will have 10 to 20 pages of requirements sources. A project with fewer than 5 pages is probably too small; your team could complete the project more easily by just building it than by designing it, so you won't appreciate the benefit of UML. A project with more than 50 pages is probably too large: the models will be huge and hard to organize until you have more practice.

Once you have your requirements sources gathered and checked into version control, ensure that each team member has access to them.

Categorizing of Requirements

A *requirement* is simply an expectation: a feature, behavior, or performance goal expected from a system. Requirements are what the end user or customer or other stakeholder[2] expects, and they are how your system will be judged.

But there are requirements, and then there are requirements. "Save us money" is different from "Let me maintain my schedule," which is different from "Get some experience with .NET on this project, so that we can decide whether to use it on other projects." Each is a requirement, but they impact your process in different ways.

A major part of requirements analysis is to categorize what you learn about the requirements, so that everyone can agree which requirements are features to implement, and which affect the features that you implement.

---

2. Courtesy of Gary K. Evans, here are some useful definitions for these different people: an *end-user* is the actual consumer of the system's services. A *customer* is someone who pays for the system and its development. The customer may not be an end-user. A *stakeholder* is any person or group with a vested interest in the outcome of the project. Stakeholders may come in both "supportive" and "hostile" flavors.

Following the example of Wiegers,[3] I like to define seven categories of requirements information:

- **Business requirements.** These provide the high-level "vision" of the system. They explain the compelling reason for the system, including the expected costs and the expected benefits. At the highest level, these define what would be expected from a successful system.

- **User requirements.** These are the vision made concrete. They tell what users need to get their jobs done, including the processes they will perform in these jobs.

- **Functional requirements.** These are the user requirements, made even more concrete. They define the functions that designers and developers must implement to satisfy the user requirements. Thus, each functional requirement traces directly to one or more user requirements.

- **Nonfunctional requirements (NFRs).** When I mentioned these once, a friend (whose name is withheld for his own protection) cynically remarked, "We meet all of those: none of our code functions." Well, these aren't about lack of functionality; they're about requirements that aren't themselves functions to be implemented, but rather are limitations that affect one or more user or functional requirements. For instance, "Maintain a schedule" is a functional requirement; "Do not let the schedule consume more than 10MB of disk space" is an NFR that affects that functional requirement. There are many kinds of NFRs, including performance targets (resource and performance requirements), quality targets (maximum number and severity of defects), maintenance targets (standards of maintenance and configurability), and interoperability targets (existing systems and standards with which the system must comply).

- **Constraints.** Whereas NFRs limit how you can implement certain functions, constraints limit your development process itself. Perhaps you could solve the problem easily if you hired a database guru, but you have a hiring freeze. Perhaps you could solve the problem in one-fifth the time if you worked in a productivity environment like Rational XDE, Visual Studio .NET, and .NET, but marketing has decided that the bulk of your customer base is on Unix boxes. Perhaps there are political realities, in which executives not directly affected by the success of your project have the power to redirect your efforts for their own ends. Like NFRs, constraints affect user and functional requirements, but at the management level more than at the design and implementation level.

---

3. Karl E. Wiegers, *Software Requirements*, p. 8

- Constraints may be divided further into categories:

  - *Operational constraints* define limits on your organization's ways of doing things. For example, you may have ISO 9000 rules that define your development process, and you risk losing ISO certification if you violate them.

  - *Statutory constraints* define legal mandates you must follow. For instance, developers working on health care systems in the U.S.A. must be aware of HIPAA, a set of regulations that define how security and privacy must be maintained for patient records.

  - *Contractual constraints* define obligations you face under contracts. For instance, your client may require that you have outside quality auditors.

  - *Fiduciary constraints* define the financial risks and limits that your organization will accept. For instance, they may only be willing to commit a certain amount of dollars to a project.

  - *Database constraints* define limitations imposed by your database system and existing data. For example, you may have to interoperate with a large existing database, and your client may require that you keep it up to date with your new work.

- Other categories of constraints are possible.

- **Actors.** An actor represents any outside system that interacts with the system you're designing (see Chapter 2 for more details). No, these aren't requirements *per se*, but a well-analyzed set of requirements should identify all actors and document what is known about them.

- **Domain objects.** These are any object or entity that the customer expects your system to either represent or maintain (see Chapter 2 for more details).

Meet the Martins

In the earlier chapters of this book, I was mostly in what I call "Martin the Instructor Mode": I was trying to teach you principles and techniques, with just a little bit on my personal modeling practices. In this case study, I am definitely in "Martin the Practitioner Mode": I'm showing you specifically how I would tackle an analysis and design problem for a .NET project. My UML students have learned to tell the difference between these modes: Martin the Instructor wants to show you that there are a lot of successful ways to solve problems, and to describe some of them; Martin the Practitioner wants to show you what works for him.[4] These aren't the only practices that work, by any means; but they are successful for me as applied here.

In terms of documenting your requirements, certain development processes define detailed document templates to be filled out for each type of requirement. While I think these templates can be overkill if each field of each form is considered mandatory, they are useful suggestion lists to help you think about what to document. (For examples, see Wiegers,[5] the Three Amigos,[6] Schneider and Winters, [7] Cockburn,[8] and Texel & Williams.[9])

For any given project, you will need to determine the right level of documentation for your project, and then stick to it. (As you're working through the exercises presented in this book, you should probably lean toward lightweight documentation, because you want to focus on your modeling skills; but you may find that you need more documentation as you progress.)

One useful technique for categorizing the requirements is to have every team member read every requirements source, with each team member focused on a different kind of requirement. For example, one team member would look for business requirements, one would look for actors, and so on. This focus lets each team member do just two tasks: comprehend the requirements, and identify and

---

4. This habit of speaking of myself in the third person has been described as "Bob Dole Syndrome," after a famous habit of former Senator Robert Dole (R-Kansas); but I go Senator Dole one better, speaking of myself as *multiple* third persons. Hey, they're *my* personae, and I'll do what I want with them.

5. Karl E. Wiegers, *Software Requirements*

6. Ivar Jacobson, Grady Booch, James Rumbaugh, *The Unified Software Development Process* (Addison-Wesley, 1999)

7. Geri Schneider and Jason P. Winters, *Applying Use Cases: A Practical Guide, Second Edition* (Addison-Wesley, 1998)

8. Alistair Cockburn, *Writing Effective Use Cases* (Addison-Wesley, 2000)

9. Putnam P. Texel and Charles B. Williams, *Use Cases Combined with Booch/OMT/UML: Process and Products* (Prentice Hall, 1997)

catalog *one* type of information. This is easier than trying to comprehend every kind of requirement within the sources.

Each team member can produce a summary report or catalog of their particular kind of requirement; and then all team members can review these, looking for inconsistencies. You should also look for overlap: the same requirement categorized in two different ways, such as an actor that is also listed as a domain object. When you see inconsistencies and overlap, the team should meet to hammer out the details. These conflicts indicate that team members understood things in inconsistent ways, and resolving them will improve communications among the team.

Exercise 501: Categorize Your Requirements

Read through the requirements sources for your chosen sample project and place the requirements into one of the categories described previously, so you may understand the features that you must implement and the context of those features.

Determining Dependencies Among Requirements

Once you've categorized your requirements, the next stage is to determine which requirements are dependent upon others, based on your requirements sources. In particular, you should look for user requirements, functional requirements, and domain objects that are affected by NFRs and constraints. Using a spreadsheet, a database, or a more sophisticated requirements tool (such as Rational RequisitePro), you can define a trace matrix that shows everyone how requirements affect each other. This will be a valuable aid in assessing the impact of requirements changes, particularly after development has begun.

For instance, Figure 5-2 is a sample trace matrix for the KMS project.

Req.	Type	Kennel Worker	Pet Owner	Reserve pen	Search for dates	Pen	Reservation	Reservation must be on-line	Check pet status	Update Pet Status
Kennel Worker	Actor									X
Pet Owner	Actor			X	X		X		X	
Reserve pen	User Req	X			X	X	X	X		
Search for dates	Func Req	X	X			X	X	X		
Pen	Dom Obj		X	X			X			
Reservation	Dom Obj	X	X	X	X			X		
Reservation must be on-line	NFR			X	X		X			
Check pet status	User Req	X								
Update Pet Status	User Req	X								

Figure 5-2. Sample trace matrix for the KMS project

Collaboration within your team to build the trace matrix is another useful way to resolve different perceptions of what the requirements mean.

Exercise 502: Find Dependencies Among Your Requirements

Using a spreadsheet or another tool, build a trace matrix. Make a row and a column for each requirement, and then put an X in each cell that marks the row and column of two related requirements.

Diagramming Requirements

Based on the requirements analysis so far, the next stage is for you to create a set of UML diagrams that reflect these requirements. I won't talk about this process any further here, because over the next couple of chapters we'll be looking at this stage in detail. We'll be using Use Case Diagrams, Activity Diagrams, and occasionally, during this stage, Class Diagrams as well.

Reviewing Requirements

Once you've begun the process of creating Use Case and Activity Diagrams, no doubt you'll have found gaps in your requirements sources. Here's where you close the loop: you can use *your* diagrams as a means to communicate the gaps in the requirements. You're using the pictures as a tool for, yes, communications: communicating what you understand, what you don't understand, and what you *might* understand if they can clarify matters for you.

When the number of unanswered questions starts to diminish, you're ready to start building. (In almost all cases, you must accept that not all requirements can be known in advance; but you do want to have confidence that you have the bases covered.) No one can tell you exactly when this is; but here are some useful rules of thumb:

- All existing use cases are diagrammed.

- 90 percent or more of the use cases have primary and alternate scenarios defined in detail.

- 90 percent or more of the scenarios have Activity Diagrams.

- The Requirements Delta is less than 10 percent. The *Requirements Delta* is the ratio of change in requirements (new requirements, deleted requirements, and changed requirements) over the total number of requirements over a given period (a couple of days for small projects, a couple of weeks for large ones).

- For mission-critical systems, no analyst or client or other team member is raising any red flags. Uncertainty is expected at this stage; certain failures aren't. Remember Morton Thiokol and the Space Shuttle Challenger disaster:[10] when engineering judgment tells you that someone is going to get killed, pay attention.

---

10. Roger M. Boisjoly, "Ethical Decisions—Morton Thiokol and the Space Shuttle Challenger Disaster," The Online Ethics Center for Engineering and Science Web site (http://onlineethics.org/essays/shuttle/bois.html)

Now the preceding numbers are just guidelines. If yours is a high-risk project, you might want to tighten those margins (say, >95 percent/>95 percent/<5 percent).[11] If your project needs to move quickly and you can afford to waste money on rework, you might want to loosen those margins (say, >80 percent/>80 percent/<20 percent). But the key is to decide on your targets in advance, and get everyone to agree to them at the start of analysis (in writing, if possible), *before* the pressure begins to start cranking out code. That way, you will have some control over the risks of both premature development and the never-ending requirements phase.

Requirements: A .NET Perspective

As we'll discuss further in Chapter 6, the requirements process is not specific to a given platform or environment. Where possible, your requirements process should be platform neutral, and should be used to help select the best platform for the project, where "best" is defined by a number of factors:

- Can you get the job done on the chosen platform or platform combination? Does the platform simplify a lot of your work, or does it require that you do the entire job manually? Because of the vast scope of the .NET Framework, there is a lot of infrastructure you can easily reuse.

- What do your users expect? If you walk into the typical office environment with anything but a Windows/.NET solution, you'll have an uphill battle; but if you walk into a newspaper office and your system doesn't run on a Macintosh, the battle will be even steeper. Because .NET is ubiquitous (or will be soon), familiarity can be a strong argument for a .NET solution.

- Will your typical end user have one machine, or will the application cross machines? If the work is distributed across multiple machines, will they all have the same environment? As discussed in Chapter 2, two applications that are both running on .NET and can communicate via .NET Remoting will usually communicate more efficiently than will applications in a homogeneous network communicating via Web services.

---

11. In this case, I use "high risk" to mean mission critical (lives are at stake) or financially risky, or legally risky, or any other situation in which it may almost be better to build no system than to build the wrong system. We'll discuss risk management in more detail in upcoming chapters.

So these questions become some of the NFRs and constraints that you must identify to determine your overall requirements. For the purposes of this book, of course, assume that you choose .NET as your platform wherever possible.

Summary

In this chapter, I've given you a quick overview of the requirements analysis process. When developing a new system, everything springs from getting the requirements right, and here, communication is key.

As a starting point in the requirements gathering stage, you can use sources such as vision documents, functional specifications, and interviews with end users. Next, you should think about how to organize the requirements into categories such as business requirements, user requirements, functional requirements, and so on. Once your team has categorized your requirements, you should review them together to ensure that there are no inconsistencies, and then create a matrix that documents the dependencies between each of them. The next stage is to start diagramming the requirements—a process that we'll look at in detail in Chapters 6 and 7. Before you consider your set requirements complete, it's important to go through a review stage with your customer to make sure that you haven't overlooked anything.

CHAPTER 6

Step 1: Define Your Requirements

Y OU SAW IN THE last chapter how to gather requirements, categorize them, and document the dependencies between them. In this chapter, we'll move on to Step 1 of Five-Step UML: defining requirements as a set of Use Case Diagrams, using the Kennel Management System as an example.

I'll start off by showing you how to identify lists of actors and domain objects. Next, I'll go on to show you how to determine which use cases are initiated by each actor, and draw the corresponding Use Case Diagrams. You'll then learn how to refine these diagrams by adding the associated domain objects to them.

Finally, once we've got a complete set of Use Case Diagrams for the Kennel Management System, I'll discuss the general topic of requirements further, from the point of view of managers, testers, and documenters.

But before we get started, a quick note about the case study . . .

The Kennel Management System

The requirements of the Kennel Management System (KMS) are based on the specification included as Appendix A. Throughout this and subsequent chapters, I'll reference sections of Appendix A by paragraph number. Appendix A shall serve as an *initial* specification; but we'll learn more about the KMS as the case study evolves.

It's worth taking some time to look at that specification now—we'll be following this case study over the next few chapters, so that you can see in detail how each step of Five-Step UML works in a real-world case study.

Everything You Know Is Wrong

Many of the KMS diagrams earlier in this book were created *not* as part of a complete KMS design, but rather as examples to illustrate particular points in UML. In other words, they were instructive, not necessarily correct. To make good models of the project spec, I may have to contradict what you've seen in earlier chapters.

But that's OK. "Do I contradict myself? Very well then, I contradict myself, (I am large, I contain multitudes.)"[1]Consistency is not the goal; communication is the goal.

One of Scott Ambler's *Agile Modeling* principles is "Discard temporary models."[2] His point is much the same as the design-and-fix principles I have discussed earlier: on the road to a good solution lie a lot of bad solutions, and he sees the cost of preserving the bad solutions to often be higher than the value of keeping them.

So for this case study, we're starting from scratch. If an earlier diagram is useful, we may re-create it; but I'm not going to try to enforce consistency with the earlier diagrams.

A Word of Warning: Work Ahead!

In later chapters, I'll concentrate on individual actors and individual use cases, in order to save some of the forests we'd have to cut down if I included the whole thing. In this chapter, however, I'm going to show you the complete first step, and this is for a realistically sized case study. For some programming languages, you can get quite a long way learning the syntax by writing "Hello World" applications and little GUI calculators, but one of the problems with UML is that to understand how it works, and to understand the importance of modeling, you need to apply it to a reasonably complex problem, or you're just left thinking, "Why am I doing this? I could have coded this already!" I also want to give you an idea as to what level of detail you need to drill down to, the numbers and types of actors you might have to work with, how you might organize them, how they correspond to the different use cases, and so on. But fear not! I'll ease up on the scope after this, when I focus in more narrowly on different parts of the system in the later steps of the process.

Because the remainder of this book focuses on .NET and on a process based on UML, I'll present a lot of diagrams and references to the spec; but I won't necessarily include a lot of commentary. (Insert sigh of relief here.) *And* I'll skip a lot of intermediate diagrams, presenting only finished results. I'll reserve most of my comments for diagrams that do one or more of the following:

- Display new UML syntax

- Demonstrate useful ways to plan and organize a model

---

1. Walt Whitman, "Song of Myself," *Leaves of Grass* (Bantam Classics, 1983), stanza 51

2. Scott Ambler, *Agile Modeling: Effective Practices for eXtreme Programming and the Unified Process* (John Wiley & Sons, 2002), pp. 64–65

- Are useful in planning, testing, documentation, and management

- Pertain to .NET

If a diagram doesn't fall into one of these categories, don't expect a lot of commentary; but I *will* make an effort to provide simple, clear diagrams (clear to those who have read this far in this book, at least). Because the purpose of UML, after all, is communication.

Identifying and Organizing Actors

When identifying potential actors, you should start by reviewing your requirements sources, such as your functional specification. Each entity[3] that is described as doing something or responding to something is a potential actor.

One technique is to look for the subjects of sentences—for example, "The salesperson shall update the customer profile to reflect the new information." In this sentence, "salesperson" is the subject, and is also the actor that will ask the system to do something.

Another technique (which was particularly useful for the KMS example) is to review the glossary in the spec and ask about each entry, "Does this item ask the system to do something? Or does it do something for the system?" For example, in the KMS spec (section 1.2) we read, "Care Giver: A kennel worker whose primary duties are the care and feeding of pets and the cleaning of pens and facilities." We might assume from this that "Care Giver" will be one of our actors.

Yet another technique is simply to read the spec and build a "cast list": a list of people or things that do things involving the system.

No technique is perfect. You'll miss some actors, and you'll identify others that really shouldn't be there. Thus, you'll need a good review process, and a few good rules of thumb:

- If in the final analysis the candidate actor has no use cases, it may not be an actor at all; and if it also has no communications from use cases, it's definitely not an actor.

- If the candidate actor does nothing but hold information, it's probably a candidate object, not an actor. (Candidate objects are discussed later in this chapter, in the section "Identify and Organize Domain Objects.")

---

3. This is not an entity in the sense commonly used in database modeling (i.e., a table and records that represent one kind of data). Rather, I use "entity" here because actors may be people or things, so I wanted a term that encompassed both.

- If the actor name is too specific (i.e., "Bob, the Second Shift Supervisor"), you should try to identify the role behind that name (which in this example might be "Supervisor", but it might also be some particular work role that Bob fills but that isn't represented in his title).

- If the actor name is too general (i.e., "User"), you should break the actors up into more specific actor names based on particular roles. Only tolerate such general actors for use cases that are generally available to a wide range of users.

Here is the candidate actor list I came up with from my analysis:

Accountant	Kennel Staff
Breeder	Kennel Worker
Care Giver	KMS Workers
Contractor	Other Franchises
Credit Company	Other Operators
Customer	Others
End User	Owner of Sandy's Pets
Facility	Pet Handler
Facility Staff	Pet Owner
Five-Step UML Company, or FSU (That's us, the team that is analyzing and building the KMS.)	Pet Owner Representative
	Pet Tag (Why is this an actor? Because it informs the system about the pet's location.)
Franchise	Pet Worker
Franchise Group	Receptionist
Franchise Owner	Registration Authority
Franchisee	Sandy's Pets
Franchising Consultant	Supervisor
Groomers	Vendor
Home Office	Veterinarians
Kennel Owner	

That's quite a list of potential actors; but some of these are pretty obscure. For instance, "Others" are referenced in sections 2.6 to 2.8 of the spec: "Allows pet owners and others to . . ." This is an indicator that these requirements are too vague. Who is allowed to view PetCams? Only registered owners? Only owners and representatives? Or everyone, because everyone loves dogs (and puppies!), and it makes great advertising?

Through interviews with end users and domain experts (I've saved you the tedium of those interview meetings for this case study), we're able to refine our actor set. For instance, in the KMS example, I've decided that I *do* want to let any visitor view PetCams, so I've defined the **Visitor** actor to represent someone who visits the Sandy's Pets Web site but doesn't work for or with Sandy's Pets. The resulting set of actors is depicted in Figure 6-1.

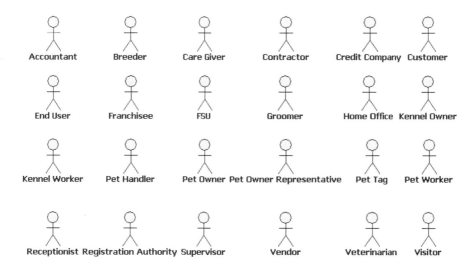

Figure 6-1. KMS actors

Whoa, we've already got a pretty cluttered picture there, and it will only get worse when we add relations between the actors. This picture is well beyond **The 7 ± 2 Rule**, which I talked about in Chapter 3.

In order to get some structure into this diagram, we can do two things:

- Add in some stereotypes, so that we can distinguish particular varieties of actors. (Recall from Chapter 3 that a stereotype is not a Jeff Foxworthy "redneck" joke; it's a way of extending UML by defining your own dialect for specific modeling needs.)

- Organize the actors into packages using the Actor Hierarchy Pattern (which we'll meet shortly).

The next two sections examine these steps in more detail.

KMS Actor Stereotypes

For the KMS system, I've used the following actor stereotypes:

System

The **System** stereotype denotes any external computer system or software with which the KMS must interact. One example in the KMS is the **Credit Company**, a banking system.

Timer

The **Timer** stereotype represents any regularly occurring event that must be processed. At this point, we haven't found any requirements for timers in the KMS; but experience tells me that we may before we're done.

Event

The **Event** stereotype denotes any programmatic event that must be processed (other than timers, which have their own stereotype).

Pet Worker

The **Pet Worker** stereotype denotes any human actor who interacts directly with pets. This stereotype helps us to recognize which actors may be responsible for the health and safety of a pet, and which are not involved in pet-related duties.

Now that we've adopted this stereotype, I suspect that we can dispense with the **Pet Worker** actor. At first, that seemed like a possible base class actor for a lot of other actors; but as I reviewed some of my actor diagrams (which we'll look at later in this chapter), I discovered that many of these actors already had base class actors. While UML doesn't make it illegal for a class or actor to have multiple base classes (unlike .NET and Java and some other OO environments, in which such *multiple inheritance* is illegal), this can lead to confusion. So for this case study, we'll use **Pet Worker** as a stereotype, not as an actor.

The Actor Hierarchy Pattern

When I walk into a new consulting project, I like to walk in with some commonly occurring structure already in place. This establishes a template process, giving me places to put things. I like to have separate requirements and architecture models already initialized. I like to have a **Domain Model** package. And I like to have the Actor Hierarchy Pattern in the requirements model.

What Is a Pattern?

Patterns are a popular analysis-and-design tool in software development. They are a description of a commonly occurring analysis-and-design problem, together with a description of a known solution to the problem, including a discussion of limitations on the solution and when it might not apply.

Many patterns books describe patterns as the problem statement and the solution in combination, but I like to separate them. The problem statement is a sort of "interface" to a problem, whereas the solution is a sort of "implementation." By thinking of the problem and solution as separate pieces, you are able to plug in different solutions to a single problem until you find one that fits.

In essence, patterns are "best practices" formally described as an aid to study and application. A formal study of a pattern usually follows a template or *pattern language* that defines the elements needed to completely understand the pattern. For example, a pattern language might specify that you must include these elements (based on *A UML Pattern Language*[4]):

- **Name.** Succinct and memorable "tag" for the pattern
- **Problem.** Describes problem to which the pattern may be applied
- **Context.** Describes the context in which the problem may arise
- **Forces.** Considerations and constraints that affect the applicability of the pattern
- **Solution.** Describes how the pattern is applied and the problem is resolved
- **Resulting context.** Describes how the context is changed after the pattern is applied
- **Discussion.** Additional notes and diagrams

---

4. Paul Evitts, *A UML Pattern Language* (Que, 2000), pp. 22–23

But in this book, when I mention patterns, I'll only show the results—not the formal descriptions—so that I can save space and time. For readers who want to learn more about patterns, I recommend *A UML Pattern Language, Design Patterns*,[5] and *Analysis Patterns*.[6]

One new source of information about patterns is the pattern work being done by Microsoft. See http://www.microsoft.com/practices for their latest work.

The Actor Hierarchy Pattern is a way of organizing actors, a way that I find useful across most of my projects. Hopefully you'll also find it a useful starting point for organizing the actors in your own projects. It can be visualized in Figure 6-2.

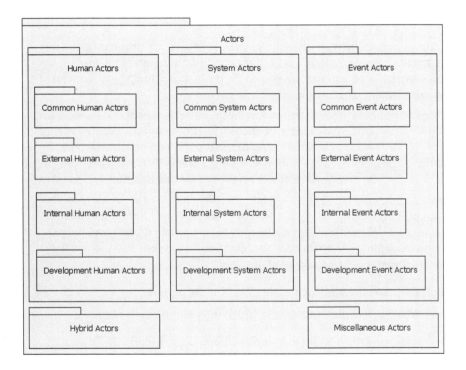

Figure 6-2. The Actor Hierarchy Pattern

5.   Erich Gamma, Richard Helm, Ralph Johnson, and John Vlissides, *Design Patterns: Elements of Reusable Object-Oriented Software* (Addison-Wesley, 1995)

6.   Martin Fowler, *Analysis Patterns: Reusable Object Models* (Addison-Wesley, 1996)

This diagram shows the packages of actors contained within other packages, all contained within a top-level **Actors** package. My requirements models always start with these packages. (If I find that there are no actors in a given package, I can always delete it from the final model; but I can save time during requirements gathering if all of the packages are there, just in case.)

For some of these packages, we'll have many different actors from our case study, and for others, none. So that you can see how it all fits together, though, I'll step through all of the different packages in this section, and describe each one in more detail.

Actors Package

In the Actor Hierarchy Pattern, the **Actors** package contains no actors, but is instead only a container for other packages.

Human Actors Package

The **Human Actors** package contains four packages, each of which contains actors that represent people and organizations that interact with the system:

- **Common Human** Actors

- **External Human** Actors

- **Internal Human** Actors

- **Development Human** Actors

Common Human Actors Package

The **Common Human Actors** package contains actors that represent people who can't easily be described as internal or external (which I'll describe next). That often means these are base actors from which both internal and external actors are derived. For the KMS thus far, that's a *very* small set, as shown in Figure 6-3.

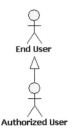

Figure 6-3. Common Human Actors package

The **End User** actor represents any end user of the system. The **Authorized User** actor represents users whose identity must be verified before they can perform tasks. Common use cases such as security authorization shall be assigned to one of these actors.

Note the use in Figure 6-3 of the closed arrowhead to indicate an inheritance (generalization) relationship: **End User** is a base actor from which **Authorized User** is derived. You'll be seeing this notation throughout this chapter.

Where Did the Authorized User Come From?

From my head, of course. But seriously: as I started analyzing the KMS use cases, I saw that *most* should involve some level of user security, whereas only a few didn't. So I realized that there were two classes of end users: **End Users** and **Authorized Users**, and I updated the model accordingly. Then I interviewed the customer (What, you missed *another* interview? You have to keep up, here!) and persuaded them that we needed this distinction.

External Human Actors Package

The **External Human Actors** package contains actors that represent people outside our client organization who interact with the system. Remember: *all* actors are external to the system you're developing. That's the definition of an actor. Here, though, I'm talking about actors that are even more external: outside not just the system, but the organization as well.

In the case of the KMS, this package contains actors that represent people who don't work for the Sandy's Pets home office or for its franchisees. Looking at these actors, we can count 11. That's not *too* excessive for one diagram; but if you go back and look at the list of actors for the KMS, you may spot some useful sub-packages. These are shown in Figure 6-4.

Figure 6-4. External Human Actors package

Next, I'll describe each of these subpackages in more detail.

Owner Actors

The **Owner Actors** package contains actors that represent the customer and pet owner, as shown in Figure 6-5.

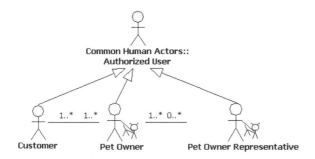

Figure 6-5. Owner Actors package

What's with Those Numbers?

In Figure 6-5, notice the number ranges attached to the associations between some actors: **1..*** and **0..*** between **Pet Owner** and **Pet Owner Representative**, for example. These are the UML way to show *multiplicity:* the number of things of a given type that participate in a relationship.

You might simply call this *cardinality,* just like it has been called in computer science for half a century and in mathematics for centuries; but the UML authors felt they needed a new term to represent the *range* of allowed cardinality values. Either that, or they like a word that makes me trip over it every time I say it in a class.

Multiplicity is expressed in the form Lower Bound ... Upper Bound.

A zero (0) indicates that sometimes the actor is not present, and thus the relationship is optional. If only a single value is specified, then the multiplicity is given by that value. For example, 1 means that there is a one-to-one relationship. An asterisk (*) indicates an unspecified number, and a single asterisk (with no range specified) is equivalent to **0...***.

You'll often specify multiplicity in Class Diagrams, and sometimes in Use Case Diagrams, Component Diagrams, and Deployment Diagrams.

As per the KMS spec, a **Pet Owner** may be a **Customer**, and vice versa; but nothing stops a **Customer** from representing and paying for multiple **Pet Owners**. For example, a parent might have multiple children who are all **Pet Owners**; yet the parent is responsible for the bills, and is thus the **Customer**. Also, one **Pet Owner** may work with multiple customers (I'm not sure how, but we don't want to rule this out).

You can also see from this diagram that a **Pet Owner** may designate one or more **Pet Owner Representatives** who are allowed to check a pet in and out.

Finally, note that each of these actors is an **Authorized User**.

What's with That :: Name?

Notice how the name of Authorized User appears: **Common Human Actors::Authorized User**. This optional format for names allows you to indicate the package in which a diagram element resides (if it's not part of the current package).

Supplier Actors

The **Supplier Actors** package contains actors that represent vendors and contractors, and the corresponding diagram for this package is shown in Figure 6-6.

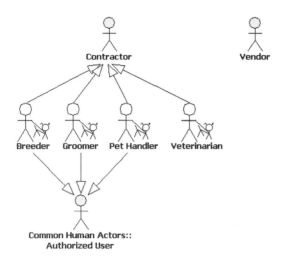

Figure 6-6. Supplier Actors package

Note how three of the different types of **Contractor** are expected to be **Authorized Users** of the system; but as per the spec, we don't require **Veterinarians** to be **Authorized Users**.

Other External Human Actors

Figure 6-7 shows the additional external human actors I came up with for the system.

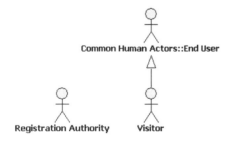

Figure 6-7. Other External Human Actors package

Note that I've made **Visitor** an **End User**, not an **Authorized User**. We decided earlier that **Authorized User** is where security use cases apply. Because we want to allow visitors to view the PetCams as a form of advertisement, we don't require them to have a user ID and password.

Internal Human Actors Package

The **Internal Human Actors** package contains actors that represent people who work for the client organization and who interact with the system.

In the case of the KMS, that means people who work for Sandy's Pets or its franchisees. If you look back at the list of actors shown in Figure 6-1, you can count eight. Again, that's not excessive for one diagram; but you may also notice some useful subpackages, as shown in Figure 6-8.

Figure 6-8. Internal Human Actors package

Let's now analyze each of these **Internal Human Actors** packages.

Sandy's Pets Staff Actors

Figure 6-9 shows the diagram for the **Sandy's Pets Staff Actors** package.

Figure 6-9. Sandy's Pets Staff Actors package

So far, all the use cases involving the **Home Office** actor don't identify any more specific staff. Thus, we'll have a general actor to represent anyone from the **Home Office** who interacts with a franchise.

Franchise Staff Actors

The **Franchise Staff Actors** package is shown in Figure 6-10.

Figure 6-10. Franchise Staff Actors package

So far, all the use cases involving the franchise don't identify any more specific staff. Thus, we'll have a general actor to represent the **Franchisee**, along with anyone from the franchise who interacts with the **Home Office**.

Kennel Staff Actors

The **Kennel Staff Actors** package appears in Figure 6-11.

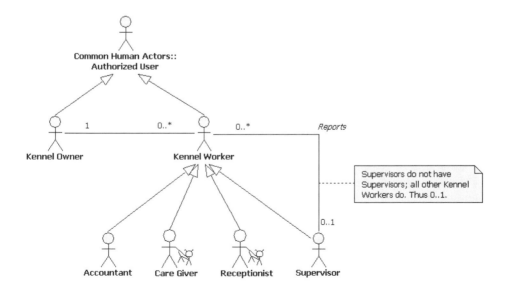

Figure 6-11. Kennel Staff Actors package

Note that **Kennel Worker** is an **Authorized User**, and therefore **Accountant, Care Giver, Receptionist,** and **Supervisor** are all **Authorized Users.**

Development Human Actors Package

The **Development Human Actors** package contains actors that represent people who work for the development organization and who interact with the system. You should include development actors, if you want to model maintenance and upgrade tasks that may only be performed by the development team.

In the case of the KMS, that's the Five-Step UML Company, or FSU (i.e., me). So far in this example, we have no known tasks of this type; but just in case, we'll define a general FSU actor, as shown in Figure 6-12.

Figure 6-12. Development Human Actors package

System Actors Package

The **System Actors** package, like the **Human Actors Package** discussed previously, contains four subpackages, each of which contains actors that represent external software and other computer systems that interact with the system:

- **Common Systems Actors** package

- **External Systems Actors** package

- **Internal Systems Actors** package

- **Development Systems Actors** package

Recall that we've developed the system stereotype to indicate actors that are systems, rather than people.

Common System Actors Package

The **Common System Actors** package contains actors that represent systems that can't easily be described as internal or external (as discussed in the section "Miscellaneous Actors Package" later in this chapter). That often means that these are base actors from which both internal and external actors are derived.

For the KMS thus far, we haven't identified any common system actors.

External System Actors Package

The **External System Actors** package contains actors that represent systems outside of the client organization and which interact with your system.

In the case of the KMS, we've identified one, as shown in Figure 6-13.

Credit Company

Figure 6-13. External System Actors package

For the KMS, I've tentatively decided that we can treat banks and credit companies the same, because many credit companies *are* banks (and vice versa). If we later find this to be a problem, we could add **Bank** to this diagram.

Internal System Actors Package

The **Internal System Actors** package contains actors that represent systems within the client organization and that interact with the system.

For the KMS thus far, we haven't identified any internal system actors.

Development System Actors Package

The **Development System Actors** package contains actors that represent development systems that interact with the system.

For the KMS thus far, we haven't identified any development system actors.

Event Actors Package

Like the **System Actors** package and the **Human Actors** package that we've already seen, the Event Actors package contains four subpackages:

- **Common Event Actors** package

- **External Event Actors** package

- **Internal Event Actors** package

- **Development Event Actors** package

Each of these contains actors that represent programmatic events to which the system must respond. These include timers elapsing, sensors triggering, alarms raising, etc. Recall that earlier we developed the **Event** stereotype to represent actors that were events, rather than people or external systems.

Common Event Actors Package

The **Common Event Actors** package contains actors that represent events that can't easily be described as internal or external (as discussed in the section "Miscellaneous Actors Package" later). That often means these are base actors from which both internal and external actors are derived.

For the KMS thus far, we haven't identified any common event actors.

External Event Actors Package

The **External Event Actors** package contains actors that represent events from outside of the client organization.

For the KMS thus far, we haven't identified any external event actors.

Internal Event Actors Package

The **Internal Event Actors** package contains systems actors that represent events within the client organization.

For the KMS, we've identified one such event, as shown in Figure 6-14.

Pet Tag

Figure 6-14. Internal Event Actors package

Development Event Actors Package

The **Development Event Actors** package contains actors that represent events issued by the development organization. For example, you might need to send out automated upgrades.

For the KMS thus far, we haven't identified any development system actors.

Hybrid Actors Package

The **Hybrid Actors** package contains actors that represent entities that can't easily be classified as people, systems, or events (as discussed previously). That often means these are base actors that define roles filled by some combination of people and systems and events.

For the KMS thus far, we haven't identified any hybrid actors.

Miscellaneous Actors Package

The **Miscellaneous Actors** package contains actors that don't fit *any* of the preceding categories. Often an actor in this category belongs in one of the other packages, but you haven't yet decided which one.

For the KMS thus far, we haven't identified any miscellaneous actors.

> ## Exercise 601: Organize and Relate Your Actors

Building on Exercise 501, in which you categorized your requirements, organize your actors into packages, and define the relations between them.

Identifying and Organizing Domain Objects

The next stage of the process is to review the requirements sources to identify potential domain objects. Each entity that must be represented or maintained is a potential domain object. A good place to start is by reviewing the spec and looking for such entities.

One technique is to look for the nouns that aren't subjects. For instance, in the sentence, "The salesperson shall update the customer profile to reflect the new information," "customer profile" and "new information" are both objects within the sentence. ("New information" is not very specific, and most likely refers to something in a previous sentence. When the term isn't specific, find the specific term to which it refers, and use that.)

Another technique that was particularly useful for the KMS spec was to review the glossary and ask about each entry, "Does the system maintain information about this object? Or does it create this object?" For example, in section 1.2 you can find the entry, "Grooming Schedule: A specific kind of pet schedule, having to do with when a pet gets groomed." You could imagine that the KMS will need to maintain information about the Grooming Schedule, so we should make it a domain object.

No technique is perfect. You'll miss some objects, and you'll identify others that really shouldn't be there. Thus, you'll need a good review process, and a few good rules of thumb:

- If in the final analysis the object is not involved in any use cases, it's not a domain object.

- If the candidate object asks the system to do something or does something for the system, it's probably an actor, not a candidate object.

For the KMS, I ended up with the following candidate object list:

Account
Availability
Bill
Birth
Breeding
Appointment
Breeding Schedule
Building
Charge
Contract
Contract Status
Contracted Work
Contractor
Assignment
Contractor
Schedule
Contractor Services
Diagnoses
Electronic Order
Exercise and Play
Activity
Exercise Area
Exercise Schedule
Exotic Pet
External Account
Facility
Facility Map
Feeding Schedule
Food
Franchise
Franchise Account
Franchise Books
Franchise Group
Franchise Notice
Grooming
Schedule

Grounds
Inventory
Kennel
Kennel Supplies
Kennel Worker
Schedule
Live Food
Log
Log Entry
Log Events
Log Observations
Med Schedule
Meds
Offspring
Order
Owner Information
Paper Order
Parent
Payable Account
Payment
Payroll
Pedigree
Pen
Pen Assignment
Pen Schedule
Pet
Pet History
Pet ID
Pet Information
Security
Pet Location
Pet Owner History
Pet Owner ID
Pet Owner
Information
Security

Pet Owner
Password
Pet Owner Record
Pet Record
Pet Schedule
Pet Status
Pet Supplies
Pet Tag
Pet Tag Sensor
Pet Vital Stats
PetCam
Prescriptions
Private Supplies
Receipt
Receivables
Account
Reception Building
Reservation
Run
Schedule
Shipment
Signatures
Special Offers
Task Assignment
Time Card
Time Period
Treatment
Vendor Information
Vendor Order
Vendor Schedule
Veterinary
Schedule
Worker Record

Gee, and you thought the actor list was long!

Through interviews, you can refine and pare down your domain object set. (I'll spare you the Everything Diagram of the domain objects for the KMS, because it's just too large to bother with.) Next, we'll organize our domain objects.

KMS Domain Object Stereotypes

Recall that before we organized our actors, we defined actor stereotypes. Shouldn't we do the same for our domain objects?

Not necessarily. It's easy to go overboard with stereotypes; and it's *especially* easy to use them where you really should use base classes and derived classes. So don't try to guess in advance which domain object stereotypes you'll need.

For the KMS, however, I've defined one: **User Interface**, as you saw in Chapter 2.

The **User Interface** stereotype indicates a form or Web page or other mechanism for communicating with end users.

If you find that you need other stereotypes, define them when the time comes to use them.

The Domain Object Hierarchy Pattern

Just as I have a standard organization for my actors, I like to organize my domain objects according to the Domain Object Hierarchy Pattern, as shown in Figure 6-15.

This diagram shows the packages of objects contained within other packages, all contained within a top-level **Domain Model** package.

The two main subpackages are **Represented Objects** and **Maintained Objects**. The division between represented objects and maintained objects is one I find useful for categorizing domain objects, but it can take some practice to apply. For instance, is a schedule a represented object or a maintained object? My usual answer is that it's maintained; the computer system is used to create and maintain the schedule. I know, however, of one business that is computerized, but still clings to manual methods for certain tasks, and that includes the schedule. Their schedule is hand drawn on a big whiteboard for all to see. If I were to create a computer system for that business, I would consider the schedule to be a represented object.

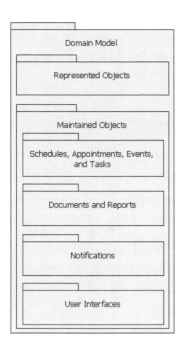

Figure 6-15. The Domain Object Hierarchy Pattern

So my basic rule is simple: does the real object exist within the system? If so, it's a maintained object. Does the real object exist outside the system, with information about it stored within the system? If so, it's a represented object.

As with the Actor Hierarchy Pattern, you may find the Domain Object Hierarchy Pattern a useful starting point for organizing the domain objects in your own projects, so let's spend the rest of this section looking at each of these packages in more detail, using the KMS as our example.

"Do I Have to Organize According to These Patterns?"

Not at all! The Actor Hierarchy Pattern and the Domain Object Hierarchy Pattern aren't always the best way to organize any particular model. The purpose of patterns isn't to *dictate* solutions, but rather to *suggest* solutions. When they apply, they save you a lot of effort, because they're already thought out. When they don't apply, they may still inspire you to a better solution. The Actor Hierarchy Pattern and the Domain Object Hierarchy Pattern are almost always good starting points, but they're only a start.

Domain Model Package

In the Domain Object Hierarchy Pattern, the **Domain Model** package contains no objects, but is instead only a container for other packages, namely

- **Represented Objects** package

- **Maintained Objects** package

Represented Objects Package

The **Represented Objects** package contains all of the physical objects that must be represented within the system. If a domain object exists in the physical world or in a computer system outside your own, and you have to track information about it in your system, it's a represented object; your system represents the object, but doesn't actually contain the real object itself. (Contrast this with maintained objects, which are discussed in the next section.)

If you examine the list of identified objects for the KMS, you can count 34 represented objects, far too many for a single diagram. So we need to group them into subpackages, as shown in Figure 6-16.

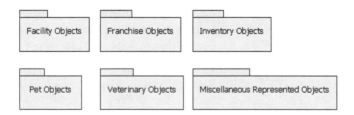

Figure 6-16. Represented Objects package for the KMS

Let's take a closer look at each of these packages.

Facility Objects

The **Facility Objects** package contains objects that represent the grounds and physical layout of a facility, as shown in Figure 6-17.

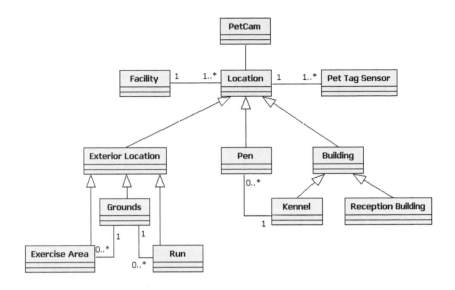

Figure 6-17. Facility Objects package

In this diagram, you can see that I've added two more domain objects to my original list: **Location**, to represent any location where kennel business may take place, and **Exterior Location**, as a contrast to **Building**.

Franchise Objects

The **Franchise Objects** package contains objects that represent a franchise, as shown in Figure 6-18.

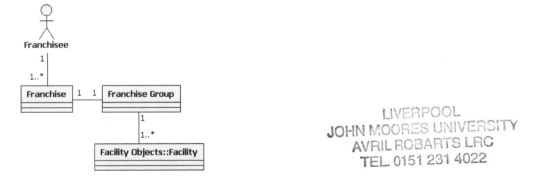

Figure 6-18. Franchise Objects package

Note that there are two different ways of viewing our requirements. One view is that a **Franchise** either has zero **Facility** objects and one **Franchise Group** (which has **Facility** objects); alternatively, it has one **Facility** and zero **Franchise Group** objects. This seems cumbersome; so instead, I chose to model a **Franchise Group** for each **Franchise**, and each **Facility** belonging to a **Franchise Group**.

Inventory Objects

The **Inventory Objects** package contains objects that represent inventory and supplies, as shown in Figure 6-19.

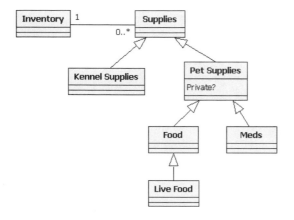

Figure 6-19. Inventory Objects package

Notice that I've added one domain object, **Supplies**, to represent supplies in general. Notice also that, having realized that **Private Supplies** didn't make a very useful class, I've modeled this as a **Private?** attribute for **Pet Supplies**.

Private?

If you phrase the attribute as a question, your stakeholders will more likely recognize that it needs an answer. If you follow a more common approach—say, **IsPrivate** or simply **Private** as a Boolean—then nondevelopers might not recognize that the attribute must be true or false. Save the more programmatic names for the design stage.

Pet Objects

The **Pet Objects** package contains objects that represent pets, as shown in Figure 6-20.

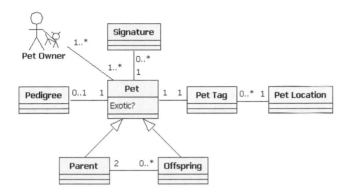

Figure 6-20. Pet Objects package

As with **Private Supplies**, I decided that **Exotic?** should be an attribute of a **Pet**, not a separate class.

Veterinary Objects

The **Veterinary Objects** package contains objects that represent veterinary objects, as shown in Figure 6-21.

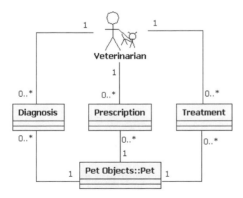

Figure 6-21. Veterinary Objects package

Where's Exotic?

Remember that **The Model Rule** tells you that not every detail has to appear in every diagram. While **Exotic?** is relevant to Figure 6-20, I don't think that information is relevant to Figure 6-21. So I left it off this diagram.

Miscellaneous Represented Objects

The **Miscellaneous Represented Objects** package contains objects that don't fit easily into the other represented object packages, as shown in Figure 6-22.

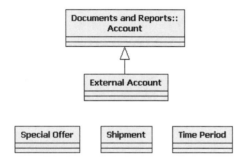

Figure 6-22. Miscellaneous Represented Objects package

Note that **External Account** is derived from **Account**, a maintained object. This is a convenience. I could have put **Account** (and related classes) into a separate package, and then define **Internal Account** (a maintained object) and **External Account** (a represented object) to both derive from it. But that seemed like added complexity for little benefit. It's easier to go with the model as shown in Figure 6-22.

Maintained Objects Package

If a domain object exists only within your system, it's a maintained object; your system maintains the real object itself. The **Maintained Objects** package contains the following subpackages, each of which contains objects that have information that must be maintained within the system:

- **Schedules, Appointments, Events, and Tasks** package

- **Documents and Reports** package

- **Notifications** package

- **User Interfaces** package

Let's take a look at each of those packages in more detail, and see what they contain for the KMS example.

Schedules, Appointments, Events, and Tasks Package

The **Schedules, Appointments, Events, and Tasks** package contains objects that represent schedules and chronologies and their contents.

If you examine the KMS spec, you can count 17 such objects, so we need to organize them into subpackages, as shown in Figure 6-23.

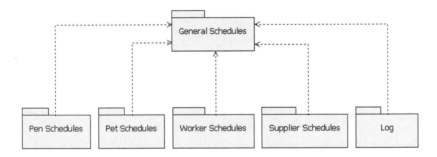

Figure 6-23. Schedules, Appointments, Events, and Tasks package

General Schedules

The **General Schedules** package contains objects that represent the common features of schedules, as shown in Figure 6-24.

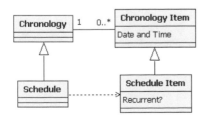

Figure 6-24. General Schedules package

Note that I've added a **Schedule Item** class to represent items within schedules. I've also added **Chronology** and **Chronology Item** as base classes that represent events in time. **Schedule** is a record of events expected to happen. (As you'll see later, **Log** is a record of events that *have* happened.)

Pen Schedules

The **Pen Schedules** package contains objects that represent schedules for when pets will check into and out of the kennel, as shown in Figure 6-25.

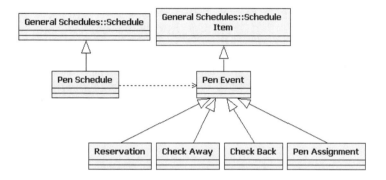

Figure 6-25. Pen Schedules package

Pet Schedules

The **Pet Schedules** package contains objects that represent schedules for working with a pet, as shown in Figure 6-26.

Note that **Pet Schedule** doesn't have a direct dependency on any **Schedule Item** objects; unlike the more specific kinds of pet schedules, such as **Breeding Schedule**, **Feeding Schedule**, etc.

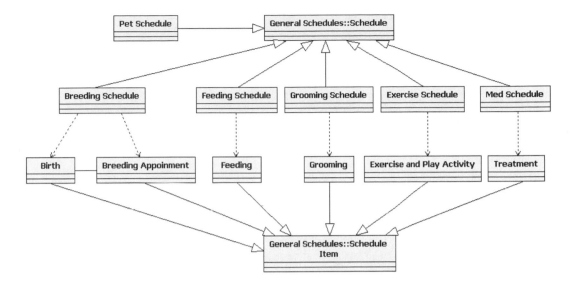

Figure 6-26. Pet Schedules package

Worker Schedules

The **Worker Schedules** package contains objects that represent schedules for a **Kennel Worker**, as shown in Figure 6-27.

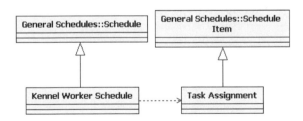

Figure 6-27. Worker Schedules package

Supplier Schedules

The **Supplier Schedules** package contains objects that represent schedules for contractors, vendors, and other suppliers, as shown in Figure 6-28.

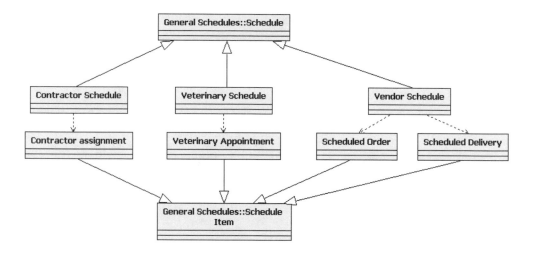

Figure 6-28. Supplier Schedules package

Log

The **Log** package contains objects that represent the kennel log, as shown in Figure 6-29.

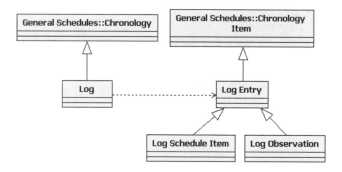

Figure 6-29. Log package

And that completes all of the packages within the **Schedules, Appointments, Events, and Tasks** package.

Documents and Reports Package

The **Documents and Reports** package contains objects that represent documents and reports and their contents.

If you examine the KMS spec, you can count 27 such objects, so we need to organize them into subpackages, as shown in Figure 6-30.

Figure 6-30. Documents and Reports package

Let's take a closer look at each of these packages.

Accounts

The **Accounts** package contains objects that represent accounts, as shown in Figure 6-31.

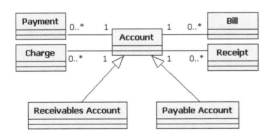

Figure 6-31. Accounts package

Facility Info

The **Facility Info** package contains objects that represent workers and other information at a facility, as shown in Figure 6-32.

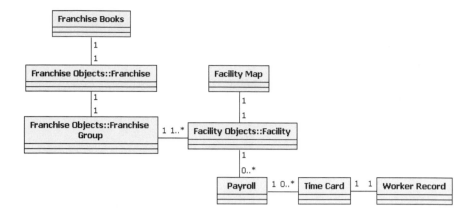

Figure 6-32. Facility Info package

Orders

The **Orders** package contains objects that represent orders, as shown in Figure 6-33.

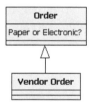

Figure 6-33. Orders package

Note that rather than modeling the two different domain objects that I identified earlier, **Paper Order** and **Electronic Order**, I turned the distinction into an attribute of the **Order** domain object, from which **Vendor Order** derives.

Owner Info

The **Owner Info** package contains objects that represent owners, as shown in Figure 6-34.

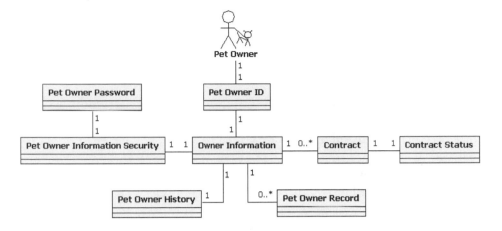

Figure 6-34. Owner Info package

Pet Info

The **Pet Info** package contains objects that represent pets, as shown in Figure 6-35.

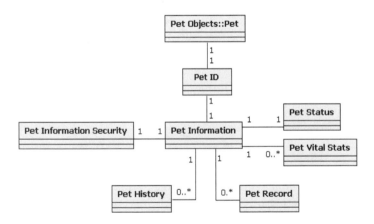

Figure 6-35. Pet Info package

Supplier Info

The **Supplier Info** package contains objects that represent suppliers, as shown in Figure 6-36.

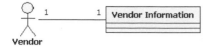

Figure 6-36. Supplier Info package

Notifications Package

The **Notifications** package contains objects that represent information notifications and their contents. At this point, we've identified only one, as in Figure 6-37.

Figure 6-37. Notifications package

User Interfaces Package

This package contains objects that represent forms and Web pages and other means of communicating with users. At this point, we haven't identified any; but trust me, we will.

....

Is That All There Is?[7]

If you think this collection of domain objects seems small—**Supplier Info** and **Notifications** are a bit sparse, for example—you're right. This is just a first pass, based on a simple reading of the spec. Further analysis would likely add a lot to this collection.

On the other hand, if this collection of domain objects seems large ... well, this is an example of a principle that I teach my students: *There are no small problems.* Or rather, the small problems have been solved already. If it's a small problem, some COTS (Commercial Off The Shelf) product will probably address the need. In our business today, any project we take on is larger than it appears at first glance.

---

7. Alan L. Bean, *From the Earth to the Moon,* "Part 7: That's All There Is," videocassette (HBO Studios, 1998)

Any project. Outside of classroom exercises and similar "canned" problems, there is **no project** so small that you can't learn more by building at least a simple model. (For example, when I selected the Kennel Management System as an example, I guessed that it might have a half-dozen actors and maybe a dozen domain objects.)

Indeed, for those of you who think this collection of domain objects is too large, I have bad news: it's not large enough. It's simplified, so that it can serve as a case study and tutorial. Fowler's *Analysis Patterns* includes better ideas for some of these objects. In particular, Fowler's Accountability and Inventory and Accounting Patterns[8] are far more useful than my simplistic **End User/ Authorized User** and **Inventory and Account** arrangement. But to explain *why* those are superior took Fowler 54 pages; and what he ended up with works well, but it looks confusing until you understand the reasons. So rather than try to reproduce Fowler's 54 pages of reasoning, I'll simply encourage you to read *Analysis Patterns*, and I'll stick to the simplistic objects for this case study.

Exercise 602: Organize and Relate Your Domain

Building on Exercise 501, in which you categorized your requirements, and using your requirements sources, organize your domain into packages, and define the relations between them. Also define the relationships between domain objects and the actors that work with them.

Identifying and Diagramming Use Cases for Each Actor

The next stage of the process involves the review of requirements sources to identify use cases for each actor. Along the way, you'll probably discover new actors and domain objects, and you'll need to update your requirements model.

With so many actors and domain objects, you can probably guess that you'll need some sort of organization scheme to keep them straight; and you may even guess that this involves another pattern.

---

8. Martin Fowler, *Analysis Patterns: Reusable Object Models* (Addison-Wesley, 1996), pp. 17–34 and 95–132

The Use Case Hierarchy Pattern

Because the primary benefit of use cases is a focus on end-user needs, I like to produce one diagram and one package of use cases for each actor. Following on from our earlier organization of actors into a hierarchy of packages, it's useful to organize your use case packages along similar lines, in a Use Case Hierarchy Pattern, as shown in Figure 6-38.

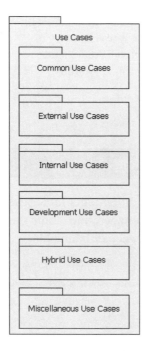

Figure 6-38. The Use Case Hierarchy Pattern

This diagram shows the packages of use cases contained within a top-level **Use Cases** package. Within each package will be one subpackage for each actor from the corresponding actor packages.

A Lesson in User-ese

The Use Case Hierarchy Pattern gave me a useful lesson in learning to speak the user's language, not my language. I was visiting a client—a research laboratory that was collaborating with a number of other labs in California—and I drew this pattern on the board to show the organization. And as was my habit when drawing by hand, I abbreviated a lot. Specifically, instead of "Use Cases," I wrote "UCs" everywhere. And my clients looked at my drawing and said, "So which is it? UC Davis, UC Berkeley, UC Irvine . . .?" In their world, "UC" meant "University of California," their partner labs.

They said that they could learn to adapt, but I refused to ask that of them, and I erased and redrew my diagram. Always, always, *always* learn to speak user-ese if you want to understand user needs.

Next, I'll describe these packages in more detail, and see how the use cases from our KMS case study fit in.

Common Use Cases Package

The **Common Use Cases** package contains packages of use cases required by actors that can't easily be described as internal or external.

Looking at the model so far, we can count two such actors—the **End User** and the **Authorized User**—with use case packages as shown in Figure 6-39.

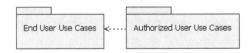

Figure 6-39. Common Use Cases package

Let's now analyze each of these packages in more detail.

End User Use Cases

The **End User Use Cases** package depicts the requirements that are common to all end users. Although you'll find in the spec only one reference to users in general, further interviews have revealed that Sandy's Pets would like to use the Web site for promotions. This leads to more requirements, as shown in Figure 6-40.

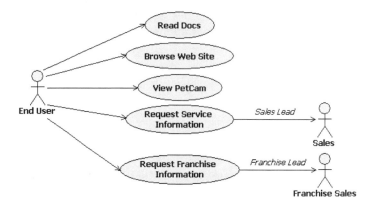

Figure 6-40. End User Use Cases package

Note that along the way we've identified two new sales actors that respond to sales leads.

Authorized User Use Cases

The **Authorized User Use Cases** package depicts the requirements that are common to all authorized end users. Recall that although **Authorized Users** aren't mentioned in the spec at all, they were identified as a result of interviews and the realization that some operations require user authentication and security. Further analysis tells us that the only *common* requirements for authorized users are all about security, as shown in Figure 6-41.

Note the appearance of a new domain object, **User Profile**, which is used to store a password and other information about a user. We also require, therefore, a use case, **Change User Profile**, to allow the user to alter such information.

A little further reflection tells us that there's more to user security than this: some of our users will be viewing information across the Web, while others will be working from local .NET desktop applications on the corporate network, PetNet. Local users may be authenticated based on their Windows user credentials, while remote users must supply authentication information as part of an ASP.NET request.

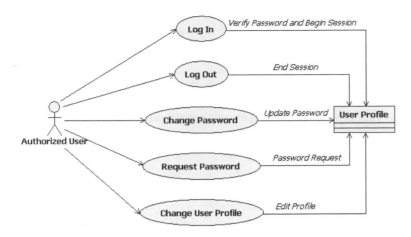

Figure 6-41. Authorized User Use Cases package

So do we model these security requirements as two use cases each, one local and one remote? Nope. Let's take the **Log In** use case first, as an example. We're going to model this as *three* use cases: one general use case and two specific use cases, as shown in Figure 6-42.

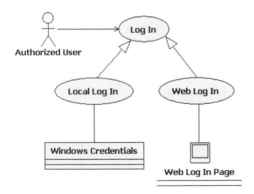

Figure 6-42. Log In Use Cases package (and an example of use case generalization)

Note that two new domain objects are identified: **Windows Credentials** to reflect the logged-in Windows user, and **Web Log In Page** to represent the form the Web used by the **Authorized User** to log in.

Use Case Generalization

We've already examined generalization for classes, actors, and interfaces earlier in the book, in Chapters 1 and 4. Generalization (or inheritance) indicates that a base class provides some common or general behavior shared by one or more derived classes, each of which provides more detailed and specific behavior.

Use case generalization is a similar concept, though not as familiar as class generalization. In use case generalization, a base use case defines the general rules for the use case, while the derived use cases build on and override some of these rules.

You depict generalization of use cases much as you depict generalization of classes: with a closed-headed arrow from the derived use case to the base use case, as shown in Figure 6-42.

So, for our **Log In** use case, the rules might be

1. Get the user identity.

2. Verify the user's access rights.

3. Display valid options for this user.

Then in a **Local Log In** use case, the rules might be

1. Get the Windows identity for the currently logged in user.

2. Verify the user's access rights.

3. Display valid options for this user.

While for a **Web Log In** use case, the rules might be

1. Display a log-in form.

2. Get the log-in information.

3. Access the Windows identity for the log-in information.

4. If the log-in information doesn't correspond to a valid Windows user, redisplay the log-in form with an error message, and repeat from Step 2.

5. Verify the user's access rights.

6. Display valid options for this user.

The basic logic is the same in both derived use cases; but each adds to that logic in appropriate ways.

Local and remote log out are illustrated in Figure 6-43.

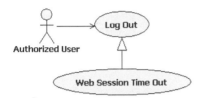

Figure 6-43. Log Out Use Cases package

In this case, there's not much difference between a manual log out locally and one via the Web; each should involve closing or serializing any user state information and freeing up any resources in use. But over the Web, we have to deal with the possibility of users disconnecting without ever logging out. Because the Web doesn't have persistent connections, we'll never know if the user is gone or not; but a common solution is to close any session where no activity has occurred within a time-out interval. Thus, we add a special derived use case for that situation.

Finally, let's look at the other three **Authorized User** use cases—**Change Password**, **Request Password**, and **Change User Profile**. The processes involved for changing passwords and user profiles are pretty similar, whether local or on the Web, and emailing a user password is something only a Web user would request. (Local users who lose their passwords won't be able to log into Windows, and would have to contact their system administrator for assistance. That's out of our hands.) So we don't need separate diagrams for the remaining use cases.

External Use Cases Package

The **External Use Cases** package contains use cases required by actors that are outside of your client organization.

Looking at our KMS model so far, we can count 12 such actors, with use case packages as shown in Figure 6-44.

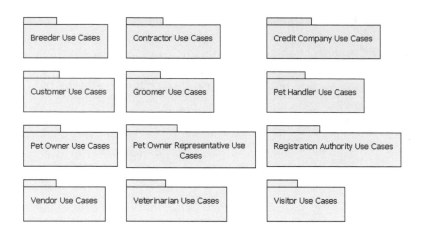

Figure 6-44. External Use Cases package

Let's take a closer look at each of these packages.

Breeder Use Cases

The **Breeder Use Cases** package depicts the requirements for the **Breeder** actor, as shown in Figure 6-45.

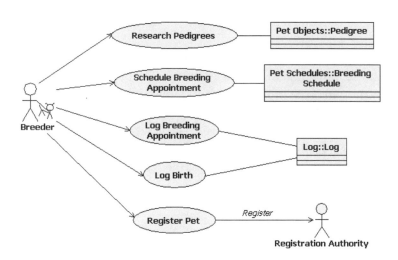

Figure 6-45. Breeder Use Cases package

Contractor Use Cases

The **Contractor Use Cases** package depicts the requirements common to all
Contractor actors, as shown in Figure 6-46.

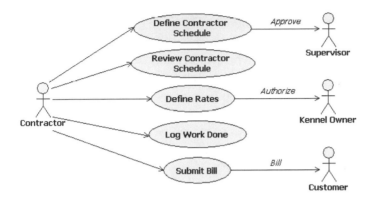

Figure 6-46. Contractor Use Cases package

Note that, in defining the **Contractor** use cases, we've revealed a basic contradiction in the spec. The definition of **Contractor** says

> *Contractor: A worker who is not employed by the home office or a franchise,
> but who does contracted work for either, using their own facilities and/or
> tools and setting their own schedule and rates.*

But in section 2.2, it says

> *2.2 Contractor Operations. Allows contractors to check their assignments
> and record services.*

And in section 3.5.1, it says

> *Contractor scheduling (Critical). Allow a supervisor to schedule contractor
> services.*

On the one hand, contractors are supposed to create their own schedules.
On the other hand, contractors have "assignments" that are scheduled by supervisors. This sort of contradiction is all too easy to make when crafting the spec,

even for a small project like the KMS. In larger projects, it's impossible to avoid them: the paper documents are just too vast to keep 100 percent consistent. As discussed in Chapter 1, one benefit of modeling is **The Outline Effect**: by creating the model, you gain new perspectives on the spec, and can more easily spot contradictions and inconsistencies. (If you think this is the only contradiction in my spec, you're more optimistic than I am.)

In this case, further interviews were needed to resolve the contradiction. In those interviews, we learned that Internal Revenue Service codes very specifically define who qualifies as a contractor and who qualifies as an employee. To stay on the safe side of the IRS, the Sandy's Pets policy is that contractors *must* set their own schedules. So the requirements spec has been revised:

> *2.2 Contractor Operations. Allows contractors to define their schedules and record services.*

> *Contractor scheduling (Critical). Allow a supervisor to negotiate and approve contractor schedules, and to arrange other contractors if an acceptable schedule can't be negotiated.*

Yes, contractors can set their own schedule; but if Sandy's Pets doesn't like the schedule, they can always find another contractor. So a contractor has to be open to negotiation on schedules. (Welcome to the world of contracting.)

Figure 6-46 depicts these requirements after we've resolved the contradiction.

Credit Company Use Cases

The **Credit Company Uses Cases** package depicts the requirements for the **Credit Company** actor. A review of the spec shows that the only requirements defined so far are to approve or reject charges. Because those actions will only take place when you request them—i.e., as part of a use case initiated by another actor—they don't constitute use cases in and of themselves. Thus, this is an empty package at this time.

Customer Use Cases

The **Customer Use Cases** package depicts the requirements of the **Customer** actor, as shown in Figure 6-47.

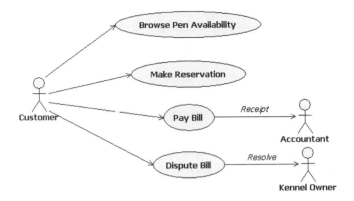

Figure 6-47. Customer Use Cases package

Feature Creep?

Note that a requirement appears, **Dispute Bill**, that isn't explicitly stated in the spec. I don't like feature creep—the gratuitous adding of features beyond what the customer requests and needs in the first place—but this arose during a requirements interview I just held with myself:

MARTIN THE ANALYST: It says here that you want customers to pay their bills.

MARTIN THE CLIENT: Of course!

MARTIN THE ANALYST: But what happens if a customer thinks their bill is wrong?

MARTIN THE CLIENT: That never happens.

MARTIN THE ANALYST: Never?

MARTIN THE CLIENT: *Well . . .* it *almost* never happens. And when it does, we work with the customer to resolve it.

MARTIN THE ANALYST: So anyone can resolve a customer's bill problem?

MARTIN THE CLIENT: Oh, no! Oh, we trust our people, you know; but these disputes are a delicate matter. If we're too forgiving, we could lose money, and go out of business if we keep making that mistake. If we're too hard-nosed, we could lose a customer, and go out of business if we keep making *that* mistake. As the kennel owners, we're the ones responsible for the health of the business; so we want to handle these disputes at the top.

MARTIN THE ANALYST: OK, so should you handle disputes for *all* customers, even at the franchise kennels?

MARTIN THE CLIENT: Hmmm . . . no, that could get to be too much. Each kennel owner should handle their own disputes.

MARTIN THE ANALYST: OK, then why don't we let customers file disputes online, *especially* because some of your customers will make their primary contacts through the Web, not through their local franchise. This way, we can codify your best practice—handle disputes by routing to the kennel owner—and ensure that it's practiced consistently across the organization.

MARTIN THE CLIENT: Yeah, that makes sense! That's a great catch! My word, man, you're brilliant!

MARTIN THE ANALYST: Well, if I'm so brilliant, why do you have so many oversights in your spec?

MARTIN THE CLIENT: Because *you* may be brilliant, but *I* am a dolt.

Note that section 3.4.1 of the KMS spec defines several methods for a customer to browse availability, as shown in Figure 6-48.

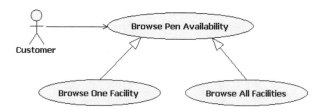

Figure 6-48. Browsing availability

(Section 3.4.1 also defines local versus online browsing; but because local browsing is always the responsibility of the **Receptionist**, it's not relevant in this context.)

Note also that the definition of **Exotic Pet** tells us that:

Operations involving exotic pets may require supervisor approval.

Although not explicitly stated anywhere (another requirement slips through the cracks, but is rescued by **The Outline Effect**), certainly "operations" should include making reservations: a **Supervisor** must ensure that Sandy's Pets has the right equipment and training to handle any exotic pet, as shown in Figure 6-49.

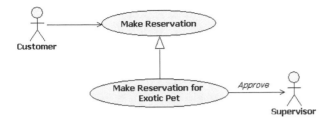

Figure 6-49. Exotic pet reservations

Groomer Use Cases

The **Groomer Use Cases** package depicts the requirements for the **Groomer** actor. Further study reveals that these requirements are entirely described by the **Contractor** use cases (Figure 6-46). Thus, no new diagram is required.

Pet Handler Use Cases

The **Pet Handler Uses Cases** package depicts the requirements for the **Pet Handler** actor, as shown in Figure 6-50.

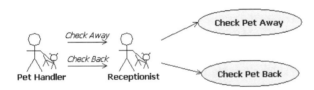

Figure 6-50. Pet Handler Use Cases package

Note how the KMS spec defines a **Pet Handler**:

A person (possibly contracted by a pet owner, possibly by a kennel owner) who takes a pet to pet shows and is responsible for the pet during the shows.

This sounds very consistent with the definitions for **Check Away** and **Check Back:**

Checking Away: The process of removing a pet from the kennel temporarily, for a home visit, a vet visit, or a pet show. The pet leaves, but its pen remains assigned to it.

Checking Back: The process of returning a pet to the kennel from a home visit, a vet visit, or a pet show.

But in section 3.4.4, the spec defines the specific process of checking away and back:

Check Away (Critical). Allow a receptionist to request a pet from a care giver, receive the pet from the care giver, place the magnetic tag in the Away stack from an owner, get a signature from the owner or representative, and turn the pet over to the owner or representative.

Check Back (Critical). Allow a receptionist to sign for a pet, receive the pet from an owner or representative, retrieve the tag from the Away stack, attach the tag to the pet, and turn the pet over to a care giver for return to the assigned pen.

All of the actual interaction with the KMS is performed by the **Receptionist** (and possibly by the **Care Giver**), *not* by the **Pet Handler**. This leads to Figure 6-50, where the **Pet Handler** communicates with the **Receptionist**, and the **Receptionist** communicates with the KMS. So it makes sense to move these use cases into a package for the **Receptionist** (which you'll see later); and once that is done, there's nothing for a **Pet Handler** to do. When we convert the requirements model to an architectural model, I suspect we'll lose **Pet Handler** entirely, because the **Pet Handler** has no relevance to the KMS.

Pet Owner Use Cases

The **Pet Owner Use Cases** package depicts the requirements for the **Pet Owner** actor. First note that, as with the **Pet Handler** actor, check in and check out activities will all be performed by the **Receptionist**, as will the delivery of private supplies; so for simplicity, those are omitted from Figure 6-51.

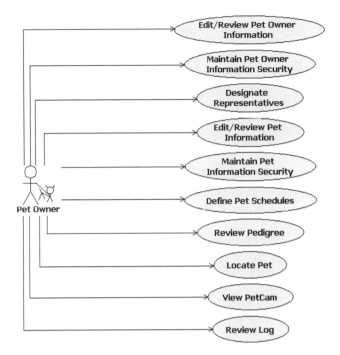

Figure 6-51. Pet Owner Use Cases package

Note that the requirements specify that a **Pet Owner** must be able to define multiple schedules, as shown in Figure 6-52.

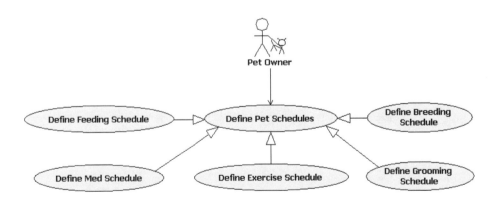

Figure 6-52. Pet Owner Scheduling Use Cases package

Pet Owner Representative Use Cases

The **Pet Owner Representative Use Cases** package depicts the requirements for the **Pet Owner Representative** actor. A review of the KMS spec shows that these requirements are merely a subset of the **Pet Owner** requirements, so no new diagram is needed.

Registration Authority Use Cases

The **Registration Authority Use Cases** package depicts the requirements for the **Registration Authority** actor. A review of the KMS spec shows that this actor never makes any requests from our system (it only responds to requests), so no diagram is needed.

Vendor Use Cases

The **Vendor Use Cases** package depicts the requirements for the **Vendor** actor. A review of the KMS spec shows that this actor never makes any requests from our system (kennel workers enter and maintain all vendor information), so no diagram is needed.

Veterinarian Use Cases

The **Veterinarian Use Cases** package depicts the requirements for the **Veterinarian** actor, as shown in Figure 6-53.

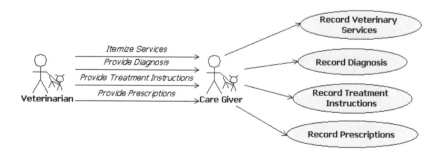

Figure 6-53. Veterinarian Use Cases package

Note that, as with the **Pet Handler**, all of the **Veterinarian** use cases are performed through staff, in this case the **Care Giver** actor. Thus, these use cases shall be relocated to the **Care Giver** package.

Visitor Use Cases

The **Visitor Use Cases** package depicts the requirements for the **Visitor** actor, as shown in Figure 6-54.

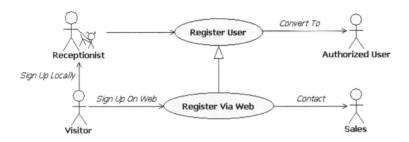

Figure 6-54. Visitor Use Cases package

Remember that **Visitor** wasn't even in the KMS spec, but rather was discovered during analysis; so we'll have to work a little harder to identify its requirements. Because the **Visitor** actor is an **End User**, most of its requirements are captured in the **End User Use Cases** diagram (Figure 6-40). But there's one other important requirement for **Visitor** actors: the ability to become **Authorized User** actors. Figure 6-54 shows that there are general rules for signing up a new user (carried out locally by a **Receptionist**) and specific rules for a **Visitor** that signs up online.

Internal Use Cases Package

The **Internal Use Cases** package contains use cases required by actors within your client organization.

Looking at our KMS model so far, we can count 12 such actors, with use case packages as shown in Figure 6-55.

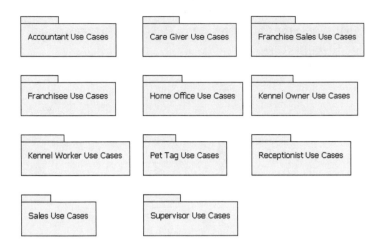

Figure 6-55. External Use Cases package

Let's take a closer look at each of these packages.

Accountant Use Cases

The **Accountant Use Cases** package depicts the requirements for the **Accountant** actor, as shown in Figure 6-56.

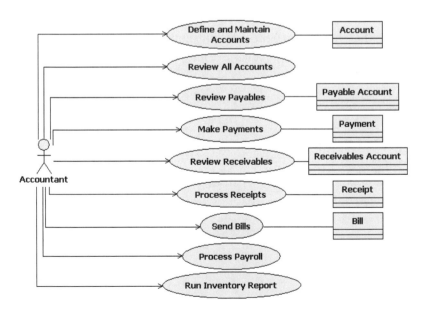

Figure 6-56. Accountant Use Cases package

Care Giver Use Cases

The **Care Giver Use Cases** package depicts the requirements for the **Care Giver** actor, as shown in Figure 6-57.

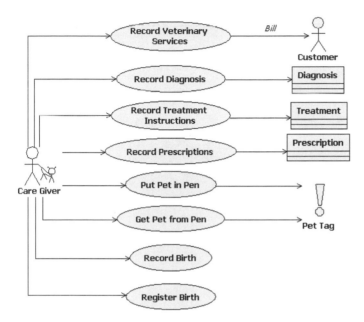

Figure 6-57. Care Giver Use Cases package

Franchise Sales Use Cases

The **Franchise Sales Use Cases** package depicts the requirements for the **Franchise Sales** actor, as shown in Figure 6-58.

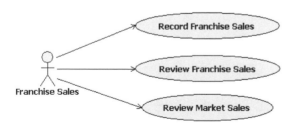

Figure 6-58. Franchise Sales Use Cases package

Note that **Franchise Sales** was an actor discovered during analysis, and thus has no explicit requirements in the KMS spec. These requirements were discovered during further interviews.

Franchisee Use Cases

The **Franchisee Use Cases** package depicts the requirements for the **Franchisee** actor, as shown in Figure 6-59.

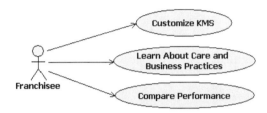

Figure 6-59. Franchisee Use Cases package

Note that the KMS spec requires various specific kinds of performance comparisons, as shown in Figure 6-60.

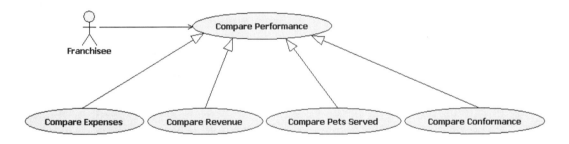

Figure 6-60. Performance comparison use cases

Home Office Use Cases

The **Home Office Use Cases** package depicts the requirements for the **Home Office** actor, as shown in Figure 6-61.

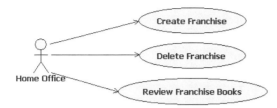

Figure 6-61. Home Office Use Cases package

Kennel Owner Use Cases

The **Kennel Owner Use Cases** package depicts the requirements for the **Kennel Owner** actor. From the KMS spec, the definition of the **Kennel Owner** says

> *Kennel Owner: The owner of a given facility. May be a franchise owner or the owner of Sandy's Pets.*

Inspection of the spec reveals no requirements for this actor, only for the **Home Office** and the **Franchisee**.

Kennel Worker Use Cases

The **Kennel Worker Use Cases** package depicts the requirements for the **Kennel Worker** actor. As the most general actor in Sandy's Pets, the **Kennel Worker** has 20 use cases, too many for a single, coherent diagram. Thus, these use cases are depicted in separate diagrams as shown in Figures 6-62 to 6-67.

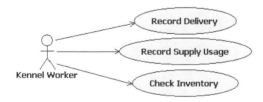

Figure 6-62. Kennel Worker Inventory use cases

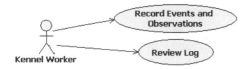

Figure 6-63. Kennel Worker Logging use cases

Figure 6-64. Kennel Worker/Pet Owner use cases

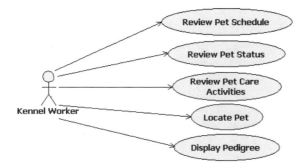

Figure 6-65. Kennel Worker/Pet use cases

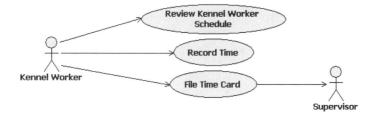

Figure 6-66. Kennel Worker Schedule use cases

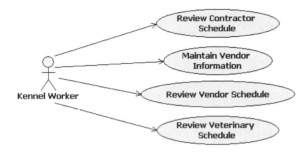

Figure 6-67. Kennel Worker/Supplier use cases

Pet Tag Use Cases

The **Pet Tag Use Cases** package depicts the requirements for the **Pet Tag** actor, as shown in Figure 6-68.

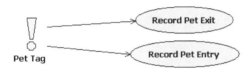

Figure 6-68. Pet Tag Use Cases package

After researching the pet tag technology, we've learned that the tags are simple devices that only record that a tag has passed a sensor, *not* the direction that it passed. Thus, we need two sensors at every exit or entrance (we'll call these *portals*), one for each side of the portal; and the pet's location will be deduced by looking at which sensor triggered first and which triggered last, indicating a movement from one side of the portal to the other. After grumbling a bit about having to pay for twice as many sensors, the client agreed that this was the only approach that made sense.

Receptionist Use Cases

The **Receptionist Use Cases** package depicts the requirements for the **Receptionist** actor, as shown in Figure 6-69.

247

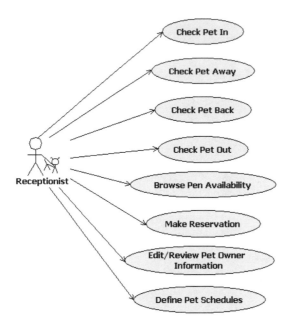

Figure 6-69. Receptionist Use Cases package

Note that the **Receptionist** has use cases in common with the **Customer** and the **Pet Owner**, because these use cases may be performed by the **Receptionist** locally or by the **Customer** and the **Pet Owner** via the Web. In the design models, we might want to derive an abstract actor that represents "the person doing these jobs," not anyone specific; but in an analysis model, those abstractions don't help your stakeholders to understand the requirements, and may hinder them.

So in the analysis model, I prefer to present this duplication of effort. If anybody asks "Aren't these the same use case?" *then* I can ask whether they *are* the same use case. (If nobody asks, then I will.) Do the **Receptionist** and the **Customer** or the **Pet Owner** do these tasks in the same way with the same user interface? If so, then I can show this by introducing the abstract actor, at a time when the stakeholders are ready for the concept. If not, then I have learned something important about the requirements, and I need to define separate use cases.

Sales Use Cases

The **Sales Use Cases** package depicts the requirements for the **Sales** actor, as shown in Figure 6-70.

Figure 6-70. Sales Use Cases package

Note that **Sales** was an actor discovered during analysis, and thus has no explicit requirements in the KMS spec. These requirements were discovered during further interviews.

Supervisor Use Cases

The **Supervisor Use Cases** package depicts the requirements for the **Supervisor** actor. Like the **Kennel Worker**, the **Supervisor** has 20 use cases, too many for a single, coherent diagram. Thus, these use cases are depicted in separate diagrams, as shown in Figures 6-71 to 6-74.

Figure 6-71. Supervisor Contract use cases

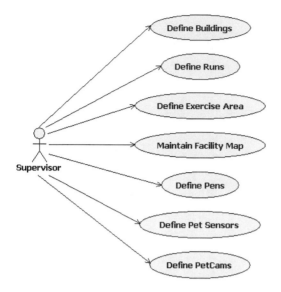

Figure 6-72. Supervisor Facility use cases

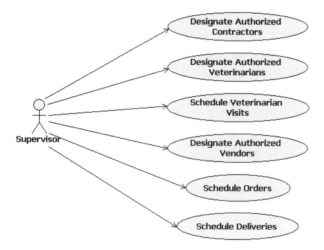

Figure 6-73. Supervisor/Supplier use cases

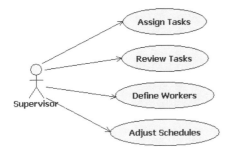

Figure 6-74. Supervisor Task and Worker use cases

Development Use Cases Package

The **Development Use Cases** package contains use cases required by actors within the development organization.

Although we'll eventually need development use cases to reflect our mainte-nance tasks for the KMS, none are stated nor even implied at this time.

Hybrid Use Cases Package

The **Hybrid Use Cases** package contains use cases required by actors that represent entities that can't easily be classified as people, systems, or events.

For the KMS thus far, we haven't identified any hybrid actors.

Miscellaneous Use Cases Package

The **Miscellaneous Use Cases** package contains use cases required by actors that can't easily be classified within other packages.

For the KMS thus far, we haven't identified any miscellaneous actors.

Exercise 603: Add Use Cases for Your Actors

Building on Exercise 601, in which you organized and related your actors, define a package for each actor, and then define use cases for each actor. Also define which other actors participate in those use cases. Draw the Use Case Diagrams for each actor.

Next, identify which domain objects are created or maintained in each use case, and draw the corresponding Use Case Diagrams.

Finally, organize your use case packages.

Reviewing Domain Objects to Ensure All Necessary Use Cases

By this stage of the process, you should have already identified and organized your actors and domain objects, and diagrammed your use cases. Next, you should review your requirements sources again, to verify that you have all the use cases necessary to support each domain object.

For our KMS case study, however, that's a lot of work, and mostly redundant with what you've seen so far. It's a necessary step for a thorough analysis—if you skip it, you'll be sorry, so don't blame me!—but it's not very useful as a tutorial. You would learn a few key kernels of overlooked information in the course of reviewing a multitude of mostly familiar diagrams.

So for this book, I'm only going to pick one representative domain object and show how drawing its Use Case Diagrams helps us to find overlooked requirements.

The domain object I'll select for this stage is **Task Assignment**. While building the requirements model, I've begun to believe that task assignments are *the* key element of the KMS: if we want to duplicate the success of Sandy's Pets in other locations, we have to ensure that every worker knows what to do next, and that every supervisor knows what has been done and what needs doing. We can't replicate home office expertise without automating much of that expertise. And I've developed a sneaking suspicion that some key aspects of assignments are being overlooked.

Looking at use cases that involve **Task Assignment** objects, I found too many for a simple diagram. But I found that these may be simply divided into "pre-task" use cases (Figure 6-75) that involve creating and scheduling tasks before the tasks begin and "post-task" use cases (Figure 6-76) that describe information about tasks that have been completed.

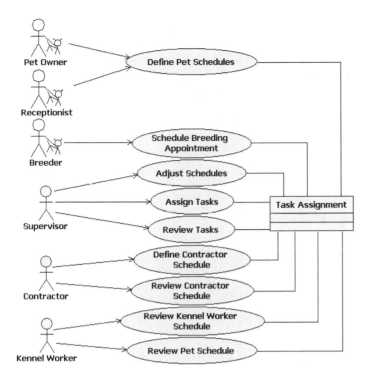

Figure 6-75. Pre-task use cases

Figure 6-76. Post-task use cases

NOTE Recall that we're stepping though this process simply to identify missing requirements. Figures 6-75 and 6-76 shouldn't be read to imply that these two sets of use cases rely solely on the **Task Assignment** domain object to realize their functionality. Rather, we're just collecting together all those use cases that are associated with the **Task Assignment** object. There is a many-to-many relationship between use cases and domain objects.

By examining these diagrams, we can spot the gap in the requirements: we have no use cases that relate to a task actually being performed. This leads us to ask our clients two questions:

- **Do you want kennel workers and contractors to update the system when they start a task?** The answer, we learn, is yes. We want supervisors and customers and others to be able to know what tasks are currently being done for a given pet, and we want supervisors to know what tasks are being performed by the kennel workers. We'll add an **Activate Task** use case that is invoked by **Kennel Worker** and **Contractor** actors.

- **Do you want supervisors to know when a task is overdue?** The answer to this one is "sort of." A kennel must be run on a schedule, but precision is just about impossible: pets don't always cooperate, and tasks take more or less time depending on a number of factors. And experience has shown that when a supervisor watches every little minute of a worker's time, the worker is *less* productive because they rush through tasks and end up having to do a lot of rework. So the client wants to define a "time window" for each task, and alert the supervisor *and* the worker if a task is not activated within that window. To perform the alert, we'll need a new **Task Timer** actor.

These new use cases are depicted in Figure 6-77.

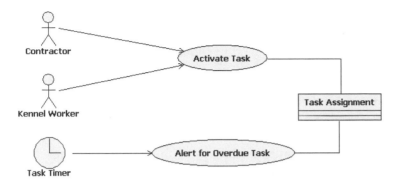

Figure 6-77. Task use cases

I hope this example shows how looking at domain objects and related use cases will reveal gaps in your understanding (and I have no doubt whatsoever that there are gaps yet to be found). It's important to remember, though, that these diagrams are *not* comprehensive pictures of the behavior of any given use case in the diagrams. Rather, they are comprehensive pictures of which use cases affect a particular domain object. It's important to label these diagrams clearly so that readers understand the purpose and don't misconstrue the diagrams. (You may also want to draw diagrams that show each use case and the objects it affects; but I felt that was overkill for this example.)

Exercise 604: Relate Use Cases to Your Domain Objects

Building on Exercises 602 and 603, in which you organized your domain and added use cases for your actors, draw the Use Case Diagrams for each domain object, and verify that you have all necessary use cases for that object.

A Manager's View of Requirements

Software development management may be defined by six interrelated activities:

- **Staffing.** This is the process of selecting the right personnel and enough personnel to do the work.

- **Planning.** This is the process of estimating the amount of work to be done, determining an effective order in which to do it, and scheduling the work. The order of work and the schedule depend in part on the available staff.

- **Tracking.** This is the process of reviewing the progress made and comparing it to the plan.

- **Reporting.** This is the process of publishing the results of tracking, with a particular emphasis on making others aware when the plan is off track so that they may deal with any dependencies that are disrupted by the lateness.

- **Correction.** This is the process of identifying ways to address problems with the plan and with the work.

- **Risk management.** This is the process of looking ahead for possible problems and preparing corrective action in case a particular problem arises.

In this section, I'll be discussing these activities in relation to the requirements analysis stage. In later chapters, I'll be continuing along this theme with further "Manager's Views" sections, where you'll learn how your models help to drive the activities just listed. For the purpose of this section, I'm assuming that you're a manager who is responsible for these activities.

Staffing

Your initial staff should consist of yourself, some sort of analysts to gather client needs, and some sort of architects to identify possible technical issues. Perhaps you call the analysts "product managers" or "domain experts" (or maybe even "marketers"); but they are the people who work most closely with the client to identify the user needs. Perhaps you call the architects "lead programmers" or "tech leads"; but they are the people who define the basic structure of the system. All three groups should have skill in requirements analysis and modeling—or at least be literate in requirements terminology and Use Case Diagrams—so as to provide review and feedback on the analysts' work. This initial analysis team will gather requirements as described in Chapter 5 and analyze them as discussed in this chapter (and refine them as described in Chapter 7).

Once the analysis team has gathered and modeled the bulk of the use cases, examine your actors, your domain objects, and your use cases with an eye to which particular skills you'll need. Inspired by Brooks,[9] I suggest the following common roles for your consideration.

Analysts

New requirements crop up throughout the life of the project; and one of the classically poor ways to handle them is to *not* analyze them as thoroughly as you analyzed the initial requirements. Some of your analysts should stay involved as the project progresses.

Architect

Architecture work continues throughout the life of your project (if only in response to new requirements), so some of your architects should stay involved as the project progresses.

Database Administrator (DBA)

The DBA designs, implements, and maintains the database for the system. If your system involves more than a handful of persistent domain objects, you'll need at least one DBA, and possibly a DBA team.

User Interface Designer

The UI designer designs, implements, and maintains the user interfaces for the system. If your system involves *any* user interfaces, you *need* a good UI designer. It's far too easy to build a bad user interface, and difficult to build a really good one; and as I mentioned in Chapter 2, you're weird (or at the least, your developers are weird). You're better than average at comprehending large volumes of information, and you're practiced with using cumbersome programming and management

---

9. Frederick P. Brooks, Jr., *The Mythical Man Month* (Addison-Wesley, 1995), pp. 29–37. Brooks discusses what he calls "The Surgical Team," a ten-person team specialized into roles to provide maximum support to one chief programmer. Brooks' "surgeon" and "copilot" may be an early version of the pair programming approach.

tools. You aren't the best judge of what makes a usable user interface, but a good UI designer should be.

Web Designer

A Web designer is a specialized UI designer who understands both the metaphors of the Web and the capabilities and limitations of current Web technology. If your system involves any Web access, you need a good Web designer.

Designer

The designer should have strong modeling and design skills and a firm grasp of programming. The designer is responsible for fleshing out the initial design efforts of the architects. If your system involves coding, it involves designing, whether you put effort into it or not. You need a designer.

Coder

The coder writes code. Duh! But in particular, you need a person with enough design and modeling literacy to grasp the requirements, architecture, and component models, implement them faithfully, *and* recognize their shortcomings and work out better solutions, *and* recognize their limitations and flesh out the details. The coder is no mindless drone, but rather a skilled individual who makes the abstract concrete. If your system involves coding, you need a coder. (If your system doesn't involve coding, why are you reading this book?)

Tester

The tester reviews models and code, looking for ways to break them; and then breaks them and breaks them and breaks them until they just won't break any more. Every bug they find is one less bug that a customer finds and one less developer stranded in a warehouse at 3 a.m. A good tester is my best friend. The tester should have enough modeling literacy to understand both how the system is supposed to work (for building acceptance tests) *and* how it might break. You need a tester. No, I take that back: you need a *good* tester, and we developers are usually lousy testers, especially of our own code. Get a good tester on your team.

Documenter

The documenter explains what your system does. If you have users (other than the developers themselves), you need a good documenter.

Technology Specialist

The technology specialist is a designer or coder who is expert in a particular technology that may be new with this project, or may just be difficult to master. If you're using such technologies, you need a tech specialist.

Librarian

The librarian maintains records for the team, including archived versions of documents and models and code. If your team has one person, you don't need a librarian: one person can organize artifacts well enough for their own needs. If your team has two people, you *might not* need a librarian: if I didn't write the code, I know you did, so I can ask you questions about it. If your team has three or more people, you no longer know who has the answer to any given question, and you need a librarian to at least set up the archiving and retrieval policies, along with the infrastructure (configuration management tools, etc.). As your team gets larger, librarian becomes more and more of a full-time job.

Toolsmith

The toolsmith maintains your development tools, and more importantly, looks for new tools that could be useful for your specific needs, and either purchases them (if commercially available), downloads and configures them (if available as Open Source), or designs and implements and tests them (if you need unique tools). These tools (especially custom-crafted tools) can really add to your productivity, if done well and applied well. The flip side is that a poorly built or poorly understood tool can lead you down an unproductive dead end. I don't know that any project *needs* a toolsmith; but it can be good business strategy to include a good toolsmith so that your teams can become very efficient at common tasks over time.[10]

---

10. If your team is working in Visual Studio .NET, your toolsmith should pick up Les Smith's *Writing Add-Ins for Visual Studio .NET* (Apress, 2000). This book has revealed all sorts of things I never knew about VS .NET add-ins, and gives you the skills to write some really powerful custom tools for VS .NET.

Manager

This is you, of course. Make sure your team really has a manager, *not* another programmer. I plan to show that you have more than enough work on your plate, and you'll have *no* time for coding. Don't count on yourself for any code unless you can afford for that code to be late, rushed, and eventually thrown out as unworkable.

"But I Don't Have All Those People!"

Many teams don't have enough people to individually cover all of these responsibilities. That's normal, and it's OK. Think of all those positions we just looked at, from analyst to toolsmith to manager, as roles that people can play. They are, in essence, the actors in a model of the software development process, the jobs that must be accomplished. Determine which roles you need, and assign them to people based on their skill sets and interests. If some people have to fill multiple roles, that's fine; but be sure that each role is adequately covered (and that no person has too many roles to fulfill).

Now if you find that your people don't have the *skills* for these roles, you have a bigger problem. Development of any sizable projects requires all of these skills. You need to hire new people; or even better, you need to train the people you have. Your people's brains are close to the entirety of your capital assets, *and* they're easier to grow than almost any other asset. The cost of training each team member—*real* training, not just corporate policies or fuzzy motivational training—for one week per year is less than the cost of new hardware, less than the cost of new facilities, *and* less than the cost of hiring new people, while the benefit of the new training multiplies across project after project. Grow those skills, and grow those brains.

In the case of the Kennel Management System, I examined the actors, domain objects, and use cases; and I determined that the following staff is needed: a manager, analysts, architects, DBAs (because we're considering over 100 different domain objects), UI designers, Web designers (because there are significant Web requirements), designers, coders, testers, documenters (especially because there are requirements for instructional materials), and librarians (there are already a lot of documents to archive, and more are on the way). There is no immediate need for toolsmiths; but we may decide to add them for long-term leverage. And because the KMS will be a .NET solution, we'll need some .NET technology specialists.

How Do You Know It's a .NET Solution?

Well, because .NET is in the title of this book, of course. It wouldn't be very consistent to do a non-.NET solution. What a question.

Actually, I should say, "What a question!" I think that at this stage, it's an *excellent* question. It can be a horrible mistake to pick the technology before you understand the problem (unless, of course, the customer *requires* a particular technology). One of the things you should expect from your architects at this point is to look at the use cases and the domain objects. Then they should recommend the technology that's the best fit for the requirements *and* that best fits your skill sets and your strategic vision for the future and your cost goals. Fit the solution to the problem, not the other way around.

Now if you read the spec for this case study, you might almost think that the requirements were *designed* to be a good fit for .NET.

Now how many people do you need for each role? That ties into the related management activity of *planning*.

Planning

As described previously, planning consists of estimating the amount of work, determining the order of work, and scheduling the work. We'll examine each of these tasks in the following sections.

Estimating the Work

In the ideal world (and occasionally in academia, R&D, or mission-critical system development), a job "takes as long as it takes" (and as much money and resources as it takes). In the real world, the time involved in the effort is a cost that must be managed and recouped. In the real world, the budget for an effort is finite and must be accounted for. And in the real world, resources must be planned and scheduled. Resources that are idle or that are spent on failed efforts are lost forever.

The key tool in managing your key resources—your time, your people's time, your budget—is an estimate of how many resources you'll need, and for how long. This estimate provides your justification for accepting the project (or for running away screaming); and once the project is underway, it provides a gauge to indicate how you're progressing. And if you don't make the estimate, someone else will make one for you, and hold you to it. Here's a classic conversation you do *not* want to have:

MIDDLE MANAGER: How long will it take?

PROJECT MANAGER: I don't know.

MIDDLE MANAGER: But how long will it take?

PROJECT MANAGER: But I don't know.

MIDDLE MANAGER: Oh, come on, you must have some idea.

PROJECT MANAGER: Nope. Sorry.

MIDDLE MANAGER: But you *must* have some idea.

PROJECT MANAGER: If I did, I'd tell you.

MIDDLE MANAGER: But I need this for my report to the executives. They insist.

PROJECT MANAGER: Then I feel very sorry for you.

MIDDLE MANAGER: Oh, just give me a date.

PROJECT MANAGER: All right: 10 years, a hundred million dollars. We won't go over that.

MIDDLE MANAGER: Oh, get real!

PROJECT MANAGER: That is real. We won't go over 10 years or a hundred million.

MIDDLE MANAGER: Ha, ha, very funny. Look, just give me a date I can put in this report. *I won't hold you to it.*

And therein lies the trap. You believe that promise, maybe even the middle manager believes that promise, and you give an estimate just to shut him up. And the next day, it's written in stone, published in the annual report, and promised to the customer. The *right* answer isn't "I don't know," it's "I don't know, but I'll tell you in 2 days." Or 2 weeks. Or for really long projects, maybe even 2 months. That middle manager really does have to report something to the executives; and you're reminding him that you can't make an estimate without adequate study, *and* you're telling him when he can expect an answer for the executives. To a good middle manager, this is sufficient.

"But They Don't Ask Me for an Estimate. They Just Tell Me When It's Due. (Some Time After That, They'll Tell Me What They Want Us to Build.)"

It doesn't matter. Make an estimate anyway. There are at least four reasons why you should make an estimate:

1. You might find the schedule is attainable. Whew! What a relief! (You might also find that helpful elves have written all your code while you slept. It's about as likely.)

2. You might make stakeholders realize that the schedule is too tight, and get them to pull back before the ship hits the iceberg. (Not *quite* as unlikely as helpful elves; but there are organizations where this will *never* happen.)

3. Your warnings of doom might help your coworkers and clients and other stakeholders to make contingency plans in case the ship sinks. This requires you to publish your estimates, which may not make you popular, but is a responsible and ethical way to treat your coworkers and clients. And besides . . .

4. If you see an iceberg ahead and the captains won't change course, you have a chance to jump ship. Find another job as soon as possible, long before the disaster looms (and the estimate will let you see that iceberg from a *long* way away). That way, no one can blame the disaster on you, because things were fine when you left. (This is a favorite tactic of some corporate sales personnel: sell an undeliverable system that will take 18 months to collapse, then leave after 6. "It's not my fault. Those developers just couldn't do the job I sold. But my idea was great, so pay me more money." At least *your* hands will be clean when you leave.)

Don't skip the estimate, and don't endorse an unrealistic estimate. That way madness lies.

Your primary estimating technique is to estimate honestly. A dishonest or optimistic estimate will *always* fail. Modern estimating techniques are made up of a large number of smaller estimating elements; and these techniques count on the low estimates balancing out the high estimates, yielding a more accurate overall estimate. If you let people coax you into wearing rose-colored glasses, the final picture will look rosy indeed. It will also look nothing like reality.

And where do you get all these smaller estimating elements? Well, from your UML model, of course:

- Look at each domain object. Does it have to be persisted? There's a database table, or an XML file, or some other persistent storage.

- Does the domain object have to be represented in the code? There's a class.

- Do you need to manage collections of instances of the domain object? There's perhaps another table, perhaps another class, perhaps both.

- Does the domain object represent a user interface? There's a form or Web page that has to be designed and implemented.

- Look at each actor. How does your system interact with it? There's another user interface, or perhaps a programmatic interface.

- Do you have to maintain information about the actor? There's perhaps another table, perhaps another class, perhaps both.

- Do you need to manage collections of instances of the actor? There's perhaps another table, perhaps another class, perhaps both.

- Look at each use case. The use case represents one or more operations that you must implement. Each operation is an estimating element, as is the algorithm that ties the activities together. Consider the scenarios that may occur within the use case, and contemplate useful operations. (You'll see more on scenarios, activities, and algorithms in Chapter 7.)

- Each use case also defines one or more test cases (one for each scenario) that must be implemented and applied.

- Each use case also defines one document section that must be produced, with a size that varies with the number of scenarios.

- Each use case and its scenarios may suggest new domain objects, and thus perhaps new tables and classes.

Other estimating elements are possible; but these should certainly give you the idea. In the case of the KMS, we've already identified 27 actors, 104 domain objects, and 129 use cases. When the number of actors, domain objects, and use cases starts to stabilize (i.e., when the Requirements Delta starts to drop to acceptable levels, as described in Chapter 5), we should have plenty of estimating elements with which to work.

What do you do with these estimating elements? Well, that depends on the specific estimating technique you select. (Actually, in *Rapid Development*, McConnell recommends redundant estimation: use at least *three* different techniques at once.[11] If the techniques agree, you can have real confidence in your estimate; or if the techniques yield significantly different results, you can study the results to see if one technique has identified risks that you might otherwise have missed.)

Some specific estimating techniques include

---

11. Steve McConnell, *Rapid Development: Taming Wild Software Schedules* (Microsoft Press, 1996), p. 179

- **Analogy to past efforts.** Of course, this works best when you have a good, honest history of those past efforts *and* when your team is roughly the same team that performed those past efforts *and* when those past efforts have some similarities to the current project. If all of these are true, analogy can be a powerful estimating technique.

- **Seat of the pants.** What works poorly when applied to the whole project works somewhat better when applied to the individual estimating elements. In one of my classes, a student gave an estimate of 2 weeks for him to implement a particular feature. Then he and his team spent 5 minutes designing the elements that would go into that feature, and they gave estimates to each element. The resulting estimate was 14 to 37 weeks. He looked at the original problem description, and said, "It sounds like 2 weeks." And he looked at each individual element, and said, "14 would be *really* pushing it, and we'd better think about at least 20." And he swore that was the last time he would give an estimate without building some amount of relevant models first.

- **Distributed estimation.** You make each person provide the estimates for the pieces they will produce, using whatever techniques they think will work best.

- **Pessimistic estimation.** Similar to distributed estimation, but you make each person estimate the efforts of *others* on whose work they depend. This tends to counteract unwarranted confidence: we never expect our own code to let us down, but we all know that other people's code lets us down all the time.

- **Outside estimation experts.** Estimation is a skill. Sometimes you can hire it. The experts won't know your organization as well as you do, but they'll have experience with a wide range of estimating challenges. They can give a useful outside perspective as part of redundant estimation.

- **COCOMO II.** Boehm et al. have designed the COCOMO II model, an ambitious effort to quantify both the size of your project and the skills and capabilities of your team. It requires that you make many measurements of your organization. It also includes ways to tailor the model to your team over time, improving your accuracy.

- **Function points.** Not as ambitious as COCOMO II, function points are only about measuring your project, not your team. (In fact, they can serve as an input to COCOMO II estimating.) Function points quantify all the discrete elements of your system and try to estimate the number of "units" of functionality to be implemented.

You should prefer techniques based on automated tools, because they remove much of the subjectivity and optimism that can infect an estimate. They also make the estimating process more repeatable and predictable, and may guide you through the process. Boehm's *Software Cost Estimation with COCOMO II* includes a CD with an implementation of the COCOMO II model.[12] McConnell's company, Construx, produces Construx Estimate.[13] My own practice is to use a function-point estimating spreadsheet based on material from Garmus and Herron's *Function Point Analysis*[14] and charts in McConnell's *Rapid Development* that map function points to development effort.[15] What I like about this approach is that it yields both an estimate of the effort *and* an estimate of optimum team size.

Applying this spreadsheet to the current model of the KMS, I get an initial estimate of 13 months for a team of eight full-time equivalent employees, or FTEs. An FTE represents one person working full time, two people working half-time, etc. Because my spreadsheet doesn't (yet) have any C# or .NET data, I had to use Visual C++ data to produce that estimate. Because I find .NET to be a significantly more productive environment than Visual C++ and Windows, I might be comfortable reducing that estimate; but because I'm assuming a lot of the team will need to learn .NET and UML, I'll leave the estimate where it stands for now. I'll adjust it when we get some experience under our belts.

So now let's revisit the staffing issue with respect to the KMS. There are 12 roles to fill: manager, analyst, architect, DBA, UI designer, Web designer, designer, coder, tester, documenter, librarian, and .NET technology specialist. And I have set the staffing level at eight. One of those eight is the manager, and one is a documenter. Ideally, one person should act as a full-time analyst to maintain a clear vision of user needs, especially as requirements shift over time. That leaves five FTEs. I like to have at least two testers, so that they may review each other's work. (Also, research shows that a one-to-one or one-to-two tester-to-developer ratio is essential for adequate testing.) That leaves only three FTEs to cover architect, DBA, UI designer, Web designer, designer, coder, and .NET technology specialist. With so many tables, one person should be a nearly full-time DBA. And we certainly need an architect.

So that leaves one FTE for UI designer, Web designer, designer, coder, and .NET technology specialist. Not a good plan. Let's rethink this. First, because the UI is partly Web and partly desktop, one person can deal with both. And on a team this small, *everyone* will have to be .NET technology specialists, as much as they can be. We may want to contract a .NET specialist as an occasional consultant

12. Barry W. Boehm et al., *Software Cost Estimation with COCOMO II* (Prentice Hall, 2000)

13. Available at http://www.construx.com.

14. David Garmus and David Herron, *Function Point Analysis: Measurement Practices for Successful Software Projects* (Addison-Wesley, 2000)

15. Steve McConnell, *Rapid Development: Taming Wild Software Schedules* (Microsoft Press, 1996), pp. 188–196

to steer us around missteps. We'll want people to overlap roles some: the architect and DBA should double as assistant analysts; the architect should help review the database; the DBA and UI designer should help review the architecture; and the analyst and DBA and UI designer should all function as designers and coders. That still leaves me with a gut feeling that we could use another designer/coder, and that implies probably another tester. The role of librarian has been left out, so someone should have that as a secondary responsibility (perhaps one of the testers, because they need ready access to all artifacts for testing anyway). In the long run, we'll probably need one or two more FTEs than indicated by my estimating spreadsheet.

Ordering the Work

Once you have an estimate—and perhaps before you have a final staff—you can begin to determine an order of work. Look at your use cases and determine whether any are obviously precursors of others. The objects for those will need to be implemented first, along with any user interfaces and the use cases themselves. Also try to gauge the priorities of individual use cases, so that you may implement the most critical features earliest. You're not trying to get a complete order of work, merely some guidelines to apply in building the schedule.

Scheduling the Work

Next, build a schedule, based on your order of work, your staff—don't forget to allow time for vacations, sick days, personal days, and training; and realize that experienced managers usually assume that no more than 80 percent of an FTE's time is productively spent on the project—and your size estimates for individual elements. Because use cases represent behavior that is visible from the outside and important to end users, your schedule should always be stated in terms of use cases being implemented. Your internal schedule may reflect the finer-grained details within a use case; but it's the use cases that are meaningful to your stakeholders.

Tracking

Once you have your estimate and your schedule, you're in a position to begin tracking the work. Each estimating element or use case has got a scheduled start time and a scheduled completion. You can check the status of these to see that things are proceeding on a timely schedule, with an eye to reporting and correction.

Reporting

Another key to a successful project is visibility: team members and stakeholders have to have access to the status of the project at all times. In particular, they have to know what may be wrong, so that they can plan around it. Errors and missteps happen, and are unavoidable; but every mistake becomes worse when the people affected by it are unaware of it until they're slapped in the face with it. Ignorance may be bliss, but it's also a lousy way to run a project.

Externally, you report your progress in terms of use cases: which have begun implementation, which are pending, which are late, which have developed problems, and so on. Again, the use cases are the most meaningful level of functionality to your outside stakeholders.

Internally, you can report your progress with finer granularity: domain objects, scenarios of use cases, database tables, and other estimating elements. These are more meaningful to the team.

Correction

Once your project status is visible, your next task is to correct any deviations from the schedule. Perhaps you can reassign some staff. Perhaps you can reprioritize some use cases. Perhaps some use cases need to be analyzed in further depth. Perhaps your estimates need to be adjusted.

But in all cases, the key to correction is this: go back to the beginning. There's a natural impulse to do something *now* to immediately react to the problem; but that impulse can lead you astray. Don't just do something, stand there. There's something you thought you understood, but you didn't; and until you find what that something is, you can't make the *right* correction. Go back to your requirements sources and study the relevant sections. Look at the model for those sections, and see what you may have overlooked. Revise your estimate, your dependencies, and your plan. In every step, you'll be able to apply new perspective that you and your team have gained by working on the problem; so look for ways that the model and the estimate and the schedule don't fit with what you've learned. *Then* you'll understand where to apply corrective action. Remember: a bug isn't fixed until you understand where it came from and *then* understand how to correct it; and that applies to process and model bugs as well as to code bugs.

Constant Reevaluation

You may wonder if this process of reanalysis and reestimating ever ends. The answer is no, not as long as the project lasts. It is unrealistic to expect to know the final shape of things before you're done; but your picture can continuously improve, *if* you keep revisiting your assessment and planning tasks to incorporate what you have learned.

For inspiration, think of NASA's manned space flight program. When NASA launched Apollo capsules to the Moon, they didn't just point the nose, press a button, and wait to land. They had an overall mission plan, but that plan was not set in stone at the start of a voyage. Instead, at predictable intervals along the trip, they took attitude and distance and velocity checks, and then adjusted the flight plan to fit their current status. In this way, the Apollo landings got ever more precise; and even in the case of Apollo 13—where a catastrophic O_2 tank explosion sent the craft tumbling, crippled their power supply, and vented gases that kept pushing them off their flight path—this rigorous discipline of assessment and correction brought the crew home against unimaginable odds.

Sometimes when I use this analogy, a cynic will say, "Yeah, but our job's not rocket science." They're right. Despite the tragedies of Apollo 1, the Challenger explosion, and the Columbia breakup, the manned space flight program's missions have close to a 99 percent success rate. Most likely, the cynical teams can't claim similar success rates. Maybe we should learn from the rocket scientists.

Risk Management

Another key management task is risk management: knowing what your most likely risks are, and already having a plan in place for them. That saves you energy, because these risks can be handled almost automatically. (You'll need that energy for the completely unexpected problems that will somehow slip past your risk management.) When you have your use cases and your domain objects, ask your team for individual opinions on which use cases look risky to them, and how, and what might be done to handle those risks. Gather that feedback, look for the largest or most likely risks, and prepare plans in depth for those risks.

A Tester's View of Requirements

As a software tester, your task is to define tests and test suites, apply the tests, assess the results, and report the state of the system. From your perspective, each use case defines a test suite: one or more tests for each scenario of the use case, plus additional tests to try to break the use case. You can then organize these test suites in the same hierarchy as the use cases themselves.

When reporting test results, you should always relate them to the use cases and actors and domain objects affected. This will put the test results into context, helping your stakeholders to understand the magnitude of test failures and the health of the system.

A Documenter's View of Requirements

As a software documenter, your task is to describe how the system operates. The actors and use cases serve as a road map to what you need to document. The domain objects indicate important concepts that users of the system must understand. You might organize your user documentation by actor, or perhaps by the actor packages in the requirements model; or you might find a more natural way to present the information. But you should understand the actors and the Use Case Diagrams to understand the thought behind the system.

This won't be enough to let you write the documents, of course, but it will let you start designing an outline, a style guide, and other foundations of the documentation. You'll be able to explain the system's behavior in more depth when the team refines the requirements, as in Chapter 7.

Summary

In this chapter, I've talked about the first step of Five-Step UML. During this step, your first task is to identify all your actors and domain objects from your requirements sources. To help you better organize these elements, I showed you two hierarchical patterns (one for actors and one for domain objects), which I find useful and which can be adapted to many different projects. At the very least, they should serve as a useful starting point for you. Next, you need to look at each actor in turn and identify all of the use cases initiated by this actor, documenting these as Use Case Diagrams. As you go along, you should look at what domain objects are also associated with the use case, and whether there are any other actors involved. Sometimes it can help at the end of this stage to look through all of your domain objects in turn, and think about which use cases are associated with them, to make sure that you haven't overlooked any other use cases.

As an illustration of the whole process, I showed you how this step works in practice analyzing the use cases for the Kennel Management System. From the number of actors and domain objects that we identified from this fairly simple example, you can get an idea of the level of complexity that is uncovered in any project when you begin modeling it in detail.

The model created at this stage can help everyone involved in the project. In particular it's important for the manager, in terms of planning, to be able to use it to make a first estimate of the amount of work, in order to determine the schedule and the staffing requirements. Obviously, this estimate will need to be revisited and revised as more is learned about the system.

In the next chapter, you'll be moving on to Step 2 of Five-Step UML, where you'll focus on the use cases developed in Step 1, refining the various scenarios and documenting them as a set of Activity Diagrams.

CHAPTER 7

Step 2: Refine Your Requirements

IN THE LAST CHAPTER, I discussed Step 1 of Five-Step UML, and looked in detail at how to define the requirements of the Kennel Management System (KMS) using a set of Use Case Diagrams.

You'll move on in this chapter to look at the second step of the process, which involves studying our use cases in more detail in order to refine the requirements of a system. The use cases will inevitably throw up more questions, so you can expect to carry out more user interviews at this stage of the process.

Once again, I'll walk you through the KMS as an example, using our work from the last chapter as a starting point. In Step 2, we'll be developing Activity Diagrams to show how the different scenarios in each use case work. Towards the end of the chapter, I'll show you how UML will help you to manage, document, and test the requirements.

Before we get started, though, I'll just explain a little about the examples in this chapter. We won't be following through every single use case that we documented in the last chapter. For starters, we've already seen the relevant Activity Diagram notation back in Chapter 2, and also many of the diagrams we'd draw will be "predundant" (that's redundant in advance) with the same diagrams that we *will* draw in Chapter 8 when we add swimlanes. Drawing them here would consume a lot of space without telling you as much as you'll learn in Chapter 8. The big lesson, in case you haven't figured it out, is that any real-world project that's worth doing is likely to need at least one "refine the requirements" step. So instead of trying to refine the entire requirements model in this book, I'll concentrate on one example use case. I'll use this both to demonstrate the process and to demonstrate particular stereotypes that I find useful when I'm working with use cases and Activity Diagrams.

Identifying and Diagramming Scenarios for Each Use Case

From the KMS case study, the use case that I've selected to examine in detail in this chapter is the **Define Contractor Schedule** use case, initiated by the **Contractor** actor.

As you may recall, our requirements review in the last chapter revealed that this use case has to be performed by the **Contractor**, *not* by the **Supervisor**, as the spec suggests; but that still leaves the question of how the **Contractor** defines a schedule. How does the **Contractor** know what services need to be scheduled? Further interviews have revealed that the **Supervisor** *does* have a role to play: the **Supervisor** needs to define the tasks to be performed by a particular **Contractor**, so that the **Contractor** can select and schedule tasks from this list. This is reflected in Figure 7-1.

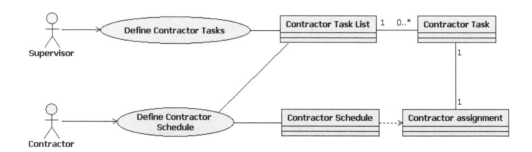

Figure 7-1. Contractor task use cases

The **Contractor Task List** is a list of **Contractor Task** objects to be performed. When the Contractor performs **Define Contractor Schedule**, he or she converts a task from the list to an assignment in the schedule.

Included Use Cases

If you stop to think about the user interface for the two use cases in Figure 7-1, you'll probably conclude that both use cases require an actor to be able to review a **Contractor Task List**. From there, it's only a small step to decide that this review process should be substantially the same for both use cases. You can show behavior that's common between two or more use cases as an included use case, depicted with dependencies with **«include»** stereotypes, as demonstrated in Figure 7-2.

When the included use case cannot stand on its own but instead may only be included, it is called an *abstract use case*, and its name is shown in italics, as in Figure 7-2.

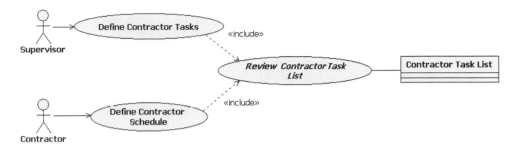

Figure 7-2. Contractor task use cases, including common review behavior

So the Primary Scenario for the **Define Contractor Schedule** use case is for the **Contractor** to review the task list, select a task, add it to the schedule, and submit the schedule to the **Supervisor** for approval. Recall that I also referred to this as the "Happy Path" in Chapter 2, because in this scenario everything goes as we like and as we expect.

In interviews, we've also learned that **Contractors** can have two different payment rates for services: a standard rate table that a **Supervisor** can use in selecting **Contractors**, and specific rates for specific tasks. This allows the **Contractor** to charge extra for difficult tasks or to offer discounts for special circumstances. Thus, the Primary Scenario might appear as shown in Figure 7-3.

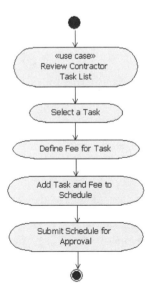

Figure 7-3. Primary Scenario for Define Contractor Schedule use case

What's with that «use case» Stereotype?

That's a Martin-the-Practitioner stereotype, my way of indicating that one activity represents the entire behavior of a given use case. In this example, the activity represents the included use case from Figure 7-2, **Review Contractor List**. Similarly, I might use the **«use case»** stereotype to indicate the behavior of a base use case within the flow of a derived use case.

Now that we've seen what happens in our ideal Primary Scenario, where we assume that everything goes as planned, we need to define more complex Alternate and Exception Scenarios by playing the "What could go wrong?" game, looking at each activity and asking if the flow might branch after it.

For instance, look at the first activity, **Review Contractor Task List**. What could go wrong? Well, suppose the list is empty. In that case, it doesn't make sense to assign tasks to the schedule. We can revise the Activity Diagram shown earlier to look like Figure 7-4.

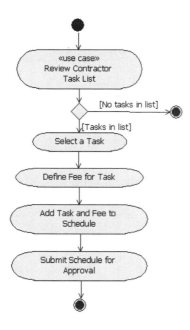

Figure 7-4. Define Contractor Schedule use case, first revision

Next, we should ask whether a **Contractor** wants to schedule only one task at a time. Probably not: **Contractors** will want to schedule a number of activities in a row, and *then* submit their schedules. Thus, we need a loop, as shown in Figure 7-5.

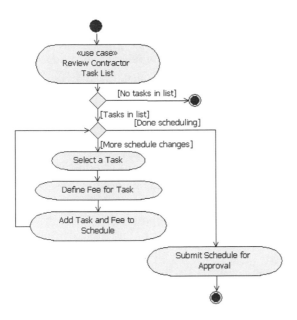

Figure 7-5. Define Contractor Schedule use case, second revision

Next, we should consider if a **Contractor** is ever allowed to change their mind: can they construct a schedule, and then decide not to submit it? The client says, "Sure!" So that means we need the concept of rolling back the changes, as in Figure 7-6.

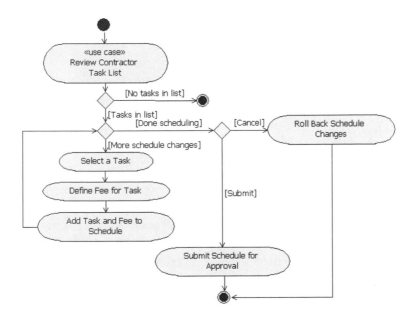

Figure 7-6. Define Contractor Schedule use case, third revision

But this is still a one-way process: the **Contractor** can only add to the schedule and then commit those changes or roll them back. We could ask whether the **Contractor** should be able to remove tasks from the schedule as well; and the client again says, "Sure!" (More likely, the client says, "Well, of course. That's obvious. Why did I have to tell you that?" A large part of requirements refinement is identifying the obvious with perfect 20-20 hindsight, when no one bothered to point it out in the first place, because it *was* obvious—to them.)

We then ask if there's anything else **Contractors** should be able to do as part of defining a schedule; and the client says, "Well, they have to be able to reject tasks that they're not interested in performing. That way, the supervisor will know to find another contractor." At this point, our diagram is starting to look a little cluttered; so we'll add subactivity states, as shown in Figure 7-7.

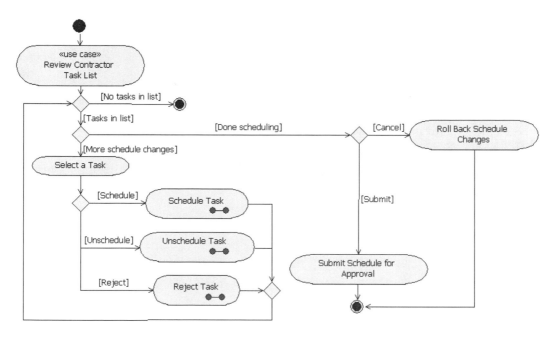

Figure 7-7. Define Contractor Schedule use case, fourth revision

Recall that you first met subactivity states back in Chapter 2. A subactivity state merely implies a nested Activity Diagram. There are more activities going on inside the subactivity state than are indicated on the main diagram; you can draw a separate Activity Diagram for each subactivity state. The notation that Rational XDE uses for this is a small icon in the bottom-right corner to indicate nesting.

What's with the Layout of Those Subactivity States?

That's what I call the *Case Pattern:* when there are many possible transitions from a single branch that will likely be coded with what Pascal and VB programmers would call a *case statement,* and what C, C++, Java, and C# programmers would call a *switch statement.* (I'm revealing my Pascal roots here by how I name the pattern.) The C# code for such a statement would look something like this:

```
switch (boolean_expression)
{
    case CHOICE1 :
    {
        // Process choice 1.
    }
    break;
    case CHOICE2 :
    {
        // Process choice 2.
    }
    break;
    ...
    case CHOICEn :
    {
        // Process choice n.
    }
    break;
    default :
    {
        // Process default or unexpected choice.
    }
    break;
}
```

In a case statement, there are a bunch of labeled choices, each followed by a bunch of statements appropriate to the choice. And my coding preference is to make each block of handler code a separate operation, so that the code remains uncluttered. So my modeling preference is to model the logic with a pattern that has a similar layout: a branch followed by a column of possible activities, each with a labeled transition that tells when you would choose that activity. Ultimately, the activities all rejoin in a merge.

Then, after further interviews to better understand these new subactivity states, we end up with the diagrams shown in Figures 7-8 to 7-10.

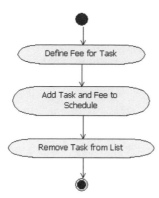

Figure 7-8. Schedule Task subactivity state

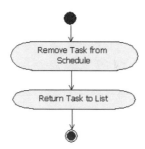

Figure 7-9. Unschedule Task subactivity state

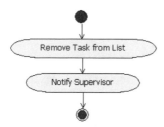

Figure 7-10. Reject Task subactivity state

Doubtless, we could refine each of the activities yet further (for instance, we could show how to handle an invalid **Contractor** fee); but these examples should be sufficient for now.

The diagram as shown in Figure 7-7 is once again getting pretty complex, and we're not done yet. So we need to look for ways to simplify it. One practice that I often find useful for simplifying Activity Diagrams is to turn loop bodies into subactivity states, as demonstrated in Figure 7-11.

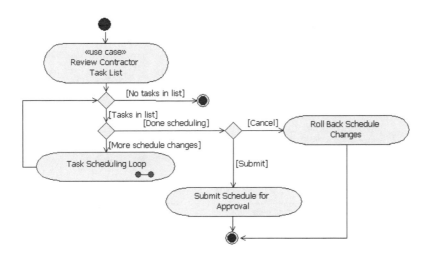

Figure 7-11. Define Contractor Schedule use case, fifth revision

Then the loop body would appear as in Figure 7-12.

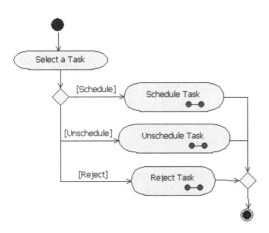

Figure 7-12. Task scheduling loop body

Looking at Figure 7-11 (and thinking about our overall list of **Contractor** use cases), I see one more question for our client: what happens if the **Supervisor** rejects the **Contractor** schedule? All right, two more questions: for that matter, what if the **Supervisor** *accepts* the schedule? Does the **Contractor** wait around for instantaneous approval? "Absolutely not!" says the client. "Who knows when the supervisor may be available? We have to email the final decision to the contractor, and then update the kennel schedule if the contractor schedule is approved." This is reflected in Figure 7-13.

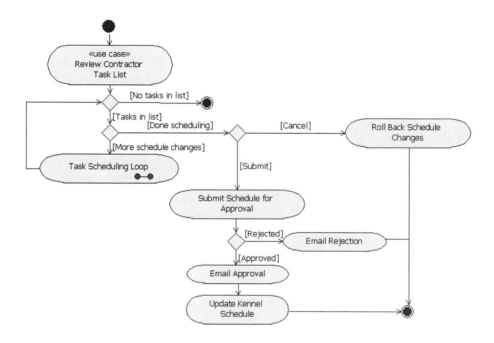

Figure 7-13. Define Contractor Schedule use case, sixth revision

We could probably refine this a little bit further; but then we'd soon be into implementation, not business rules or even architecture, so let's stop here.

In this example, we started with a simple statement of a required feature ("Define Contractor Schedule"); we identified five simple activities that describe that feature as the client expects it to work; and through lots of questions and diligence, we ended up with an algorithm of seven activities (one of which is a loop with more detailed activities within) and four decisions that describe that feature as it *may* work. That one simple statement hid a lot of detailed requirements knowledge. You can see from this simple example how much more detail you start uncovering by working with Activity Diagrams.

Exercise 701: Elaborate Your Use Cases

Building on Exercises 602 through 604, in which you organized your domain, added use cases for your actors, and related use cases to your domain objects, define the Primary and Alternate Scenarios for each use case, and verify that you have correctly captured the business rules and related requirements.

A Manager's View of Refined Requirements

The manager's view of these refined requirements is, I'm afraid, mostly bad news. As I just described, the refined requirements pretty much always reveal a wealth of detail you hadn't foreseen; and somehow, that new detail never seems to make the estimate smaller, only larger. Your precious estimates and schedules go right out the window.

What do you do? How do you cope with this "unexpected" scope creep (which, as I said, is pretty much expected)? I can see a few successful approaches:

Don't provide your first estimate and schedule until after refining your requirements. McConnell (among others) even argues[1] that you should fund the development effort in two phases: a requirements/quotation phase (maybe even proceeding all the way through to an initial architecture), and a design/construction phase. The client pays for the first phase, then decides whether the resulting analysis and quotation justify pursuing the effort. The client may even hand the design to a different team to implement (though Ambler argues against this, saying that a design is idiosyncratic to the team that created it[2]). This two-phase contract may seem a bit radical to clients who are used to just passing out a spec and requesting a quote; but it's not at all unusual in the physical contracting world. When clients want a new building built, they first contract an architecture firm to draw up plans, and they pay the architects for that work; and then they solicit bids from contracting firms to build the building according to the plans. Or maybe they contact a prime contractor, and the prime contractor subcontracts the architectural work; but in either case, the architects get paid for the up-front analysis and design, whether the building is completed or not. Yes, the two-phase

---

1. Steve McConnell, *Software Project Survival Guide* (Microsoft Press, 1997), p. 38
2. Scott W. Ambler, *Agile Modeling: Effective Practices for Extreme Programming and the Unified Process* (John Wiley & Sons, 2002), p. 147

contract is a bit radical for many software projects. Sadly, so is on-time and on-budget delivery of projects. Try *hard* to persuade your managers and clients to accept two-phase contracts as a way to minimize risks.

Put wide error margins in any estimate that precedes the refinement of the requirements. McConnell argues that –75 percent/+300 percent is a pretty good way to cover most eventualities in such early estimates.[3]

Revise your estimate after refinement, and then negotiate feature trimming to fit the agreed-upon schedule. No one will be happy: they'll accuse you of going back on your word, and maybe even of bait-and-switch. Well, as the old saying goes, suck it up! You're the bearer of bad news, and the bearer of bad news always gets stuck with the pointy end of something sharp. No matter. When you can see that the scope is beyond the schedule, you *know* you're going to have to trim some features. You can either trim them now, when things are calm and you can take time to reassess priorities; or you can trim them after the deadline has passed, when tempers are short and key features still aren't implemented. Other "fixes"—mandatory overtime, hiring highly paid consultants, throwing more bodies at the problem, buying "amazing wonder tools that will solve all your problems"—are all proven ways to make the project even later *and* buggier. Trim now and make your schedule with a smaller but better project, or trim later in a haphazard fashion leading to a late and buggy project. Those are your only choices.

Cancel the project. It's bad to bite off more than you can chew; but it's far worse to try to swallow it. Spit the project out, count how much time you saved by *not* choking on the thing, and go find another project to chew on. (This works well with the two-phase contract structure described previously: there's a natural break between the two phases, during which all parties can decide whether the second phase is worth pursuing.)

Find another job. If someone in power insists that there's another option besides options 1 to 4, the project has already failed. All that's left is a long, miserable exercise in proving the failure. You have better things to do with your life.

Staffing

The refined requirements may certainly reveal new staffing needs for the project, as you realize that particular activities require special skills, or simply more bodies.

---

3. Steve McConnell, *Rapid Development: Taming Wild Software Schedules* (Microsoft Press, 1996), p. 168

Planning

As stated earlier, you'll need to completely overhaul your estimate after refining your requirements. Remember that estimation is a continuous process throughout the life of the project. From the revised estimate, define a new order of work and a new schedule.

Tracking

The new estimate and schedule shall define new estimating elements that must be tracked. You may even discover new use cases that must be tracked, as shown in Figure 7-1.

Reporting

The new tracking requirements imply new reporting, as discussed in Chapter 6.

Correction

The new tracking requirements imply new opportunities for correction, as discussed in Chapter 6.

Risk Management

The number one new risk implied by the requirements refinement is the increased scope, as discussed previously. The nature of the new risk varies depending on how you decide to manage the increased scope:

- If you choose to deal with the scope change via a two-phase contract, your major new risk is that the client won't choose to continue the project after quotation. There's also a business risk that the client won't choose to pay for the quote; but that's for the business folks to handle, and beyond the scope of this book.

- If you choose wide estimating margins, your new risk is that the margins just tightened up, probably toward the high side. This will make some stakeholders nervous, and may cause them to push for drastic, rash measures to correct this predictable problem (which really needs no correction—yet).

- If you choose to trim features, you add two new risks: that you won't be able to reach agreement on what to trim; and that you'll trim features that are actually essential to the success of the project.

- If you choose to cancel the project, there's a risk that some stakeholders won't understand that failing early is a victory compared to failing late, because it costs less and leaves time to try new projects. They may become risk averse; or they may choose not to work with your group in the future, even though you made a responsible business decision.

- If you choose to quit, there's a risk that you won't find another job.

A Tester's View of Refined Requirements

For a tester, these refined requirements define your individual test cases. Recall from Chapter 6 that each use case defined a test suite of one or more test cases; now the scenarios within a use case define test cases for the corresponding suite. The activities also help to identify prep work that must be done prior to a test being run.

As an example, let's look at the diagrams for the **Define Contractor Schedule** use case that we've been studying in this chapter. We can identify the following test cases:

1. No tasks for this contractor. Prep work: empty the task list.

2. Contractor cancels schedule changes. Prep work: put tasks in the list so that the contractor may make changes.

3. Contractor cancels a schedule that includes rejected tasks. Prep work: put tasks in the list so that the contractor may make changes. Note here that the clever tester has detected a flaw in this analysis: the model shows that we'll notify the supervisor immediately upon rejecting a task, *even if* the changes are later rolled back. One of two changes must occur: either rejecting a task can't be rolled back (ugh!); or these notifications must be deferred until the schedule is submitted to the supervisor, and most likely are included as part of the schedule submission. The tester doesn't even bother detailing this test case until a decision is made. Let's assume that after some discussion with the client, we decide to queue the notifications for reporting with the schedule, so we'll modify Figure 7-10 as shown in Figure 7-14.

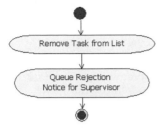

Figure 7-14. Reject Task, first revision

4. Contractor submits an empty schedule. Prep work: put tasks in the list so that the contractor may make changes. Oops! We never discussed how to handle this one, either. Time for more model updates. This tester is certainly earning their pay.

5. Supervisor rejects the schedule. Prep work: put tasks in the list so that the contractor may make changes.

6. Supervisor approves the schedule. Prep work: put tasks in the list so that the contractor may make changes.

7. Contractor schedules a task. Prep work: put tasks in the list so that the contractor may make changes.

8. Contractor unschedules a task. Prep work: put tasks in the list so that the contractor may make changes; schedule one or more tasks.

9. Contractor rejects a task. Prep work: put tasks in the list so that the contractor may make changes.

And this is probably not all! A good tester will find even more test cases within these diagrams.

A Documenter's View of Refined Requirements

For a documenter, the refined requirements define the stories you must tell, which will often overlap the test cases identified by the testers. Recall from Chapter 6 that your use cases helped you to define an outline for your documentation; now the scenarios within a use case define more detailed steps that must be included in the outline and thus in the docs. The activities also help to identify screen shots that will be needed.

Again, let's look though our diagrams for the **Define Contractor Schedule** use case as an example. We can see at least the following scenarios that must be documented:

1. No tasks for this contractor. Screen shots: main screen; an empty task list screen.

2. Contractor cancels schedule changes. Additional screen shots: a task list screen that shows changes; a confirmation dialog box to confirm canceling.

3. Contractor submits an empty schedule. Additional screen shots: an error dialog box.

4. Supervisor rejects the schedule. Additional screen shots: the supervisor's dialog box, which allows approval or rejection; the notice sent to the contractor (possibly more than one kind of notice).

5. Supervisor approves the schedule. Additional screen shots: the notice sent to the Contractor (possibly more than one kind of notice); the changes to the task list.

6. Contractor schedules a task. Additional screen shots: changes to the task list and schedule.

7. Contractor unschedules a task. Additional screen shots: changes to the task list and schedule.

8. Contractor rejects a task. Additional screen shots: changes to the task list; the notice to be sent to the supervisor.

A good documenter will probably find even more scenarios and screen shots within these diagrams.

Summary

In this chapter, you have worked through Step 2 of Five-Step UML in some detail. At this stage of the process, you need to look at all the use case diagrams that you created in Step 1 in order to refine your requirements. What this means in practice is that you should break out the use case into individual steps that illustrate the separate activities involved in realizing the use case, and document these activities as UML Activity Diagrams.

One of the advantages of this type of diagram is that it allows you to put in branches, showing what different activities may occur at different stages of the process depending on whether certain conditions are satisfied, which allows you to express several different scenarios in one diagram. You can also indicate a looping structure with Activity Diagrams, or even structures like a case statement.

Sometimes an Activity Diagram gets too cluttered, particularly if you try to include too much information on it. In this situation, I recommend nesting your Activity Diagram by hiding some of the detail inside subactivity states.

In this chapter, we've worked only through one use case completely as an illustrative example, but you can see how lengthy this process can get when you carry it out for every use case you identified in Step 1. Some use cases will be quite simple, but even on a small project, it's easy to see how much more information you'll uncover about your requirements when you carry out this step. You need to work out how you're going to manage this expansion in requirements, and toward the end of the chapter, I outlined some techniques to help you do this. Because the aim of this step is to understand your requirements in more detail, this expansion in scope is an almost inevitable result, so you should expect it and plan for it.

Finally, we looked at how this increase in detailed information about requirements would affect some of the different members of the team. In particular, the manager needs to focus on how the uncovering of new levels of details in the requirements will affect the estimation of the work that needs to be done. I offered you some different ideas on how you might tackle this. Furthermore, the documenter needs to document the different scenarios identified, whereas the tester can use them to work out some test cases.

In the next chapter, you'll see how to further refine your Activity Diagrams, during Step 3 of Five-Step UML.

CHAPTER 8

Step 3: Assign Your Requirements to Components and Interfaces

WITH THE **KMS** case study, I've been so far focusing on requirements. In Chapter 6, we worked through Step 1 of Five-Step UML, documenting the requirements for the KMS as Use Case Diagrams. In Chapter 7, we delved into more detail on just one of those Use Cases during Step 2 of the process, refining the requirements by looking at the different possible scenarios and documenting them in the form of Activity Diagrams.

In this chapter, you'll move on to Step 3 of Five-Step UML, which is an important step in the move from a requirements model to an architectural one. During this phase, you begin to focus in more detail on how you're going to go about building a solution. I'll show you how to take the refined requirements from Step 2 and use them to identify useful services and user interfaces.

For our KMS case study, we'll be adding swimlanes to the example Activity Diagrams from Chapter 7 and to a number of new Activity Diagrams. The aim of this is to give us a basis of the architectural design in Chapter 9.

As in the last chapter, I won't try to break down every use case here, because I only want to come up with enough swimlanes to demonstrate how to design a .NET architecture. Instead, I have opted to concentrate on some representative use cases for a range of actors—skipping from actor to actor and use case to use case, looking for interesting examples. The full set of diagrams will be found in the online model as it evolves.

Moving from a Requirements Model to an Architectural Model

Your first step in this effort is to define a new architectural model from the requirements model. With a tool like Rational XDE, you can do this by making a new model and then using the clipboard to copy the contents from one model to another.

This architectural model allows you to make changes in the use cases and activities and other elements to conform to and define the architecture without losing all the requirements and business rules knowledge you've gained along the way. As I discussed in Chapter 1, it's important to maintain a separation between your analysis and design models, because they communicate to different audiences.

But it's important that the architectural elements reflect the requirements. Even as you change things, it's important that there be traceability back to the user needs. After all, you don't want to build the wrong system.

Your next step is to define a *bridge model:* a model that contains no elements of its own, but depicts the relationships between elements of other models. I like to put all of these relationships in this separate bridge model so that the individual models remain uncluttered and stand on their own. Usually you only want to look at one model at a time; but in those rare cases where you want to see relations between them, you can look at the bridge model.

The bridge model is by no means a requirement for your UML use. Rather, I find it a convenient artifact of how many UML tools work, allowing me to tie two UML models together without cluttering up either model.

The requirements and architecture packages of the bridge model may be depicted as shown in Figure 8-1. Here, the darker shaded packages indicate the requirements model, whereas the lighter packages are the architectural model.

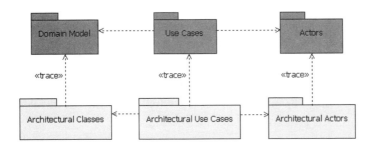

Figure 8-1. Requirements and Architectural packages

The top packages contain the actors, domain objects, and use cases that comprise the requirements model you've developed so far, whereas the bottom packages contain the architectural representations of the same concepts, which start out identical, but will vary as the architecture evolves. The «trace» dependency tells you that the requirements packages contain information that is necessary to understand the architecture packages; and if the requirements change, the architecture will have to change to accommodate the new requirements. (Dependencies were discussed in Chapter 2.)

Similarly, you can add diagrams that show how high-level functionality in the requirements may be comprised of finer-grained operations as the architecture gets closer to design. Often, this indicates the difference between user requirements and functional requirements, as discussed in Chapter 5. For instance, Figure 8-2 shows how in the KMS a simple user requirement becomes four functional requirements (and thus, a change in that user requirement is automatically a change in the functional requirements).

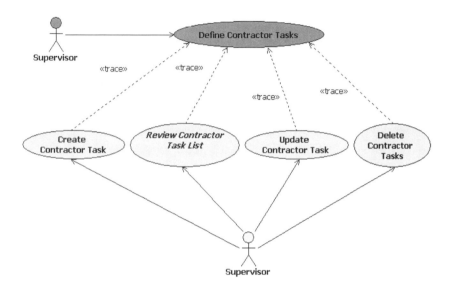

Figure 8-2. Contractor Tasks: user requirements and functional requirements

CRUD

A common analysis pattern is CRUD: Create, Review, Update, and Delete, which is illustrated in Figure 8-2. As Schneider and Winters point out,[1] different practitioners have different views on whether CRUD is one use case or four. Schneider and Winters argue that CRUD is best modeled as four use cases. You'll see that they're right, as you get close to implementation: each part of CRUD is one function that designers must design, developers must code, testers must test, and documenters must explain. But often during initial requirements gathering, it's easier to treat CRUD as one use case. As I described in Chapter 2, use case analysis may be applied at different levels of granularity as the system evolves.

---

1. Geri Schneider and Jason P. Winters, *Applying Use Cases: A Practical Guide, Second Edition* (Addison-Wesley, 2001), pp. 98–99

At this point, you might be asking yourself whether I really draw all those Trace Diagrams. All right, I'll admit it: the answer is no, not always. As I said in Chapter 3, I only draw pictures that I feel answer useful questions. Often, these Trace Diagrams are obvious: Figure 8-1, for example, is one I wouldn't draw (unless I found that someone was confused without it). But Figure 8-2 is a little less obvious: it shows that one user requirement yields multiple functional requirements, with all the management and process burdens that come with those requirements. So I might draw that one. Then again, I might not: I might simply rename my user requirement as **Contractor Task CRUD** (see sidebar "CRUD"), and trust that everyone knows that that implies four functional requirements.

Besides drawing pictures that answer questions, there are two other reasons why I might draw the Trace Diagrams:

- To provide placeholders for Activity Diagrams and related information. For example, each of the separate Create, Review, Update, and Delete use cases might have its own complex logic. I could capture this logic in an Activity Diagram for each use case.

- To support automated requirements management. Some automated requirements tools (such as Rational RequisitePro) can incorporate and maintain these trace dependencies, notifying you when a change in one requirement means that you must revisit other requirements.

Remember that the bridge model is definitely a secondary model: useful for showing how two models are related, but not very useful on its own. Don't spend too much time on it except where it clarifies matters. Think of it as a mental scratch pad for yourself.

Adding Swimlanes to Your Activity Diagrams

Recall that in Chapter 2, you saw how to add swimlanes to your Activity Diagrams to indicate which parts of the system will be responsible for what behavior. At this stage, you want to identify both internal and user interfaces, and use these as the headings for each swimlane, before dragging the various activities, along with related branches, merges, and so on, into those swimlanes. Remember to search for implicit requirements and back-end activities as you add swimlanes in your architecture model. Sometimes you'll find yourself adding and removing swimlanes, and producing different versions of your swimlaned Activity Diagrams before you hit on the right design.

For the rest of this section, I'll show you some examples from various use cases from the KMS case study, so that you can get a clearer idea of how this works in practice. In particular, I'll be focusing on the **Define Contractor Schedule** and **Review Contractor Task List** use cases that we looked at in the last chapter, and also a few new ones: **Request Password**, **View PetCam**, and **Logging**.

So let's get started . . .

Define Contractor Schedule

We'll start with the example use case from Chapter 7, **Define Contractor Schedule**, and see what it looks like when we add swimlanes. The result is shown in Figure 8-3.

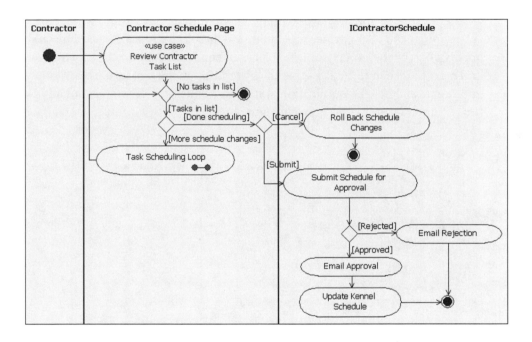

Figure 8-3. Define Contractor Schedule use case, swimlaned

Looking at this picture, you see an actor (**Contractor**), a user interface (**Contractor Schedule Page**), and an interface to scheduling services (**IContractorSchedule**). This is a fairly simple division of responsibility and it becomes clear that there's at least one swimlane missing: a swimlane to represent the supervisor who approves or rejects a schedule. And that leads to a new question (and, naturally, yet more requirements gathering): how does the supervisor learn of the schedule and decide to approve or reject it?

There are two common approaches to a problem like this:

- **Push.** The system directly notifies the supervisor to take action, and then processes the supervisor's action. The supervisor may receive the notification delayed in time, but the approval process is still conceptually driven by the contractor's action.

- **Pull.** The supervisor decides at some point to review a list of all schedules that await approval, and approves or rejects them when they get around to it. This approach implies new use cases—new functional requirements, most likely—that show how the supervisor reviews and approves schedules.

Let's suppose that the development team is fond of push approaches; and sure enough, our client agrees with them. We therefore choose an email mechanism whereby the supervisor will receive an email message for the schedule, and can approve or reject the schedule by replying to the message. This implies another swimlane for a notification system that will notify the supervisor and process their response, as shown in Figure 8-4.

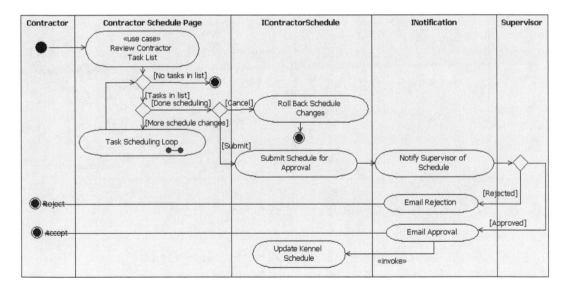

Figure 8-4. Define Contractor Schedule use case, swimlaned, first revision

Note how this diagram also identifies one new activity, **Notify Supervisor of Schedule**. The **IContractorSchedule** interface is responsible for submitting schedules, but not for notifying people; for that, you need an additional activity under the **INotification** interface.

Because we're starting to identify an architecture, you should consider what these swimlanes represent. Some represent actors, whereas others represent various interface constructs, such as user interfaces of programmatic interfaces. In the .NET environment, I like to add stereotypes to the swimlanes that represent the underlying .NET technologies, as shown in Figure 8-5.

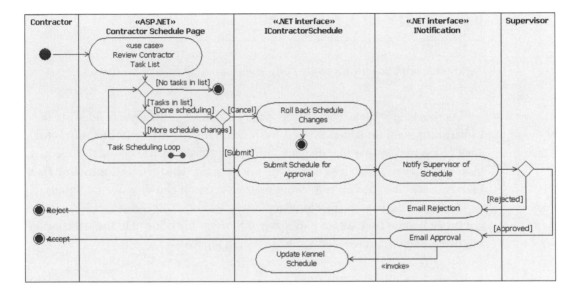

Figure 8-5. Define Contractor Schedule use case, swimlaned, second revision

These stereotypes reflect the preliminary design decisions, and may change when we design the architecture in Chapter 9; but they will help you to think about how swimlanes may interact both within and between machines.

Looking inside the loop body subactivity state (**Task Scheduling Loop**), which I introduced in the last chapter, we can identify more swimlanes, as shown in Figure 8-6.

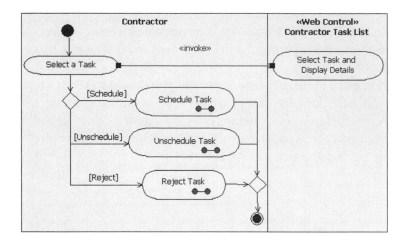

Figure 8-6. Task Scheduling loop body, swimlaned

As this loop is really user driven, pretty much all of the logic resides in the **Contractor** swimlane, but we've added a swimlane to represent the **Contractor Task List**, a Web control that displays the available tasks and details on the selected task. You'll see more of this control when we dig into the **Review Contractor Task List** use case later; but for now, what matters is that it can display task details.

Let's now dig into the three subactivity states shown in Figure 8-6. First, we've got the **Schedule Task** subactivity state, which was introduced in the last chapter (Figure 7-8). You can see swimlanes shown in Figure 8-7.

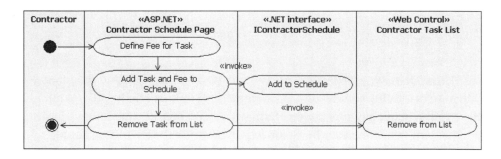

Figure 8-7. Schedule Task subactivity state, swimlaned

Note the two back-end activities added for the swimlanes discovered earlier.

Looking at the **Unschedule Task** subactivity state (originally depicted in Figure 7-9), you can see swimlanes as shown in Figure 8-8.

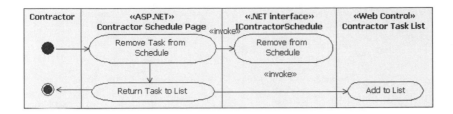

Figure 8-8. Unschedule Task subactivity state, swimlaned

Again, note the two back-end activities added for the swimlanes discovered earlier.

Looking at the **Reject Task** subactivity state (originally depicted in Figure 7-10), you can see swimlanes as shown in Figure 8-9.

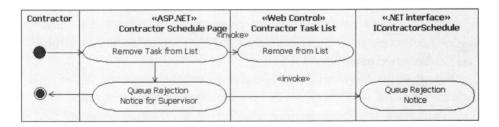

Figure 8-9. Reject Task subactivity state, swimlaned

Note that removing a task from the list is the exact same process as depicted in the swimlaned Activity Diagram for the **Schedule Task** subactivity state shown in Figure 8-7. Here, we've also discovered one back-end activity for the **IContractorSchedule** swimlane.

Review Contractor Task List

So far we've dug into all the constituent activities that were inside the **Define Contractor Schedule** subactivity state, **Task Scheduling Loop**, shown in Figure 8-5. Now we need to examine another activity from that diagram in more detail, **Review Contractor Task List**. Recall from Chapter 7 that this activity represents an included use case, a set of common behavior included in other use cases. We want to show the behavior within that use case, broken into swimlanes as demonstrated in Figure 8-10.

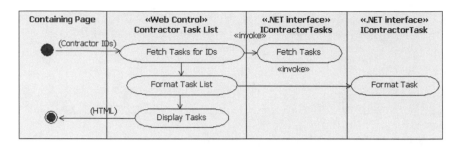

Figure 8-10. Review Contractor Task List activity, swimlaned

In this diagram, the first swimlane represents any ASP.NET page containing the **Contractor Task List**. This page will be responsible for passing in one or more Contractor IDs to use as keys in looking up tasks. In the case of a contractor defining a schedule, this will be the single ID that identifies the contractor. In the case of a supervisor, this will be one or more IDs for contractors whose work the supervisor wants to review. Because a Web control is required to render its contents as HTML, the **Contractor Task List** returns an HTML stream to the **Containing Page**, as indicated in the diagram.

Note that this diagram identifies two new interface swimlanes: **IContractorTasks**, which represents the set of all contractor tasks, and **IContractorTask**, which represents a specific contractor task. The **Fetch Task** activity will return a number of **IContractorTask** objects, and then the **Format Task List** activity will loop over these, formatting each one.

Request Password

Let's go back now to one of the use cases of the **Authorized User** actor, which we looked at in Chapter 6, namely the **Request Password** use case (illustrated in Figure 6-41). In this use case, authorized users may request that their password be emailed to them in case they forget it.

For this example, we'll go for a security procedure similar to many commercial Web sites:

- The user may provide a user name and request that a password be emailed to the email address previously registered for that user name.

- If the user name can't be found, the system will display an error message.

- If for any reason the password may not be delivered, the system will ask the user a previously registered secret question for that user, and request an answer.

- If the secret answer is valid, the system will allow the user to define a new email address, and it will again attempt to email the password.

....

Please Don't Try This at Home!

Note: I am *not* a computer security expert. It's very likely that this password procedure has gaping holes you could drive a Mack truck through. *Please* don't implement this procedure in your systems. Find a real security expert to advise you on user and password security!

....

Now that we know more about the behavior of this use case, we can illustrate it in the form of an Activity Diagram, broken into swimlanes as demonstrated in Figure 8-11.

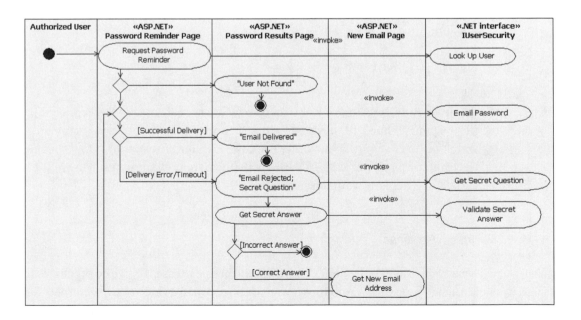

Figure 8-11. Request Password activity, swimlaned

Looking at this picture, you can see swimlanes that represent three ASP.NET pages: one for requesting a password reminder, one for displaying the reminder results (and the secret question, when appropriate), and one for requesting a new email address.

The diagram also shows a new **IUserSecurity** interface to encapsulate all user security information: the ASP.NET pages never directly access the password or the correct secret answer, because all of that information is maintained within a secure component accessed through the interface.

View PetCam

Here, we're going to examine another use case, which we first met in Chapter 6, this time the **View PetCam** use case, initiated by the **End User** actor (see Figure 6-40). Further analysis indicates that this is a general use case with two derived use cases, as shown in Figure 8-12.

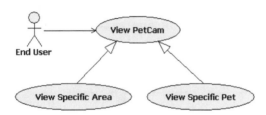

Figure 8-12. View PetCam

In one use case, the viewer selects to view a specific area of the kennel: the puppy pen, perhaps, or maybe the exercise runs, because the viewer wants to watch puppies at play. In the other use case, the viewer selects to view a specific pet: their own pet, perhaps, or perhaps there's a show champion staying in the kennel and her fans want to see her.

Base Use Case

Next we'll examine the behavior within the base use case. The basic process is to launch a video window on the viewer's desktop, open a video stream, connect the video stream to the video window, and switch the video stream to the desired PetCam. This behavior can be broken into swimlanes as shown in Figure 8-13.

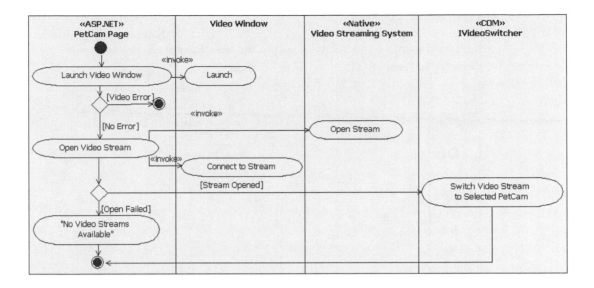

Figure 8-13. View PetCam activity, swimlaned

Looking at this picture, you can see one swimlane that represents an ASP.NET page which launches the viewer's favorite video player on the viewer's desktop, and another swimlane that represents the video player itself.

We have two other swimlanes that represent commercial video systems: one for video stream management, and one for switching video input sources. The **Video Streaming System** is a high-performance native Win32 component distributed as a DLL. We apply a **«Native»** stereotype to its swimlane to indicate that we'll have to use .NET's native DLL-wrapping mechanisms to control this system. The **Video Switcher** is distributed with a simple COM interface, so we apply a **«COM»** stereotype to indicate that we'll use .NET's COM Interop mechanisms to control the switcher.

Keep Telling Yourself: "It's Only an Example"

Compared to what I know about Web cams, I *am* a computer security expert. The operations shown previously are based on my reading of market literature, not on any actual experience with the technology. If you know this technology, please feel free to come up with a better set of interactions.

View Specific Area

Next we'll examine the behavior within the **View Specific Area** use case, as depicted in Figure 8-14.

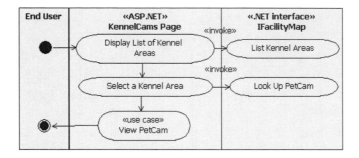

Figure 8-14. View Specific Area use case, swimlaned

The major swimlane in this diagram is a page that lists the available KennelCams (a new marketing buzzword: KennelCams are just PetCams, listed by area instead of by pet). It does so by using the new **IFacilityMap** interface to list all the areas available, and then to find the PetCam for the selected area. The rest of the behavior is encapsulated in the **View PetCam** activity, which represents the base use case.

View Specific Pet

Next we'll examine the behavior within the **View Specific Pet** use case, as depicted in Figure 8-15.

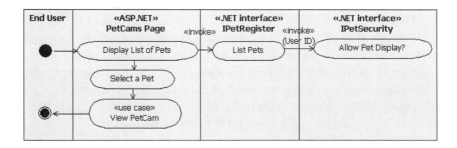

Figure 8-15. View Specific Pet use case, swimlaned

Besides the page that lists the available PetCams, this diagram introduces two new swimlanes. The first, **IPetRegister**, provides services related to the **kennel** registry (e.g., the list of pets currently registered in the kennel). The second, **IPetSecurity**, provides control over a pet's information as specified by the pet owner (as shown in Figure 6-51). In this particular example, the pet owner has previously provided a list of user IDs for users who are allowed to view information on the pet, *including* the information that the pet is registered in the kennel. A pet owner can also allow users to see the pet without regard to user ID. The **IPetRegister** interface uses the **IPetSecurity** interface to generate a list only of those pets that are visible to the specified user. (Note: if a pet owner chooses to hide a pet's information, the pet may still be seen on KennelCams, but will not be named or otherwise identified.)

Logging

Further discussion of the logging requirements reveals the need to log in more detail than was previously understood. In particular, we need to log when a task starts, when it ends, and when it is late. This means that, in addition to the logging use cases that we uncovered back in Chapter 6 (see Figure 6-63), we have more logging use cases, as shown in Figure 8-16.

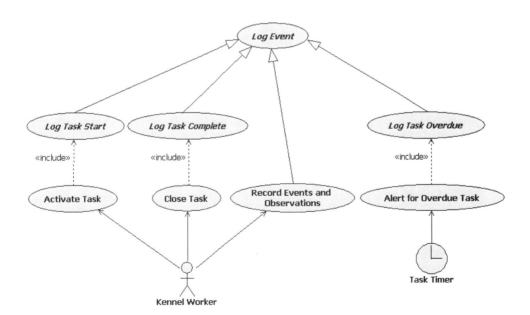

Figure 8-16. Logging use cases

As you can see from the diagram, we have one abstract base use case for logging, and then a number of more specific derived use cases.

You've probably noticed that in this diagram, three of the derived logging use cases—**Log Task Start**, **Log Task Complete**, and **Log Task Overdue**—don't seem to be reused anywhere else. Why are they included use cases? Why aren't they just part of the including use cases? Why can't the including use cases just include **Log Event**?

Although the most common reason for included use cases (by far) is to show common behavior, it's legal to have a use case that is included in only one other use case, as shown in Figure 8-16. My reason for separating the logging use cases from the task use cases was to emphasize exactly what gets logged in each case. If the task use cases directly included **Log Event**, I feel it would be less clear that there are four particular kinds of log events.

For simplicity, however, we'll concentrate here only on the general use case. Its behavior is shown in Figure 8-17.

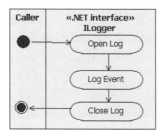

Figure 8-17. Log Event use case, swimlaned

Well, that's certainly simplicity! But it serves two purposes that I wanted served.

First, it demonstrates the use of a **Caller** swimlane to represent the code that calls a particular interface. In the more specific use cases, the **Caller** may be an ASP.NET page, or it may be another interface.

Second, it introduces **ILogger**. This is an interface that I suspect will be architecturally interesting when we get to Chapter 9 (because a lot of components may use the logger); and it also gives us a nice, round 20 user interfaces and interfaces, which I believe will be enough to make Chapter 9 interesting.

That means that with this final diagram, you're ready for Chapter 9. But before we move on, I'll spend the latter part of this chapter taking a quick overview of this step in our Five-Step process, from the point of view of the manager, the tester, and the documenter.

Exercise 801: Swimlane Your Activity Diagrams

Building on Exercise 701, in which you elaborated on your use cases, add swim-lanes to each Activity Diagram. Document each swimlane as an actor, an interface, or a user interface, and document the responsibilities of each.

A Manager's View of Swimlanes and Interfaces

The manager's view of the swimlanes and interfaces should build on the view of refined requirements. The process of adding swimlanes shouldn't have revealed too many new requirements, and it should start giving your architecture team confidence that they can devise a suitable solution.

Staffing

Earlier, you speculated about services your system would need, and thus skills that your team would need. Now, as your architects identify and classify swim-lanes and interfaces, you should know your skill needs much more precisely.

Planning

Even though the requirements likely haven't changed much, it's time to revise your estimate and schedule. In this phase, you make some concrete decisions about things that were only surmises before. The good news is that for the first time, you might even see your estimate decrease: if your system is simpler than you feared, you'll start to recognize that now.

Tracking

The new estimate and schedule shall define new estimating elements that must be tracked.

Reporting

The new tracking requirements imply new reporting, as discussed in Chapter 6.

Correction

The new tracking requirements imply new opportunities for correction, as discussed in Chapter 6.

Risk Management

Now you can start addressing more technical risks:

- If your system is designed around Commercial Off The Shelf (COTS) components, are those components well supported? Will the vendor go out of business at the worst possible moment?

- Is your user interface vision becoming too difficult to use? You may have identified a number of forms and Web pages. Which ones are most critical?

- Does your team understand all the technologies implied by your swimlanes?

These and other technical risks will become more prominent as you flesh out the architecture in Chapter 9.

A Tester's View of Swimlanes and Interfaces

For a tester, the swimlanes indicate isolated units of functionality, units that you may test with—surprise!—unit tests. Each swimlane should lead to a unit test suite for the component it represents; and each activity within a swimlane may become a subsuite, or simply a unit test.

A Documenter's View of Swimlanes and Interfaces

As a documenter, you may have little or no interest in the swimlanes. These will be important if you have to write technical documentation; and they may help you to more precisely identify the screen shots you'll need. But these diagrams start to reveal how the system is built, instead of how it works; and most users don't want to understand that part of the system.

Summary

In this chapter, I've walked you through Step 3 of Five-Step UML. In this stage of your modeling work, you need to look at assigning the various actions involved in the Activity Diagrams developed during Step 2 to the various components that will make up your system—for example, Web pages, Web controls, and .NET interfaces. You can indicate the responsibilities of these different components using swimlanes on your Activity Diagrams.

I illustrated in detail how this works with some examples from our KMS case study, namely some of the **Contractor** Activity Diagrams that we developed in the last chapter, together with some earlier use cases from Chapter 6. That has given us enough components and interfaces to get started organizing an architecture for the KMS in the next chapter.

CHAPTER 9

Step 4: Design Your Architecture

NOW THAT YOU'VE worked through the first three steps of Five-Step UML, you've seen how to design and refine requirements using Use Case Diagrams and Activity Diagrams, and, by adding swimlanes to the Activity diagrams, you began to identify the components and interfaces for your system.

Now it's time to examine these interfaces and user interfaces, and define an architecture that supports them. That's what we do in Step 4 of Five-Step UML. The UML we'll need in this chapter will consist of Component Diagrams that show how the system is constructed and connected and how users interact with it. The main stages involved in designing the architecture are

- Identifying and organizing all your interfaces and user interfaces

- Assigning interfaces and user interfaces to components

- Organizing your components into an overall system architecture

In this chapter, I'll be examining each of these stages in more detail, in particular looking at how they relate to our KMS case study. Along the way, I'll also discuss some common architecture patterns that may be useful to you in your development work.

Note that I won't define the entire architecture for the KMS in this book, but will concentrate instead on the 19 interfaces identified in Chapter 8 and on the components identified in the KMS spec. By concentrating on part of the system in detail like this, you should get a better idea of the overall process, and how you can apply it to your own modeling work.

Why Are There Components in the Requirements Spec?

I have no idea, but it happens all the time: in the process of defining their needs, users and clients try to define the solution to those needs as well.

Depending on the source of your requirements, there can be a number of reasons for this:

- The users are concerned about easy user interfaces, and they've specified components that they believe reflect the UI.

- The users have tried to analyze the system in terms of areas of related functionality, and they believe that those are natural ways to structure the system as well.

- The users are requesting additions and modifications to an existing system, and the components that they describe reflect and fit within the existing components.

- The users are following some document template from some book or process guide, and the template indicates where you put components. (This is actually one of the major reasons that there are components in the KMS spec.)

Regardless, if components are already specified, it never hurts to use them as a starting point for your architecture. Like all design, architecture is a sloppy, iterative process that starts from vague ideas and evolves into concrete design decisions.

What Do I Mean by "Architecture?"

Unfortunately, *architecture* is a term with a wide range of definitions. (Some people seem to think that architecture is spelled n-t-i-e-r.) Different people use the term different ways, but I think most will accept certain common tasks as part of architecture:

- Decomposition of a system into various subsystems

- Definition of the relations among and communications between the subsystems

- Assignment of functionality to the various subsystems

The Unified Process—and certain other processes—identifies at least two more architectural tasks:

- Preliminary design of critical subsystems

- Preliminary design of critical functionality

In the Unified Process, the architecture process is broadly defined as analysis and design of "architecturally significant" elements of the problem and solution: those key elements that could shape the entire solution. In essence, it's about identifying what "looks like trouble." I think this is a very useful, pragmatic definition; but it's beyond the scope of this book. (For much more on this topic, see the Three Amigos' *Unified Software Development Process* [Addison-Wesley, 1999].) So to keep things simple, I'll try to focus primarily on architecture as the modular structure of the system; but what you'll see is that thoroughly defining this modular structure almost inevitably requires you to delve into some deeper behavioral questions, leading you closer to the Unified Process view of architecture.

Gathering and Documenting Your Interfaces

Before you can gather interfaces, you need a place in which to gather them. Because these are the means by which the architecture is stitched together, I prefer that these be placed in a new top-level package called **Interfaces**. This package can be shared among many models, but it should be controlled as part of the architecture model.

Let's see how this works for our KMS case study. Based on the work in Chapter 8, we add the interfaces (formerly represented simply as swimlanes) to the model, as shown in Figure 9-1.

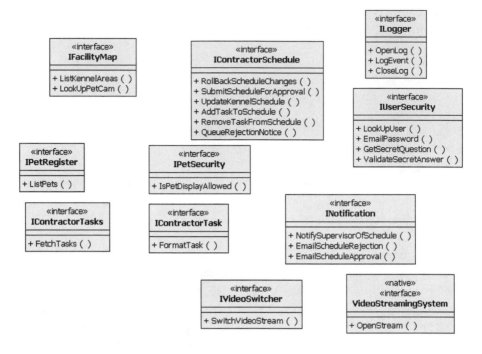

Figure 9-1. Initial KMS interfaces

Hmmm . . . getting pretty cluttered, and we haven't really analyzed any of these in depth yet. I'm not *positive* that I'd subdivide and organize for just 11 interfaces, as you see here. Once you start looking at a problem in more detail, however, and really analyze your interfaces in detail, it's likely that number of interfaces will only grow. So it's worth dividing these interfaces into packages.

When dividing your interfaces into packages, a useful technique is to think of functionality that is common or related, and then package the interfaces accordingly. So for our KMS example, I'll group together the following interfaces:

- Because I'd like to keep the pet-related functionality together, I'll create a **Pet Interfaces** package, although so far this contains only one interface, **IPetRegister.**

- **IContractorTasks** is a list of **IContractorTask** interface instances, and an **IContractorSchedule** should reference **IContractorTask** interface instances. So I put all of those in a single package, **Contractor Interfaces.**

- I want to isolate the video subsystem to keep it simple, so I put **IVideoSwitcher** and **VideoStreamingSystem** in their own package, **Video Interfaces.**

- I expect that security functions will share a lot of common code, so I put **IPetSecurity** and **IUserSecurity** in a **Security Interfaces** package.

- I expect that certain functionality will be broadly applicable across the entire system, so I put those interfaces in an **Infrastructure Interfaces** package. At this point, that package contains the **ILogger** and **INotification** interfaces.

- Two interfaces seem unrelated to the rest, and seem to have no common functionality. So I stuck each in its own package, suspecting that more will be added to those packages later. I put the **IPetRegister** interface in the **Pet Interfaces** package, and I put the **IFacilityMap** interface in the **Facility Interfaces** package.

These packages are shown in Figure 9-2.

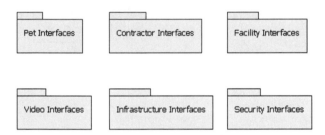

Figure 9-2. KMS interface packages

It's likely that, as the design evolves, I'll find some of this packaging is wrong, or incomplete. I'll repackage the interfaces as needed. In the end, I often find that each package corresponds to one component in the architecture.

Now, if you're going to settle on a good architecture, it's time to add meat to the interfaces. You need more than just names of activities: you need to decide what information is passed to and returned from each interface operation, as well as the specific mechanism for each interface. To do these tasks, we'll explore each of these packages in more detail in the sections that follow.

Pet Interfaces

This package is very simple (so far), containing only one interface: **IPetRegister**, the interface for maintaining information on the pets currently registered in the kennel. As we did with the swimlanes, we'll stereotype this as a .NET interface.

The **IPetRegister** interface currently contains only one method, **ListPets**. The purpose of this method is to produce a formatted list of pets in the kennel registry. Recall from the **View Specific Pet** use case, which we looked at in the last chapter, that this method should return *only* those pets whose names the end user is authorized to display. That seems wrong to me: the name **ListPets** implies listing all the pets; and I hate misleading names. I can see two ways to design that restriction. First, we could change the name to something clearer for the usage, such as **ListPetsForDisplay**. Although cumbersome, that's accurate. Second, we could pass a parameter, such as **ForDisplay**, that tells the operation when to filter the list and when to return the entire list. That works, but it strikes me as a lousy name, and too special purpose. After a little thought, I decided that I like the second approach, but I don't like the parameter name. Instead, I prefer the concept of "public" and "private" lists, which makes the operation a little more widely useful. To implement this idea, we'll need to change the method's parameter to a Boolean named **PublicOnly**.

We also need to select a format for returning the list, such that it can be easily displayed in the **PetCams Page** and perhaps elsewhere. In the .NET world, a very common mechanism for passing structured data is XML, so let's have the method return an **XmlDocument**, a class (from the .NET **System.Xml** namespace) that reads and writes and otherwise manipulates XML documents.[1] This decision also implies that **IPetRegister** depends on **XmlDocument**, because it must know how to create and return it.

These decisions add up to create the diagram in Figure 9-3.

Figure 9-3. The Pet Interfaces package

Note the use of the **«.NET interface»** stereotype.

---

1. There's just no room to do justice to the topic of XML here. If you don't know XML, it's enough to know that XML is a structured, tagged text format for documents and elements of documents. Tags are delimited with **<AngleBrackets>** and closed with **</AngleBrackets>** (note the "/"). Between the delimiters are found the values of the tags; and within the opening delimiter, you can have attributes for a tag. It's common to have a schema file that defines the legal tags and attributes and relations for a particular type of XML document; but it's not required, and I won't bother with a schema for this book. You'll see samples of XML documents in Chapter 10. For much more on the topic of XML, see Soo Mee Foo and Wei Meng Lee, *XML Programming Using the Microsoft XML Parser* (Apress, 2002).

Contractor Interfaces

This package contains three interfaces (all with a **«.NET interface»** stereotype):

- **IContractorSchedule** to represent a schedule of contractor tasks

- **IContractorTasks** to represent a list of contractor tasks

- **IContractorTask** to represent the tasks themselves

A little thought reveals that these interfaces are very closely related: the purpose of an **IContractorTasks** object is to retrieve **IContractorTask** objects; and an **IContractorSchedule** object should build a schedule out of **IContractorTask** objects (perhaps stored in an **IContractorTasks** object; but for now, that's a design decision, not an architecture decision).

The IContractorTask Interface

Let's first look at the simplest of these interfaces: **IContractorTask**. It currently contains only a single method, **FormatTask**. As we saw in the last chapter, the purpose of this method is to format a given task for HTML output.

On further reflection, XML might be even more appropriate, so we could contemplate whether the method should return an **XmlElement** object to represent the task. This *sounds* really clever: we could build an XML document up piece by piece. But past experience with the XML document object model (XML DOM) has given me advance warning that this could lead to problems. How so? Well, under XML DOM, XML elements can't be created on their own, only within an existing document. So for **FormatTask** to work with an XML document, we could follow one of three strategies:

- Create the **XmlElement** object from the document outside of **FormatTask** and pass the element to the operation.

- Pass the document to **FormatTask** as an argument, so that **FormatTask** can create an element as needed.

- Give up on returning an **XmlElement**, and simply return a string; but that then requires you to manually format and concatenate the collected strings.

Speaking for myself, I'm too lazy to write my own XML concatenation logic and whenever possible, I'll choose to use .NET's built-in code rather than my own, so I wouldn't recommend the latter approach. Of the other two approaches,

I prefer the second: it allows **FormatTask** to decide that (for whatever reason) no element is needed; whereas the former approach *always* creates an element, needed or not.

And now, knowing how we plan to implement this, we find that **FormatTask** doesn't really need to return anything at all: because the operation can work on the document directly, the return is superfluous.

The IContractorTasks Interface

Looking at **IContractorTasks**, I begin to suspect our work on the **Contractor Activity Diagrams** is incomplete. Figure 8-10 doesn't show how the **Contractor Task List** Web control formats a list of tasks. What's missing here is a mechanism for iterating through a list of tasks, formatting each in turn. Well, if **IContractorTasks** represents a list of contractor tasks, then it ought to include the list behavior as part of the interface itself.

.NET already defines a number of useful interfaces for collections, including one for a collection that may be enumerated: **IEnumerable**. This interface and the related interface, **IEnumerator**, form an implementation of the **Iterator** pattern identified by Gamma et al.,[2] which is a mechanism for stepping through the elements of a collection in order, without knowing anything about how the collection is implemented (nor even what "in order" means, only that there *is* an order). The **Iterator** pattern for a collection allows calling code to ask for an iterator, which may be reset to the start of the collection, moved through the collection, and used to read the current element of the collection. In .NET, **IEnumerable** is an interface a collection may implement, and **IEnumerator** is an iterator through the collection. **IEnumerator** may be implemented by the collection itself, or it may be implemented by another class. (The point of interfaces, after all, is to make those implementation decisions invisible and irrelevant to calling code.) So a common example of the implementation of **IEnumerable** and **IEnumerator** might look like Figure 9-4.

---

2. Erich Gamma, Richard Helm, Ralph Johnson, and John Vlissides, *Design Patterns: Elements of Reusable Object-Oriented Software* (Addison-Wesley, 1995), pp. 257–271

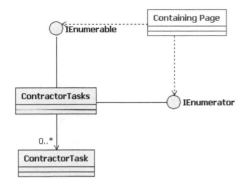

Figure 9-4. An example of the structure of a collection with IEnumerable and IEnumerator

So using **IEnumerable** and **IEnumerator**, we could revise the diagram in Figure 8-10 to create the two new swimlanes, as shown in Figure 9-5.

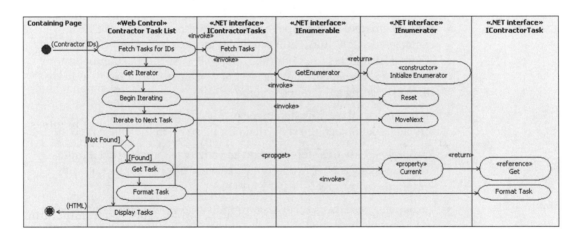

Figure 9-5. An example of using a collection with IEnumerable and IEnumerator

The **GetEnumerator** method of **IEnumerable** is responsible for creating and returning an **IEnumerator** interface that enumerates through the underlying collection. Once you have the **IEnumerator** interface, its **Reset** method resets the enumerator to before the start of the collection, and its **MoveNext** method moves the enumerator ahead one item. **MoveNext** returns **true** if there was a next item, **false** if it has reached the end of the collection. So a simple loop of **MoveNext** calls will step you through the collection.

What's with Those Funky Stereotypes?

In Figure 9-5, I introduce some new stereotypes for transitions and for activities. I find some of these to be useful for modeling .NET systems in particular, and others useful for modeling in general:

- **«return».** I use this stereotype on a transition between swimlanes to indicate that the originating swimlane is not necessarily calling any code on the target swimlane, but is simply returning the target swimlane for use by other activities and swimlanes. I commonly use this in conjunction with my **«invoke»** stereotype to indicate a return from **«invoke»**. For example, the **GetEnumerator** method is invoked in Figure 9-5, and the **IEnumerator** interface is returned. I may also use this in conjunction with the **«reference»** stereotype (see the last entry in this list) to indicate that I'm creating a reference to some object.

- **«constructor».** I use this stereotype on an activity to indicate the constructor of an object, the steps that take place when the object is created.

- **«property».** I use this stereotype on an activity to indicate that it represents accessing a .NET property. I usually use this in conjunction with **«propput»** or **«propget»** (see the next entry in this list).

- **«propput».** I use this stereotype on a transition when setting the value of a .NET property. Similarly, I use the **«propget»** stereotype on a transition when getting the value of a .NET property.

- **«reference».** I use this stereotype on an activity to indicate that I'm creating a reference to some object. For example, in Figure 9-5, the **Current** method of **IEnumerator** returns a reference to an **IContractorTask** interface.

Remember, as with most stereotypes, these are part of a particular dialect of UML. I present them here to communicate certain ideas, which is (of course) my goal in using UML. If you find them useful, great; if not, no problem.

But Figure 9-5 is needlessly complicated: we don't want **IContractorTasks** to *contain* a collection, we want it to *be* a collection. Similarly, we want **IContractorTask** to be "responsible" for its membership in the collection. We can accomplish both of these goals through generalization, as shown in Figure 9-6.

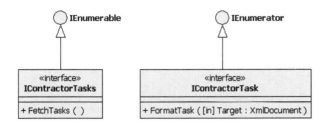

Figure 9-6. Generalization of contractor task interfaces

This allows us to redraw the diagram in Figure 9-4 as shown in Figure 9-7.

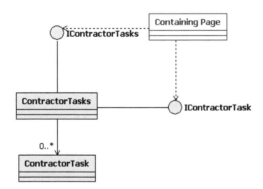

Figure 9-7. Contractor tasks and associated interfaces

Finally, this allows us to redraw our swimlaned Activity Diagram in Figure 9-5 in a much simpler fashion, as shown in Figure 9-8.

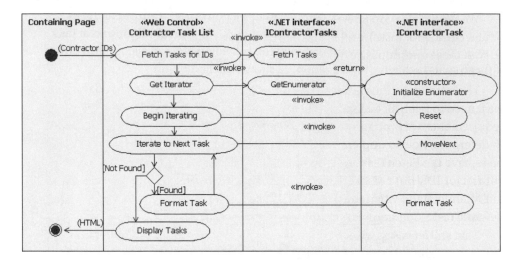

Figure 9-8. Displaying contractor tasks through the contractor task interfaces

Remember, I told you that trying to precisely define the interfaces between components would necessarily entail doing some deeper design work. Sometimes it's the only way to answer the interface questions.

Figures 9-5 and 9-8 also point out another aspect of the **IContractorTasks** interface: it doesn't represent just a list of tasks, but more specifically a list of tasks assigned to a list of contractor IDs. We need to determine a format for that list of contractor IDs, and we have many possible choices:

- Create a simple **ContractorID** class and a related collection class, and pass the collection around.

- Create an **IContractorID** interface and a related collection interface. This would leave the implementation of the interfaces at a lower level.

- Pass the contractor IDs as a collection of strings.

- Pass the contractor IDs as one long concatenated string.

- Pass the contractor IDs as an XML document.

- Make the list of contractor IDs a property of the **IContractorTasks** interface.

We should also consider whether we ever want to fetch all tasks (not just particular contractor tasks), and if so, whether that should be a separate method. To answer these questions, we need once again to consider our implementation in a little more depth.

The latter questions are easier questions, for me. I foresee that it's *likely* that we'll need to fetch all tasks at some point (indeed, had we fully analyzed the requirements, we probably would have already found the need), so we only need to determine how to implement that functionality. One approach would simply be to have the **FetchTasks** operation return all tasks if it has not passed a list of contractor IDs; but I dislike optional parameters. It's too easy for a programmer not to understand when the parameters need to be supplied. So we'll add a **FetchAllTasks** operation for that purpose.

That still leaves us with the question of how to pass the list of contractor IDs. For that, we should consider how these will be used. The **Contractor Task List** Web control in Figure 9-8 is hosted in an ASP.NET Web page; so the list must be provided in a format consistent with what we expect from Web pages. Thinking about the user interface, it seems plausible that the supervisor will select a number of contractors from a list control; and the selection within that control will be passed in an HTTP request as a set of values for that control. In ASP.NET, when we retrieve these list control parameters, they are returned as a string that is a comma-delimited list. Because this is the format that will be most convenient to read from the HTTP request, we'll use it as the input parameter for **FetchTasks**. Note that this conveniently defers (for now) the question of what a contractor ID looks like. As long as it can be represented as a string, that's good enough.

The IContractorSchedule Interface

That leaves us with a final contractor interface, **IContractorSchedule**, which is an interface for building and maintaining schedules. Because it will be used in the stateless world of Web pages, we'll probably need some sort schedule ID to determine which schedule to maintain. Consistent with the decision for contractor IDs, we'll pass these as strings. In fact, because much of the KMS is Web-based and the Web is at heart a text-based protocol, we'll make this a general rule: all unique element IDs in the system are passed as strings. We'll add the necessary ID parameters to the methods of **IContractorSchedule**, ending with a final diagram of the interfaces in this package as shown in Figure 9-9.

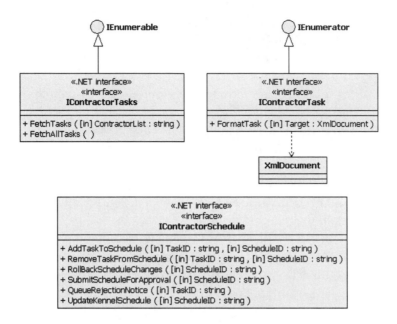

Figure 9-9. The Contractor Interfaces package

Facility Interfaces

This package currently contains only one interface (with a «.NET interface» stereotype): **IFacilityMap**, representing a map of a kennel facility. This interface contains two operations.

The first is an operation to return a list of kennel areas. As with the **ListPets** operation of **IPetRegister**, we'll choose to have this operation work on an XML document. In this case, we'll make the operation send back the document as its return value, so that the document may be entirely created and filled within the operation.

The second is an operation for finding a PetCam, given an area ID. The area ID will be a string, of course; but in what format will information about the PetCam itself be returned? Well, without knowing the details of the video system (remember, I'm making this video streaming technology up as I go along), I'm going to postulate that it's some sort of handle to a stream within the streaming system. It happens that .NET provides a structure, **IntPtr**, to represent such handles used in native code. This sounds like a good return type for this operation.

With these decisions in mind, this package would look like what is shown in Figure 9-10.

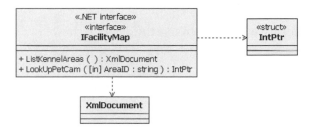

Figure 9-10. The Facility Interfaces package

Video Interfaces

This package contains the interfaces for controlling the video system (as described in regard to Figure 8-13): **IVideoSwitcher**, representing a third-party COM interface to allow switching between video streams, and **VideoStreamingSystem**, a DLL of functions for opening and controlling streams. Both should involve **IntPtr** objects to represent stream handles. You can add the COM interface to a VS .NET project, and VS .NET will automatically generate a wrapper class that will make the COM interface look like a .NET interface. For native code operations in DLLs, .NET defines a special attribute, **DllImport**. When this attribute is applied to an operation, .NET does not generate code for the operation. Instead, it generates code to load a specific DLL, and then translates all calls to that operation into calls to a function within that DLL. So my practice is to create a class that represents the DLL, with each function within the DLL being a static method of the class. Following this practice, the code for the **VideoStreamingSystem** would look something like this:

```
class VideoStreamingSystem
{
    [DllImport("MyVideoLibrary.DLL", EntryPoint="OpenStream",
ExactSpelling=true,
                CallingConvention=CallingConvention.StdCall)]
    public static extern IntPtr OpenStream(int StreamNumber);
}
```

Because the **OpenStream** operation is static, it may be called with code that looks like this:

```
IntPtr streamHandle = VideoStreamingSystem.OpenStream( 1 );
```

And the interfaces in this package will then look like the diagram shown in Figure 9-11.

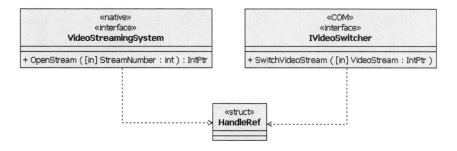

Figure 9-11. The Video Interfaces package

Infrastructure Interfaces

This package contains two interfaces for common functionality that will be useful in many parts of the system. One of these, **ILogger**, records events that happen at given points in time. The other, **INotification**, provides notification of events and decisions.

ILogger is the easier of these two interfaces. It has methods for opening and closing the log and for recording a log entry. A log entry should include a source ID (representing either a person or an automated system), a time, and details.

As it has been used so far, **INotification** is probably too specific to justify calling it part of the infrastructure. It has only been used to send schedule-specific messages via email. It should really be more general purpose: it should support any text message, and it should support multiple mechanisms for notification (email, paging, pop-up messages, printouts, etc.). The target of a message should indicate the preferred method of notification, and the notification system should select the appropriate mechanism without the caller having to know the details.

Given these choices, the interfaces in this package are depicted in Figure 9-12.

```
          «.NET interface»
           «interface»
           INotification

+ NotifyTarget ( [in] TargetID : string , [in] Contents : string )
```

```
          «.NET interface»
           «interface»
             ILogger

+ OpenLog ( )
+ LogEvent ( [in] SourceID : string , [in] Time : DateTime , [in] Details : string )
+ CloseLog ( )
```

```
   «struct»
   DateTime
```

Figure 9-12. The Infrastructure Interfaces package

Security Interfaces

This package contains two interfaces for managing security: **IPetSecurity** and
IUserSecurity. The pet security interface determines whether to display a pet's
name (based on a user ID). The user security interface manages user IDs, passwords,
and secret questions and answers. These interfaces are depicted in Figure 9-13.

```
          «.NET interface»
           «interface»
           IPetSecurity

+ IsPetDisplayAllowed ( [in] UserID : string ) : bool
```

```
          «.NET interface»
           «interface»
           IUserSecurity

+ LookUpUser ( [in] UserID : string )
+ EmailPassword ( [in] UserID : string )
+ GetSecretQuestion ( [in] UserID : string ) : string
+ ValidateSecretAnswer ( [in] UserID : string , [in] Answer : string ) : bool
```

Figure 9-13. The Security Interfaces package

Interfaces and Classes in UML 2.0: Ports

UML 2.0 introduces *structured classes,* classes with internal structure and behavior. As I read about UML 2.0, I can't really see a lot of difference between the concepts of components and of structured classes; but I'm still researching. One major difference, I suppose, is that a component need not have structure inside—indeed, need not be Object Oriented in any sense—as long as it has well-defined interfaces that other components can use. But a structured class is specifically a class with objects "inside" it, along with structured relations between those objects. So for right now, I'm thinking of structured classes as particular ways to envision Object-Oriented components.

One other important new concept has been introduced to work with structured classes: *ports.* The idea of a port is like an interface, but more: a port defines a set of interfaces, including ones that the structured class provides and ones that the structured class *requires;* and more importantly, it also defines the protocols through which these interfaces can be used to do work. Whereas the methods of an interface are task oriented, the protocols of a port are more goal oriented. Many UML architects have discovered that it's not enough to specify the operations available through an interface, because the implementers need to know how to *use* the operations, not just call them.

Although no UML tool today supports the concept of ports, you can model the port concept as a container class with the relevant interfaces as nested classes inside the container. You can also nest Interaction Diagrams (Collaboration and Sequence Diagrams) inside the port to document the protocols. You can then give the container class a «**port**» stereotype, along with a custom icon. The standard icon for a port is a solid square that sits on the edge of a structured class and is associated with an object within the structured class, as shown in Figure 9-14.

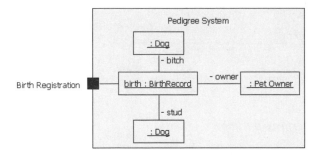

Figure 9-14. An example of a UML 2.0 structured class, with a port

Building on Exercise 801, in which you swimlaned your Activity Diagrams, document your interfaces. Define the operations, parameters, return values, and protocols to support the responsibilities of each interface. Define relations between the interfaces, and package and organize the interfaces as appropriate.

Gathering and Documenting Your User Interfaces

In this section, we'll go through a similar process as in the last section, but this time focusing on the user interfaces.

In any project, you'll need a place in which to gather your user interfaces, just as with your interfaces. These user interfaces represent what the Unified Process calls *boundary classes:* classes that represent the boundary between the system and what lies outside. But unlike interfaces—which may be contracts between parts of the system, and thus must be maintained consistently between the parts—these user interfaces are "one sided" in a sense. If you change them, you have to change the code that implements them, but you don't have to change any code that uses them (although test plans and documentation are another matter). So each user interface *could* be maintained solely within the component that implements it, rather than at the architectural level.

The user interfaces we've identified so far in the KMS case study play very specific roles in the requirements themselves, and are expected to gather particular information that will be needed in other parts of the architecture. So we'll place them in a new top-level package called **User Interfaces**. This package can be shared among many models, but it should be controlled as part of the architecture model.

Then, based on our work in Chapter 8, we'll add the user interfaces (formerly represented simply as swimlanes) to the model, as shown in Figure 9-15.

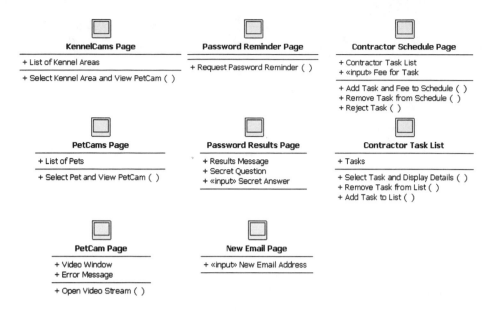

Figure 9-15. Initial KMS user interfaces

Note how, in reviewing the user interface swimlanes, I've also reviewed the information displayed within and maintained within each user interface. Here, information displayed to the user is modeled as attributes, and information provided by the user as attributes with an **«input»** stereotype. As you'd expect, actions that the user can take through a user interface are modeled as operations of that user interface.

The user interfaces identified so far are (barely) few enough to make a comprehensible diagram by themselves. As we add more user interfaces in further analysis and design, we'll certainly find more than can easily be displayed in a single diagram or understood as a single set. We'll need to package these, much as we packaged our interfaces earlier in the chapter. One likely set of packages is displayed in Figure 9-16.

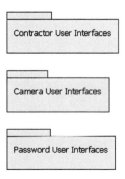

Figure 9-16. KMS user interface packages

We can further analyze these user interfaces as we need (and as time permits) in order to

- Identify types and formats for information displayed.

- Identify types and formats for information entered.

- Create prototype screens.

- Design the flow of operations with and between user interfaces, using Activity Diagrams and Sequence Diagrams, as appropriate.

But usually, these are user interface design concerns, and not architecturally significant. So for now, we'll move on to component assignment.

Exercise 902: Gather and Document Your User Interfaces

Building on Exercise 901, document your user interfaces. Define the fields, inputs, and operations to support the responsibilities of each user interface. Define relations between the user interfaces, and package and organize the user interfaces as appropriate. Define the target mechanism for the user interface: Web-based, desktop, or some other mechanism.

Assigning Interfaces and User Interfaces to Components

Once all of the interfaces and user interfaces have been organized into packages and documented, you need to find a place in your architecture model to show the relations between components and interfaces.

For our KMS case study, we'll add a package, **Architectural Components**, to our model, which will represent the components and the roles they play within the architecture. (Later, we'll give each component its own model to reflect its design in detail; but we're not there yet.) Then we'll add an architectural overview diagram to that package, and we'll add all of the interfaces and user interfaces, as shown in Figure 9-17.

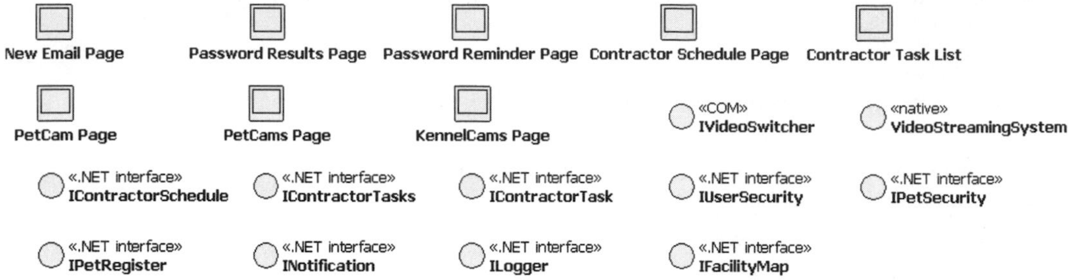

Figure 9-17. KMS interfaces and user interfaces

Well, this diagram might not tell us much, but it's only a start. Now we need to begin assigning these elements to components. We can think in terms of three broad kinds of components:

- UI components that provide user interfaces

- Functional components that provide rules, behavior, structure, and storage for the UI components

- Hybrid components that have aspects of both UI and functional components (I'll try to avoid such hybrid components, though they may be the most sensible solution for very simple components.)

We'll start with the more straightforward task: assigning the user interfaces to UI components, and then we'll move on to assigning interfaces to the functional components. Once we've done that, we'll see what other components we have to add to our model.

Assigning User Interfaces to UI Components

When you begin to assign your user interfaces to UI components, you have to make some technology decisions. (That's a big part of what architecture is about, anyway.) To wit: how is each user interface going to be implemented? Some possibilities include

- A desktop form: possibly stand-alone, possibly one form of many provided by a given component.

- A custom control, designed to be hosted within a desktop form to provide custom user interface capabilities.

- A Web form, for access via Web browsers. You may want to further specify whether the form is specific to desktop browsers or generalized for handheld browsers such as some cellular phones and PDAs.

- A Web control, designed to be hosted within a Web form to provide custom user interface capabilities expressed as HTML.

- A console application, consisting of a number of questions to be asked and answered.

- A batch input, consisting of a collection of records (a file or a stream, most likely) to be submitted for processing.

- A voice interface, consisting of a set of messages and responses.

- A telephone interface, consisting of a set of menus or prompts, and to which the user responds by pressing telephone keys.

- An image scanner, through which a user can input images.

- A barcode scanner, with which a user can scan bar codes.

- User input devices such as joysticks, trackballs, digitizing pads, waldoes, etc.

- Hybrid combinations, such as a handheld barcode scanner with a built-in PDA on which the user can run Web forms.

In our KMS case study, all of the user interfaces identified so far are designed for Web use: **Contractor Task List** as a Web control, the rest as Web forms. We could model each individual form as an individual component, but although this is a valid way to model ASP.NET pages, it doesn't scale well: as the number of pages in a complex system grows, so does the number of components, which means the architecture gets unnecessarily complex. A better approach is to define a component that represents an entire Web site or Web folder (with, naturally, a **«Web folder»** stereotype). Thus, the user interfaces from Figure 9-17 might be assigned to components as shown in Figure 9-18.

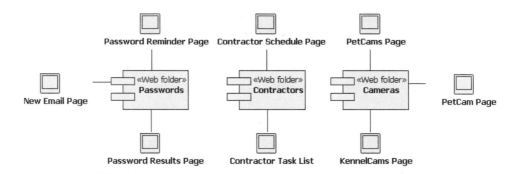

Figure 9-18. KMS user interfaces and Web folder components

Then if we wish, we can show the individual ASPX pages within these components in separate diagrams. You've already seen how classes can have associations between them; and in Chapter 4, you also saw that associations can be navigable, indicating a "flow" or "ownership" relationship. Although it's less common, you can also have associations and navigability between components. Thus, to see these components in more detail, we can show each Web folder containing the ASPX pages that provide its user interfaces, as demonstrated in Figures 9-19 to 9-21.

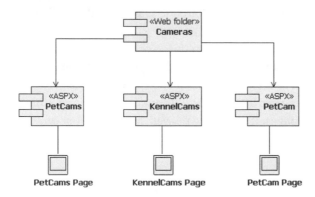

Figure 9-19. KMS camera user interface components

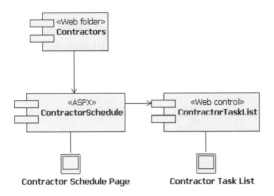

Figure 9-20. KMS contractor user interface components

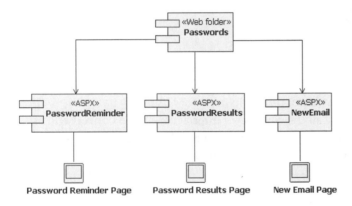

Figure 9-21. KMS password user interface components

Note the use of two new stereotypes: **«ASPX»** to represent the code-behind class for an ASP.NET page, and **«Web control»** to represent the code that interprets the contents of a Web control and renders those contents as HTML. Note also how the **«Web control»** component is referenced by an **«ASPX»** component, reflecting how the actual control resides within the Web page.

Assigning Interfaces to Functional Components

Next, we need to assign our interfaces to functional components. In this instance, we have fewer technology decisions to make for the KMS than we did for user interfaces: we've decided to build a .NET application, so most of our functional components will be .NET components. The rest are Commercial Off The Shelf (COTS) components, so you don't have to decide how to implement them.

(In other systems where .NET is not mandated, you may have to make many more technology decisions to define your architecture.) Thus, the interfaces from Figure 9-17 might be assigned to components as shown in Figure 9-22.

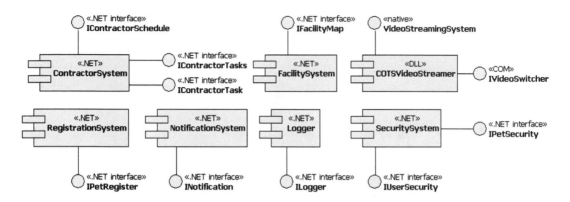

Figure 9-22. KMS interfaces and components

How did I arrive at these component definitions? Simply by trying to group related interfaces. Certainly all the contractor interfaces work in concert and on common data, so it makes sense for them to all be provided by a single component. Similarly, I decided to have a central component for all security, so I assigned the security interfaces to it. And the two video interfaces are COTS, remember, so we're stuck with how they're implemented: a DLL with some native API functions and with a COM interface for embedding in windows. The remaining interfaces all seemed unrelated to any other interfaces (so far), so each got its own component. (Note also that, much as I predicted earlier, the interface packages ended up very closely analogous to the final components.)

Notice the use of two new stereotypes: «.NET» to indicate a generic .NET component, and «DLL» to indicate a native API DLL. You'll also commonly use more specific .NET stereotypes: «ASPX» and «Web control», as described previously; «class library» to indicate a .NET library of classes designed solely for use within other components; «Web service» to indicate a Web service, as described in Chapter 4; and «.NET service» to indicate a service that runs independently and may be controlled through the Win32 service API.

Adding User-Specified Components

Next, let's consider the components identified in Section 2 of the functional spec for the KMS. Again, we shouldn't reject these out of hand simply because they're not requirements: they may make a useful starting point (we can think of them as candidate components); and it may not hurt to meet customers' expectations of how the system will be built (unless those expectations aren't feasible). So let's consider the following:

- **Accounting Operations.** It's certainly true that we'll need accounting functions, so we'll add this component.

- **Contractor Operations.** We already have a **ContractorSystem** component, so this is covered.

- **Facility Information.** We already have a **FacilitySystem** component, so this is covered.

- **Franchise Information.** We'll need a way to manage franchise information, so we'll add this component.

- **Inventory Operations.** We'll need a way to manage inventory, so we'll add this component.

- **PetCam.** We already have the **Cameras** Web folder to represent the user interface through which PetCams are accessed; and we also have the **COTSVideoStreamer**, the third-party library for running the cameras and accessing the streams. It's possible we'll find a need for a third video component; but for now, we'll leave this candidate component out.

- **Pet Information.** We currently have one "pet" interface, **IPetRegister**, and it has been assigned to a component; but after a little thought, we can see that interface is more about registration and kennels than about pets themselves, which is why we assign it to a component called **RegistrationSystem**. That means that we don't (yet) have a component for pet information itself. We'll add this component.

- **Pet Location.** We haven't even begun to investigate the pet location architecture, and we know you'll need *something* for that; so we'll add this component.

- **Reception Operations.** Here's another area we've missed so far, so we'll add this component.

- **Reservation Operations.** We already have the **RegistrationSystem**, so this is covered.

- **Supervisor Operations.** Surprisingly, we haven't analyzed any supervisor architecture yet. We'll add this component.

- **Vendor Information.** Here's another area we've missed so far, so we'll add this component.

- **Veterinary Information.** Here's yet another area we've missed so far, so we'll add this component.

So the new components are those depicted in Figure 9-23.

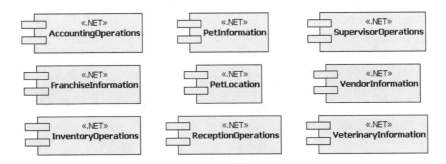

Figure 9-23. User-specified KMS components

Note also that these user-specified components are mostly described in terms of behavior and user interaction. In other words, they're most likely just UI components. As we analyze and architect more thoroughly, we may very likely find that there are multiple functional components lying beneath these UI components, or that some of these will work best as hybrid components.

Add What's Missing

Finally, we should look at all our components, and think about what's missing. Often, a focus on external requirements leading in is better at catching user interface components and those just behind the user interface than it is at catching "deeper" components that provide low-level services and foundations for the system. So we need to consider whether any components are obviously missing from our KMS case study; one obvious answer is a database. For simplicity's sake, we'll treat the database as one component for now, which is shown in Figure 9-24.

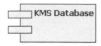

Figure 9-24. Missing KMS component

Starts with *D*, Ends with *B*, Two Letters ...

One very common "missing" component is the database. Most of the analysis and design to this point has focused on requirements and behavior and functionality, not on implementation and persistence. So it's likely that any storage you require is simply the responsibility of your existing components.

So should you show the database as a component in the architecture? There are various answers, depending really on how you view the role of architecture:

- Yes, because the architecture is supposed to reflect every component in the system.

- No, because the architecture is only supposed to reflect the architecturally significant components in the system, and the storage mechanisms lie "beneath" the level of architecture.

- Yes, because you want to interact with the database in a common, consistent fashion, making those interactions a matter of architectural significance.

- No, because you want to avoid overdesign: you want each team to determine their own database needs and implement only the minimum database functionality they need.

- Yes, but only as a big black box.

- Yes, and you want each table of each database modeled as a separate component so that you can see which other components interact with each table.

No one answer is right for every project, but I prefer to include the database as a big black box when I develop the candidate architecture, then evolve that into individual tables as the architecture solidifies.

Exercise 903: Assign Your Interfaces and User Interfaces to Components

Building on Exercises 901 and 902, define components to provide your interfaces and user interfaces. Define the implementation language and target operating system for each component, and verify that those choices support the protocols and mechanisms selected for your interfaces and user interfaces.

Identifying Dependencies from the Activity Diagrams

Once you've identified all your components, you should combine all the existing Component Diagrams (for the KMS, that's Figures 9-18, 9-22, 9-23, and 9-24) into an Everything Diagram, an overall architecture diagram. Next you need to add the actors that will use the user interfaces. Then, by looking at the swimlaned Activity Diagrams from Step 3, you can add the dependencies, as implied by the transitions between swimlanes (recall we did this back in Chapter 2). Where you can make reasonable hypotheses, you should add dependencies to and from the user-specified components and the missing components as well.

Then take two ibuprofen[3] and a break, because your picture probably looks as ugly as the one for our KMS system does, shown in Figure 9-25.

---

3. Or aspirin, or acetaminophen, or ginseng tablets, or whatever analgesic works best for your headaches.

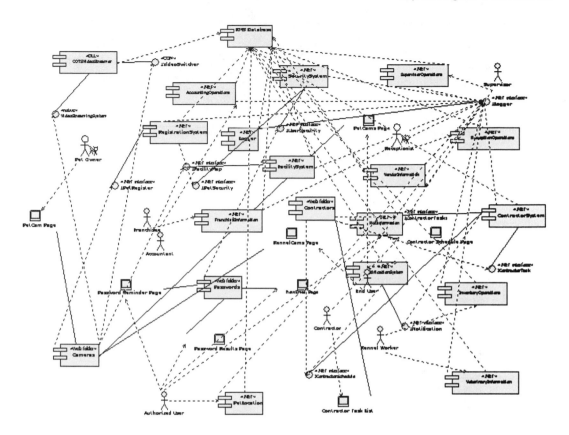

Figure 9-25. KMS architectural overview

Well, I did warn you that an Everything Diagram would be difficult to read.
That's why your next move is to make your diagram readable, as described next.

Organizing the Architecture

The first step from a cluttered and confusing Everything Diagram to some kind of coherent architecture is to simplify things by removing some components, and rearranging the rest to clarify the relationships.

Much as I like having the actors play a role in the architecture and in the Component Diagrams, I can see one clear way to simplify Figure 9-25: remove the actors and user interfaces from the overview. (Trust me: they'll reappear on Detail Diagrams.) We can also remove the **Logger** component from the overview. This improves matters slightly, as shown in Figure 9-26.

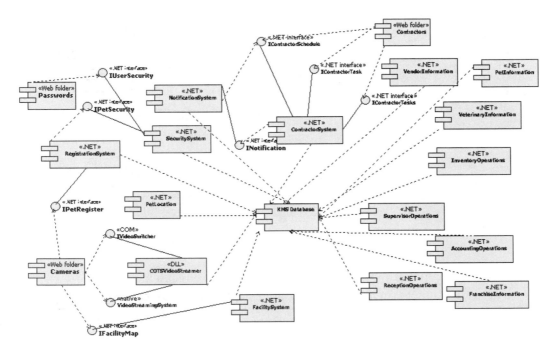

Figure 9-26. KMS architectural overview, revised

But it's not enough of an improvement. To simplify things further, we can step away from a detailed architecture diagram, and instead produce a conceptual architecture diagram.

In a conceptual architecture diagram, you omit interfaces for the sake of simplicity, and instead you simply add dependencies between the components. This flies in the face of all the reasons for using interfaces (e.g., to keep components loosely coupled), but it's useful just for this overview diagram, because it hides duplicate interface dependencies among components.

In this fashion, we can produce the simpler diagram shown in Figure 9-27.

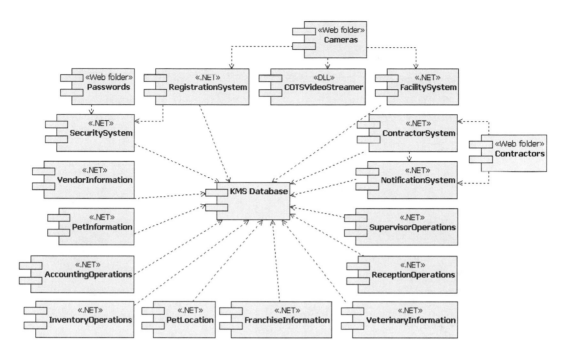

Figure 9-27. KMS architectural overview, second revision

But it's *still* not enough of an improvement. Now you could certainly keep removing components to simplify the picture; but if you remove enough components, it's hard to still call this an overview diagram.

What's *really* wrong here is that we have no particular organizational plan in mind. This is where architectural experience can help, by suggesting useful ways to organize the system. But if you don't have personal architectural experience, you can rely on something almost as good: architectural experience captured as architectural patterns. So, before we go on to devise an architecture for the KMS, let's take a look at some common patterns first.

Architectural Patterns

There are many well-studied architectural patterns. Some are interactive, specifying the mechanisms and protocols by which components interact, while others are organizational, helping to organize the components and the relations between them.

The following are a few organizational patterns:

- Monolithic

- Two-Tier

- Three-Tier

- N-Tier

- Layered

- Pipes and Filters

- Hierarchical

- Broadcasts and Listeners

- Switchboard

- Hybrid

I'll discuss each of these in the following sections.

Monolithic

In a Monolithic architecture, the entire application is one component, as shown in Figure 9-28.

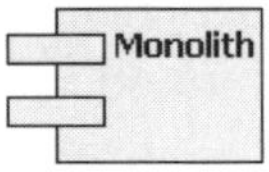

Figure 9-28. A Monolithic architecture

Two-Tier

In a Two-Tier architecture, (aka Client-Server), user interface and business rules are separated from the data storage, as shown in Figure 9-29.[4]

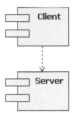

Figure 9-29. A Two-Tier architecture

Three-Tier

In a Three-Tier architecture (aka **Model-View-Controller,** aka **Boundary-Control-Entity**), the user interface is separated from the business rules, which are separated from the data storage. The user interface can interact with the business rules, and the business rules can interact with the data, but the user interface can't directly interact with the data. A simple Three-Tier architecture is depicted in Figure 9-30.

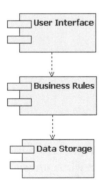

Figure 9-30. A Three-Tier architecture

---

4. For a lot more on client-server development, see Jeff Levinson and Steven J. Houglum, *Building Client/Server Applications Under .NET: An Example-Driven Approach* (Apress, 2003).

N-Tier

An N-Tier architecture is the generalized form of the Two-Tier and Three-Tier architectures: components are organized into tiers of services—possibly including multiple components in each tier— and components in a given tier can only interact with components in the next "lower" tier, as shown in Figure 9-31.

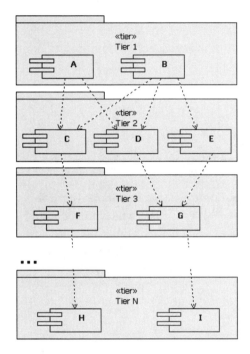

Figure 9-31. An N-Tier architecture

Layered

A Layered architecture is a looser form of N-Tier: components are organized into layers of services, and components in a given layer can only interact with components in lower layers, as shown in Figure 9-32.

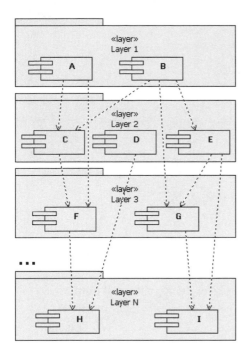

Figure 9-32. A Layered architecture

Pipes and Filters

A Pipes and Filters architecture pattern functions well when a number of components must work on a given data stream in sequence, each modifying the stream and passing it along. The components can be arranged in one long pipeline, or they can split the stream into multiple pipelines. The first component in the pipeline receives or creates the stream, and the last component in any pipeline writes or transmits the stream. In the case of a single pipeline, this pattern may be viewed as a degenerate form of N-Tier, in which each tier contains exactly one component, and there's usually one common interface used to pass from tier to tier. A linear Pipes and Filters architecture is shown in Figure 9-33.

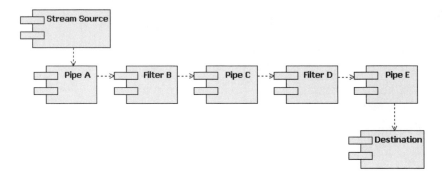

Figure 9-33. A Pipes and Filters architecture

Hierarchical

With a Hierarchical architecture, the system is made up of a small number of components. Each component may contain a number of subcomponents, and each subcomponent may itself contain subcomponents, and so on. The component space is thus broken into a strict hierarchy. Any component may interact with its subcomponents (if any), its peer components (if any), and its parent component (if any), but with no other components. Figure 9-34 shows a simple Hierarchical architecture.

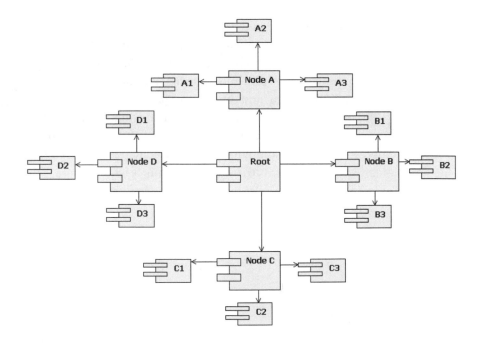

Figure 9-34. A Hierarchical architecture

Broker

The Broker architecture pattern allows for a rather disjointed organization, and possibly a dynamic organization as well. In this pattern, a single broker component receives all requests for interaction, and then forwards each request to an appropriate destination component. When results are returned, the broker is again responsible for routing the response to the correct component. The broker may be configured dynamically to define the routing for particular requests; or in a publish-subscribe fashion, each component can request that particular interactions be routed to it. (If more than one component asks to receive a particular kind of interaction, the broker can be designed to send a copy to each, or it can have rules for determining priority among the subscribers.) A simple Broker architecture is shown in Figure 9-35.

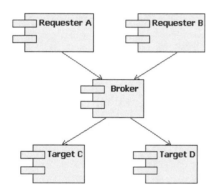

Figure 9-35. A Broker architecture

Broadcasts and Listeners

The Broadcasts and Listeners architecture pattern is even more disjointed than Broker: a component can request an interaction using a well-known channel (such as a TCP broadcast port); and then any listener on that port can respond to the request. This is shown in Figure 9-36.

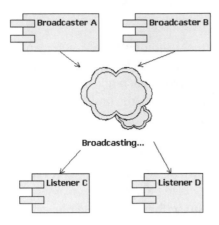

Figure 9-36. A Broadcasts and Listeners architecture

Switchboard

The Switchboard architecture pattern is a little *less* disjointed than Broker, though it's similar: a switchboard component receives a request for interaction, finds an appropriate destination component, and establishes a connection between the two components. After that, the two components may communicate directly, without any intercession from the switchboard. A simple Switchboard architecture is shown in Figure 9-37.

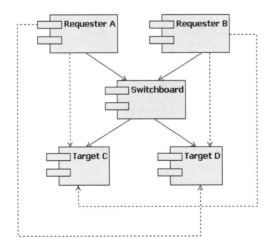

Figure 9-37. A Switchboard architecture

Hybrid

The Hybrid "pattern" simply indicates that you use different patterns to organize different parts of the architecture.

Choosing the KMS Architecture

A full discussion of why you would choose any particular architectural pattern is well beyond the scope of this book,[5] so I'm going to keep it simple. Despite all the fancy, interesting patterns available, I'm going to settle on the good old reliable N-Tier pattern for the Kennel Management System. The tiers in this case will be UI, Hybrid, Control, and Data, as shown in Figure 9-38.

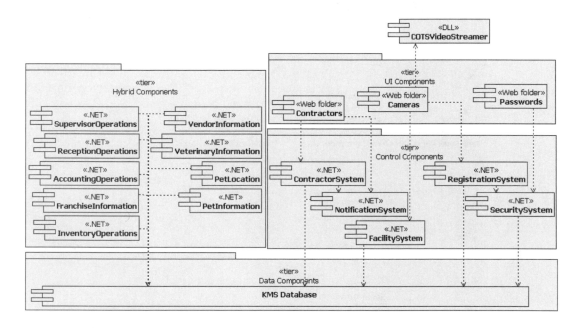

Figure 9-38. KMS N-Tier architecture

---

5. Readers interested in learning more about architecture have a number of resources available. I recommend Frank Buschmann et al., *Pattern-Oriented Software Architecture, Volume 1: A System of Patterns* (John Wiley & Sons, 1996); Douglas Schmidt, *Pattern-Oriented Software Architecture, Volume 2, Patterns for Concurrent and Networked Objects* (John Wiley & Sons, 2000); Martin Fowler et al., *Patterns of Enterprise Application Architecture* (Addison-Wesley, 2002); and the .NET architecture work from Microsoft at http://msdn.microsoft.com/architecture.

The **COTSVideoStreamer** component is modeled outside of any of the tiers for two reasons. First, it really isn't something you're building and maintaining, so it belongs elsewhere (perhaps in a package of COTS components). And second, well, I just couldn't make it fit very easily.

Context Diagrams

Once you've decided on an architecture for your system and organized your components into a useful overview of the system, you need to try to understand each component in more detail. To do this, it helps to draw a Context Diagram, which is a Component Diagram centered on one component, and showing the other components and actors with which it interacts.

Let's look at an example from the KMS case study. Figure 9-39 shows a Context Diagram for the **Passwords** Web folder.

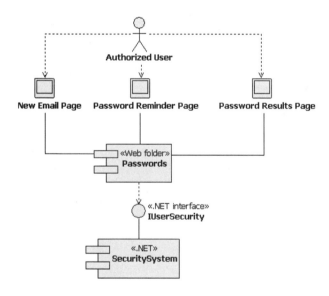

Figure 9-39. Context Diagram for the Passwords Web folder

Context Diagrams can be useful for the teams designing each component, allowing them to easily see just those components that directly relate to their work; but frankly, 19 more of these diagrams won't add much to this book, so let's leave it there for now.

Sometimes you might find that, as you design your components in more detail during Step 5 of Five-Step UML, a particular Context Diagram would be useful for you. If this happens, you can always add it at that stage.

> ### Exercise 904: Define the Dependencies
> ### Between Your Components

Building on Exercises 801 (in which you swimlaned your Activity Diagrams) and 903 (in which you assigned your interfaces and user interfaces to components), identify and define the dependencies among your components. Select an architectural pattern, and organize your components within that pattern. Draw one or more Component Diagrams to reflect your component architecture.

A Manager's View of Architecture

In Step 4 of the Five-Step process, your view of the architecture as a manager should start getting pretty detailed, and perhaps pretty complex. Now that your architects have a firm architecture in place, you can start the detailed planning and staffing of your project.

Staffing

So far, you've identified key skill needs, based on your swimlanes. Now you have precise components defined; and based on the activities assigned to the interfaces of a particular component, you and your architects can identify precisely which technologies will be used within that component. Once you know the technology skills required for each component, you can assign each component to an individual or team with the necessary skills (or the necessary time and budget to learn those skills).

Planning

Once again, it's time to revise your estimate. In this phase, you've developed a concrete architecture, including selecting core technologies, approving COTS components, and exploring particularly difficult design issues. You've learned a lot, so it's time to reflect that newfound knowledge in the estimate.

It's also time to update your schedule: both because your estimate has changed, and because you're now in a position to see conflicts in the schedule. Earlier, you simply prioritized the use cases and tried to schedule their implementation.

Now you know that the implementation of those use cases will involve particular components assigned to particular individuals and teams; and now you'll be able to tell when you're counting on people to work on two different things at the same time. (Hint: *They can't do that!* Not if you want them to succeed at either one.) So now you'll be faced with unfortunate trade-offs, and you'll have to work with analysts and users and other stakeholders to reprioritize and reschedule some of the functionality of the system.

Tracking

The new estimate and schedule shall define new elements that must be tracked. In particular, now you can track the progress of particular teams on particular components, interfaces, and operations. You're able to track to a very fine degree— perhaps too fine. You may find that trying to track to as fine a degree as is theoretically possible will consume all your time, and thus be pragmatically impossible. But you might ask the individual or team responsible for each component to do this microtracking for you. In particular, you might build automated systems so that they can update the status of these fine details as part of the process of working on them.

Reporting

The new tracking elements imply new reporting, as discussed in Chapter 6. Now you can report the progress of individuals and teams on particular components, so that you can see how work is proceeding along parallel paths.

Correction

The new tracking elements imply new opportunities for correction, as discussed in Chapter 6.

Risk Management

Now you can address both technical and process risks:

- You've started designing particular roles and tasks for specific COTS components. Do those components fulfill all your expectations? Have you written sample code to prove it?

- Your user interface is becoming tangible. Have you built UI prototypes? Have you reviewed these with real users to ensure they make sense?

- Are people assigned to components and technologies that fit their skills? If not, is there adequate time and budget to train them?

- Which are the critical components? Who's working on them? Have you considered what will happen if these people leave? How are you training others on the design of these critical components?

- Have you identified any conflicts in the schedule? Have you resolved them? Were use cases reprioritized and rescheduled in the process? Does everyone know of and accept the reprioritization and rescheduling?

These and other technical and process risks may shape the design and code work you'll do in Chapter 10.

A Tester's View of Architecture

For a tester, the components and interfaces indicate precise targets for unit tests. Each interface should include a unit test suite; and each method of an interface should become a subsuite, or simply a unit test.

The definitions of the components and the interfaces in the architecture can help your testing in another way: you now have the specs for any test shims you may need. A *test shim* is a component that stands in place of another component to provide predictable, controllable behavior in place of the component, and perhaps in advance of the other component being completed. You may sometimes use a test shim to test *other* components that interact with the component for which you designed the shim.

A Documenter's View of Architecture

As a documenter, you probably have little or no interest in the architecture, unless you have to write technical documentation to describe the components to be deployed. In more complex architectures, however, you may need to write documents for how components are integrated into the system. For example, one purpose for a Broker architecture is to make it easy to define new requester and new target components, and even to define new types of requests. If the architecture team chooses a Broker architecture, there is probably a requirement that the system be extensible by end-user programming. In that case, you'll probably have to document the extension mechanism, which means documenting the

Broker architecture. So you should review the architecture strictly from a viewpoint of flexibility: if it's flexible from a user's point of view, that flexibility requires documentation.

Summary

In this chapter, I've been talking about Step 4 of Five-Step UML, where you begin to design the architecture of your system.

The swimlaned Activity Diagrams developed in Step 3 are your starting point. These help you to identify the different interfaces and user interfaces required for your system. It can be helpful at this stage to organize these interfaces and to document them in Package Diagrams. Next, you need to assign components to each interface and user interface. You should also look through your requirements sources, such as a functional specification, to make sure that you have identified all of the components you'll need. Make sure you've also considered what your database requirements will be. If you don't want to delve too deeply into your database architecture at this stage, you can always simply model this as a "black box" to include on your Component Diagrams.

The final stage of Step 4 is to organize all of the Component Diagrams together to form an "Everything Diagram," making sure that you've identified dependencies between your components. Now, you'll notice that things can get a little out of hand at this stage, with a crazy cluttered diagram that no one can understand. In order to bring some coherency to your overall architecture, you'll need to think how you're going to organize your components overall. Here, you should learn from the experience of others and familiarize yourself with some useful architectural patterns. You're probably already familiar with N-Tier design, but other architectural patterns can be useful, depending on what kind of system you're creating.

Finally, as with each step in the process, you can see that when you drill down into the details of your model, you start uncovering more functionality, more requirements than you had earlier established. In the last part of this chapter, we spent some time examining how you need to keep reevaluating your plans with regards to staffing, scheduling, risk management, testing, and documentation as you learn more about the design of your system.

Now that we've identified our components and designed the overall architecture, we'll move on in the next chapter to the final step in the Five-Step process, component design.

CHAPTER 10

Step 5: Repeat to Design Your Components

YOU'VE ALREADY COME a long way down the road of developing a UML model for a new system. In the first two steps of Five-Step UML, you focused on requirements, documenting and refining them using Use Case Diagrams and Activity Diagrams. In Step 3 of the process, you developed swimlanes for your Activity Diagrams, and used those in Step 4 to identify interfaces and components, which you then organized into an overall architectural design.

During Step 5 of the process, it's time to dig inside some of those components identified in Step 4, and analyze and design them at the class and object level. In this chapter, I'll be using some of the techniques you've been learning throughout the book, but this time you'll see how to apply them at the level of the individual component. I'll guide you in developing Use Case and Activity Diagrams that depict the responsibilities of the components, followed by Class Diagrams that depict the structures of and the relationships between the classes within the components.

Again, we'll be following the KMS case study through this final step of the process, but I won't delve into the design of every component in this chapter. Instead, I'll concentrate on one user interface (UI) component and one "middle-tier" component. I'll call this middle-tier component a service component, because it provides services—i.e., interfaces—used by other components. I'll concentrate on what looks like the richest area of the architecture so far, the contractor components.

Designing the UI Component

In the last chapter, we identified the need for a **Contractor Schedule Page**, an ASP.NET page for contractor information, and a **Contractor Task List**, an ASP.NET Web control for displaying contractor tasks. These UIs, their contents, and their responsibilities are summarized in Figure 10-1.

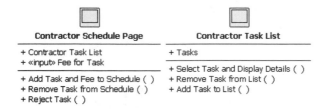

Figure 10-1. Contractor UIs

Together, the UIs shown in Figure 10-1 make up the **Contractors** Web folder component that we'll design in this chapter. As you can see, each UI has

- Attributes that describe its contents

- **«input»** attributes that describe information it provides

- Operations that describe what a user can do through it

Making a New Design Model for the Component

The first step in designing any component is to define a new model for it. This **design** model allows you to define the component in more depth than is necessary for an architectural perspective. Just as you separated requirements from architecture concerns with separate models, so you should separate architectural roles from design details via separate models. But the architectural model will drive your design model by defining the requirements for each individual component.

In the case of the **Contractors** Web folder component from our KMS example, we'll add a **Contractors Web** model.

Making Prototype UIs for the Component

Your next step in designing a UI component is to create prototypes for it. Prototypes allow you to review and discuss how you'll present the contents of each UI and how the system will interact with the user.

For our KMS example, let's start with the prototype for the **Contractor Task List**, which is shown in Figure 10-2.

Before Friday - Ladi - Needs undercoat pulled
Week of 17th - Patches - Needs claws trimmed
Week of 17th - Patches - Needs cut and shampoo
Ladi is going to the vet next week, and we want her coat pulled before then so he can check how her scars are recovering.

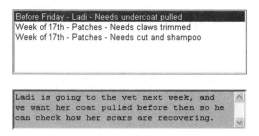

Figure 10-2. Prototype Contractor Task List

This Web control consists of two nested controls. The first control is a list of the tasks. For the purposes of the prototype, that list contains three pieces of information: the date period by which the task must be performed (remember that your rules—your entire purpose for the **Contractor Schedule Page**, in fact—require that contractors be able to define their own schedules for tasks), the name of the pet, and a summary of the task to be performed. The second control is a text box that shows details of a selected task.

Next we'll prototype the form that contains the control, as shown in **Figure 10-3.**

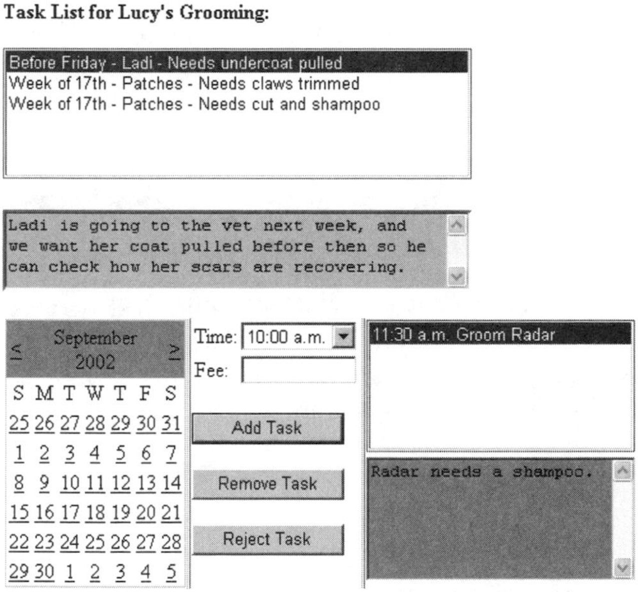

Task List for Lucy's Grooming:
Before Friday - Ladi - Needs undercoat pulled
Week of 17th - Patches - Needs claws trimmed
Week of 17th - Patches - Needs cut and shampoo
Ladi is going to the vet next week, and we want her coat pulled before then so he can check how her scars are recovering.
September 2002
S M T W T F S
25 26 27 28 29 30 31
1 2 3 4 5 6 7
8 9 10 11 12 13 14
15 16 17 18 19 20 21
22 23 24 25 26 27 28
29 30 1 2 3 4 5
Time: 10:00 a.m.
Fee:
Add Task
Remove Task
Reject Task
11:30 a.m. Groom Radar
Radar needs a shampoo.

Figure 10-3. Prototype Contractor Schedule Page

As I built this prototype, I realized that the UI requirements were incomplete (something I hoped would have been caught in reviews before I ever got this far, but you can never be sure). When we add tasks to the schedule, it's not enough to just know the fee, as shown in Figure 10-1; we also need to know a date and time. Here, I've used the standard ASP.NET calendar control for selecting dates, and a drop-down list filled with times (in half-hour increments) for selecting times.

Also, if we're going to allow the contractor to remove tasks from the schedule through this page, we need to display the contractor's current schedule. I chose to display that schedule as a list with details, as I did with the **Contractor Task List**; and it's very likely that I'll turn this schedule list into a Web control as the project evolves, but not at this time.

So Figure 10-1 might be revised to include the new attributes for Date, Time, and details of the contractor's current schedule, as shown in Figure 10-4.

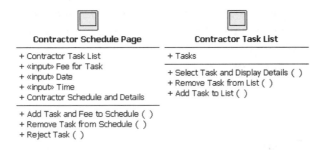

Figure 10-4. Contractor UIs, revised

Exercise 1001: Prototype Your UIs

Building on Exercise 902, in which you gathered and documented your user interfaces, create prototype layouts for your UIs. For each UI, ensure that it displays the accepted fields, has input fields for expected inputs, and has controls and mechanisms for invoking each expected operation.

Defining the UI Requirements

Once you've got your UI prototypes sorted out, you'll need to add use cases that depict how the user interacts with the component. You might organize these use cases by actor, much as I did with the original requirements model during Step 1 in Chapter 6; but often a UI component (like the **Contractors** Web folder) is aimed at a single actor role, so a simple **Use Cases** package may be enough of an organization.

That's the approach we'll take for the KMS model. For our initial use cases, we'll start with the UIs themselves, as shown in Figure 10-5.

Figure 10-5. Contractor component use cases

Both of these use cases may be refined to reflect the smaller steps that can be performed through the UI, indicated by its inputs and operations. This is depicted in Figures 10-6 and 10-7.

Figure 10-6. Detailed contractor schedule use cases

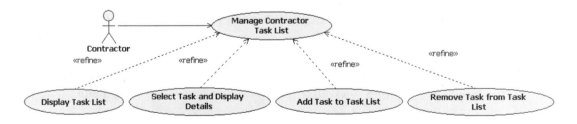

Figure 10-7. Detailed contractor task list use cases

Note the use of the **«refine»** stereotype on dependencies, which I've added to indicate that the new use cases provide more detail for the existing use cases.

Note also that, as in these examples, many UIs have an implied use case that represents displaying their contents.

Next, let's look at the diagrams that show only the refined use cases, as demonstrated in Figure 10-8.

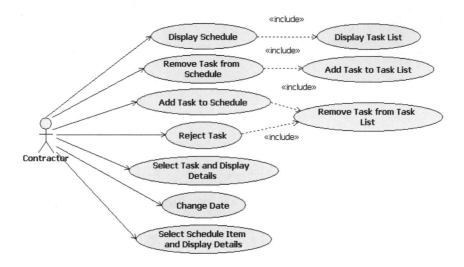

Figure 10-8. Detailed contractor use cases

Because the **Contractor Task List** UI is contained within the **Contractor Schedule Page** UI, it made sense to combine the details into a single diagram. If these were two completely separate UIs—or if you were exploring how the **Contractor Task List** is reused in other pages—then you might see a benefit in keeping the Detail Diagrams separate.

Note that this diagram shows that a task can get deleted from the task list for two reasons: because the contractor adds it to the schedule, or because the contractor rejects it.

You might argue that Figures 10-5 through 10-8 don't really tell us much new. They're really representations of Figure 10-4 (and earlier diagrams), expressed as use cases. But "expressed as use cases" has some value. As always, a focus on use cases is a focus on specific user needs and interactions. It's about requirements. And it also provides you with placeholders for more detailed requirements, as in the next step.

But can you skip these component use cases? Yes, you can. If you feel like you already understand the UI requirements of the component and you don't need placeholders for the detailed requirements, you can skip them. Or, as you'll see later in the chapter, I'll explore an entirely different way to model and detail these requirements.

Exercise 1002: Define Use Cases for Your UIs

Building on Exercise 1001, in which you prototyped your UIs, create detailed use cases for your UIs. Identify the actors performing each use case, along with other actors and interfaces that participate.

Refining the UI Requirements

Now that you have your component requirements captured as use cases, you can turn each requirement into an algorithm via an Activity Diagram. Whereas our development of Activity Diagrams in Chapter 7 focused on business rules, this time we'll be focusing on implementation rules.

For the rest of this section, we'll be developing each of the detailed use cases identified in Figure 10-8 into their corresponding Activity Diagrams.

Display Schedule Use Case

In the **Display Schedule** use case, we need to determine who our contractor is (we'll use a simple cookie mechanism[1] to identify the contractor—not very secure or robust, but simple enough for this example), and then display the contractor's schedule and the list of tasks delegated to that contractor. This leads to Figure 10-9.

---

1. For those new to Web programming, *cookies* are tiny files stored on the client's machine to associate a name with a value. Not all browsers support them, and some Web users distrust them (for reasons far too convoluted for me to even attempt to explain here) and disable them. It's usually not a good idea to rely on cookies for Web sites that will serve a wide range of users and browser types; and in fact, ASP.NET can largely make it irrelevant whether you use cookies or not. But in this particular case, you'll be using persistent cookies—cookies that remain on the client's machine for a fixed length of time after a session—as a way to identify contractors each time they visit the site.

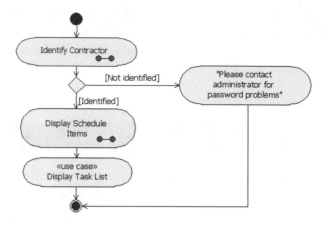

Figure 10-9. Activity Diagram for Display Schedule use case

The **Display Task List** activity shown in this diagram has a «**use case**» stereotype, indicating that it represents a use case, which I'll discuss in the next section, but first, let's look at the two activities—**Identify Contractor** and **Display Schedule Items**—that are subactivity states (as indicated by the icon in the lower-right corner). More detailed rules for these subactivity states are shown in Figures 10-10 and 10-11.

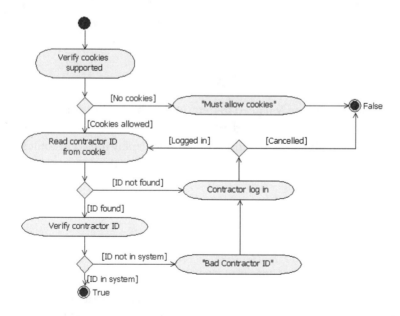

Figure 10-10. Activity Diagram for Identify Contractor activity

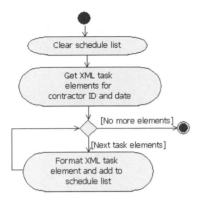

Figure 10-11. Activity Diagram for Display Schedule Items activity

Display Task List Use Case

In the **Display Task List** use case (which is a use case for the **Contractor Task List**, remember), we need to display the list of tasks assigned to a particular contractor but not yet put on that contractor's schedule. This reveals a possible missing attribute for this UI: the contractor ID. We *could* let the Web control do just what the Web page does: read a cookie for the ID. But this is duplicating cookie fetching logic; and duplicate code is code I just don't trust. So I think it makes more sense to make the contractor ID a property of the control, and have the Web page update the property. This means our earlier diagram illustrating the **Contractor** UIs needs to be updated, as shown in Figure 10-12.

Figure 10-12. Contractor UIs, second revision

Note the **«property»** stereotype: this is a common .NET stereotype to indicate that a data value is actually a .NET property.

If you're *really* diligent, you might notice that none of the Activity Diagrams so far show the Web page updating the value of the contractor ID property.

We could redraw our Activity Diagram for the **Display Schedule** use case (shown previously in Figure 10-9) to add this explicit update, as shown in Figure 10-13.

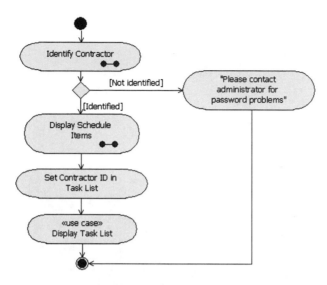

Figure 10-13. Activity Diagram for Display Schedule use case, revised

Now we have enough information to show the details of the **Display Task List** use case, as demonstrated in Figure 10-14.

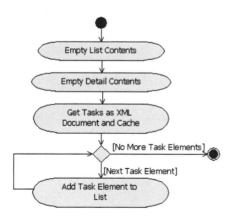

Figure 10-14. Activity Diagram for Display Task List use case

In this diagram, we call our service component to get the list of tasks as an XML document, and then walk through that document and add the individual tasks to the list. We also cache the list, for the purposes of displaying details later.

Remove Task from Schedule Use Case

In the **Remove Task from Schedule** use case, we need to figure out which scheduled task is selected (if any) and remove it from the schedule. Then we need to add its details back into the task list. Now we could reconstruct the task list entry from the schedule details, or we could simply give the task list a task ID and let it reload the item. I prefer the latter approach, because it lets the control be responsible for knowing what information is relevant, and it doesn't require the page and the control to agree on what's relevant. So this algorithm would look like the diagram in Figure 10-15.

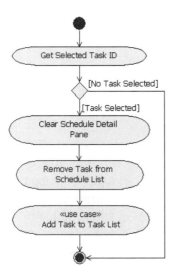

Figure 10-15. Activity Diagram for Remove Task from Schedule use case

Note that the **Add Task to Task List** activity in this diagram has the **«use case»** stereotype, so let's take a look at that use case next.

Add Task to Task List Use Case

In the **Add Task to Task List** use case, we'll take a task ID, call our service component, and add that component into our cached list and into the visible list, as shown in Figure 10-16.

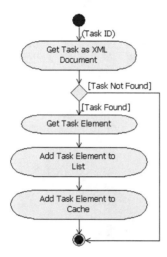

Figure 10-16. Activity Diagram for Add Task to Task List use case

Note that I've added a parameter, **Task ID**, to the initial transition.

Using parameters in Activity Diagrams is a convenient way of indicating data used within or between activities without taking up space with an object icon. Make sure you don't go to extremes, however, by showing too many parameters. Usually, if data is simply passed from one activity to the next, I don't bother to show it on a diagram like this. If data is used by two or more nonsequential activities and I want to indicate this, then I show it as an object icon; but if data is passed into or out of the diagram, then I show it as a parameter.

Note also that the **Add Task Element to List** activity should look familiar. You saw the same activity in Figure 10-14. That hints at common behavior, which can be modeled as an abstract included use case. Thus, our earlier diagram illustrating the detailed **Contractor** use cases (Figure 10-8) can be modified, as shown in Figure 10-17.

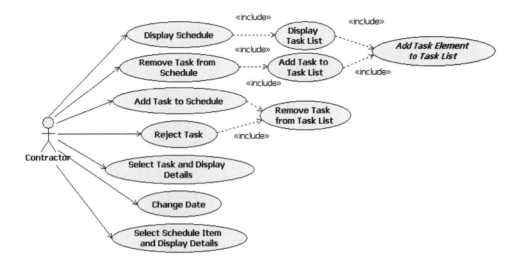

Figure 10-17. Detailed contractor use cases, revised

We could also revise Figures 10-14 and 10-16 to add the **«use case»** stereotype to the **Add Task Element to List** activity; but that's very straightforward, so I won't bother showing those changes here.

Let's take a look at that use case now.

Add Task Element to Task List Use Case

In the newly discovered use case, **Add Task Element to Task List**, we need to extract the deadline, the pet name, and the summary, and then add them to the list, as shown in Figure 10-18.

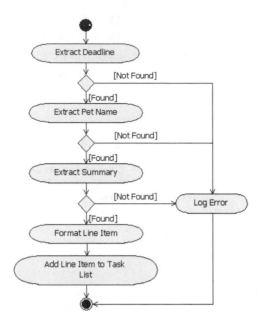

Figure 10-18. Activity Diagram for Add Task Element to Task List use case

This diagram shows that we need to program defensively: expecting the possibility of poorly formatted XML elements, and logging if we find them.

Add Task to Schedule Use Case

In the **Add Task to Schedule** use case, we need to figure out which task list item is selected (if any) and remove it from the task list. Then we need to add its details to the schedule at the specified time. As we did when adding to the control, we'll read a task ID from the control and let the page load the item from the service component. So this algorithm would look like the diagram in Figure 10-19.

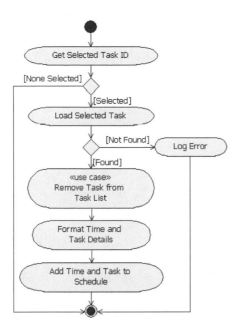

Figure 10-19. Activity Diagram for Add Task to Schedule use case

Remove Task from Task List Use Case

In the **Remove Task from Task List** use case, we'll look up a task ID in the task list cache. If it's found, we'll delete it from the cache and from the list, as shown in Figure 10-20.

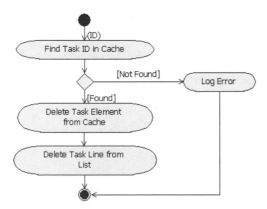

Figure 10-20. Activity Diagram for Remove Task from Task List use case

Reject Task Use Case

In the Reject Task use case, we'll find the selected task ID, and then remove it from the task list, as shown in Figure 10-21.

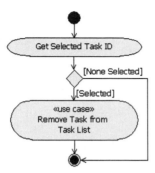

Figure 10-21. Activity Diagram for Reject Task use case

Select Task and Display Details Use Case

In the **Select Task and Display Details** use case, the contractor selects a line in the task list, and the control displays the details in the detail pane, as shown in Figure 10-22.

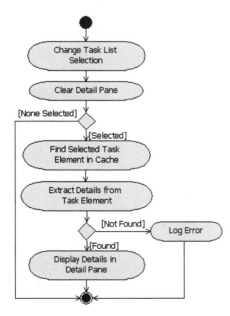

Figure 10-22. Activity Diagram for Select Task and Display Details use case

Change Date Use Case

In the **Change Date** use case, we need to look up a new date, and then display the schedule items for that date. Now, that step sounds suspiciously like the **Display Schedule Items** activity from the first use case we looked at, **Display Schedule** (see Figure 10-11). In fact, it's the same logic. So we can turn the activity behind Figure 10-11 from a simple subactivity state to an included use case, which we'll call **Display Schedule Items for Date**. Let's have a look once more at the detailed **Contractor** Use Case Diagram to see how this fits in. The modified diagram is shown in Figure 10-23.

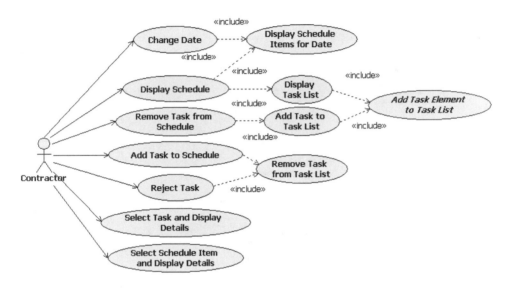

Figure 10-23. Detailed Contractor use cases, second revision

The Activity Diagram for this new included use case is the same as the one for our **Display Schedule Items** activity, shown in Figure 10-11, and using our new included use case, we can model the rather simple behavior of the **Change Date** use case, as shown in Figure 10-24.

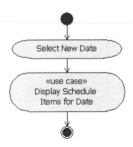

Figure 10-24. Activity Diagram for Change Date use case

373

Note that for working with dates, we'll most likely be using the .NET **System.DateTime** struct, a useful type that supports easy date operations and conversion to different display formats, including localized formats.

Select Schedule Item and Display Details Use Case

In the **Select Schedule Item and Display Details** use case, the contractor selects a line in the schedule list, and the page displays the details in the detail pane, as shown in Figure 10-25.

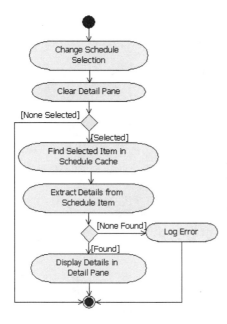

Figure 10-25. Activity Diagram for Select Schedule Item and Display Details use case

Phew! That was a lot of work; and that's just working through the use cases for one component. You can see from this section how we can reuse the technique we used in Step 2 to help us in figuring out exactly how our components should work. In the next section, we'll continue examining the Contractor UI component, this time using the techniques from Step 3.

Exercise 1003: Refine the Use Cases for Your UIs

Building on Exercise 1002, in which you defined use cases for your UIs, refine these use cases. Create Activity Diagrams that reflect the behavior in detail, including algorithms, exception handling, etc.

Assigning the UI Responsibilities

Now that you have required functions captured as algorithms in Activity Diagrams, you can assign responsibility within the algorithms by adding swimlanes to the Activity Diagrams. Recall that we looked at the process of assigning swimlanes to Activity Diagrams in detail in Step 3 of the Five-Step UML, but whereas then your focus was primarily on actors, interfaces, and UIs, now you need to add in objects where appropriate.

In our KMS case study, the major objects we'll be looking at during this stage of the process will be the Web page, the Web control, the service component, and the XML documents. To hold the classes for these objects, we'll add a **Classes** package to the **Contractors Web** model, as shown in Figure 10-26.

Figure 10-26. Overview of the Contractor Web model

For the rest of this section, I'll be stepping through some of the more significant Activity Diagrams documented already in this chapter, and adding swimlanes to them.

Display Schedule Use Case

By adding swimlanes to the Activity Diagram for the **Display Schedule** use case (see Figure 10-13), we discover two of our expected classes, plus an error page, as shown in Figure 10-27.

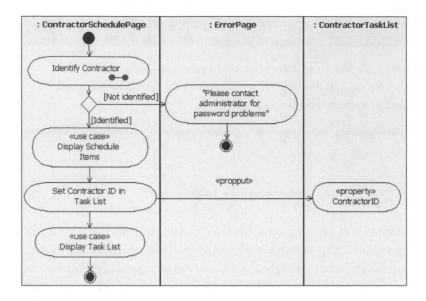

Figure 10-27. Activity Diagram for Display Schedule use case, with swimlanes

Here, we've added an extra terminal state to emphasize that if the contractor can't be identified and the user is redirected to the **ErrorPage**, they won't be returned to the **ContractorSchedulePage**.

Identify Contractor Subactivity State

Remember that we also developed Activity Diagrams for the subactivity states. In adding swimlanes to the Activity Diagram for the **Identify Contractor** subactivity state (Figure 10-10), we discover the need for new objects to represent the session state and other Web-related information. This new swimlaned Activity Diagram is shown in Figure 10-28.

As you can see in this diagram, the first activity involves the verification of cookie support: we have to check whether cookies are supported, and read them if they are. Because ASP.NET is being targeted—and because I know a little bit about how ASP.NET handles session state and related information—I know that this information is accessed through the **System.Web.HttpApplication** class.

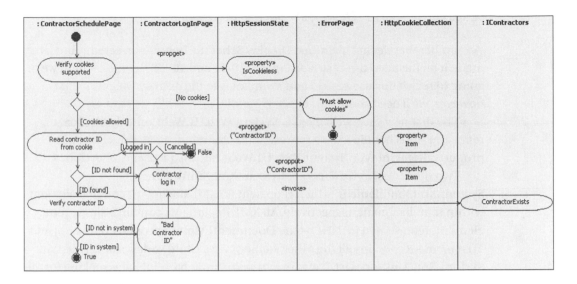

Figure 10-28. Activity Diagram for Identify Contractor activity, with swimlanes

A common practice (and the practice in code generated by the ASP.NET AppWizard) is to derive a **Global** class from **System.Web.HttpApplication**. This **Global** class can override generic functions from its base class to provide the unique behavior of your Web app. **System.Web.HttpApplication** represents the running Web app, across all user sessions. It also provides a property, **Session**, of type **HttpSessionState**. This represents the session state of the current user, and provides information such as browser support for cookies, through the **IsCookieless** property, which we use as part of our for **Identify Contractor** activity, shown in the preceding diagram.

There's also a shortcut to the current session state: **ContractorSchedulePage** is derived from **System.Web.UI.Page**; and the base class has a **Session** property to access the session state. The **Page** class is important for another reason when it comes to cookies: cookie values may change from HTTP request to request, so they're not accessible through the **Session** property. Instead, they're accessed through the **Request** property of the **Page** class, a value of type **System.Web.HttpRequest**. That class has a **Cookies** property for accessing the cookie collection.

Notice the addition of a new Web page, **ContractorLogInPage**, which manages logging in if the cookie is not found. A brand new interface, **IContractors**, is also added to manage the collection of all contractors.

Display Schedule Items for Date Use Case

Remember that we first identified **Display Schedule Items** as an activity, but later made it an included use case (see Figures 10-11 and 10-23). In this section, we're going to revisit this use case to add swimlanes to the Activity Diagram. First, however, we'll need some new classes.

The first new class we'll need is **System.Web.UI.WebControls.ListBox**, to represent the schedule list. To represent the items in the list, this class has a property, **Items**, of type **System.Web.UI.WebControls.ListItemCollection**.

Two other classes we'll use are **System.Xml.XmlDocument** and **System.Xml.XmlElement**, which represent an XML document and one element within that document, respectively. All XML documents contain a single root element, represented in .NET as the **DocumentElement** property of the object. That element contains all the other elements in a **ChildNodes** property of type **System.Xml.XmlNodeList**. Now we *can* walk through **ChildNodes** looking for all the schedule items; but there's an easier way to find them. **System.Xml.XmlElement** has an operation, **GetElementsByTagName**, that will extract all the elements of a specific type. We can use this operation to extract the task elements.

Before we can actually redraw our Activity Diagram, it may be useful to work out the format of the XML documents we'll be passing around. Rather than draw up a formal XML schema, I'll simply provide and discuss the following sample task list document:

```
<?xml version="1.0" ?>
<TaskList>
    <Task>
        <TaskID>00000001</TaskID>
        <Deadline>Friday Noon</Deadline>
        <PetID>DOG00001</PetID>
        <Job>Shampoo and Cut</Job>
        <Details>
        Ladi is going to a show, so she needs to be trimmed for conformation.
        </Details>
    </Task>
    <Task>
        <TaskID>00000002</TaskID>
        <Deadline>Monday</Deadline>
        <PetID>DOG00002</PetID>
        <Job>Nail trim</Job>
        <Details>
        Patches needs his nails trimmed. He doesn't enjoy this, so it will take
                some time.
        </Details>
    </Task>
</TaskList>
```

UML and XML

One unfortunate misconception I face as a UML instructor is when people know about Hypertext Markup Language (HTML) and eXtensible Markup Language (XML) and even Standard Generalized Markup Language (SGML, the basis for HTML and XML), and they assume UML must be part of that family of markup languages. Before I can teach them UML, I have to first explain that UML has nothing to do with XML.

But in a sense, that's not true. Although UML and XML have very different purposes and uses, they have some common concepts. They're both *languages*, after all, for communicating ideas. And the XML ideas of schema and element correspond fairly closely to the UML ideas of class and object:

- An XML schema element describes the legal format for a category of XML document elements: what the category name is, what its contents are, what attributes describe an element of the category, and what elements an element of the category may contain or reference.

- A UML class describes the structure and behavior of a class of code objects: what the class name is, what its attributes are, what operations it can perform, and what other objects it contains or relates to.

The two ideas are not perfectly aligned: an XML element can be created without a schema to define it (unless you enforce schema validation); and a UML object can perform operations. Still, the ideas are similar enough that you can pretty easily model an XML schema or an XML document with UML. For example, the schema for the preceding document could be modeled as shown in Figure 10-29.

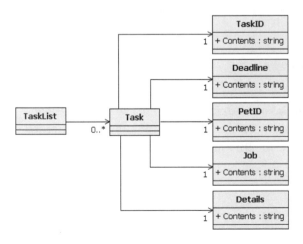

Figure 10-29. Class Diagram for XML task document

Similarly, given a class model in UML, it's fairly easy to devise an XML schema that represents the classes and relations in the model. Rational ROSE and some other tools will automatically generate XML schemas from models and vice versa.

The document element in the preceding XML document is a **TaskList**, a container for multiple **Task** elements. Each **Task** contains a **TaskID**, a **Deadline**, a **PetID**, a **Job**, and **Details**. The **PetID** is used to look up the pet's name (and other information, if needed). The other elements should be self-explanatory.

Now we have the foundation to add swimlanes to our earlier Activity Diagram for Display Schedule Items (Figure 10-11), producing the diagram in Figure 10-30.

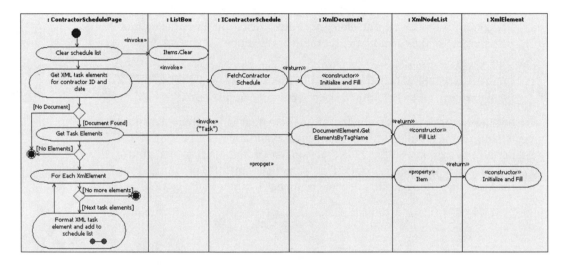

Figure 10-30. Activity Diagram for Display Schedule Items use case, with swimlanes

As I started to tie to specific classes and operations, I realized that the algorithm from our earlier Activity Diagram (Figure 10-11) was too simplistic. It needed to include the steps of fetching the document element from the XML document and fetching a given task from the task collection. I also realized that the activity, **Format XML Task Element and Add to Schedule List**, was too complex to stand as a single activity, yet also too complex to include in Figure 10-30; so I converted that activity into a subactivity state, with its algorithm as shown in Figure 10-31 (with swimlanes).

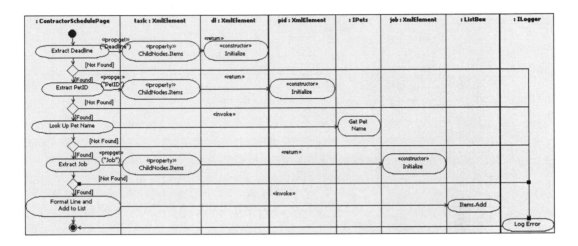

Figure 10-31. Activity Diagram for Format XML Task and Add to Schedule activity, with swimlanes

Notice that two new interfaces are discovered: **IPets**, representing a collection of pets, used here to get the name of a pet given the ID; and **ILogger**, used for logging errors.

Remove Task from Schedule Use Case

When we add swimlanes to the **Remove Task from Schedule** Activity Diagram (see Figure 10-15), we can see a little more of how a **ListBox** is manipulated, as shown in Figure 10-32.

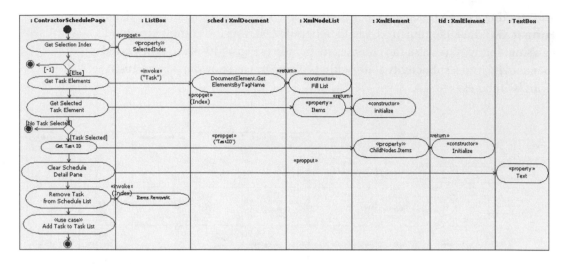

Figure 10-32. Activity Diagram for Remove Task from Schedule use case, with swimlanes

Now here I'm using the index of an item in the list box as an index into a list of XML elements.

That's it for the swimlaned Activity Diagrams for now—I'm not going to bother detailing the rest of the use cases, because we won't be seeing anything new or interesting in terms of the UML used or the process.

In the next section, we'll take some of the classes we've identified here, and use them to start organizing a structure for our UI components.

Exercise 1004: Assign Responsibilities for the Activities of Your UIs

Building on Exercise 1003, in which you refined your UI use cases, add swimlanes to the Activity Diagrams for your UIs. Document each swimlane as a form, a control, a class, an interface, or an actor, and document the responsibilities of each.

Designing the UI Structure

So far in the component design, you've worked out the Activity Diagrams for your components, and added swimlanes to them, thus assigning responsibilities to classes and interfaces. Now you can design the structure of those components. In the last chapter, you focused on the organization of the components and their interfaces in Component Diagrams, whereas now you'll work on Class Diagrams, looking at the structure inside of the components.

In our KMS case study, we'll start this stage of the process with the collection of classes and interfaces identified from the swimlanes in the diagrams presented earlier in this chapter (those related to the contractors UI). These are shown in Figure 10-33.

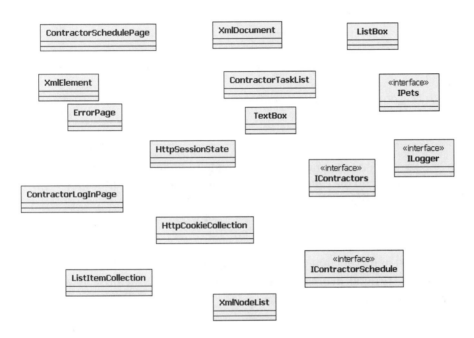

Figure 10-33. Contractor Web classes

This collection is a little large, and a little disorganized. So our next step is to package the classes. The easiest to package are the ones that come from the .NET Framework. Those can be packaged according to their namespaces: **System.Web**, **System.Web.SessionState**, **System.Web.UI**, **System.Web.UI.WebControls**, and **System.Xml**. Then we'll add another package for Web pages, another for Web controls, and another for Web applications. We'll also add a package for useful XML extension classes. Finally, we'll migrate the newly discovered interfaces back into the architecture.

With these packages, we'll end up with the diagram in Figure 10-34.

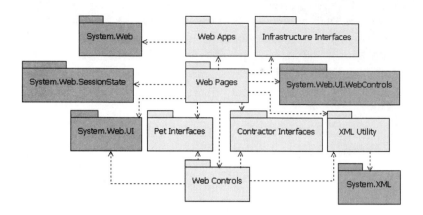

Figure 10-34. Contractor Web class packages

 NOTE   In this diagram the darker shaded packages refer to .NET classes, and the lighter ones to packages containing components from the KMS.

For the rest of this section, we'll be looking at the classes in these packages. I won't show every detail of every class, but will instead focus on those details that have appeared in earlier diagrams.

Web Pages Classes

The **Web Pages Classes** package contains the three Web pages, as shown in Figure 10-35.

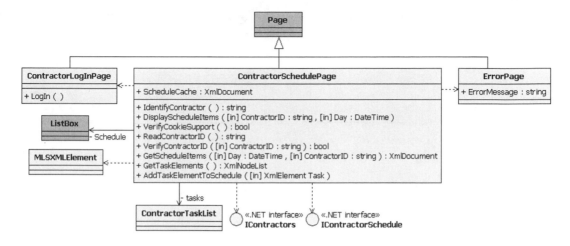

Figure 10-35. Web Pages classes

The **ContractorSchedulePage** depends on **MLSXMLElement**, a new class you'll see later in this chapter. This class will simplify reading subelement contents from an XML element. Note also the added dependencies of **IContractors** and **IContractorSchedule**. The first dependency is based on the swimlanes for the Activity Diagram for the **Identify Contractor** activity (Figure 10-28). The second dependency is one I'm sure we'll need when we add swimlanes to the Activity Diagram for the Add Task to Schedule use case (Figure 10-19).

Web Apps Classes

The **Web Apps Classes** package contains the one class, as shown in Figure 10-36.

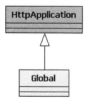

Figure 10-36. Web Apps classes

The **Global** class has yet to appear in any of these diagrams; but experience with ASP.NET applications tells me that we'll run into it many times before the design is complete.

Web Controls Classes

The **Web Controls Classes** package contains one control with two embedded controls and a cached **XmlDocument**, as shown in Figure 10-37.

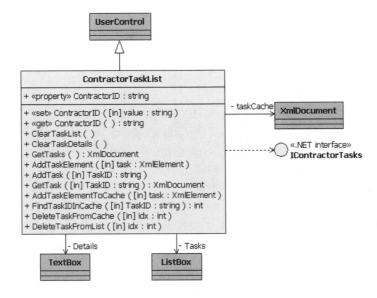

Figure 10-37. Web Controls classes

Note the added dependency on **IContractorTasks**, which we'd discover when we add swimlanes to the Activity Diagram for the **Display Task List** use case (Figure 10-14).

XML Utility Classes

The **XML Utility Classes** package contains a new kind of XML element, as shown in Figure 10-38.

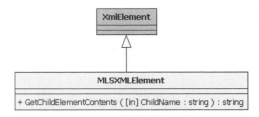

Figure 10-38. XML Utility classes

If you look back at our swimlaned Activity Diagram for the **Format XML Task and Add to Schedule** activity (Figure 10-31), you can see a lot of design effort spent on the repetitive, mechanical task of finding a single child element within a parent and extracting its contents; and I foresee that we'll need to do that a lot more as the design evolves. So rather than duplicate these mechanical steps throughout the design and code, we need to make a new derivative of **XmlElement** that can do this work automatically. As we design further, we'll likely find more repetitive behavior to move into this derived class.

NOTE   I've named the derivative class by prefixing the original name with my initials. This is a common habit I follow when I'm extending an existing class only by adding some utility functions specific to my design and my style of coding.

Exercise 1005: Define the Class Structure for Your UIs

Building on Exercise 1004, in which you assigned responsibilities for the activities of your UIs, package and organize the classes for your UIs, and define the relations between the classes. Draw the Class Diagrams to depict these relations. Ensure that each class contains the necessary attributes and operations to support its responsibilities.

Designing the Service Component

We've spent the first half of this chapter focusing on the design for a UI component, namely the Contractor Schedule Page for the KMS. Next, we'll step through this whole process again, but this time, we'll be designing the service component, the **ContractorSystem**. Because I've shown you the whole process once already, however, I won't go into quite so much detail in this section.

In the last chapter, recall that we organized our contractor interfaces into a package (Figure 9-9). The interfaces in this package were **IContractorSchedule**, for maintaining contractor schedules, **IContractorTasks** for maintaining a list of tasks, and **IContractorTask** to represent a single task. In designing the UIs earlier in this chapter, we discovered one more interface, **IContractors**, for representing the collection of all contractors.

These interfaces and their responsibilities are summarized in Figure 10-39.

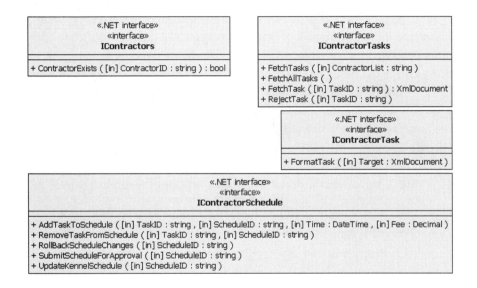

Figure 10-39. Contractor interfaces

Note that this figure shows additional operations and parameters as appropriate for the diagrams drawn so far. Note also that, on reflection, I decided that rejecting tasks is a function of the tasks, not of the schedule. So I've updated the architecture accordingly.

Making a New Design Model for the Component

The first step, remember, is to define a new model for this component. In this case, we'll add a **ContractorSystem** model.

Refining the Service Requirements

The functional requirements of the service component are defined by its interfaces and by their operations and attributes. In this section, I'll show you how we design the algorithm for each of the operations by looking at the relevant Activity Diagrams.

But first, we'll need places to hold these algorithms in the model (and eventually, in the code, of course). We could follow the example from Chapter 2, treating the interfaces as actors and the algorithms as use cases; but while that's a useful metaphor for getting people thinking about analysis and design and requirements, there are easier ways to organize the model as it gets close to code. Instead, we need to think ahead just a little bit, considering how the contractor interfaces will be realized by the **ContractorSystem** component. The most common and easiest OO solution is to have a class or classes realize each interface. So we'll add a class behind each of the interfaces: a class for contractors, a class for schedules, and a common class for task lists and for tasks. Then we'll add the individual interface methods to the classes, resulting in the diagram in Figure 10-40.

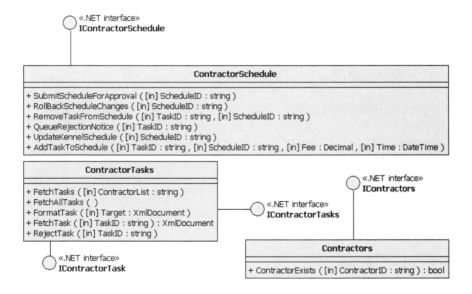

Figure 10-40. Interface classes for the ContractorSystem component

Now we can attach an Activity Diagram to each interface method of the classes, as shown in the diagrams that follow. For this stage of the process, I'll focus on just a couple of typical operations, to give you an idea of how this all works.

Contractors.ContractorExists Operation

In the **Contractors.ContractorExists** operation, we want to find if a specified contractor exists. Our component will need to talk to the **KMS Database** to gather this information (the back-end tier not indicated in our overall N-Tier architectural model, Figure 9-38). The algorithm is as depicted in Figure 10-41.

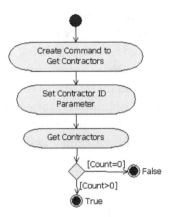

Figure 10-41. Activity Diagram for ContractorsExist operation

ContractorTasks.FetchTasks Operation

In the **ContractorTasks.FetchTasks** operation, we want to retrieve all tasks for one or more contractors, with the result formatted as an XML string. The algorithm is as depicted in Figure 10-42.

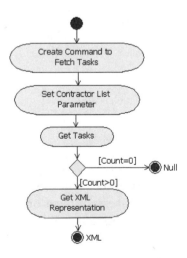

Figure 10-42. Activity Diagram for FetchTasks operation

Exercise 1006: Refine the Responsibilities for Your Service Components

Building on Exercise 901, in which you gathered and documented your interfaces, refine the operations of your interfaces. Create Activity Diagrams that reflect the behavior in detail, including algorithms, exception handling, etc.

Assigning the Service Responsibilities

Now that you have the required functions of your service component captured as algorithms in Activity Diagrams, you can add swimlanes to assign responsibility. The major objects in this component will be the classes that provide the interfaces (as shown in Figure 10-40) and classes that provide the data. And that leads you to an important strategic decision: how are you accessing the database?

As I explained in Chapter 2, I like to model the database itself as an object with a number of contained objects (the tables) and a number of operations (stored procedures). Treating databases as objects lets them fit very naturally into the rest of the design; and working primarily through stored procedures lets the database designers package up efficient SQL solutions in OO ways. It's usually far more efficient to apply logical and mathematical operations to an entire set of database records in SQL code than to fetch the records and then apply the operations to one record at a time. For one thing, SQL is optimized for operation on sets of records. For another thing, a single, powerful SQL call represents one round-trip from the application to the database and back, as opposed to one round-trip per record. I know this to be true as a rule, but I'm nowhere near good enough as a SQL programmer to write good, efficient SQL code. The stored procedure bridges the gap between my OO expectations and the relational SQL world.

So should you call these stored procedure "operations" of the database "object" directly from your interface class? You could, but that spreads the database mechanisms all throughout the component. That makes the system less maintainable *and* less amenable to change. The issue of change is important, because different databases and different database technologies require different means of access. If you want to be able to change your mind on the database technology, it's important to encapsulate the database access code.

And how do you encapsulate code? With objects and classes, of course. You could make one class that represents access to the entire database, but that would be shortsighted: the database may be too large to comprehend as one big chunk.

For our KMS example, we'll add classes to represent access to the various tables and services provided by the database. The .NET Framework actually presents a wide range of database classes for various purposes; but for now, we're interested in responsibilities, not implementation. So we'll defer selecting the specific classes and mechanisms until the next section.

Contractors.ContractorExists Operation

Adding swimlanes to our earlier Activity Diagram for the **Contractors.ContractorExists** operation (Figure 10-41), we get the diagram shown in Figure 10-43.

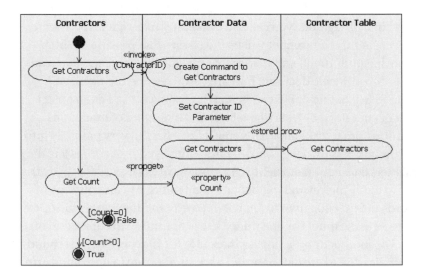

Figure 10-43. Activity Diagram for ContractorsExist operation, with swimlanes

ContractorTasks.FetchTasks Operation

Adding swimlanes to our earlier Activity Diagram for the operation **ContractorTasks.FetchTasks** (Figure 10-42), we get the diagram shown in Figure 10-44.

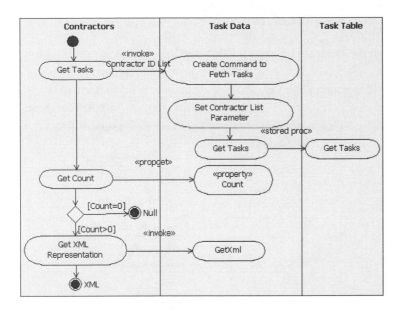

Figure 10-44. Activity Diagram for FetchTasks operation, with swimlanes

Exercise 1007: Assign Responsibilities for the Activities of Your Interfaces

Building on Exercise 1006, in which you refined the responsibilities for your service components, add swimlanes to the Activity Diagrams for your interfaces. Document each swimlane as an interface realization, a class, or an interface, and document the responsibilities of each.

Designing the Service Structure

Now we're ready to decide the specific classes and mechanisms we'll use to access the database, but first let's take a moment to examine the database options that .NET provides.

The .NET Framework actually provides two different (but related) mechanisms for database access: data sources and data sets. We'll examine these mechanisms in the following sections, before we return to our KMS case study.

Data Sources via Data Providers

Data access through data sources involves making database connections through connection objects, issuing commands through command objects, and reading results through reader objects in a forward-only fashion. This mechanism is suited for scenarios in which your code connects to and interacts with the database in a continuous, live-update method. The major .NET classes for data sources are shown in Figure 10-45 (with a *lot* of detail omitted).

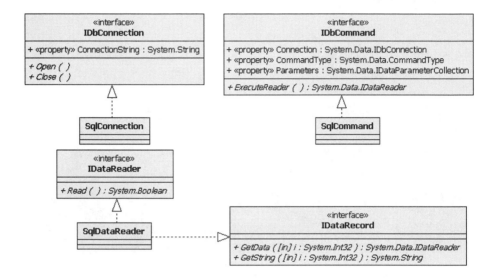

Figure 10-45. Class Diagram for .NET data sources

The major .NET data access functionality is defined by interfaces, which are then implemented by specific classes for specific data sources:

- The **IDbConnection** interface represents a mechanism for connecting to a particular data source. The **SqlConnection** class implements **IDbConnection** for accessing SQL Server databases.

- The **IDbCommand** interface represents a request or command to a specific source. It requires an **IDbConnection** interface to find the data source; and through its **ExecuteReader** operation, it produces an **IDataReader** to read through the resulting data. The **SqlCommand** class implements **IDbCommand** for driving SQL Server databases.

- The **IDataReader** interface represents a mechanism for iterating through a set of data records. The **SqlDataReader** class implements **IDataReader** for reading a SQL Server result set.

- The **IDataRecord** interface represents one record in a set of data records. The **SqlDataReader** class also implements **IDataRecord** for reading a SQL Server result set.

A common approach to reading data with these classes might look like the diagram in Figure 10-46.

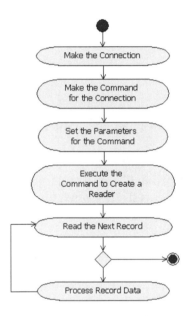

Figure 10-46. Activity Diagram for .NET database reading

Data Access via Data Sets

Data access through data sets involves issuing commands, filling in a collection of resulting objects, and then working through that collection instead of through the database itself. Data sets use data sources to fill the sets, but then stand on their own, independent of the sources. This mechanism is suited for scenarios in which your code must connect to and interact with the database only initially, but must then work with the resulting data. This may be more efficient in terms of network round-trips (though it may be less efficient if you're going to request a large number of records and then only process a small subset—a questionable approach anyway, if efficiency is your concern). It may also just be easier to use.

In particular, data sets will automatically convert their contents to XML documents, which is much easier than creating your own XML documents.

The major .NET classes for data set access are shown in Figure 10-47 (again, with a lot of detail omitted).

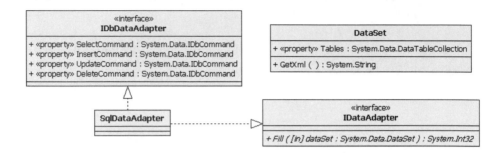

Figure 10-47. Class Diagram for .NET data sources

As with data sources, the major data set functionality is defined by interfaces and classes behind those interfaces:

- The **IDataAdapter** interface represents a bridge that fills a data set from a data source. The **SqlDataAdapter** class implements **IDataAdapter** for filling in data sets.

- The **IDbDataAdapter** interface represents common database operations (Select, Insert, Update, and Delete) for use in a data adapter. It uses **IDbCommand** objects (and thus, **IDbConnection** objects behind the scenes) to access the data source. The **SqlDataAdapter** class also implements **IDataAdapter** for accessing SQL Server data sources.

Finally, the **DataSet** class is a base class for data sets that represent particular table or result set formats. A **SqlAdapter** can fill such a set from a **SqlCommand**.

Because data sets will automatically convert to XML (and thus save you a lot of busy work) and because they pass results as whole sets rather than as individual rows (which makes more sense across component boundaries), you'll use data sets as the base classes for your data classes.

Service Structure

Returning to our KMS example, we're now ready to design our service structure in detail. Note that I've taken a few leaps here, adding in classes that I expect we'll discover in further analysis and design. The structure appears as shown in Figure 10-48.

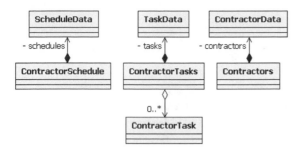

Figure 10-48. Class Diagram for the ContractorSystem

Aggregation, Composition, Association, and Dependence

I've already talked about the concepts of association and dependence, and you've seen them both represented in many UML diagrams from the KMS case study, but Figure 10-48 introduces some new relationships: aggregation and composition. These are deep, detailed UML notation and concepts, the meanings of which are summarized here:

- **Aggregation** is a whole-part or collection-contents relationship between objects of two classes. If one object contains other objects as replaceable or removable parts, then the containing object *aggregates* the other objects. In UML, this is indicated by an unfilled diamond on the containing end of an association between the classes. According to Figure 10-48, a **ContractorTasks** object aggregates zero or more **ContractorTask** objects. Because this is an aggregation, a **ContractorTask** may be removed from or added to a particular **ContractorTasks** object.

- **Composition** is a stronger, more permanent whole-part relationship between objects of two classes. If one object contains another object as a fixed, nonremovable part, then the containing object *is composed of* the other object. In UML, this is indicated by a filled diamond on the containing end of an association between the classes. According to Figure 10-48, a **ContractorTasks** object composes a **TaskData** object. Because this is a composition with multiplicity 1 (implied, because no multiplicity is shown), there is only one **TaskData** object within a particular **ContractorTasks** object throughout its lifetime.

To summarize, aggregation implies containment, but containment doesn't imply aggregation. For example, the room I am sitting in contains me, but it isn't made up of me. Sometimes the concepts of *dependence, association, aggregation,* and *composition* can be confusing. It's very often true that you *could* use more than one to model a particular idea, so sometimes people worry about which is the right relationship to use. So I'd like to present Table 10-1 for suggested uses.

Table 10-1. Dependence, Association, Aggregation, and Composition

Relation	Meaning	Example	C++ Code
Dependence	Uses	I have a dependence on the class **Canoe**: I know how to paddle one. If you loan me a canoe, I can travel with it. But I don't actually own a canoe. If you can find me, that gives you no help at all in finding any particular canoe. If A is dependent on B, that means that a change in B may require a change in A.	#include
Association	Has	I have an association with the class **Automobile**: I not only know how to drive one, but I actually own one. If you can find me, you can find my car through our association (i.e., the title and registration that identify the car as mine).	Instance Data (unspecified)
Aggregation	Contains	My car aggregates four objects of class **Tire**: the tires are not just associated with the car, but are part of it; yet any given tire may be removed and replaced. The tires and the car may exist independently of each other. An aggregation implies containment but not integration: an egg carton aggregates the eggs inside it, but the eggs are not part of the carton.	Instance Data: Pointer
Composition	Persistent Contains	My car is composed of an object of class **Frame**: the frame is an integral part of the car; and if you replaced the frame, you would be (in effect) replacing the car as well. The car and the frame don't exist independently of each other. A composition implies integration: the whole and the parts are inseparable in some sense.	Instance Data: Member Variable, Const Data Pointer, Const Reference

Note the last column of the table, "C++ Code." This column shows the code concepts I use when explaining these relations to C++ programmers:

- **Dependence** means your class **#include**s the header file for another class. Your class can then create, pass, and manipulate objects of the second class.

- **Association** means your class includes an instance of another class. Given an object of your class, there's always a way to find an object of the other class (unless that object is null). Association is nonspecific: it might mean containing a member variable of the second class, or it might mean containing a pointer to an object of the second class; but you haven't made up your mind yet. To be more specific, use aggregation or composition.

- **Aggregation** means your class includes a pointer to an object of another class. Your object and the second object may be created and destroyed independently of each other, and your object may aggregate different objects at different times through a given aggregation.

- **Composition** means your class includes a member variable of another class. Your object and the second object are created and destroyed together, and your object may not compose any other object through that particular composition.

The problem with these definitions, though, is that they fall apart under .NET. First, except in C++, there's no concept of header files: all classes in the current project and any referenced project may be used by any classes within the project. Second, except in unsafe code, there's no concept of pointers. And third, except for structures, all classes are memory managed and garbage collected, and thus all contained objects may exist independently of their containers.

Some .NET modelers always use aggregation, because objects may always exist independently. Others always use composition, for simplicity. Still others always use association. And the code generated by most .NET tools is the same for either association, aggregation, or composition, so there's no reason to say one approach is "right." Similarly, many .NET modelers avoid dependence altogether, because it doesn't affect the code either way.

My practice, though, is to use all of these relations to convey meaning to the *reader*, not to code generators. And I think the original UML meanings are useful in this regard, and I try to follow them. I use dependence when a class is passed as a parameter, returned as a result, or used as a temporary variable inside a method (though this latter use may be too detailed to show up in the design). I use association to indicate a relation, but not a whole-part relation. I use aggregation to indicate a dynamic whole-part relation. And I use composition to indicate a static whole-part relation.

Another important design decision you have to make with any system that connects to databases is how you will manage connections. Will you have a single connection for an entire application? Will you create a new, unique connection every time you need to talk to the database? Will you create a persistent connection for each client object? Will you have a pool of connections available for use in various parts of your application? There are many possible design decisions; but the one decision you can't afford to make is to not decide. Database connections can be scarce resources. If you choose not to manage them, you'll create unforeseen bottlenecks in your application.

We want to keep our KMS example simple, so each interface class in the **ContractorSystem** component will have its own **SqlConnection** for its requests. (This is far from the most efficient database strategy available, but it lets me avoid synchronization, an issue that's too large for this book.) To simplify matters further, we'll derive a new base class, **KMSDataSet**, which contains the **SqlConnection** for each derived class. These relations are shown in Figure 10-49.

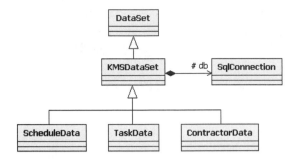

Figure 10-49. Class Diagram for ContractorSystem data sets

Here I've made the connection protected, so that each derived class may use it directly. Note that the UML visibility symbols (+, -, ~, #) were discussed in Chapter 4.

Exercise 1008: Define the Class Structure for Your Interfaces

Building on Exercise 1007, in which you assigned responsibilities for the activities of your interfaces, package and organize the classes for UIs, and define the relations between the classes. Draw the Class Diagrams to depict these relations. Ensure that each class contains the necessary attributes and operations to support its responsibilities.

An Alternative Approach: Using VS .NET and Rational XDE

You *can* follow all of the steps I describe throughout Chapter 10. In fact, depending on the power of your UML tool, I *encourage* you to follow all of these steps.

But I don't follow them myself.

Remember my guideline from Chapter 3: **Do What Works.** And remember the digression that followed that rule, in which I explained that my preferred modeling tool, Rational XDE, lets me work from the code to the model instead of from the model to the code. Well, component design is where these powerful features of XDE really change the way I work. A good tool like XDE lets you work in the model and the code simultaneously, changing overall design aspects in the model, changing implementation details in the code, and then automatically synchronizing the model and the code. It's not model then code, nor even code then model: it's model and code in parallel. This power really changes my entire approach to UML modeling, by letting me express each thought in the tool where it's easiest to express. "Do what works" in this case means "Use the best, easiest tool for any given task." So in this section, I'd like to show you how I'd *really* do the work in this chapter.

Designing the ContractorWeb with VS .NET and XDE

To begin designing the **ContractorWeb**, I'll use the **Add New Project** dialog box in VS .NET to add a new C# project of kind **ASP.NET Web Application** to my VS .NET solution. I'll name this project **ContractorWeb**, and VS .NET will generate the following files for me:

- **AssemblyInfo.cs.** This file defines attributes for the assembly that contains this project.

- **ContractorWeb.vsdisco.** This file contains an XML-format Dynamic Discovery Document, which describes the component for discovery services (a topic that's beyond this book).

- **Global.asax.cs.** This file allows visual and code editing of **Global**, a class derived from **System.Web.HttpApplication** (and described previously in this chapter). Visual editing seems a little odd for a nonvisual object like **Global**. (Don't blame me; I didn't write VS .NET.) It allows you to add components—database connections, database commands, error logs, and a range of other components—to your **Global** object by dragging and dropping. Code editing simply allows you to edit the **Global** class directly.

- **Web.config.** This file contains an XML-format configuration file that controls how ASP.NET processes the Web app.

- **Webform1.aspx.** This file allows visual editing of a Web page within the Web app. The default name is useless, so I change the name to the name of one of the Web pages I know I'll need. Referring to Figure 10-4, that means **ContractorSchedulePage** in this case.

- **Webform1.aspx.cs.** This file contains the code behind **Webform1.aspx.** The *code behind* concept in ASP.NET has gotten a lot of attention because it's new and different from the old ASP approach, but it's actually very simple. This file is compiled into a DLL and loaded onto the Web server; and when the Web server needs to process requests and events for this form, the requests and events are passed to the DLL for processing. This gives ASP.NET coding a look and feel and approach that is *very* similar to desktop app coding, and very simple. When you rename **Webform1.aspx,** this file will be automatically renamed to be consistent.

After I build the shell of the Web app, I'll add the two other pages discovered earlier in this chapter: **ContractorLogInPage** and **ErrorPage.** Then I'll use the **Add New Item** dialog box to add the **ContractorTaskList** Web user control. This will add the following files to the project:

- **ContractorLogInPage.aspx.** The file for visually editing the contractor login page.

- **ContractorLogInPage.aspx.cs.** The code behind the contractor login page.

- **ErrorPage.aspx.** The file for visually editing the error page.

- **ErrorPage.aspx.cs.** The code behind the error page.

- **ContractorTaskList.ascx.** This file allows visual editing of the Web control.

- **ContractorTaskList.ascx.cs.** This file contains the code behind **ContractorTaskList.ascx.** Like code behind for a Web page, this file is compiled into a DLL and loaded onto the Web server. When the Web server needs to process requests and events for this control, the requests and events are passed to the DLL for processing.

Once I have the Web page and the control defined, I'll use VS .NET's visual editing tools to draw the basic contents and controls (like I did in drawing Figures 10-1 to 10-4). Drawing the page and the controls is significantly faster than trying to design them with UML. Again, use the right tool for the job. I'll also add handlers for each UI event: button clicks, list selections, etc.

And *then* I'll build my UML model, by letting XDE reverse engineer it for me. XDE only captures the structure, not the behavior, so there's still a lot of work to do; but after reverse engineering and then creating diagrams that reflect the model, I'll end up with the diagrams in Figures 10-50 and 10-51.

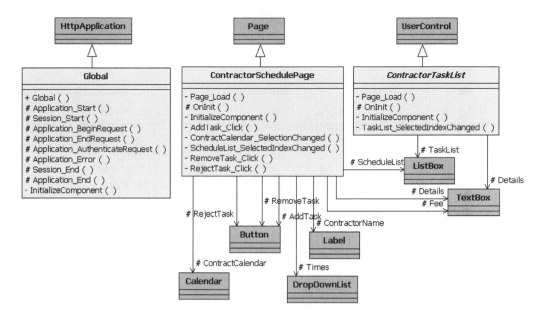

Figure 10-50. Reverse-engineered Class Diagram for ContractorWeb main pages

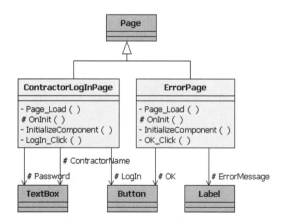

Figure 10-51. Reverse-engineered Class Diagram for ContractorWeb support pages

Note that the associations from the Web page and the Web control to the control classes are all prefaced with a pound sign (#). Recall from Chapter 4 that this indicates that these relations are *protected*: derived classes can see and use these relations, but outside classes can't. So in code created with the VS .NET form designers, outside classes can't directly manipulate the controls within a page or a control.

Once I have a reverse-engineered model, I can analyze and diagram the requirements for the UI, much as I did earlier in the chapter (Figures 10-5 through 10-32); but now when I draw these diagrams, I can do so with a basic design structure in mind. It may change the diagrams in subtle ways, because I'll draw them to fit the code structure, as opposed to fitting the code to the structure after the fact. That's all right, because now the code and design are evolving in tandem. I'll also revise these two reverse-engineered UML diagrams (Figures 10-50 and 10-51) to add things I learn about the classes through refining the requirements, such as the **ContractorID** property in the **ContractorTaskList**. (It's actually easier to add a property through XDE than through the code, in my opinion: XDE can automatically generate a member variable to hold the property value.) And eventually, I'll discover dependencies on interfaces and dependencies and associations between classes, as shown in the earlier Class Diagrams of the Web Pages classes and Web Controls classes (Figures 10-35 and 10-37). Plus I'll find the need for class **MLSXMLElement**, as shown in Figure 10-38. And I'll find the need for all the operations internal to these classes. After I find these design issues, I'll end up with revised Class Diagrams as shown in Figures 10-52 and 10-53.

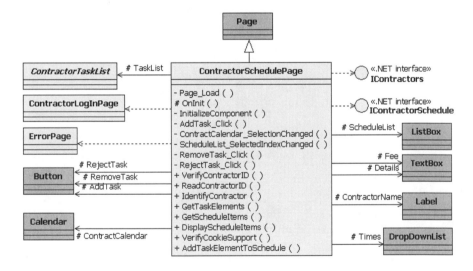

Figure 10-52. Class Diagram for ContractorSchedulePage

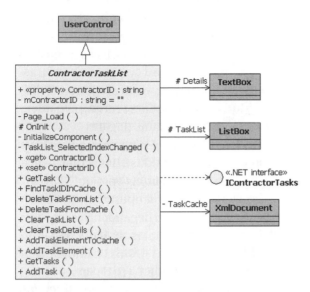

Figure 10-53. Class Diagram for ContractorTaskList

Next I'll synchronize my code and my model to reflect my changes. And then I'll review Figures 10-9 through 10-32 and write the code within the methods to fit the Activity Diagrams.

Designing the ContractorSystem with VS .NET and XDE

To begin designing the **ContractorSystem**, I'll use the **Add New Project** dialog box in VS .NET to add a new C# project of kind **Class Library** to my VS .NET solution. I'll name this project **ContractorSystem**, and VS .NET will generate the following files for me:

- **AssemblyInfo.cs.** This file defines attributes for the assembly that contains this project.

- **Class1.cs.** This file contains the code for one class in the class library, with a default name of **Class1**. Eventually, I'll rename both the class and the file to the name of a class in the design.

Next I'll add *another* class library, but delete the class file from it. Why another class library? Remember from back in Chapter 9, I wanted to keep my interface definitions as an independent part of the architecture, not part of any given component. This lets me impose stricter architectural control over these interfaces, while letting the component teams have control over how they implement the interfaces. Well, this new class library, **KMS Interfaces.dll**, represents the interfaces in terms of .NET code. (The clients of interfaces and the suppliers of interfaces can all reference this library for the interface definitions.) Once I've created the library, I'll reverse engineer an XDE model from it, drag the interfaces from the architecture model, and synchronize the model, generating the code definitions for the interfaces. Then I'll compile this DLL, and the .NET interfaces are ready for use in my other projects.

Next, I'll add classes to support the **ContractorSystem** interfaces, as shown earlier in this chapter (Figures 10-39 and 10-40). And then I'll analyze the operations of these classes, as shown in the Activity Diagrams for the **ContractorSystem** component (Figures 10-41 through 10-44). And then I'll design the major structure of my classes within the **ContractorSystem**, as shown in the earlier Class Diagrams (Figures 10-45 and 10-48).

At this point, I'll be ready to design my database classes; but this is another area where VS .NET and Rational XDE change my work habits. XDE includes powerful extensions to UML for modeling databases, database tables, and database relations. These extensions allow you to generate data models from databases or database scripts, and vice versa. Thus, just as with the C# code, you can work with the database and the model simultaneously, changing whichever seems easier.

To me, it seems easier to model the data the way I envision it, and then to generate a database and stored procedures from the data model. So I'll add an XDE data model to my solution. Then I'll add a database (a component with a **«Database»** stereotype) and a schema (a package to contain the tables), as shown in Figure 10-54.

Figure 10-54. KMS data model

Within the schema package, I'll add tables: classes (with a stereotype of «**Table**») that represent tables within the database. Some of the KMS classes are shown in Figure 10-55.

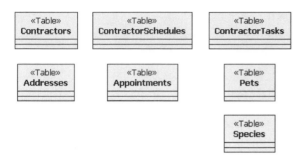

Figure 10-55. KMS database tables

Contractors will have addresses (possibly more than one each). I'll maintain contractor schedules and tasks, as well as appointments to perform a specific task at a scheduled time for a specific fee. One defining characteristic of a contractor task is that it involves a pet. And each pet has a species.

Next, I'll add columns: attributes (with stereotype «**Column**») to reflect the database columns within each table. Earlier, I decided to pass IDs as strings throughout the system. I'll capture this in the database by making IDs eight-character **CHAR** fields (a SQL fixed-length character string). The rest of the columns will be **VARCHAR** fields (a SQL character string with a maximum length) or other types as appropriate. I'll also make the ID field for each table into a unique primary key (i.e., a value that may be used to uniquely identify a particular table in the database).

In response, XDE will automatically generate two operations that represent the constraints on this key: one with a «**Primary Key**» stereotype, and one with a «**Unique Constraint**» stereotype. (The default names for these constraints are in the form **Constraint***n*. I usually rename them as **PK_***ColumnName* and **UC_***ColumnName*.) With all columns and keys added, the tables will look like Figures 10-56 through 10-58.

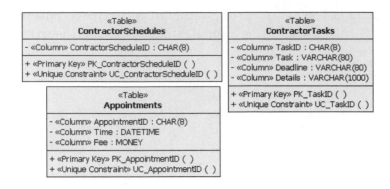

Figure 10-56. KMS schedule tables, with columns

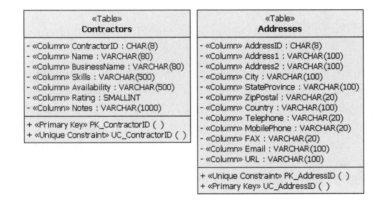

Figure 10-57. KMS contractor tables, with columns

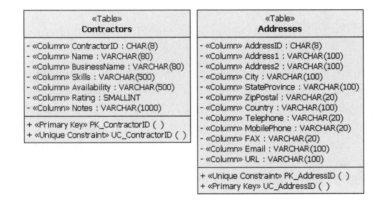

Figure 10-58. KMS pet tables, with columns

Note that I used two new SQL data types in Figure 10-56: **DATETIME**, representing a specific date and time; and **MONEY**, representing an amount of money. Also note that I used the SQL data type **BIT** to represent a simple true/false value in Figure 10-58.

Next I'll add the associations that show the relations between these tables. XDE defines four kinds of relations between tables:

- **Identifying.** This is a relationship in which the parent or referencing record must exist in order for the child or referenced record to exist.

- **Non-identifying.** This is a relationship in which the referencing record need not exist in order for the referenced record to exist.

- **Many-to-many.** This is a relationship in which the referencing record may refer to multiple referenced records, and vice versa.

- **Self-referencing**. This is a relationship in which records in a table may refer to other records in the same table.

XDE indicates these relationship types with stereotypes where appropriate. Figures 10-59 through 10-61 show the relations among the tables.

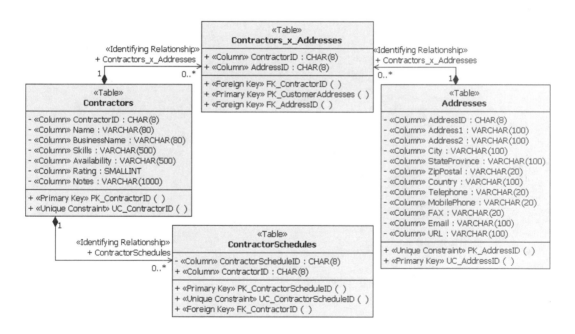

Figure 10-59. KMS contractor tables, with associations

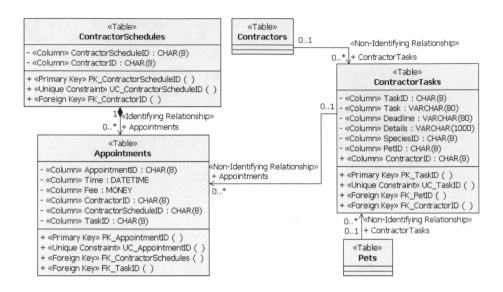

Figure 10-60. KMS schedule tables, with associations

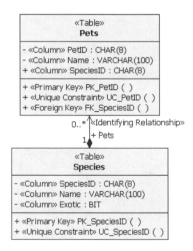

Figure 10-61. KMS pet tables, with associations

Notice in Figure 10-59 that when I added a many-to-many relation between **Contractors** and **Addresses**, XDE automatically added a cross table **Contractors_x_Addresses**, to maintain the list of relations between the two tables. Notice also that XDE automatically added foreign key columns and foreign key constraints (operations with **«Foreign Key»** stereotypes) to indicate that the relations are keys. (As with primary keys and unique constraints, XDE

named these **Constraint*n***. I usually rename them as **FK_*ColumnName*** or
FK_*TableName*.)

Next I'll need to design my stored procedures. XDE models a stored procedure
as a class with a «**Stored Procedure Container**» stereotype. Within the class is one
operation (with a «**Stored Procedure**» stereotype) that defines the signature of
the procedure. In this analysis so far, I've identified two stored procedures, as
shown in Figure 10-62.

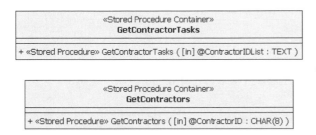

Figure 10-62. KMS stored procedures

After I have my database tables and relations and my stored procedures
designed, I'll build the database from the model. XDE will do this for me automatically: it will generate Data Definition Language (DDL) scripts, or it will directly
create or update the SQL database. First I need to mark each table or stored procedure as residing in my new database. XDE indicates this using the realization
arrow, as shown in Figure 10-63.

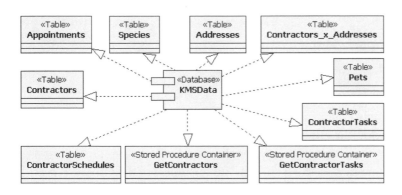

Figure 10-63. KMS database elements

Next, I'll generate the database from the data model, and then write the
stored procedures, as shown here:

```
CREATE PROCEDURE "dbo"."GetContractors" @ContractorID CHAR ( 8 )
AS
if (@ContractorID is null) or (@ContractorID = '')
    select * from Contractors
else
    select * from Contractors where (ContractorID = @ContractorID)
GO
CREATE PROCEDURE "dbo"."GetContractorTasks" @ContractorIDList TEXT
AS
if (@ContractorIDList is null) or (@ContractorIDList like '')
    select * from ContractorTasks
else
    select * from ContractorTasks
        where (@ContractorIDList like ('%'+ContractorID+'%'))
GO
```

And from these, I'll generate **DataSet** classes using the tools in VS .NET. I'll use the **Add New Item** dialog box in VS .NET to add a new data set file, **TaskData.xsd**. This file allows me to visually edit the **DataSet** class, dragging and dropping SQL elements onto it. I'll drag and drop the **GetContractorTasks** stored procedure, and VS .NET will automatically generate a **DataSet** class to hold the stored procedure results. (This class is stored in **TaskData.cs**, a code-behind file for the data set.) After this, I can create and use **TaskData** objects within my projects. I can also reverse engineer this file into the **ContractorSystem** design model.

There's a lot more I could do here, but now it's all of a very similar nature: find the easiest tool to express what I want to do, do the work in that, and then synchronize with other tools. The combination of VS .NET and XDE makes this tool swapping very easy, far easier than doing all the work straight from the model *or* straight from the code.

A Manager's View of Component Design

Depending on your development process and your team structure, component design may fall below the radar for the project manager. Instead, it's the province of the tech leads for the individual component teams. In other team structures, the project manager may *be* the tech lead. But regardless of the structure, management at the component design level becomes a different process from management at the requirements and architecture levels. The emphasis shifts from forecasting to monitoring, and from deciding what to do and how to do it to making sure it gets done.

Staffing

By this stage, your staff is more or less defined. Now you need to decide how to parcel out work to them. Rule One is simple: give work to the people who know how to do that work (or can learn within your time frame). But after Rule One, there's a sharp difference of opinion. It's common design wisdom that good design comes from individuals. As Brooks wrote:

> *I will contend that conceptual integrity is the most important consideration in system design. It is better to have a system omit certain anomalous features and improvements, but to reflect one set of design ideas, than to have one that contains many good but independent and uncoordinated ideas. . . . Conceptual integrity in turn dictates that the design must proceed from one mind, or from a very small number of agreeing resonant minds.[2]*

Yet in the very next sentence, Brooks points out at least one of the realities that undermine this approach:

> *Schedule pressures, however, dictate that system building needs many hands.[3]*

Most projects are just too large for a single mind. But there's another problem with a single designer: *sound* design comes from groups, not individuals. Even the best designers have blind spots, so you need overlapping coverage from many minds.

Resolving this paradox—conceptual integrity versus overlapping coverage—leads to the difference of opinion, different ways of staffing the design effort:

- One approach is to assign different design tasks to individual programmers, then have the team review each design and the resulting code. This requires a cyclic process: design, review, code, review, repeat. This is a classic "orchestrated" approach, heavy on design and review to ensure that no surprises slip into the system and no requirements are overlooked. Teams that follow this approach must have regular, punctual, repeatable work habits, or the process falls apart: reviews will be skipped or short-changed because people are too busy or aren't ready for the reviews. In this approach, you'll use UML for the designers to capture their thoughts and then to communicate them for review. After review, the UML model conveys to the coders what they must build.

---

2. Frederick P. Brooks, Jr., *The Mythical Man Month* (Addison-Wesley, 1995), pp. 42–44
3. Ibid., p. 44

- Another approach is to assign all tasks to the whole team to flesh out the essential design, and leave detailed design and coding to individuals. This approach imposes no particular cycle or schedule to the effort, because the team members will address tasks and requirements as they see the need. This is the currently popular "agile" approach: instead of trying to foresee and prevent surprises and plan for changes, the team must be constantly ready for the unforeseen, ready to change direction on very short notice. Teams that follow this approach must collaborate and communicate well and must have the freedom to discover instead of plan. In this approach, you'll use UML for the team to discuss and refine the design until team members can see the obvious shape of the code.

- Another approach is to assign all tasks—design *and* coding and debugging—to pairs of individuals, as in Extreme Programming. Although not commonly described this way, I see this as something of a compromise between the agile and the orchestrated approaches: work is primarily done by individuals and reviewed (continuously), with the designer and reviewer trading off roles as they see fit; but there's no need for a regular, punctuated cycle, because the pairs provide most of the review benefits of the orchestrated cycle. Teams that follow this approach must be willing and able to deal with the tension of two egos in one cubicle. In this approach, you'll use UML for the pairs to agree what task they're tackling before diving into code.

In my development experience, I've seen all three approaches fail. I've seen teams that can't adjust to the orchestrated cycle, undercut reviews, and end up in chaos. I've seen teams that can't design in a group without bickering, talking at mixed levels, and getting bogged down in minutiae of notation without ever really communicating. I've seen pairs of programmers who can't stand each other for 5 minutes at a stretch, and who end up operating as lone wolves.

And I've seen all three approaches succeed. I've seen strong leaders keep their teams on the orchestrated cycle, and reviews catch major errors before they become even more disastrous. I've seen groups of individuals who become in synch, and who naturally complement each other in seeing the big picture and the detail pictures. And I've worked in a pair where I've never been as productive in catching, diagnosing, and fixing bugs as I was for that brief period.

So you need to evaluate the best approach for your team; but as I indicated earlier, UML can serve as one of the main communications vehicles for all of them. Your major staffing challenge, regardless of approach, is to ensure that team members can communicate. From my perspective (admittedly biased), that means they need a number of communications tools, including UML.

Planning

Now the planning effort shifts from how long tasks should take to how much you can do in the next short interval of time. You have time estimates from earlier stages; now you have to ascertain how to realistically meet those estimates.

One key tool for this is your UML model. When you sit down at the start of a development cycle and try to evaluate whether a task may fit the time frame, create a preliminary design or elaborate the design you already have. You don't want a finished design, just enough of an idea to see if there's hope. If the design looks large and complex, you know you've got a problem. And if you can't get a preliminary design in time for planning the work, you know you're in trouble: a task you can't design in summary up front is a task you can't fit in one development cycle. It's just too complex.

It's also time to update your estimate and your schedule: as you get into detail design, you'll discover some extraneous design issues and some missing pieces. Communicate these to the project manager, so that they may update the overall estimate and schedule while you continue planning and designing.

Tracking

As your development cycle proceeds, you can track the progress of individual design elements against the expected schedule.

Reporting

As your development cycle proceeds, you can report the progress to the project manager, again letting the PM worry about schedule impact while you worry about correction. Team members should update each model element to reflect its progress and completeness.

Correction

Now your model can serve as a guide to reviewing and correcting the design and implementation of individual components. When problems pop up, always fall back to the design first, to ensure there are no fundamental flaws in your thinking. Then use the design as a check in reviewing your code, ensuring that the code you wrote is the code you intended to write.

Risk Management

As your detail design proceeds, you can find and explore architecture and schedule risks:

- Does your component have all the information needed by your design? Or does the architecture need to change to provide you with missing parameters?

- Do you have different, conflicting design approaches, some complex but powerful, others simple but limited? If so, when should you choose power and when should you choose simplicity?

- You're making your UI into a reality. How do users react to it? Does it present the information they need? Can they provide the information *you* need? Is it too complex for them to use?

A Tester's View of Component Design

For a tester, the component design may form "the wall," the line where your concern stops. You're testing how the code works, not how it's built.

Yet there may be a valuable role for you to play. A common practice in agile development and many other processes is for developers to write unit tests within their code itself, allowing the code to be self-testing. This allows a constant "temperature reading" on the code: if the code is failing its own tests, it hardly needs to be subjected to *your* tests. And it's a good division of labor: you likely don't have time to read every line of code and design tests for it, whereas each developer can (in theory) squeeze in time for these unit tests. In fact, in Extreme Programming, these tests are used as the main criteria for whether a chunk of code is done or not.

But one common complaint about this sort of unit testing is that developers usually are lousy testers. Their tests are not nearly comprehensive enough, certainly not up to your own standards. Developers don't learn the sort of coding strategies and techniques that you know. Now Fowler argues that's an acceptable problem:

It is better to write and run incomplete tests than not to run complete tests.[4]

---

4. Martin Fowler et al., *Refactoring: Improving the Design of Existing Code* (Addison-Wesley, 1999), p. 98

His point here, if I may interpret, is that complete tests may take so much time and effort that they never get implemented; but incomplete tests can be created with much less effort, and can then be run frequently so as to catch many simple mistakes. But I think there's a middle ground between incomplete tests and complete tests that are never written and run (or complete tests that you as a tester have to write). And the path to that middle ground is UML. You can read the code designs much more quickly than you can read the code itself; and then you can apply your testing skills to suggest unit tests that the developers can write. Furthermore, the developers may use UML to design the tests themselves, and you can help to review those test designs. In this fashion, you become something of a coach or mentor, helping the developers to become better testers.

A Documenter's View of Component Design

As a documenter, unless you have to write technical documentation to describe the design, your main interest in detailed design involves the refined UI design and the detailed logic behind it. The developers should now be able to provide you with complete screen shots and with detailed Activity Diagrams that describe what happens when the user performs various operations. They should also provide Activity Diagrams with swimlanes to show the flow of operations between pages and elements of the UI.

Summary

In this chapter, you've worked through Step 5 of Five-Step UML, which focuses on component design. As a starting point for this step, you should take the component interfaces that you diagrammed as part of Step 4. For the user interface components, it's a good idea to create GUI prototypes that enable you to better understand how end users will interact with your system. The process of determining the internal structure of a component involves repeating the first four steps of Five-Step UML, but this time focusing in on the component, rather than on the system as a whole. So that means you define your component requirements in terms of Use Case Diagrams, and refine those requirements by diagramming the algorithm for each use case as an Activity Diagram. Next, you assign responsibilities to the different elements within the component (classes and interfaces) by adding swimlanes to your Activity Diagrams. Finally, by examining the communications across swimlanes, you can work out the dependencies between the classes that comprise each component, thus organizing those classes into a coherent structure illustrated in a Class Diagram.

As in previous chapters, I showed you how this all works in practice with our KMS case study, but then I let you into a little secret—that's not actually how I work at all! In the next few sections I led you through a different approach, whereby I develop both the code and the model in parallel, using Visual Studio .NET and Rational XDE.

In the final part of the chapter, I once more took a bird's eye overview of how the whole process can be managed at this stage, from planning and staffing through to documentation and testing. As ever, estimates need to be constantly reviewed as the development of the model uncovers yet more detail, but at this stage the emphasis has moved away from planning and scheduling to monitoring the progress of work and making sure that everything stays on track.

Now the model is basically designed, but there is one more aspect you need to consider: how to model your deployment; and that is the focus of the next chapter.

CHAPTER 11

Step Outward to Design Your Deployment

YOU'VE SPENT THE LAST five chapters delving into the detail of the Five-Step process, starting with requirements analysis and working through to an architectural design, and also diagrams revealing the structures of and relationships between individual classes. Along the way, you've seen how this works in practice with the KMS case study as an example.

With all that effort, you may be forgiven for thinking that your model is complete, but in this chapter, we're going to change our focus, looking outward instead of inward, to work out where and how the components are deployed. You'll learn how to assign your various components to nodes and how to design both your logical and physical deployment using Deployment Diagrams to illustrate the nodes and the communications between them. Once more, I'll be using some diagrams from the KMS case study to illustrate the process.

NOTE I'm discussing deployment after design *not* because it should occur after design, but rather because it's hard to write an asynchronous book. Ideally, deployment design coincides with or follows component architecture and may occur in parallel with detail design.

Assigning Components to Nodes

Before you can define the nodes (computational resources), you need a place in which to define them. I prefer to place my nodes in the architecture model, in a new top-level package called **Deployment**. This package can be shared among many models, but it should be controlled as part of the architecture model.

Our starting point for designing the deployment for the KMS is the overall architectural model that we created back in Chapter 9 (Figure 9-38), where we looked at how the various components were organized into an N-Tier architecture. Now we need to think about what nodes we should add to deploy our components.

For the purposes of this example, we'll add three desktop nodes and four servers (using XDE stereotypes with custom icons to show the difference), as shown in Figure 11-1.

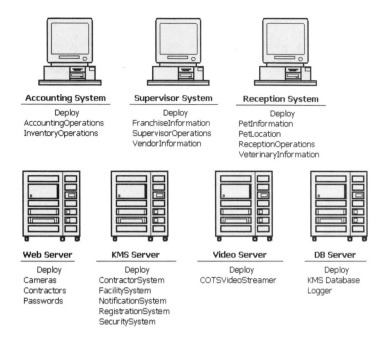

Figure 11-1. Initial KMS nodes

How did I select these nodes? Experience. Judgment. Wild guesses. *Wrong guesses.* This is just a first stab at deployment nodes, and during a process like this you should always expect to revise such a diagram as you learn more.

In the sections that follow, however, I'll review my reasoning for each node depicted in the preceding diagram, and talk about which part of the system each node is responsible for, so that you can get an idea for the kinds of systems you'll need to think about in your own development work.

Accounting System

This is a desktop system used for basic bookkeeping, plus inventory maintenance. We may find it useful to split these functions into separate nodes in large installations; but for now, we'll combine them.

Supervisor System

This is a desktop system used for all operations that are the province of the supervisor: franchise maintenance, vendor maintenance, and employee supervision.

Reception System

This is a desktop system used for all reception operations: the receptionist's work, as well as tracking pet information. We also assign the maintenance of veterinary information to the receptionist, though this task might better be performed by some other worker on a dedicated terminal.

Web Server

This is a server system for hosting all Web folders, along with their accompanying Web pages and Web controls. For throughput reasons, many projects prefer to host their Web sites on dedicated servers. I've followed this practice because it's often a good first guess for Web deployment.

KMS Server

This is a middle-tier server system for hosting all the control logic components behind our Web pages.

Video Server

This is a server system for hosting your video software. While I'm not yet certain—and this is only a hypothetical video system, don't forget—I suspect that the large number of video cameras will require a dedicated machine to manage them.

DB Server

This is a server system for hosting the database. For performance reasons, many projects prefer to host their databases on dedicated servers. I've followed this practice because it's often a good first guess for database deployment. I did add the **Logger** component to this server, for two reasons: the **Logger** will interact with the database frequently, and the **Logger** is a central service shared by many other components, just like the database.

Describing Nodes

Once you've selected a set of nodes, you can define their characteristics. To do this, you should think about the following questions:

- What type of device is a given node?

- What is its speed?

- What is its drive capacity?

- What is its memory capacity?

- What is its processor?

- What is its operating system?

- What software is preinstalled on it?

- What peripherals are attached to it?

- What ports does it have?

- Other characteristics based on the device type: page rate and dots per inch for printers, scan speed for scanners, frequency range for radio devices, etc.

The precise list of meaningful characteristics varies from device to device. You should analyze each device and document what you learn about it.

Designing the Logical Deployment

Now that you know what nodes you'll need and what kind of characteristics they'll have, next you'll need to design the logical deployment structure, which is made up of nodes and the associations between them. If two components reside on separate nodes and there is a dependency between the components, you'll need an association between the corresponding nodes.

Going back once again to our architectural Component Diagram for the KMS (Figure 9-38), we can look at what dependencies there are between our KMS components, which leads us to the Logical Deployment Diagram shown in Figure 11-2.

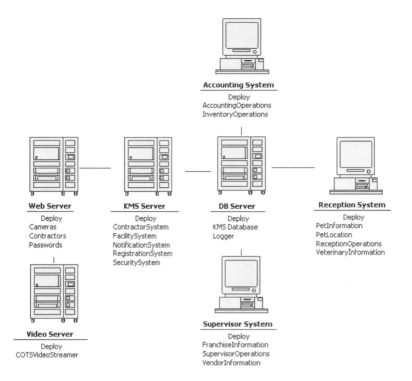

Figure 11-2. KMS logical deployment

At this stage, we should rethink some of our interfaces. Every interface that is accessed between nodes must be a remotable interface of some sort. In other words, it must be an interface that supports some form of communication (invocation, data transfer, or both) between two components that are separated across a network or some other communications channel.

For instance, according to the Context Diagram for the **Passwords** Web folder (Figure 9-39), which we developed back in Chapter 9, the **Passwords** Web folder uses the **IUserSecurity** interface to communicate with the **SecuritySystem** component. According to Figure 11-2, however, these two components will reside on separate nodes. Thus, **IUserSecurity** must be a remotable interface of some sort. In .NET, you have a number of choices for remotable interfaces:

- **Sockets.** I don't recommend this approach. It's too low level for my tastes. But if you want to use simple TCP/IP sockets—perhaps to interface with legacy applications that only support sockets—.NET provides some useful classes in the **System.Net.Sockets** namespace. This namespace provides classes for both TCP sockets (in which a listener socket waits for connection requests and then connects a client app and a server app) and UDP sockets (in which an app broadcasts messages that one or more listeners may receive).

- **Message queues.** I usually don't recommend this approach either, again, because it's too low level; but message queues can be very powerful for applications that need to communicate asynchronously and need queuing and redundancy and a number of other features. If you need this power, or if you need to communicate with existing message queue–based systems, .NET provides useful classes in the **System.Messaging** namespace. This namespace provides classes for message queues and messages, as well as for attributes that describe them. (To learn more about message queues, visit http://www.microsoft.com/windows2000/technologies/communications/ msmq/default.asp.)

- **COM+.** This is another "legacy" technology that is still very prevalent across the Windows landscape. It's a more modern, more object-like technology for remote interfaces (among other goals), and it's powerful; but it's complex. (One of the major design goals of .NET was to simplify the sort of inter- process and intersystem tasks that COM+ supports.) If you need COM+ support, .NET provides a number of useful classes in the namespace **System.Runtime.InteropServices** . VS .NET also provides a simple way to access COM and COM+ objects: you can add a reference from your project to a COM server, and VS .NET will use the classes in **System.Runtime.InteropServices** to generate wrapper classes that make COM+ objects look like well-behaved .NET objects. (Note that COM Interop isn't supported in the Microsoft Windows .NET Compact Framework.)

- **SQL/ADO.NET.** Structured Query Language (SQL) is an industry-standard data access language (with many, *many* database-specific extensions— e.g., SQL Server's T-SQL and Oracle's PL/SQL—which make it less of a standard). Most popular databases support remote access via SQL in some fashion. .NET supports SQL access through classes in the **System.Data** and **System.Data.SqlClient** namespaces. These and other namespaces make up ADO.NET, the common .NET mechanism for database access.

- **HTTP/HTML.** These protocols are the backbone of the Web, of course, building on sockets to provide a standard interface for file transfer and for hypertext markup. .NET supports HTTP through classes in the **System.Web** namespace, which is used for defining both Web apps and Web services. It supports HTML through classes in the **System.Web.UI** namespace.

- **Web services.** This is an industry-standard protocol (built on top of HTTP) for making remote processing calls by sending XML messages that conform to the Simple Object Access Protocol, or SOAP. SOAP defines XML schemas for passing request messages (including parameters) and result messages. This is a powerful technique for remote procedure calls in a heterogeneous environment, because SOAP and XML and Web services are supported on most major platforms today; but SOAP and XML and the Web services infrastructure impose a performance penalty that may be unacceptable. If performance is key, and you have .NET systems talking to other .NET systems, you'll be better off with .NET Remoting. If you're building Web services, you'll be using classes in the **System.Web** and **System.Web.Services** namespaces. These classes provide the structure of a generic Web app, along with the specific structure of a Web service.

- **.NET Remoting.** This is .NET's primary mechanism of binary interprocess communications between processes and between .NET machines. It's fast and efficient, but it's more complex and less universal than Web services. For .NET Remoting, you'll use classes from the **System.Runtime.Remoting** namespace and its many subnamespaces. These classes provide low-level support for a range of mechanisms for communicating between processes and for marshaling data between processes. (Remoting is also not supported in the .NET Compact Framework.)

Notice what's not in this list: File Transfer Protocol (FTP), Gopher, Archie, named pipes, and mailslots. FTP is an older but still common file transfer mechanism on the Internet, whereas Gopher and Archie are archaic file transfer mechanisms seldom used anymore. Named pipes are a Windows NT mechanism for interprocess communications, including those across machines, and they behave like bidirectional data streams (similar to TCP sockets). Mailslots are a unidirectional way to deliver messages to a target (similar to UDP sockets). For various reasons, the .NET team has chosen not to support these mechanisms. If you need support for them, you have more work ahead of you. Nothing in .NET prevents you from using these mechanisms, but there's no inherent support for them.

For the KMS, we'll use .NET Remoting for most of the interfaces that have to be shared between machines: **IContractors**, **IContractorSchedule**, **IContractorTasks**, **IContractorTask**, **IFacilityMap**, **ILogger**, **INotification**, **IPetRegister**, **IPets**, **IPetSecurity**, and **IUserSecurity**. We'll use ADO.NET for communication with the database and COM+ for **IVideoSwitcher**, because that was originally specified as a COM interface.

The **VideoStreamingSystem** presents more of a problem to resolve: we plan to run the video software on a dedicated machine, but **VideoStreamingSystem** is defined as a DLL. That means it doesn't execute on its own, only in the context of an application. Thus, we face a choice: we can run the **VideoStreamingSystem** on the Web browser as a DLL inside of the **Cameras** Web folder, or we can wrap the **VideoStreamingSystem** in a stand-alone .NET component and provide a .NET Remoting interface to that component. Then this new component can pass its calls through to the DLL. After proposing the first option to the Web server administrator—and after the administrator's obligatory 2-hour lecture on why it's important not to chew up Web server time on anything but Web work—

we decide to go with the second option. We'll add a new component, **VideoStreamingWrapper**, and a new .NET Remoting interface, **IVideoStreaming**.

Exercise 1101: Design Your Logical Deployment

Building on Exercise 904, where you identified your component dependencies and defined an architecture between them, identify and define nodes, and assign each component to a node. Describe the expected characteristics of each node. Draw one or more logical Deployment Diagrams to reflect your physical architecture.

Designing the Physical Deployment

Once you have your logical deployment worked out, you can work on the physical deployment.

For our KMS example, we'll start by making a copy of our Logical Deployment Diagram (Figure 11-2). We'll then hide the components and the logical associations. And finally, we'll add the physical associations. This leads to the diagram in Figure 11-3.

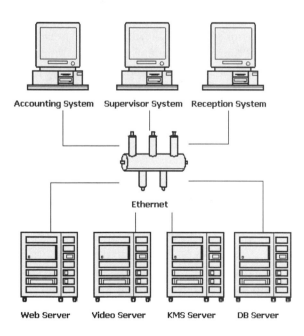

Figure 11-3. KMS physical deployment

Next we'll add other devices external to the nodes where our code resides. We'll also add multiplicity, as appropriate. The result is shown in Figure 11-4.

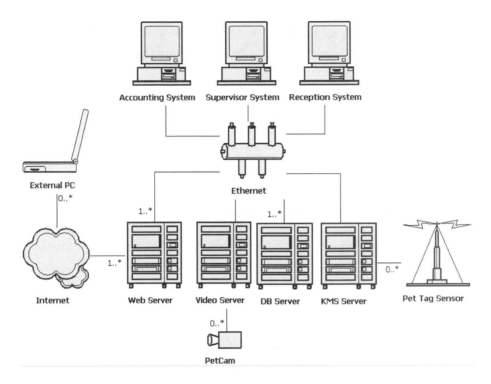

Figure 11-4. KMS physical deployment, revised

Describing Associations

We've now seen how to design the logical and the physical deployment. The next stage is to define the characteristics of the physical associations. For example:

- What is the mechanism for a given association (e.g., serial line, parallel line, coax cable, Ethernet cable, wireless, infrared, etc.)?

- What is its transmission speed?

- What is its physical protocol?

- What are its logical protocols?

There may be other meaningful characteristics for a particular physical association. Again, you should analyze each association, and document what you learn about it.

Exercise 1102: Design Your Physical Deployment

Building on Exercise 1101, draw one or more physical Deployment Diagrams to reflect your physical architecture. Describe the expected characteristics of each physical association.

A Manager's View of Deployment

Deployment design helps the project manager to understand the global view of the system. The emphasis here is on hardware, leading to new staffing and planning and risk management issues.

Staffing

Once you've identified your nodes and your associations, you've learned something more about your required skill sets. You'll need someone who knows how to program or communicate with each device, and you'll need someone who understands the remoting technologies used in your associations. Similarly, when hiring support staff, you'll need personnel who understand all of the devices in question.

Planning

Planning in regard to Deployment Diagrams is not about planning the effort of your staff. It's about planning the necessary hardware, along with planning the software to drive the hardware and interface with the devices. Devices and drivers need to be available to your team when their code needs to be deployed upon them. This is a relatively straightforward resource planning issue.

But there's another kind of hardware planning for which Deployment Diagrams can help: planning to ensure you have the necessary hardware capacity. Do you have enough memory? Enough CPU power? Enough bandwidth?

Just as there are two main elements in a Deployment Diagram—nodes and associations—there are two main categories of hardware resources that you can plan with Deployment Diagrams. These two categories of hardware resources are node resources (hardware capacity) and association resources (communications and bandwidth capacity). Each of these hardware categories are resources suited for both coarse-grained and fine-grained planning and load balancing.

Let's take a brief look at each of these situations in turn:

Node balancing (coarse-grained approach). To balance the load on your nodes, simply count the components assigned to each one, and try to equalize them. Count components that "feel large" as two, or three, or even more components. For example, the database is a large component in many systems, so I count it as three components. The Web server is also large, so I count it as two if it's dedicated to my project, three otherwise. Also recognize that some nodes are larger and more powerful than others, so that you can assign them many more components. This coarse-grained approach has far too little precision. You shouldn't purchase your hardware based on its results. But because it's coarse grained, you can apply this approach very early, as your architecture and designs are still in the concept stage. It lets you form a basic hardware strategy early on. Like the rest of the design, you'll refine the hardware spec later.

Node balancing (fine-grained approach). As your design matures, you can more clearly foresee your hardware needs. Take a given component. Look at the data elements that it stores in a given interface call or user interface action. How large, on average, is each data element? Is the number of elements fixed, or does it grow and shrink with particular actions? Looking at the use cases that involve that component, how often and how quickly do the data elements grow? These questions help you to define a storage budget for the component. Similarly, you can build budgets for memory and other consumable resources. You can also assign rough times to method calls and then multiply those times by frequency estimates to determine a rough CPU budget for the component. If you sum the resource budgets for all components on a given node, you have a rough idea of whether the node is powerful enough for the work assigned. You want a comfortable safety margin—probably a factor of three or more—to allow for unforeseen problems and to ensure smooth performance. This fine-grained approach potentially has a lot more precision. The precision is not automatic—you have to do a lot of work to build the resource budgets for each component—but the effort pays for itself the first time you find a hardware deficiency *before* shipping the system. It's far more cost effective to ship the right hardware the first time than to try to upgrade hardware in the field.

Association balancing (coarse-grained approach). To balance the load on your associations, count the interface methods assigned to each one, and try to equalize them. Again, count interface methods that "feel large" as multiple methods. At the early stage, which is when this approach is most suitable, you may not know a lot about the interface methods, so it's easiest to treat them all the same; but if, say, one method is retrieving large image files and another is returning phone numbers, it would be foolish to assume the two methods have the same impact on communications. You'll have to apply a lot of judgment in recognizing large methods and sizing them; so again, this coarse-grained approach lacks precision. But you can apply this approach very early in the architecture and design stages, looking ahead for communications bottlenecks.

Association balancing (fine-grained approach). As your interface design matures, you can examine the parameters and return values for each method and determine an average size for each value. Then you can determine frequency estimates for each scenario of each use case; and from the use cases and the Activity Diagrams, you can estimate how frequently each interface method will be called. Then multiply frequency by size to estimate the total communications budget for a given method. Sum these estimates to produce overall estimates for the communications load. Again, you want a comfortable safety margin to allow for unforeseen problems and to ensure smooth performance. If the margin looks tight, consider relocating some components to the same machine, so they won't need to communicate over the network. Consider redesigning the system so that large data is stored on the same machine as components that use the data. Consider multiple communication channels between particular nodes. In a mature design, you have the basis for a lot more precision in these estimates. They won't guarantee that you *won't* have communications bottlenecks; but if they indicate that you *do* have a bottleneck, you'd be well advised to resolve it before you ship the system.

Risk Management

The major risks involved with Deployment Diagrams include the risks identified earlier, as well as these others:

- Do your nodes have enough capacity for your components, with acceptable margins for error?

- Do you have enough nodes?

- Do you have team members with the right skills to develop for each node?

- Do you have team members with the right skills to support each node?

- Do you have team members with the right skills to develop communications code for each communication protocol?

- Do your physical associations have enough bandwidth to support their interfaces, with acceptable margins for error?

A Tester's View of Deployment

For a tester, Deployment Diagrams indicate a number of test scenarios:

- Every physical association represents a potential break in the system. Test what happens when you "pull the plug" on each association. How do the disconnected components cope with the loss of communications?

- Are the components designed to automatically reconnect when the association is reinstated? If so, test that this works. If not, test the manual mechanisms for reestablishing connections.

- Is a given association one-to-one? Test what happens when one end of the association is duplicated on the network. Can the other end find the right connection? Then test duplicating the other end.

- Is a given association one-to-many? What is the expected limit on "many"? Test what happens as you approach that limit. Test at the limit. Test *beyond* the limit.

- Is a given association many-to-many? How do the association ends find other ends? Test that this mechanism successfully connects.

- Look at the frequency estimates for use cases and scenarios that determine the load the system was designed to handle. Test that load. Test beyond that load. Test up to the safety margins and beyond.

- Look at the resource budgets for each component. Look at the static storage requirements and the expected storage growth over time. Instrument the system to ensure these budgets are not exceeded.

A Documenter's View of Deployment

For a documenter, Deployment Diagrams are useful for documenting how the hardware should be installed and connected. The logical Deployment Diagrams are useful for end-user docs, because they show the concepts of where pieces of the system reside. These form a useful overview. The physical Deployment Diagrams are useful for writing tech docs, showing precisely how the hardware should connect. Because both logical and physical Deployment Diagrams are pictures of physical things—and thus are meaningful to the average user—consider whether you might want to include these diagrams directly in your docs.

Summary

In this chapter, you've made a quick tour through the process of designing the deployment of a system, looking at the KMS case study as an example.

When thinking about deployment, you should use your component architecture as a starting point and consider what kinds of nodes you'll need to support those components. You should determine what kind of characteristics those nodes will need to have—for example, their capacity, speed, what operating system they run, and so on. The associations between the components will guide you as to the associations you'll need between your nodes, so that you can design firstly your logical deployment and secondly your physical deployment. Note that you'll need to consider what kind of technology to use for communications between components running on separate nodes.

Toward the end of the chapter, I took a step back and examined the manager's view of deployment, important aspects of which include planning what kind of hardware will be necessary and what the implications are for bandwidth. I also reviewed how you can use your model to plan node and association balancing at different stages of the model development, a process that allows you to better determine your hardware requirements. Finally, I examined what extra risks should be considered during the deployment design stage, and what implications the design held for testers and documents.

Now you've worked all the way through the complete process, from beginning to end, and you should have a good idea about how to employ these ideas in your own design and development work. As I said at the start of all this, though, Five-Step UML isn't the only way forward; indeed, it isn't even the best process out there, merely a good starting point. In order to get a better idea, then, of the different kind of methodologies used by design professionals, I'll spend the next chapter discussing some popular development processes, examining them in the form of—yes, you guessed it!—UML models.

Part Three
Beyond Code

And now, at the end of this book, we come to UML's dirty little secret . . .

UML isn't about software design.

All right, let me clarify: UML isn't about software design; it's about system design. And software is just one kind of system.

A system, in this case, is structure with behavior. In code, the structure is components and classes and relations; and the behavior is their methods and interactions, along with the use cases realized through those methods and interactions.

But UML was consciously designed to support modeling of more than just software. In fact, the Three Amigos designed UML in part to use in documenting the Unified Process (UP), their view for a customizable process for software development (and now often called the Rational Unified Process, or RUP). After all, a development team is a system: its structure is the team members, the customers, and the artifacts gathered and produced; and its behavior is the processes and activities by which the team produces the artifacts.

In this section, we'll start by looking at UML models of some popular development processes, as an example of how UML can be used to design systems and processes. I'll also give you an introduction to these processes, and discuss how UML might be used in each.

And I'll finish this section—and the main body of this book—with my last word on UML and the role it plays in communication.

CHAPTER 12
UML Models of Development Processes

THROUGHOUT THIS BOOK, I've focused on Five-Step UML, a lightweight model-centered development process, but in this chapter, I'll take a step back and examine some other common modeling processes. I'll start with the (now defunct) Waterfall Model, and then look at the Spiral Process, before moving on to a more in-depth discussion of the Unified Process. You'll also see how Five-Step UML fits in. Finally, I'll discuss the more recent paradigm of Extreme Programming.

In the models presented in this chapter, we'll focus on the activities that go into each process and on the classes and objects that result. Most of the UML you'll see in this chapter will be in the form of Activity Diagrams, which illustrate the processes as they relate to different classes and objects. We'll also look at the actors that participate in various parts of each process, shown by swimlanes in the Activity Diagrams. We'll have little use for some UML concepts, however, including the following:

- **Use cases and Use Case Diagrams.** Remember that use cases represent requirements of a system. Well, in these general models, the requirements are pretty much all the same: gather and satisfy requirements. So think of this as the sole use case for each process. The diagrams within each process describe how this use case is fulfilled.

- **Components and Component Diagrams.** Remember that a component represents a collection of related classes and objects, including the data they contain and the operations they perform. The closest analogy to components in a process might be the departments into which team members are organized, and within which objects are manipulated.

- **Interfaces.** Remember that an interface simply represents a contract or mechanism by which two components communicate. This can be a useful analogy in the team structure, defining the ways two departments interact; but this is *not* a book on departmental organization.

- **Nodes and Deployment Diagrams.** Remember that a node represents a physical location where components are deployed. The closest analogy to nodes in a process might be the buildings and locations where teams work. Again, this is *not* a book on corporate facilities management, so we won't need this analogy.

Note that all of these concepts could be useful for describing a particular implementation of a given process within your organization. They're just too specific for a general discussion such as this.

Note also that the Unified Process has a number of custom stereotypes specifically used for describing itself; but to make it easier to compare the models of the different processes, I'll avoid those UP-specific stereotypes and instead use common process stereotypes across all processes as needed. These stereotypes are as follows:

- An «**Internal Actor**» stereotype (applied to actors and swimlanes) indicates a member of your team or organization who does work within the process.

- An «**External Actor**» stereotype (applied to actors and swimlanes) indicates a person outside of your team or organization who does work within the process. Usually, this will be a client of your organization.

- An «**Internal Document**» stereotype (applied to classes and objects) indicates a document or other design artifact created within your organization. This may include specs, reports, schedules, code, etc. This stereotype appears in a Class or Activity Diagram as an open file folder with a document inside.

Internal Document

- An «**External Document**» stereotype (applied to classes and objects) indicates a document or other design artifact created outside your organization. This may include client requests, external protocols, etc. This stereotype appears in a Class or Activity Diagram as a closed file folder.

External Document

- A **«Cycle»** stereotype (applied to activities) indicates a process step that is repeated as many times as needed, refining and correcting through multiple iterations. This stereotype appears in an Activity Diagram as a clockwise arrow.

Cycle

A UML Model of the Waterfall Model

The Waterfall Model, as discussed in Chapter 2, is the oldest formal process for software development. In this very formal process, requirements are gathered, copiously documented, and then sealed. An architecture is designed, documented, and then sealed. And so on. In its purest form, it appears as shown in Figure 12-1.

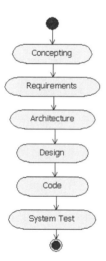

Figure 12-1. The Waterfall Model

This pure form, however, is too limiting for most projects. It assumes that every step is absolutely completed before the next step begins. On few projects can you be so certain of this, so the process is often modified as shown in Figure 12-2.

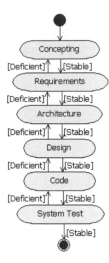

Figure 12-2. The Waterfall Model with backflow

You no longer expect a given activity to be "complete." Instead, you expect it to be "stable": complete to the best of your understanding, and not changing. Then in any activity, if you find that the preceding activity is deficient, your Waterfall has to "flow backwards."

Usually, each transition between activities is marked by the handoff of some sort of document. These documents are shown in Figure 12-3.

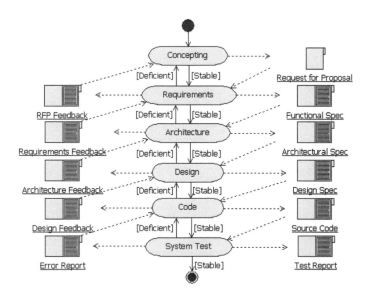

Figure 12-3. The Waterfall Model with transition documents

The transition documents are as follows:

- **Request for Proposal (RFP).** This is a document that your client prepares, describing the business requirements, goals for the system, and basic functionality. In a perfect world, this document would contain use cases, Use Case Diagrams, Activity Diagrams, and even Class Diagrams that explain the problem domain to you. If it doesn't (which is to be expected, as many clients won't be UML-aware), you may have to draw these diagrams as a way to understand and analyze the RFP.

- **Functional Spec.** This document, prepared by your analysts, converts the RFP into a set of detailed functions to be designed and implemented. Traditionally, this sort of document contains a number of narratives of system use, along with a number of definitions for terms in the domain. With UML, you can add diagrams to act as overviews and context for the text. You should create use cases, Use Case Diagrams, Activity Diagrams, and Class Diagrams for the domain (or build on the diagrams from the RFP, if it has any). You should also add more detailed Activity Diagrams until the business rules and the user interfaces and interfaces with other systems are well understood.

- **Architectural Spec.** Your architects prepare this document, building on the Functional Spec to define the component structure of the system, the interfaces between components, and the architectural pattern and rules. You'll add Interaction Diagrams (Collaboration and Sequence Diagrams) that show how the parts of the system carry out the business rules, Component Diagrams that show how components are interrelated, and perhaps Class and Database Diagrams to show the structure of key information within the system.

- **Design Specs.** Your designers prepare these documents, one for each component of the system, exploring the component structure and detail in depth. You'll add detailed Class and Interaction Diagrams, precisely specifying the structure and behavior of the code.

- **Source Code.** This is the code itself, of course, derived from the Design Specs. The programmers use the Design Specs to guide them in crafting algorithms and user interfaces and database accesses and all the other sorts of code.

- **Test Report.** Your testers produce this document, a detailed demonstration of how the code meets all tests. These tests are derived from the preceding documents, both text and diagrams. The tests themselves may be designed through UML diagrams: Interaction Diagrams to show test flow, Component and Class Diagrams to show scaffold code structures, etc.

- **Error Report.** This is a report from the testers to the programmers, indicating ways in which the code fails to meet requirements. It may reference particular documents and diagrams to help explain where the code falls short.

- **Design Feedback.** This is a report from the programmers to the designers, identifying and assessing issues about the design and any problems that might make it difficult to implement in its current definition. It may reference particular diagrams and text within the Design Spec, and it may include additional UML diagrams to demonstrate what the problems or questions are.

- **Architecture Feedback.** This is a report from the designers to the architects, identifying and assessing either questions about the architecture or problems that make the architecture unimplementable as is. It may reference particular diagrams and text within the Architecture Spec, and it may include additional UML diagrams to demonstrate what the problems or questions are.

- **Requirements Feedback.** This is a report from the architects to the analysts, identifying and assessing either questions about the requirements or tradeoffs and alternatives in how the requirements may be realized. It may reference particular diagrams and text within the Functional Spec, and it may include additional UML diagrams to demonstrate what the questions or tradeoffs are.

- **RFP Feedback.** This is a report from the analysts to the clients, identifying and assessing either questions about the requirements or tradeoffs and alternatives in how the requirements may be realized (possibly built on the Requirements Feedback document from the architects). It may reference particular diagrams and text within the Functional Spec and the RFP, and it may include additional UML diagrams to demonstrate what the questions or tradeoffs are.

As indicated by these descriptions, the Waterfall activities are usually assigned to different individuals or teams (or to different roles, with some people filling multiple roles). I could have added swimlanes to depict these responsibilities, but I think the resulting diagram wouldn't add much to your understanding. Look at some of the old systems analysis and design textbooks from the 1960s and 1970s to get a flavor of the stifling inflexibility of the process. (Back then, projects often lasted 5 years.)

Figures 12-4 through 12-6 show some common variations of the Waterfall Model. In Figure 12-4, you can see a Waterfall Model in which each component is designed as a separate, parallel project within the main project. Thus, you have one thread for each project. When the individual components are finished, you perform integration testing to ensure that the components work well together. This version of the Waterfall Model is more suited to large projects than the one shown in Figure 12-1 is, because one main benefit of component design is to allow separation of concerns and parallel, independent work.

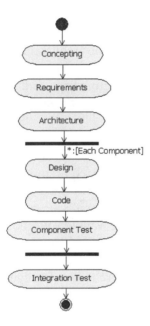

Figure 12-4. The Waterfall Model with component projects

In Figure 12-5, you can see the Staged Delivery process, a Waterfall Model broken into smaller stages to more easily manage and plan the effort. In this process, you plan the stages, along with milestones to mark the completion of each stage. At the end of each stage, you perform the component integration tests, optionally release those components, and then move on to the next stage.

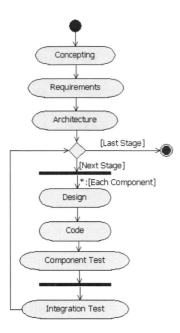

Figure 12-5. The Staged Delivery process

In Figure 12-6, you can see the Evolutionary Delivery process, a more radical departure from the Waterfall Model. Evolutionary Delivery assumes that the major risk in system development is meeting the wrong requirements. It acknowledges that requirements gathering is a difficult, inexact art, and likely cannot be done correctly in advance. Thus, Evolutionary Delivery entails understanding a preliminary, incomplete set of requirements, and designing and implementing those requirements. Then, by releasing a version of the system and gathering user feedback, you get a clearer picture of the *true* requirements. Users tell you what they don't like, and you learn which requirements you didn't really understand. Users tell you what's missing and what they can't do, and you learn which requirements they forgot to tell you. And if you work on small chunks of requirements over small intervals of time, you'll spend very little time following the wrong course.

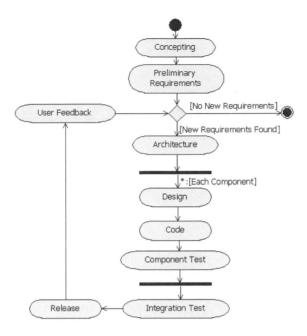

Figure 12-6. The Evolutionary Delivery process

Unlike Staged Delivery, Evolutionary Delivery has no fixed number of iterations, and only one fixed milestone at any time: the next release. Staged Delivery assumes you know the basic requirements and can break them into manageable chunks; Evolutionary Delivery assumes you *don't* know most of the requirements, but can learn them through interaction with users of the system as it progresses. Evolutionary Delivery and Staged Delivery are both influenced by Boehm's Spiral process, as are the Unified Process and Extreme Programming. So we'll examine the Spiral process next.

A UML Model of the Spiral Process

The Spiral process from Barry W. Boehm[1] is an iterative approach to software development, structuring development as a number of smaller projects that build the system in layers over time. The traditional picture of the Spiral process

---

1. Barry W. Boehm, "A Spiral Model of Software Development and Enhancement," *IEEE Computer* (May 1988), pp. 61–72

is, well, a spiral; but that picture isn't easy to draw well in UML, and isn't easy to read, either. So I'm going to take a different approach to modeling the Spiral, as shown in Figure 12-7.

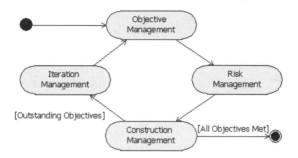

Figure 12-7. The Spiral process, iterative workflow

The Spiral process consists of four major activities, each considered to be roughly equal in import:

1. **Objective Management.** In this activity, you determine the objectives to be addressed next: the business requirements, the user requirements, the nonfunctional requirements, and the constraints. Because the Spiral process is iterative, you don't try to understand the complete set of requirements yet. Instead, you identify the requirements that you understand best; and from those, you identify the ones that are most significant (in terms of architectural impact, user priorities, etc.). This should result in a small, manageable set of objectives for the current iteration; and in the process of the current iteration, you'll learn more about the entire set of objectives.

2. **Risk Management.** In this activity, you explore the risks involved with the current objectives. You define the requirements more fully than during the **Objective Management** activity, especially nonfunctional requirements and constraints that affect the objectives, because those usually entail risks if they're violated. You build prototypes of user interfaces to ensure that they meet user expectations for clarity and ease of use and functionality. And you build prototypes of critical algorithms—database access, communications, time-critical operations, space-critical operations, etc.—so that you can be sure you know the right way to

handle each. The **Risk Management** activity should result in a very complete understanding of the current objectives, so that there are few surprises in store. You may also discover that some of your current objectives are too large for the current iteration and need to be revisited (and perhaps subdivided) in a later iteration. (Note that **Risk Management** as used here has a very specific meaning, different from what you might find in other industries such as finance.)

3. **Construction Management.** In this activity, you design, implement, and test the code to satisfy the current objectives, based largely on what you learned in the **Risk Management** activity. In early iterations, you design the revised software functionality in depth (something like the Functional Spec in the Waterfall Model). In later iterations, you design the architecture and details and tests. And in still later iterations—when you understand a set of objectives and risks and the strategies for dealing with them in depth—you implement and test the code. This becomes the first release. In later iterations, you specify and design and implement and test enhancements to this release, growing the code in layers of functionality.

4. **Iteration Management.** In this activity, you assess what you accomplished in the current iteration—what did you learn, what objectives did you meet, what objectives did you defer, what risks did you discover, what risks did you mitigate, etc.—and determine what you should accomplish next. You make detailed plans for the next iteration, and less detailed plans for future iterations.

You can see how the iterative philosophy of the Spiral process is repeated in the iterations of Evolutionary Delivery. Staged Delivery is less like the Spiral process, because Staged Delivery assumes that the requirements are largely defined in advance. By making continuous requirements discovery part of each iteration, Evolutionary Delivery becomes more like the Spiral process, analyzing and addressing new and changing requirements as the system develops. (Evolutionary Delivery is more structured than Extreme Programming, but it has a similar philosophy of continuous requirements discovery.)

But Evolutionary Delivery is rather free form, and thus not very predictable. Couldn't you get some more control and predictability and still allow for continuous requirements discovery by moving the requirements activity inside the iterations? Yes, you can; and when you do, it will look a lot like the Unified Process.

A UML Model of the Unified Process

The Unified Process is a confusing concept—and sometimes doesn't feel very unified at all—because there are actually multiple Unified Processes:

- The Unified Process is a proposal from Jacobson, Booch, Rumbaugh, and others at Rational Software for a standard software development process. It bears some superficial resemblance to the Waterfall Model; but as a more modern approach, it's more component and object oriented, and it's more iterative and incremental. It's also extremely customizable: it explicitly acknowledges that different projects require different degrees of process.[2]

- The Rational Unified Process is an integrated suite of tools from Rational for implementing, supporting, and customizing the Unified Process. While I think these are excellent tools, I find it unfortunate that many people confuse the tools with the process. Then, if they choose not to purchase the tools, they believe that the Unified Process offers no benefit to them. In this, they're quite wrong: the process is a useful approach no matter what tools you use.

- And then there's any given customization of the Unified Process. A team working on a very large project and a team working on a very small project may seem to be following entirely different processes, and yet both may claim to be following the Unified Process.

In this model, I'll describe just the basic outline of the Unified Process. For more details, I recommend *The Unified Software Development Process* from the Three Amigos.

The Four Key Characteristics

As described in *The Unified Software Development Process*,[3] the Unified Process has four key characteristics that drive its structure and how you apply the process:

1. **Use-Case Driven.** The Unified Process is driven by (and usually starts with) identifying, elaborating, categorizing, and modeling use cases. Thus, user needs are integrated into and reflected within all steps of the process.

---

2. Ivar Jacobson, Grady Booch, and James Rumbaugh, *The Unified Software Development Process* (Addison-Wesley, 1999), pp. 416–419

3. Ibid., pp. 3–8

2. **Architecture-Centric.** The Unified Process has a very broad definition of architecture, encompassing not just key elements of the system's structure, but also key use cases, key classes, key interfaces, and key methods. In the UP view, the architecture encompasses all "essential" views of the system structure, at different levels of abstraction.

3. **Iterative.** The system is analyzed, architected, designed, and implemented in cycles or iterations, mini-projects defined by identifying a set of use cases and use case scenarios that comprise a useful extension to existing knowledge and work; analyzing and identifying and managing risks within those use cases; and then architecting, designing, implementing, and testing to fulfill those use cases. (The nature of an iteration is explored further in the next section, "The Core Workflow.")

4. **Incremental.** The iterations of work can be further grouped into *increments,* marked by milestone points that indicate a particular large chunk of functionality is ready for release.

The Core Workflow

The Unified Process embraces the core philosophy of the Spiral process: that requirements gathering and analysis and design are all continuous parts of software development, rather than distinct activities performed in advance. Like Spiral, UP arranges these activities into a cycle, which forms the Core Workflow of UP, as shown in Figure 12-8.

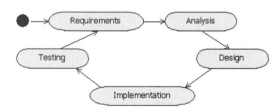

Figure 12-8. The Core Workflow of the Unified Process

Note that when I refer to an "iteration" in the Unified Process, I'm referring to one complete cycle through these five activities that make up the Core Workflow. Here, the five activities of the Core Workflow are as follows:

1. **Requirements.** Discovering, gathering, and organizing new and existing requirements.

2. **Analysis.** Analyzing, refining, and structuring the requirements, leading to early stages of an architecture. Recall from Chapter 9 that the Unified Process considers *architecture* to mean much more than code structure. Rather, UP uses the term to mean identification and elaboration of "architecturally significant" elements of the system. The concept of architectural significance thus includes the preliminary design of critical subsystems and the preliminary design of critical functionality. This is why analysis—typically thought of as a requirements activity—involves the architecture under UP. (UP has four main characteristics. It is architecture-centric, use-case driven, iterative, and incremental. You'll see these characteristics in the UP diagrams. For instance, Figure 12-8 represents the iterative nature of UP, and Figure 12-9, shown later, will represent the incremental nature.)

3. **Design.** Refining the requirements and architecture into a detailed architecture and detailed designs.

4. **Implementation.** Deriving code from the detailed designs, and refining and unit testing that code.

5. **Testing.** Designing, implementing, applying, and assessing tests to verify that the code meets the requirements. These results feed back into the **Requirements** activity, so that you can revise the requirements based on questions raised in the tests.

Unlike the Spiral process—where **Objective Management**, **Risk Management**, **Construction Management**, and **Iteration Management** form the "outer" shape of the process, with details within—the UP Core Workflow is actually an "inner" shape. These activities happen *within* larger activities of the process. In UP, all five of these workflows take place throughout the life of the project, but the proportion of time spent on each during one iteration changes as the project matures:

- Early in the project, **Requirements** consume most of the effort. **Analysis** proceeds to give structure to the requirements, and to raise architectural concerns that may lead to tradeoffs in the requirements. **Design** and **Implementation** are focused mostly on critical architecture, and perhaps on UI prototypes and other prototypes to explore the feasibility of the requirements. **Testing** is a minor effort, focused on identifying what to test and how to test to verify that the requirements are met, as well as on a testing infrastructure.

- In the middle of the project, **Requirements** are baselined, but continue to grow in response to new user needs *and* to discoveries in other activities. **Analysis** works to incorporate new requirements into the existing architecture, and to revise the architecture where it must. **Design** and **Implementation** are focused on architecture in depth and resulting code. **Testing** is focused on testing new functionality and verifying that old functionality is unbroken.

- Late in the project, **Requirements** effort drops to a minimum, handling essential change requests (and perhaps gathering nonessential requests for a next-generation project). **Analysis** similarly drops to only that needed for new requirements. **Design** is ongoing, but again focused primarily on the few new requirements. **Implementation** and **Testing** dominate the effort, pushing toward the goal of "all requirements met."

The Unified Process Phases

Early, middle, and *late* in the preceding discussion are not very specific terms. UP defines much more specific phases of the development process: Inception, Elaboration, Construction, and Transition, as shown in Figure 12-9.

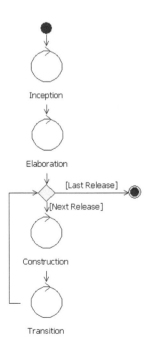

Figure 12-9. The phases of the Unified Process

I used the «Cycle» stereotype for these phases, because each represents one or more increments of effort, where an increment is the result of one iteration through the Core Workflow. Thus, each phase is cyclic until enough increments have accumulated to support transition to the next phase.

The UP phases work as follows:

- **Inception.** In this phase, you define the requirements and a candidate architecture to the point where you can assess the feasibility of the project, define initial estimates and schedules, and decide whether to take on the project or not.

- **Elaboration.** In this phase, you define the architecture in detail, setting the framework for the remaining phases.

- **Construction.** In this phase, the system is built over a number of increments and releases.

- **Transition.** In this phase, the current set of increments of the system is released to the user community for use and for feedback.

Again, each phase contains within it iterations of the Core Workflow. Next, we'll look at each activity in the Core Workflow in more depth.

The Requirements Workflow

The Requirements Workflow is depicted in Figure 12-10.

In this diagram, the swimlanes represent actors participating in the workflow:

- **System Analyst.** This actor is responsible for describing the domain and the requirements to the rest of the team.

- **Architect.** This actor is responsible for the architecture of the system.

- **Use Case Specifier.** This actor is responsible for comprehending and describing one or more use cases in depth.

- **User Interface Designer.** This actor is responsible for designing and implementing the use interfaces of the system.

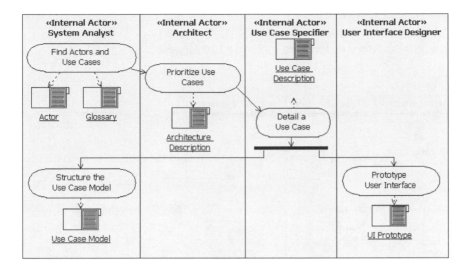

Figure 12-10. The Unified Process Requirements Workflow

The «**Internal Document**» objects in the diagram represent artifacts or work products produced within the workflow:

- **Actor.** This object represents the descriptions of one or more actors that will interact with the system.

- **Glossary.** This object represents the formal definitions of one or more domain objects within the problem domain.

- **Architecture Description.** This object represents the description of the architecturally significant elements of the system. At this time, that means primarily the significant use cases (as judged by the architect), including Use Case Diagrams and Interaction Diagrams as appropriate. This object will reappear in other workflows, with new kinds of information added to it in each workflow.

- **Use Case Description.** This object represents the descriptions of one or more use cases, including scenarios (perhaps captured as Activity Diagrams).

- **Use Case Model.** This object represents the structure and relationships of actors, use cases, and domain objects, captured in part as Use Case Diagrams, Activity Diagrams, and Class Diagrams.

- **UI Prototype.** This object represents prototype user interfaces for one or more use cases.

The Analysis Workflow

The Analysis Workflow is depicted in Figure 12-11.

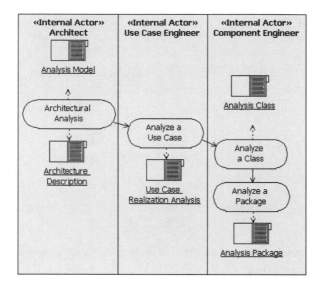

Figure 12-11. The Unified Process Analysis Workflow

In this diagram, I've added two new swimlanes:

- **Use Case Engineer.** This actor is responsible for analyzing and detailing one or more use cases.

- **Component Engineer.** This actor is responsible for specifying the responsibilities of one or more classes in one or more packages within one or more components, along with the interactions among classes.

I've also added the following **«Internal Document»** objects:

- **Architecture Description.** This object reappears in this workflow, adding the architecturally significant classes and packages and components, plus Class Diagrams and Component Diagrams. Interaction Diagrams can also be helpful explaining the purpose and method of critical use cases.

- **Analysis Model.** This object represents the packages and components and interfaces of the system, captured in Component Diagrams and Class Diagrams.

- **Use Case Realization Analysis.** This object represents the detailed analysis of one or more use cases, including detailed analysis Class Diagrams and Interaction Diagrams.

- **Analysis Class.** This object represents one or more classes or interfaces of the system, expressed at the analysis scope. This identifies the responsibilities and interfaces, but not necessarily the internals.

- **Analysis Package.** This object represents one or more packages of analysis classes, with each package possibly corresponding to a component.

The Design Workflow

The Design Workflow is depicted in Figure 12-12.

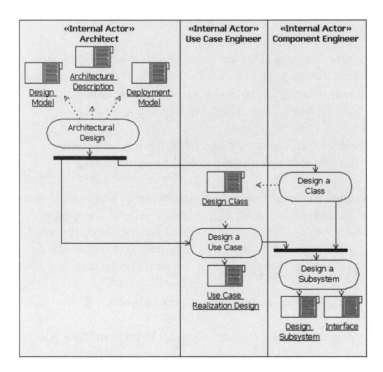

Figure 12-12. The Unified Process Design Workflow

In this diagram, you see a number of «**Internal Document**» objects:

- **Architecture Description.** This object represents the detailed decomposition into components and interfaces, captured in Component Diagrams, and Class and Interaction Diagrams for the architecturally significant elements.

- **Design Model.** This object represents the packages and components and interfaces of the system—in more depth and implementation detail than in the Analysis Model—captured in Component Diagrams and Class Diagrams.

- **Deployment Model.** This object represents the deployment of the components and interfaces to nodes and physical associations of the system, captured in Deployment Diagrams.

- **Design Class.** This object represents one or more classes or interfaces of the system, expressed at the design scope. This specifies the internals of the class: its attributes and operations and behavior in depth.

- **Use Case Realization Design.** This object represents the detailed analysis of one or more use cases, going beyond the Use Case Realization Analysis to include precise method parameters, return values, detailed logic, etc. Writing code from these diagrams should be like falling off a log.

- **Interface.** This object represents one or more interfaces, specified at a level of detail suitable for implementation in the target language.

- **Design Subsystem.** This object represents one or more components that concretely realize a set of interfaces and contain a set of design classes.

The Implementation Workflow

The Implementation Workflow is depicted in Figure 12-13.

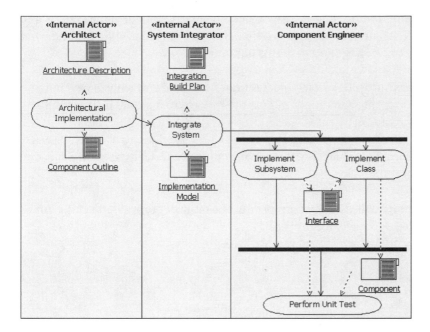

Figure 12-13. The Unified Process Implementation Workflow

In this diagram, I've added one new swimlane:

- **System Integrator.** This actor is responsible for creating integration plans to install or update the system.

You also have the following **«Internal Document»** objects:

- **Architecture Description.** This object represents updated Component Diagrams, Class Diagrams, and Interaction Diagrams.

- **Component Outline.** This object represents the detailed component and deployment structure, captured in Component and Deployment Diagrams.

- **Implementation Model.** This object represents a model of the system, and is used in later increments to help determine what has changed and what needs to be integrated with this iteration.

- **Integration Model.** This object represents a model of what is new in the system, along with details of how the new elements shall be integrated with existing elements.

- **Interface.** This object represents one or more interfaces, refined as needed during implementation.

- **Component.** This object represents one or more components, fully implemented and ready for testing.

The Testing Workflow

The Testing Workflow is depicted in Figure 12-14.

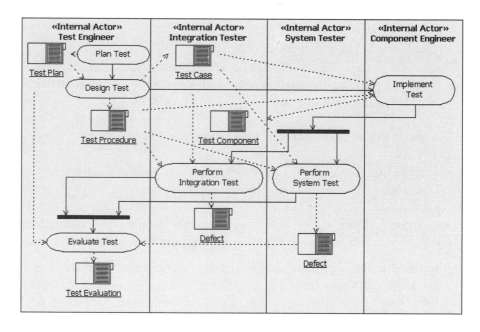

Figure 12-14. The Unified Process Testing Workflow

In this diagram, I've added three new swimlanes:

- **Test Engineer.** This actor is responsible for analyzing requirements, designs, and code to determine testing strategies and evaluate test results.

- **Integration Tester.** This actor is responsible for testing that new components work correctly with each other and with existing components in the deployment environment.

- **System Tester.** This actor is responsible for testing that each individual component works as designed.

You also have the following «**Internal Document**» objects:

- **Test Plan.** This object represents the testing strategies, test cases, and expected results used to test all or part of the system.

- **Test Procedure.** This object represents one specific set of steps to follow in carrying out a test of all or part of the system. The same test procedure may be applied in multiple test cases, with different results expected for each test case. This procedure may include Use Case Diagrams, Class Diagrams, Activity Diagrams, and other Interaction Diagrams as appropriate. It is, in essence, a model of a test, and thus may be modeled with UML.

- **Test Case.** This object represents a single test of all or part of the system, including required inputs and expected results.

- **Test Component.** This object represents a component designed and implemented specifically to test one or more components of the system, as designed in a **Test Procedure**.

- **Defect.** This object represents the results of one test case, indicating discrepancies between expected and actual results.

- **Test Evaluation.** This object represents the **Test Engineer**'s evaluation of a **Test Plan**, **Test Cases**, and **Defects**. It should include an evaluation of the severity and consequences of each defect, as well as a recommendation of whether the defects are sufficient to hold up release of the system. The **Test Evaluation** should become an input to the next Requirements Workflow.

Customizing the Unified Process

Wow, there's a lot in the Unified Process! I've identified ten participating actors—larger than a small development team—and those are only internal actors. There are external actors involved as well. I've identified 26 internal documents and artifacts, without even discussing the external documents. And trust me, I've barely scratched the surface.

This is why the Unified Process has a reputation for being large and cumbersome. But that reputation is unjustified. As I discussed earlier, you can customize UP to be larger or smaller as your project warrants. There are different types of projects—large projects and small projects, agile projects (accepting risk—in this case, a free-form development approach—for the sake of speed and responsiveness) and orchestrated projects (minimizing risk, at a cost of speed, by more precisely specifying, controlling, and reviewing development tasks)—and each type of project needs a different flavor of UP. Some ways you might customize UP include the following suggestions:

- For large or orchestrated projects, you might have very formal document templates for each kind of internal document. This helps guide workers in gathering all relevant information and answering all questions, and the consistency helps readers to understand the documents more easily.

- For small or agile projects, you might allow each type of internal document to be small and free form, making it easy and fast to prepare and maintain. You might eliminate certain documents entirely, combine other diagrams, or even capture the relevant information in the models or in the code.

- For large or orchestrated projects, you might assign multiple people to each actor role, each assigned to some subset of the whole system. Each of the UP actors might represent a whole team, with managers and reviewers and others as needed.

- For small or agile projects, individual team members may fill many of the actor roles. For a very small project, one person may fill *all* of the roles, though it's usually wise to get some outside assistance to review your work.

- For large orchestrated projects, you'll need many Elaboration increments to ensure that the system is feasible, along with many Inception increments to ensure that your architecture is correct.

- For large agile projects (not *necessarily* a contradiction in terms), you might need many Elaboration increments to understand the baseline requirements, but then have a small number of Inception increments, trusting that whatever architecture you devise in advance may be modified as needed during Construction.

- For small projects and most agile projects, you'll probably keep to a small number of Elaboration and Inception increments, trusting that the real requirements and architecture will be described and defined during Construction.

- The number of Construction and Transition increments that you need will be determined by your project's size. You'll also need to determine the basic size of each increment in terms of time. Short increments allow for more feedback, but require more end-of-transition activities that impose more frequent overhead. Long increments have less overhead, but are harder to track. You need to determine the right increment size for your needs. Agile approaches usually advocate increments 2 weeks to 1 month in length. Other projects may have increments measured in months.

- For orchestrated projects, you plan the expected Construction increments and milestones in advance, updating this plan as circumstances require.

- For agile projects, you plan no further than the current Construction increment. You define its goals and milestones, define the criteria for determining when the goals and milestones are complete, and start working. At the end of the increment, you assess which goals were and weren't met, and you make plans for the next increment.

- For agile projects, you may combine the Core Workflows as needed. For example, you might combine the Requirements and Analysis Workflows, treating them as a single workflow (analyzing requirements as you gather them). It's also possible to combine Design and Implementation Workflows to show a more code-based design process.

So really, the Unified Process is as large or as small and as orchestrated or as agile as you need it to be. Dogmatically following "all" of UP can sink a small project; but rejecting UP as "too large, too formal" can deprive you of a powerful tool for planning and organizing your development process.

If you want to learn more about the Unified Process, you can request a free RUP poster from Rational Corporation at `http://www.rational.com/products/rup/forms/poster_form.jsp?`.

A UML Model of Model-Driven Development?

Earlier in this book, I discussed Model-Driven Development: the idea that all knowledge of the system is captured in or derived from the models as much as possible. This "process" can be really just an extremely customized example of the Unified Process, wherein all of the necessary internal documents are part of the models, rather than stand-alone documents. Remember **The Model Rule**: a model is more than just the pictures, and includes information *behind* the pictures that describes and explains the elements in the pictures. When you must have stand-alone documents—source code, for example, or prototype screen shots— the model contains links to them. Thus, when you need to understand any part of the system, you should always turn to the models first, learn the overview presented in the models, and dig into details in other documents only when you need to.

Isn't this just "Agile UP"? Well, I think so, in spirit; but not in the eyes of many Agile Development enthusiasts. One core value of Agile Development is "Working software over comprehensive documentation";[4] and models fall in the category of documentation. So while many Agile Development enthusiasts use modeling, including UML, many see no value in the models once the code is produced. They see the code as the central artifact of the development process. I see the code as an essential end product, but the models are the central piece. Requirements flow in, and code and estimates and schedules and new models flow out. I find that this is agile enough for me, even if it's not Agile by some measures.

A UML Model of Five-Step UML

By comparison to the Unified Process, Five-Step UML (from Chapter 2) is a very small process, as you can see in Figure 12-15.

In this process, the artifacts produced include various UML diagrams, along with the UML elements within those diagrams and the information you learn about those elements. This is why Five-Step UML is an extremely simple example of Model-Driven Development.

---

4. The Agile Alliance, "Manifesto for Agile Software Development" (http://www.agilemanifesto.org/)

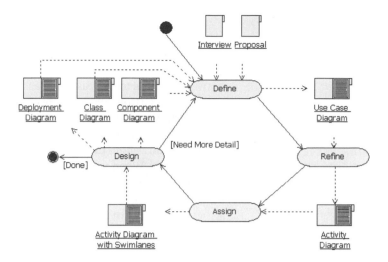

Figure 12-15. A UML model of Five-Step UML

This diagram provides you with a useful summary of all the ground we've covered in the last seven chapters. You can see graphically how the process of looping through our four phases of define, refine, assign, and design works at the different levels of focus in our system, be it the whole system, individual components, or even classes.

A UML Model of Extreme Programming

Extreme Programming (XP) is an Agile Development process based on defining, prioritizing, and realizing User Stories. The process is well suited for situations in which the customer's requirements are not very defined, but can be defined through communication and iteration. The core of XP consists of a number of iterations of effort—usually short, in the neighborhood of 2 weeks—in which stories are defined, estimated, prioritized, and implemented, as shown in Figure 12-16.

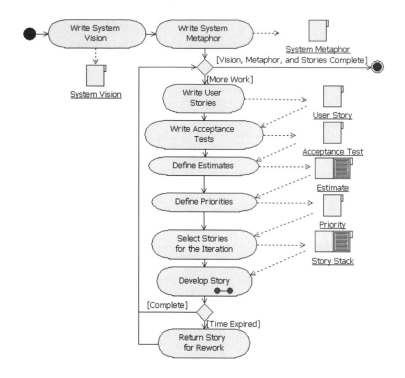

Figure 12-16. A UML model of Extreme Programming

In this process, the customer and the development team collaborate closely and very frequently to produce a number of external and internal documents:

- **System Vision.** This object represents the customer's initial statement of what the system must accomplish in order to be useful.

- **System Metaphor.** This object represents the customer's view of how the system might work. Because the customer is most likely not a developer, this view is commonly described via a metaphor, comparing the system to and contrasting it with familiar concepts. For example, the metaphor for Quicken (the personal finance manager from Intuit) might look partly like this: "Using Quicken for check management should be just as easy as writing a check. No, easier: when I write a check with Quicken, it should be entered in the check register automatically. So make it an automated checkbook with an automated check register." The metaphor helps the customer to describe the vision in more concrete terms. The metaphor is also usually the closest thing to a fixed architecture in XP: any decision that breaks the metaphor is a violation of the architecture. More traditional architectural concerns—decomposition into subsystems, etc.—are put off until development, and are subject to change whenever the team sees fit.

- **User Story.** This object represents one or more stories that the customer writes to describe scenarios of users using the system. Each story is small—a paragraph or so—and concise. User Stories are analogous to use cases, though more narrative and less formal (and usually smaller). The customer creates initial User Stories as part of specifying the project, and then adds to and revises the set of stories in response to the evolution of the system, as well as in response to newly discovered requirements.

- **Acceptance Test.** This object represents one or more precise scenarios that the customer writes to test a given User Story. It defines initial values and preconditions, along with result values and postconditions. When the Acceptance Tests for a story are all passed, the story is complete. A goal of XP is that each story should be small and detailed enough to permit only one Acceptance Test per User Story. If you need multiple Acceptance Tests, it very likely means that the User Story needs to be broken into smaller stories. In this checkbook example, the User Story "Write Check" could have many different amounts entered for the check; but it should need only one Acceptance Test, because you handle all different amounts the same. Then someone points out that you can't allow an amount that's more than the funds in the account. That seems like a new Acceptance Test, and it is; but it's a new Acceptance Test for a new User Story, "Write Overdraft."

- **Estimate.** This object represents the development team's Estimate for the effort involved in implementing one User Story. In XP, it's considered incontrovertible that developers make their own Estimates, as opposed to customers or executives or managers dictating a schedule. If developers aren't making their own Estimates, you're not doing XP. (I applaud this in theory, while knowing there are environments where this will never be accepted by executives and managers.)

- **Priority.** This object represents customers' prioritization of one or more User Stories, based both on their own needs and on the Estimates from the developers. Customers are not allowed to argue with the Estimates, but they have a right to define their Priorities based on realistic Estimates. A "must have" feature that will take 3 months may be less important than a "nice to have" feature that can be done in 2 weeks. Or it may not. Only the customer can really decide.

- **Story Stack.** This object represents the highest-priority set of User Stories that can fit within the current iteration. During the iteration, the developers will select stories from this stack, develop them, and test them.

Note the last activity in Figure 12-16: **Return Story for Rework**. This activity reflects the XP practice of putting a story back in the story collection (sometimes called the Backlog) if it can't be completed in the time allotted. The thinking behind this practice is that if the story couldn't be completed in the expected time, it wasn't properly understood. Maybe it needs to be split into smaller stories, or maybe it needs clarification from the customer. A related practice is to throw out all the code developed for that story, so that you start with a clean slate the next time you address the story. While this seems radical, XP practitioners say it keeps down the amount of bloated, nonfunctional, incomplete code. And again, there's also the thinking that if the story couldn't be realized in the time allotted, your code for that story may be heading in the wrong direction.

The subactivity state **Develop Story** represents the ongoing, day-to-day process of design, coding, and testing, as shown in Figure 12-17.

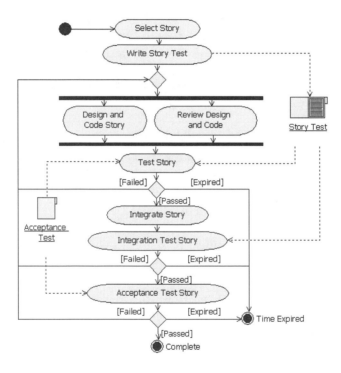

Figure 12-17. A UML model of design and coding in Extreme Programming

This diagram depicts the activities of a pair of programmers. Pair Programming is a key feature of XP: throughout an iteration, two programmers work together on all aspects of one story; and the pairs change from iteration to iteration. Each iteration, the team starts by reviewing the stories to be realized, and volunteering to implement particular stories. When two programmers both volunteer for the same story, they become a pair for that iteration.

After selecting a User Story, the pair first writes a Story Test for that story. The Story Test is based on the Acceptance Tests for the story, but it translates those Acceptance Tests into code. As much as possible, these Story Tests must be automated, and must very clearly either pass or fail. This is a discipline in XP (and other processes) known as *Test First Development:* define your tests, and then code until you pass your tests. The pair defines and creates this test; and when the code passes this test, the story is nearly done.

Once the pair agrees on the Story Test, they can design and write the code. Figure 12-17 shows this as two activities, **Design and Code Story** and **Review Design and Code**, occurring in parallel with a fork and a join. This is where Pair Programming is most important. Research shows that the most effective means of finding bugs is design and code reviews; experience shows that effective design and code reviews take a long time, are very tedious, and are difficult for most teams to maintain over the life of a project.

Many teams that start with diligent, thorough reviews will abandon them at crunch time, because the team is too busy writing and testing code. XP changes this approach by making the review a constant, ongoing part of the design and coding itself, rather than an interruption to the coding process. While one programmer designs or codes, the other watches and asks questions and makes suggestions and acts as a sounding board and a gadfly. When the programmers tire of their tasks, they take a break and then switch roles. While it's certainly true that more reviewers would catch more bugs (to a point), the most review benefit comes from the first reviewer, acting as a check to what another programmer does.

Try It, You'll Like It (Maybe ...)

Pair Programming is the largest reason why many programmers shun XP. Programmers value their privacy, and they like to work for long, uninterrupted periods. Historically, our field has attracted people who were good with numbers and math and logic and technology, but not necessarily with people. This is an ugly, unfair stereotype; but it's a stereotype based on a lot of real-world examples. For these and other reasons, Pair Programming is a deal breaker for many programmers: if they have to work in pairs, they'll find other work.

Curiously, Pair Programming is a deal breaker for other programmers, too: programmers who have actually worked in Pair Programming environments often won't go back to programming alone. They've learned that they catch more bugs faster and more easily and produce better code faster when they have a "copilot." They *like* that sort of productivity, and they don't want to give it up.

I've usually programmed solo; but long before XP was a concept in the literature, I worked on a project in which the team naturally fell into Pair Programming at crunch time. There was a lot of stress involved—a factor the XP enthusiasts never seem to mention—but I don't think I have *ever* experienced such productivity in finding bugs, diagnosing them, designing solutions, and tackling new problems. That second set of eyes counts for *a lot!* (Hi, Grieg!)

I've also worked on teams in which we did our design work as a team (like I recommended for Five-Step UML in Chapter 2). And I've seen some spectacular successes in such teams: exciting productivity, great team energy, and lots of fun.

Unfortunately, I've also seen teams in which group design efforts like this failed miserably. With the right combination of people, you can get people who criticize but never really critique, and people who never want to make a decision, and people who disagree just to be disagreeable, and people who *really* would rather be working alone; and you can spend months designing while making what feels like days of progress. And similarly, you can have pairs who just should never Pair Program. Maybe both are too strong-willed to ever concede a point. Maybe neither has the initiative to take a step forward without someone else pushing. Maybe neither has the experience to effectively review the other's work.

So if you have doubts about Pair Programming, you're not alone. But I recommend you actually try it for an iteration (or two), rather than just dismissing it outright. You can find courses on Extreme Programming that will also teach Pair Programming, and you can also find books on the subject; but if you're open minded, you can just dive in and pair off, more or less at random. As long as skill sets have enough overlap to be useful, and as long as the members of a pair are willing to patiently watch someone work or patiently listen to questions and critiques, Pair Programming is an easy practice to attempt. When it works, it will save you more than enough time to justify the "settling in" period; and when it doesn't work, you won't have to invest much time to find that out.

After the code passes the Story Test, the pair integrates the code with the master code, and then runs integration tests. These integration tests are just the set of all Story Tests that the master code has passed once. If the master code still passes all of these Story Tests, the story is ready for the customer; but if the code fails the integration tests, it's back to the drawing board for the pair.

And finally, once the code passes all tests, the story is ready for the customer, who runs their own Acceptance Tests. Once the code passes those, the User Story is complete. If somehow it still fails, the pair must work with the customer, find out what they misunderstood in the Acceptance Tests, and update their Story Test accordingly. Then they can redesign and code as needed.

Summary

Now that you've reached the end of the chapter, you should be able to see what I meant when I said earlier that UML is about *system* design. And system design must occur within a process, whether that's using some form of the Waterfall Model, or the Unified Process, as I've discussed. And each project must define its own version of these processes. This is how the Unified Process, Agile Modeling, and Extreme Programming all came to be: different ideas aimed at solving the same type of problem in different ways.

I started by talking about the Waterfall Model, which is interesting to examine, despite its manifest problems, because it allows us to see how other processes have developed out of the ideas that it expresses. One of the more successful variations was to start cycling round the different activities in the Waterfall Model using ideas from the Spiral Process. The Unified Process takes this even further, formally defining a complex iterative process and defining a set of artifacts to be produced at each stage. Despite its complexity, UP is very adaptable, and you can make it as big and bulky or as small and agile as you need. Even if you don't want to implement UP in full, it contains many useful concepts, so it's worth learning about to see what you can adapt to your own modeling work. In a way, you can look at Five-Step UML as an adaptation or a compact version of UP. At the end of the chapter, I discussed an entirely different approach, Extreme Programming, a software development process with a focus on testing, to create code with fewer bugs, and flexibility, to deal with changing requirements. Even if you don't take on board the whole process, some of the ideas from XP can be very useful, in particular the concept of pair programming.

As you learned about the different the processes presented in this chapter, perhaps you have also seen another side of UML, and understood just how flexible it is, not only in modeling software systems, but also in modeling the way in which we design such systems. UML can be (and is) used in many other areas, such as modeling business processes and organizations.

And that's what it comes down to in the end: UML is about communication, which is how we're going to wrap up in the final chapter.

CHAPTER 13

It's *All* About Communication

I WANT TO WRAP this book up with two topics: the parts of UML I didn't cover, and my view of the role of UML in the future of software development.

The Rest of UML

This book has presented a very personal view: UML as it helps me to analyze and design and build .NET systems, and as I hope it can help you. As an instructor, I find that students learn UML better and faster if they have a way to apply it, not just study it. So I've presented UML in the context of my usual development process, in the hopes that it will get you started.

But there's more to UML than just the pieces I use most often. In fact, there are pieces that some practitioners would consider essential, and yet I've barely touched on them. So who's right, me or the other practitioners? Well, by this point in this book, you should expect this answer: *all of us*. UML is a set of tools and techniques for communicating designs. If a tool helps you, use it. If a tool doesn't help you, don't use it. Don't feel you have to use it, but don't ignore what it can do for you. An auto mechanic doesn't have to use an air wrench to change the oil, but would be foolish to ignore that tool when changing the tires.

So in this section, I want to briefly introduce the rest of UML—i.e., the pieces I don't use very often—so that you'll know about them, and not be blinded by my own blinders. For each piece, I'll show an example, describe the elements, explain why I don't use it much, and explain why maybe I should use it more. The ultimate decision for you is this: do these diagrams help *you* to communicate *your* design issues? If they do, great! Use them! If not, fine; don't feel you have to use these diagrams—or any particular diagram—to use UML "correctly." One more time: if you communicate, you're using UML correctly.

Sequence Diagrams

We've seen Sequence Diagrams like the one in Figure 13-1 once or twice in this book; but this is the first time that I've formally discussed them.

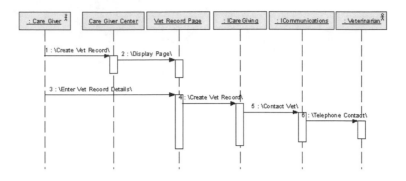

Figure 13-1. A Sequence Diagram

The purpose of a Sequence Diagram is to show the interactions between parts of the system over time, throughout one scenario of system usage. At a minimum, a Sequence Diagram consists of the following elements:

- **Time.** The most important element of a Sequence Diagram isn't an item you draw, but rather a convention you follow: time flows down the page. Items near the bottom of the page happen after items near the top. While this is natural and intuitive (at least for readers of English), it's not always obvious the first time someone sees a Sequence Diagram. Be prepared to explain this to your readers. (Although it's not standard, I find that some Sequence Diagrams are easier to read if time flows from left to right rather than from top to bottom.)

- **Objects.** These are the elements—class instances, interface instances, components, actors, or nodes—that participate in the scenario. Each object is represented by a box icon, which contains the name of the object and its class or type, separated by a colon and both underlined. If only the class or only the name is known, just show that. (If neither one is known, make one up. Sequence Diagrams are a great mechanism for exploring and selecting a structure for your system.) If the object existed before the start of the scenario, its icon appears at the top of the diagram. If the object gets created during the scenario, its icon appears in the middle of the page, at the point in time where the object is created. Object icons can be arranged horizontally any way you want; but a useful convention is to put "originating" or "client" or "outer" objects toward the left, and to put "responding" or "server" or "inner" objects to the right.

- **Lifelines.** These are dashed lines that descend down—i.e., forward in time— from the object icons. If an object exists after the end of the scenario, its lifeline extends to the bottom of the page. If an object is destroyed during the scenario, its lifeline ends at that point in the page, and is terminated with a large X.

- **Messages.** These are labeled arrows that flow from one lifeline to another, indicating that one object has requested that another object do some work. That request might represent a function call, a Web service message, an HTTP message, a socket message, or any other mechanism that one object can use for contacting another. These messages are the place where the **Time** element really becomes relevant: the flow of messages down the page indicates the order of the steps within the scenario.

- **Focus of Control indicators.** (Or Foci of Control, if you want to sound pretentious. I think of them as "activity bars.") When an object is "active" in the scenario—i.e., either doing something or waiting for an answer to some message that it sent—its lifeline is overlaid with a rectangle called a Focus of Control.

Why I Don't Use Them

- As I discussed in Chapter 2, Sequence Diagrams aren't very effective for showing complex logic. They're really a rather linear form of a diagram, and complex logic isn't linear: it has branches and loops, and it has drill-down into more detailed behavior. This logic is difficult to convey with Sequence Diagrams. Activity Diagrams, meanwhile, are explicitly designed for showing complex logic, and for showing drill-down with subactivity states, and with the addition of swimlanes, they show interactions very much as you can show in Sequence Diagrams.

- To a general audience, Sequence Diagrams are among the least familiar parts of UML. Pretty much any audience who wants your development services will be familiar with Activity Diagrams, which are really just a variation on flowcharts; but the Sequence Diagrams will be confusing to them.

- It's really easy to capture business rules and other sorts of rules with Activity Diagrams; and once those are captured, most UML tools make it really easy to add swimlanes to those diagrams to represent the objects that are responsible for each step.

- My UML tool of choice, Rational XDE, is really, really good; but rearranging message flow on a Sequence Diagram is one of its more quirky features.

So for these reasons, I tend to use Activity Diagrams with swimlanes where other practitioners will advocate using Sequence Diagrams.

Why I Should Use Them More

- There are some concepts—**«invoke»** is the biggest—that I must depict with stereotypes in Activity Diagrams, but that are "built in" with Sequence Diagrams.

- In UML 2.0, the committee will be adding **Frames**, a way to indicate sub-sections in a Sequence Diagram and to show that these Frames represent loop bodies, logical branches, etc. Depending on the UML tool, you will also be able to show or hide the contents of a Frame, allowing more or less complex diagrams. If these work well—I haven't seen them implemented in a tool yet—they may resolve the main problems with Sequence Diagrams.

- Although I consistently find that new audiences have trouble understanding Sequence Diagrams, I also find that some audiences really come to appreciate them. There's a simple, clean beauty in how these diagrams show the parts and how they interact. If I'm going to work with a given audience for a lengthy requirements gathering period, there might be an advantage in training them to get over the learning curve with Sequence Diagrams.

- My UML tool of choice, Rational XDE, allows more on-the-fly design with Sequence Diagrams and objects than with Activity Diagrams and swim-lanes. XDE makes it very easy to create new classes and new operations as I'm building a Sequence Diagram. With Activity Diagrams, I can do a small amount of class creation, and no operation creation. Worse, it allows me to assign operations to transitions within the diagram; but it allows me to assign *any* operation from *any* class, regardless of the class of the swimlane.

- Nostalgia. Sequence Diagrams were the first UML diagrams with which I really got the point of UML. So for that reason, I continue to look on them fondly. (It's possible—just barely possible—that this won't be a compelling reason for *you* . . .)

Collaboration Diagrams

Unlike Sequence Diagrams, I've barely touched on Collaboration Diagrams. Figure 13-2 contains the first one I have shown you in this book.

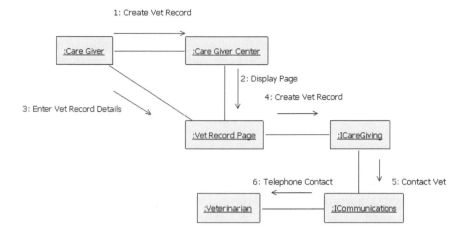

Figure 13-2. A Collaboration Diagram

The purpose of a Collaboration Diagram is similar to a Sequence Diagram: to show the interactions between parts of the system throughout one scenario of system usage. And in fact, a Collaboration Diagram can be seen as a rearrangement of a Sequence Diagram (and vice versa). But whereas a Sequence Diagram emphasizes time (which is practically nonexistent in a Collaboration Diagram), a Collaboration Diagram emphasizes which objects interact with which other objects.

At a minimum, a Collaboration Diagram consists of the following elements:

- **Objects.** These are the elements—class instances, interface instances, components, actors, or nodes—that participate in the scenario. Each object is represented by a box icon, which contains the name of the object and its class or type, separated by a colon and both underlined. If only the class or only the name is known, just show that.

- **Collaborations.** These are solid lines that connect objects. If two objects aren't connected by a collaboration, they can't interact directly. A collaboration represents the mechanism by which the objects interact: function calls, Web service messages, etc.

- **Messages.** These are arrows that flow from one lifeline to another, indicating that one object has requested that another object do some work. Adjacent to each arrow are the valid request messages that it represents.

Why I Don't Use Them

- They just don't tell me much. A Collaboration Diagram really is just a rearrangement of a Sequence Diagram; but in the act of rearranging, we obscure the time element, possibly to the point of losing it completely. I usually find that there's nothing I can read from a Collaboration Diagram that I can't read more easily from the equivalent Sequence Diagram.

- My UML tool of choice, Rational XDE, happens to not do Collaboration Diagrams. Rational's earlier tool, Rational ROSE, could create Collaboration Diagrams; but for reasons never explained to me, XDE dropped Collaboration Diagrams. Since I never use them, I've never missed them, except when teaching or writing about how *you* might use them.

Why I Should Use Them More

- A lot of very smart UML practitioners—in fact, most of the people who inspired me to master UML—think that Collaboration Diagrams are one of the most useful elements of UML. I continue to be baffled as to why; but I respect these people too much to discount their views out of hand.

- In one very, very small way, I can see Collaboration Diagrams as being more useful than Sequence Diagrams. That way is to use them as a diagram version of CRC card exercises. In CRC modeling, each Class is represented by a note card, with its **Responsibilities** written on one half of the card, and its **Collaborators** written on the other half. As a modeling exercise, team members role-play their cards to work out a scenario and to verify that each card has the correct and necessary collaborations and responsibilities to fulfill the scenario. Well, the collaboration lines in a Collaboration Diagram represent the collaborators of a given object, and the messages it receives represent its responsibilities. So I have seen some success in using Collaboration Diagrams as a more fixed, more graphical form of CRC modeling. (CRC purists will scoff at this idea. They insist that there's value in being able to pick up a card, wave it around, pass it around the room, and even rip it up. I leave that to you to decide.)

- I think it's somewhat easier to see the collaborations in a Collaboration Diagram than in a Sequence Diagram, and it's also easier to document the *valid* collaborations: if there's no collaboration line between two objects, it may be because, in your architecture, those two objects aren't allowed to interact directly (or maybe even not able to). In that case, the scenario shouldn't include any messages between them; and perhaps an intermediary object is needed.

- In a handful of cases, I have taught a student Sequence Diagrams and that student has said, "I don't get it;" and then I have taught that same student Collaboration Diagrams, and the student has said, "Aha!" Different brains approach the same problem in different ways; and it's not my job to train someone to think in a particular fashion. Well, that's not quite true. As an instructor, it's my job to teach students new tools for thinking about problems; but as a consultant, my job isn't to teach them how to think, but rather to communicate with them. If Collaboration Diagrams communicate better for some subset of my customers, then I'll be ready to use them if I can't get a point across another way.

So don't be blinded by my blinders. Experiment with Collaboration Diagrams, and see if they can help you.

Statechart Diagrams

A Statechart Diagram (colloquially a State Diagram) depicts the states and conditions of a system or of any subset of the system, along with the events that cause the system to change from one state to another (see Figure 13-3).

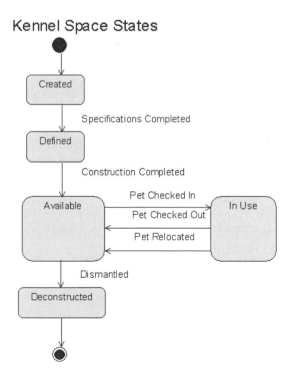

Figure 13-3. A Statechart Diagram

Based on work by David Harel, statecharts are a powerful way of documenting event-driven behavior, which is a very common behavior in modern system development. At a minimum, a Statechart Diagram consists of the following elements:

- **States.** These are the states that the system or subsystem can be in. A state is a snapshot of the system at a point in time: what it's doing, what data it contains, and what events it's expecting. Each state is represented by a rounded rectangle icon, which contains the name of the state. In more advanced Statechart Diagrams, the state may also list events that may occur while in the state, along with actions taken in response to those states. Like we saw with Activity Diagrams in Chapter 2, states can be nested: a state may itself contain a more detailed Statechart Diagram, which may be displayed within the main diagram or on a separate diagram.

- **Initial state.** This state, represented by a solid dot icon, represents where the Statechart Diagram begins, with an immediate transition to some state. There should be exactly one initial state per Statechart Diagram.

- **Final state.** This state, represented by a dot in a circle (I think of it as a target), indicates where the statechart terminates. Purists will insist that there be only zero or one final state per Statechart Diagram; but I often find it convenient to have multiple final states. Perhaps these allow me to depict different exit conditions, or perhaps they merely save me the hassle of trying to draw many different exit transitions to one final state.

- **Transitions.** These are arrows that flow from one state to another, indicating that one state has ended and another is beginning. A transition may be labeled with the name of an event that must occur before the state transition takes place; or it may be unlabeled, indicating that the transition occurs as soon as the first state is "done," however that is defined. (Note that the "bell" icons on the events in Figure 13-3 are an artifact of XDE, and aren't required for Statechart Diagrams.)

That's just a cursory look at Statechart Diagrams. The statechart notation is much richer than that, but I've just given you the basics.

Why I Don't Use Them

- Blinders, pure and simple. I just don't think in a state-and-event fashion. I probably should, but I don't. I think in a more rules-and-flow fashion.

- Novelty. I find that very few of my clients understand Statechart Diagrams. More of my coworkers do, but they're still a minority. So these diagrams require a lot more explanation, which slows down communication. And after all (in case I haven't said this enough yet): it's all about communication.

Why I Should Use Them More

- They're powerful. Nothing else captures states and events anywhere nearly as well.

- Event-driven code is the norm for my projects these days. As systems become more and more loosely coupled, events and states will become even more prominent.

- They're one of the best solutions for modeling something that the rest of UML models rather poorly: the modern graphical user interface (GUI). If you try to model a GUI as use cases, you may end up with far more use cases than you can manage. If you try to model a GUI as activities, you'll quickly find that the modern GUI allows an almost infinite variety of interactions and sequences, and that these are hard to capture as a logical flow. But if you model each form in the GUI as a state, and then if you model each click, key press, pen stroke, or spoken command within that state as an event that either is handled internally to the state or causes a transition to another state (i.e., another form), modeling the GUI suddenly becomes far easier.

Finishing Up Where I Started

As software developers, our job has never been solely about technology. Our job has always involved expressing ideas and knowledge and methods in precise physical symbols so that other users can reuse and apply those ideas, knowledge, and methods without having to master the precise physical symbols themselves—or if they do, without having to go through all the rigor and discipline and effort of applying them for themselves. All they have to master is the effort of telling the software to do what we have already mastered.

And another side of our job has been to master that which we *don't* know. We may be skilled at precise expression of ideas in physical symbols, but that doesn't make us skilled at lunar launches or color science or financial forecasting or the myriad other symbols and ideas that users want expressed in software. So we have to learn how to elicit those symbols and models from those who have them, but who lack our skills in precise expression through software. In a sense, we're translators between mental symbols and physical symbols, adding in our own mental symbols to provide an intermediary layer to allow users to make use of the physical symbols.

In other words—and you had to know that this was coming—it's all about communication.

And there's a bit of irony for you. Our field—where our entire job is precise communications—is infamous for practitioners who are *perceived* to be short on communications skills. And in fact, nothing could be farther from the truth: to have any success in software at all, you must be very, very good at precise communication, at taking an abstract set of symbols in your head and precisely communicating them to the software in such a way that the software "understands" what you understand.

So if software is all about communication, how has it come to be seen solely as a technology job? Indeed, how has it come to be dominated by technology fanatics who (in many cases) *do* have something of a problem with unstructured, imprecise communications? Why do some developers have such trouble with the nuance and the double meanings and the give-and-take and the vagaries of *human* communications?

Well, one reason is that for most of the history of software development, communicating with the technology has been hard. Very hard (though getting easier). It requires an exceptional degree of precision, and therefore it requires specialized skills not found in the general populace. As I mentioned in Chapter 2, we're weird: we handle precise communications in ways that most other people do not. This tends to set us apart. And perhaps that setting apart attracts people who are better at technology than at communications. Perhaps the time spent with precise technological tasks even causes atrophy in our other communications skills.

Another reason is that in the past, limitations of the hardware strictly constrained what we could and couldn't communicate and also put a premium on mastering obscure technical tricks and creating new technical tricks to live within the limitations of the technology. The software developer culture evolved in circumstances where technological prowess was essential in order to communicate at all.

And yet another reason: the size of projects that could fit within those limited environments was often small enough that those projects could be mastered by people who could communicate their ideas well in the software, without needing recourse to communication with others. A large number of projects were small enough and simple enough to resolve primarily through technological prowess. Well, as I tell my students, there are no simple problems left. Yes, this is a bit of an exaggeration (at this point in this book, is that a surprise?); but as a practical matter, the simple problems have been solved. Hardware today has grown so powerful as to have no meaningful comparison to the hardware of a generation ago; and yet the software problems of today strain that hardware to its limits, and there's always a backlog of problems we'd like to solve as soon as the hardware catches up. Today, no one hires a software developer to solve simple problems. They hire us for the hard problems, the really complicated problems, the problems they don't entirely understand themselves, the problems for which requirements are hazy, and success can't be clearly defined. And they're counting on us to clear away that confusion, to help them define what their needs are and what success means. They're counting on us to communicate with them because they don't know how to communicate with us. We must communicate with them and for them, leading them through the communications process to lead to the precision that the software requires.

In other words, now and for the foreseeable future, I believe that communication will be *the* key software development skill. I don't want to discount technology skills, because there are always new technological frontiers to master (like .NET today); but without communication, we'll fail to apply the technology in ways that matter. We have to communicate with our users, because we need to know what they need, how to accomplish it, what skills we must master to accomplish it, and how to recognize when we've succeeded. We have to communicate with our users in another way, through our user interfaces that allow them to access and command our software. We have to communicate with each other, because the problems are too large to solve in isolation. We have to communicate with future maintenance developers who must carry on our work when we can't. We have to communicate with mentors and educators and experts (perhaps in a disconnected fashion, through their lessons, books, examples, and presentations) to learn the new domain skills and new technology skills we must master to address user needs. When we ourselves become mentors and educators, we have to communicate to our students and readers by writing our own lessons, books, examples, and presentations. We have to communicate to testers, so that they know what and how to test, along with how to recognize success or failure. We have to communicate with documenters, so that they know what to explain and how *they* will communicate it to the users. We have to communicate with marketers and sales personnel (yes, even them) so that they understand what we can and can't deliver. We have to communicate with managers and executives to explain what they can and can't expect from the technology within constraints of time and resources.

And we have to precisely communicate with the software and the other technology, instructing it to carry out the knowledge and skills we have mastered. I sometimes call this "shipping our brains in boxes." While the metaphor is a bit gruesome, the idea is key: that software installed on my customer's machine is a proxy for my brain, sitting there and doing for that user what I could do myself if I were there—only doing much of it faster than I could do myself (and more accurately, because software is more precise and repeatable than humans usually are). And besides speed and accuracy, there's *leverage:* that software proxy for my brain can be installed on hundreds or thousands or more computers, helping far more users than I could ever help in person. We're not just working with technology, we're communicating with it, teaching it the things we know and then replicating our knowledge across the user community.

So that's my conclusion, one final time: it's all about communication. And while UML isn't the answer to your every communication need (for instance, I thought about writing this entire chapter solely in UML diagrams; but the abstract nature of diagrams just wouldn't express the precise thoughts I wanted to convey), I hope that I've shown it to be a powerful set of graphical tools for conveying complex ideas and relationships so that you can more easily communicate the skills and ideas from your users and experts to the software so that your users can apply them. Today, many UML tools will also produce the structure of your code directly from the models. In the future, UML will become a programming language, a tool for communicating with the technology directly. (Some UML tools like Compuware OptimalJ and I-Logix Rhapsody already do this in certain niches.)

So UML is a valuable way to express yourself, both to people and to machines. It's a new technology skill that will help you to apply all of your other technology skills, once you master it. Practice UML and apply it, not just by yourself, but as a means to communicate with your fellow developers and your users and everyone else with whom you must communicate. I hope that with time, UML can do for you what it has done for me: speed and smooth your communications so that you can solve more complex problems more successfully.

Part Four
Appendixes

Specification for the Kennel Management System

THIS SPECIFICATION DESCRIBES the requirements for the Kennel Management System for Sandy's Pets, a high-tech kennel providing temporary and long-term care for cats, dogs, birds, and exotic pets.

1. Business Vision

1.1 Purpose

Sandy's Pets has reached its limits as a business in its current form. With many years of pet care expertise, the owners have worked out care and business practices that allow their business to serve as many pets and customers as their current facility and staff can handle. They have been successful in growing this business, and have established a loyal clientele and a positive reputation. They have also generated significant income, and would like to reinvest this income into growing the business further.

Since their facility is currently used at maximum capacity, the owners of Sandy's Pets has decided to grow the business by franchising the name and processes to other operators across the country. They have hired a franchising consultant who has converted several other businesses into successful franchises. The consultant has identified the primary risk to this venture: their expertise may not be as easily shared as their business's name; and if the franchises are run poorly, it will damage the name of Sandy's Pets.

So the consultant has requested our assistance (as the Five-Step UML Company, or FSU) with five tasks:

- Analyze and define the Sandy's Pets care and business practices in a form that may be used to replicate those practices at other facilities.

- Design a Kennel Management System (KMS) to automate the care and business practices more fully, so that franchisees may leverage the home office expertise more easily. The consultant has persuaded the owners of Sandy's Pets that without a KMS, the franchisees likely will never be able to replicate the standards of quality and practice of the home office. Once the owners understood the need for the KMS, they decided to add new functionality to support Web operations and to allow franchisees and the home office to interoperate more closely.

- Define acceptance and diagnostic tests for the KMS.

- Define the end-user documentation that will be provided for the KMS.

- Provide estimates for the effort in completing the KMS, including all tests and end-user documentation.

Depending on the designs and estimates provided, the owners of Sandy's Pets will decide whether to commit to the franchising plan or not.

1.2 Definitions, Acronyms, and Abbreviations

This section defines all terms, acronyms, and abbreviations required to properly interpret the specification.

Account. A funds balance and a record of charges and payments. There are three kinds: franchise account, payable account, and receivable account.

Accountant. A person who maintains accounts for a franchise or for the home office.

Bank. A financial institution that maintains external accounts.

Bill. A statement of charges accrued and of payments made and due.

Bitch. A female dog (usually a breeding female or a mother).

Breed. A recognized subtype of a particular species. Breeds are usually defined by registration authorities for a given species.

Breeder. A person who researches and arranges breeding schedules for pets and registers offspring.

Breeding schedule. A specific kind of pet schedule, having to do with breeding appointments for a pet.

Building. One location at a given facility. There are usually two types: a reception building and a kennel.

Care giver. A kennel worker whose primary duties are the care and feeding of pets and the cleaning of pens and facilities.

Charge. A transaction that debits an account, possibly producing a bill.

Checking away. The process of removing a pet from the kennel temporarily, for a home visit, a vet visit, or a pet show. The pet leaves, but its pen remains assigned to it.

Checking back. The process of returning a pet to the kennel from a home visit, a vet visit, or a pet show.

Checking in. The process of assigning a pen to a pet and accepting the pet from the pet owner or representative.

Checking out. The process of delivering the pet to the pet owner or representative and removing the pen assignment.

Cleaning. The process of regular daily cleaning of a pen. Contrast with disinfecting.

Contract. An agreement between one customer and one facility to provide temporary care or long-term care for one pet.

Contracted work. Services provided by a contractor, usually billed straight to a customer.

Contractor. A worker who is not employed by the home office or a franchise, but who does contracted work for using his or her own facilities and/or tools, and setting his or her own schedule and rates. Veterinarians, breeders, and groomers are typically contractors. Contrast this with a vendor (who primarily provides supplies, not services).

Credit company. An organization that approves or rejects charges against an external account.

Customer. The person who contracts services from the facility and is responsible for charges. Usually a pet owner, but other arrangements are possible.

Delinquent. A condition in which a bill has been sent to a customer but has not been paid in full in 30 days.

Disinfecting. The process of thoroughly cleaning a pen in such a way as to prevent the spread of disease and other biohazards.

Exercise and play activities. Structured and unstructured activities and games designed to provide a pet with exercise.

Exercise area. A large fenced-in area where a pet worker and pet may interact to provide the pet with exercise.

Exercise schedule. A specific kind of pet schedule, having to do with required exercise and play activities for a pet.

Exotic pet. A pet of a species other than dogs, cats, and birds. Exotic pets may require unique pet supplies and unique pen construction that are not standard for Sandy's Pets' facilities. Operations involving exotic pets may require supervisor approval.

External account. An account not maintained within the KMS.

Facility. One location, owned either by the home office or a franchisee. Usually includes one reception building, one or more kennels, and grounds.

Facility staff. All kennel workers working at or associated with one facility.

Feeding schedule. A specific kind of pet schedule, having to do with when a pet gets fed and what foods and amounts are to be fed to the pet.

Food. Any food to be given to pets.

Franchise. An independent business operating under the name of Sandy's Pets, and subject to fees and quality and care standards established by the home office.

Franchise account. An account of charges incurred by a franchise and fees due from it, along with credits to it.

Franchise group. One or more facilities all owned by the same franchise.

Franchisee. The owner of a franchise.

Groomer. A pet worker who grooms (cleans and trims) pets.

Grooming schedule. A specific kind of pet schedule, having to do with when a pet gets groomed.

Grounds. The exterior area surrounding the buildings of a facility. Primarily consists of an exercise area and a number of runs.

Home office. The existing Sandy's Pets facility and personnel, which is offering franchises to other kennels around the country.

Home visit. When a pet under long-term care returns to the pet owner or representative, but still has an assigned pen. (Pen charges accrue during a home visit, but feeding and similar charges do not.)

Inventory. The set of all pet supplies and kennel supplies in stock.

Kennel. A building that contains one or more pens for keeping pets.

Kennel Management System. The computer software and hardware system that will manage a facility. Also known as KMS.

Kennel owner. The owner of a given facility. May be a franchise owner or the owner of Sandy's Pets.

Kennel supplies. Any supplies—cleaning, construction, etc.—that are not used for specific pets, but rather for maintenance of the facility itself.

Kennel worker. Any employee of the home office or of a franchise. Excludes contractors.

Kennel worker schedule. A specific kind of schedule, having to do with the tasks to be performed by a given kennel worker at a given time.

KMS. See Kennel Management System.

KMS Central. The computer software and hardware system that will reside at the home office and will manage relations and accounts with franchises. It will also serve as a Web host for the home office and for all franchises.

Live food. Food that must be alive when fed to particular pets, and thus requires its own pen, feeding schedule, etc.

Log. A journal of all activities at a given facility.

Long-term care. Some pets reside at a facility for months, or even years. These pets are considered to be under long-term care.

Meds. A set of medications to be given to a pet, including dosage and timing instructions.

Med schedule. A specific kind of pet schedule, having to do with when a pet gets meds and when it gets therapy.

Occupancy. The status of a pen: assigned, occupied, or vacant.

Offspring. A pet born at a facility, with at least one known parent.

Order. A request for goods or services to be provided.

Parent. The parent (mother or father) of an offspring.

Payable account. An account that records charges incurred by a franchise or by the home office.

Payment. A payment of funds into an account.

Pedigree. The recorded parentage of a pet, including ancestry and registration.

Pen. An enclosed space in which a pet resides while in short-term or long-term care.

Pen assignment. A record that a specific pen has been assigned to a specific pet.

Pet. A live animal owned by a pet owner and cared for by kennel workers.

PetCam. An online video camera that displays the activities of one or more pets.

Pet handler. A person (possibly contracted by a pet owner, possibly by a kennel owner) who takes a pet to pet shows and is responsible for the pet during the shows.

Pet history. A record of all care activities related to a particular pet.

Pet ID. A unique ID assigned to a particular pet.

Pet owner. A person responsible for a pet whenever the pet is not in short-term or long-term care.

Pet owner history. A record of all care activities related to a particular pet owner.

Pet owner ID. A unique ID assigned to a particular pet owner.

Pet owner Password. A password assigned to a particular pet. The pet owner may use this password to access pet and owner records online, as well as to check on pet status and view the PetCam.

Pet owner records. All records—accounts, history, etc.—related to a particular owner.

Pet owner representative. A person approved by a pet owner to act in the owner's stead in regards to a pet.

Pet records. All records—accounts, history, etc.—related to a particular pet.

Pet schedule. A specific kind of schedule, having to do with the tasks to be performed for a given pet at a given time.

Pet show. An external event where pets are displayed and judged.

Pet status. The current status of a pet: location, vital stats, tasks being performed, etc.

Pet supplies. Any supplies—food, bedding, etc.—that are used for specific pets, rather than for the facility as a whole.

Pet tag. A magnetically coded tag assigned to any pet to reference information about the pet and provide location information for the pet.

Pet tag sensor. One of multiple sensors placed throughout a facility to detect the location of a pet.

Pet vital stats. The current health statistics about a pet: size, weight, temperature, conscious or not, observations, etc.

Pet worker. Any worker—either a kennel worker or a contractor—who works directly with pets.

Private supplies. This is a stock of food, meds, and other pet supplies that are provided by a pet owner or representative for use only for one or more pets of that owner.

Receipt. A transaction that credits an account.

Receivables account. An account that records charges incurred by a customer.

Reception building. A building in which administrative work is usually done, and where pets are checked in and out.

Receptionist. A person who accepts pets from and delivers pets to pet owners and representatives.

Registration. The process of recording the birth of an offspring with a registration authority.

Registration authority. A body or organization with special interest in a particular species or breed that maintains bloodline histories, conformance standards, and other related information.

Reservation. An agreement to assign a particular pen to a particular pet at a particular time.

Run. A fenced-in exercise area where one pet can run and exercise as it wishes.

Sandy's Pets. The client who is contracting the KMS and related design activities.

Schedule. A list of tasks to be performed by kennel workers and contractors at particular times. There are a number of specific kinds of schedules.

Shipment. A number of pet supplies delivered to a facility.

Species. The broad biological classification for a pet.

Stud. A male dog (usually a breeding male or father).

Supervisor. A kennel worker responsible for administrative and supervisory tasks.

Temporary care. The normal pet care situation, in which a pet checks in to a facility for a short time and then checks out.

Vendor. An outside individual or organization who sells kennel supplies or pet supplies. Contrast with a contractor (who primarily provides services, not supplies).

Veterinarian. A contractor who specializes in medical treatment of pets.

Vet visit. When a pet is taken to a veterinarian, but still has an assigned pen. (Pen charges accrue during a vet visit—unless the pet does not survive—but feeding and similar charges do not.)

2. Product Overview

The KMS shall consist of the following major areas of functionality:

2.1 Accounting Operations

Provides for maintenance of accounts, payments, charges, and bills. Only onsite operations are supported.

2.2 Contractor Operations

Allows contractors to check their assignments and record services. Both online and onsite operations are supported.

2.3 Facility Information

Allows the home office and facilities to share information. Only onsite operations are supported.

2.4 Franchise Information

Allows the home office and franchisees to share information. Only onsite operations are supported.

2.5 Inventory Operations

Allows a facility to maintain and update inventories. Only onsite operations are supported.

2.6 PetCam

Allows pet owners and others to observe the pets. Only online operations are supported.

2.7 Pet Information

Allows pet owners and others to get information on pets. Both online and onsite operations are supported.

2.8 Pet Location

Allows pet workers and others to locate a pet. Only onsite operations are supported.

2.9 Reception Operations

Allows receptionists to check pets in and out. Only onsite operations are supported.

2.10 Reservation Operations

Allows pet owners and kennel workers to make and maintain reservations. Both online and onsite operations are supported.

2.11 Supervisor Operations

Allows supervisors to make and maintain task assignments. Only onsite operations are supported.

2.12 Vendor Information

Allows kennel workers to maintain information on vendors. Only onsite operations are supported.

2.13 Veterinary Information

Allows care givers to check veterinary schedules and record diagnoses, prescriptions, and treatments. Though veterinarians are contractors, they are too busy and their time is too valuable to expect them to learn the KMS. Thus, we need to allow KMS workers to maintain their information for them. Only onsite operations are supported.

3. Product Features

The following are the features required from the KMS. Each feature and subfeature is prioritized as follows:

Critical. The KMS will not be accepted without this feature.

High. This feature is expected in the first release of the KMS, but is not critical.

Low. This feature would be nice to have, but may be postponed to a future project.

3.1 Franchise Features

These features support creation and management of franchises.

3.1.1 Franchise Management (Critical)

- Create a franchise (critical). Add a new franchise in the home office records.

- Install and set up a franchise (critical). Install all software for a franchise and allow the franchisee to customize it.

- Delete a franchise (high). Remove a franchise from the home office records.

3.1.2 Franchise Learning (High)

Allow franchisee and franchisee's kennel staff to learn about care and business practices.

3.1.3 Franchise Review (High)

Review franchise books (high). Allow home office to review a franchise's books.

3.1.4 Franchise Communications (Low)

- Send franchise notices (low). Send a franchise special offers and other notices.

- Franchise comparison (low). Allow a franchisee to compare performance against other franchises. Comparisons should include expenses, revenue, pets served, and conformance to care and business standards.

3.2 Facility Features

3.2.1 Facility Management (Critical)

- Define buildings at a facility (critical). Allow a supervisor to define and delete buildings.

- Define runs at a facility (critical). Allow a supervisor to define and delete runs.

- Define a facility map (high). Allow a supervisor to define and maintain a facility map.

- Define exercise area at a facility (low). Allow a supervisor to define an exercise area.

3.2.2 Pen Management (Critical)

Allow a supervisor to define and delete pens in a kennel.

3.2.3 PetCam and Tag Sensor Management (High)

- Define tag sensors in a facility (critical). Allow a supervisor to define and delete tag sensors.

- Define PetCams in a facility (low). Allow a supervisor to define and delete PetCams.

3.3 Administrative Features

Most of these features are not considered critical, because a COTS solution may suffice; but a custom solution or integration with a COTS solution would be preferable.

3.3.1 Account Management (High)

- Define accounts (high). Allow an accountant to define and maintain accounts.

- Review accounts (high). Allow an accountant to review all accounts.

3.3.2 Accounts Payable (High)

- Review payables (high). Allow an accountant to review payable accounts.

- Make payments (high). Allow an accountant to pay on payable accounts.

3.3.3 Accounts Receivable (High)

- Review receivables (high). Allow an accountant to review receivable accounts.

- Record receipts (high). Allow an accountant to record payments received.

- Send bills (high). Allow an accountant to send bills to customers.

3.3.4 Worker Scheduling (High)

- Assign tasks (high). Allow a supervisor to assign tasks to kennel workers.

- Review tasks (high). Allow a supervisor to check the status of assigned tasks.

- Review schedule (high). Allow a kennel worker to review his or her schedule.

3.3.5 Time Tracking and Payroll (High)

- Kennel Worker definition (high). Allow a supervisor to define and delete worker records.

- Punch in and out (high). Allow kennel workers to record their time.

- File time card (high). Allow kennel workers to file their time reports.

- Review time card (high). Allow a supervisor to accept or reject time cards.

- Process payroll (high). Allow an accountant to pay kennel workers.

3.3.6 Inventory Management (High)

- Record shipments (high). Allow a kennel worker to record delivery of pet and kennel supplies.

- Record private supplies (high). Allow a kennel worker to record delivery of private supplies for a specific pet.

- Record usage (high). Allow a kennel worker to record that pet or kennel or private supplies have been consumed.

- Check inventory (high). Allow a kennel worker to check for the availability of particular supplies.

- Order supplies (high). Allow a supervisor to create paper or electronic orders for supplies.

- Run inventory report (high). Allow a supervisor or accountant to report and review the inventory.

3.4 Pet and Owner Features

3.4.1 Reservations (Critical)

- Browse availability by facility (critical). Allow a receptionist to check for pen availability at his or her own facility for a particular time period.

- Online browse availability by facility (high). Allow a customer to check for pen availability at a particular facility for a particular time period via the Web.

- Browse availability for the entire organization (high). Allow a receptionist to check for pen availability at all facilities for a particular time period.

- Online browse availability by facility (high). Allow a customer to check for pen availability at all facilities for a particular time period via the Web.

- Make reservation (critical). Allow a receptionist to make a reservation for a customer at his or her own facility for a particular time period.

- Make reservation online (high). Allow a customer to make a reservation at a particular facility for a particular time period via the Web.

3.4.2 Contract Management (Critical)

- Contract creation (critical). Allow a supervisor and customer to prepare a contract as a prerequisite for any reservation.

- Contract review (critical). Allow a supervisor to review the status of all contracts.

3.4.3 Pet Owner Information Management (Critical)

- Pet owner identification (critical). Allow a receptionist to gather owner information as a prerequisite for a contract.

- Online pet owner identification (high). Allow a pet owner to provide owner information via the Web as a prerequisite for a contract.

- Review pet owner information (critical). Allow a kennel worker to review information about a pet owner.

- Pet owner history (high). Allow a pet owner or kennel worker to review care activities related to a particular pet owner.

- Pet owner online security (high). Allow a pet owner to set and maintain security for Web access to personal and pet information.

- Pet owner representative management (critical). Allow a pet owner to designate representatives.

3.4.4 Check Pet In and Out (Critical)

- Check in (critical). Allow a receptionist to sign for a pet, receive the pet from an owner or representative, retrieve a magnetic tag from the Available stack, attach and assign the tag, and turn the pet over to a care giver for delivery to the assigned pen.

- Check away (critical). Allow a receptionist to request a pet from a care giver, receive the pet from the care giver, place the magnetic tag in the Away stack, get a signature from the owner or representative, and turn the pet over to the owner or representative.

- Check back (critical). Allow a receptionist to sign for a pet, receive the pet from an owner or representative, retrieve the tag from the Away stack, attach the tag to the pet, and turn the pet over to a care giver for return to the assigned pen.

- Check out (critical). Allow a receptionist to request a pet from a care giver, receive the pet from the care giver, place the magnetic tag in the Available stack, unassign the tag, get a signature from the owner or representative, and turn the pet over to the owner or representative.

3.4.5 Pet Scheduling (Critical)

- Scheduling (critical). Allow a receptionist to define and modify schedules for a pet.

- Online scheduling (high). Allow an owner to define and modify schedules for a pet via the Web.

- Feeding schedule (critical).

- Med schedule (critical).

- Exercise schedule (critical).

- Grooming schedule (high).

- Breeding schedule (low).

- Schedule review (critical). Allow a kennel worker to review pet schedules four ways: specific schedule (feeding, med, exercise, grooming, or breeding) for a pet; combined schedule for a pet; specific schedule for all pets; combined schedule for all pets.

- Schedule adjustment (critical). Allow a supervisor to adjust and modify schedules to resolve conflicts.

3.4.6 Pet Information Management (Critical)

- Pet information (critical). Allow a kennel worker to review information about a pet.

- Online pet information (high). Allow a pet owner to review information about a pet via the Web.

- Pet status (critical). Allow a kennel worker to review the current status of a pet.

- Online pet status (high). Allow a pet owner to review the current status of a pet via the Web.

- Pet history (high). Allow a kennel worker to review past care incidents related to a pet.

- Online pet history (low). Allow a pet owner to review past care incidents related to a pet via the Web.

- Pet location (critical). Allow a kennel worker to ascertain the location of a pet as indicated by the magnetic tag.

- Online pet location (high). Allow a pet owner to ascertain the location of a pet via the Web, as indicated by the magnetic tag.

- PetCam (low). Allow a pet owner to view over the Web a PetCam focused on the location indicated by the magnetic tag.

3.4.7 Pedigree and Breeding Management (High)

- Record breeding (critical). Allow a breeder to record breeding appointments.

- Record births (critical). Allow a care giver to record any births.

- Register births (high). Allow a care giver to register births with a registration authority.

- Display pedigree (low). Allow a kennel worker to display the pedigree of a pet.

- Online display pedigree (low). Allow a pet owner to display the pedigree of a pet via the Web.

3.5 Contractor Features

3.5.1 Contractor Management

- Contractor authorization (critical). Allow a supervisor to designate authorized contractors for particular services.

- Contractor scheduling (critical). Allow a supervisor to schedule contractor services.

- Contractor schedule review (critical). Allow a kennel worker to review a contractor schedule.

- Online contractor schedule review (high). Allow a contractor to review a contractor schedule via the Web.

- Record contractor service (critical). Allow a contractor to record services.

- Online record contractor service (high). Allow a contractor to record services via the Web.

3.5.2 Veterinary Management

- Veterinarian authorization (critical). Allow a supervisor to designate authorized veterinarians for particular pets.

- Veterinarian scheduling (critical). Allow a supervisor to schedule veterinarian visits.

- Veterinarian schedule review (critical). Allow a kennel worker to review a veterinarian schedule.

- Record veterinarian service (critical). Allow a care giver to record veterinarian services.

- Record diagnosis and results (critical). Allow a care giver to record veterinarian instructions.

3.5.3 Vendor Management

- Vendor authorization (critical). Allow a supervisor to designate authorized vendors for particular supplies.

- Vendor scheduling (critical). Allow a supervisor to schedule vendor orders and deliveries.

- Vendor schedule review (critical). Allow a kennel worker to review a vendor schedule.

3.6 Common Features

3.6.1 Logging (Critical)

Some of the pets are very valuable, and loss or injury could put the business at risk. So the logging mechanism is necessary for accountability.

- Automatic logging (critical). Make a log entry for any event in the KMS.

- Manual logging (critical). Allow a kennel worker to manually record events and observations.

- Log review (critical). Allow a kennel worker to review all log entries, filtered by pets, dates, workers, facilities, pens, buildings, pet owners, pet representatives, and other criteria, as appropriate.

- Online log review (critical). Allow a pet owner to review via the Web all log entries relevant to his or her pets.

Selected UML Tool List

THIS IS A SELECTED list of UML tools. All links were active at the time of this writing. The UML tools market is very dynamic, so many of these products change names and even owners quite often, and their sites often move to different URLs as a result.

- AllFusion Component Modeler (http://www3.ca.com/Solutions/Product.asp?ID=1003)

- Borland Together Control Center (http://www.togethersoft.com/products/controlcenter/index.jsp;jsessionid=8siqyvxsa1.www6)

- Describe (http://www.embarcadero.com/products/describe/index.asp)

- GRADE Modeler (http://www.gradetools.com/)

- MacA&D (http://www.excelsoftware.com/maca&dproducts.html)

- MagicDraw (http://www.nomagic.com/magicdrawuml)

- Microsoft Visio 2003 Professional (http://www.microsoft.com/office/visio/prodinfo/default.mspx)

- ObjectDomain (http://www.objectdomain.com)

- OptimalJ (http://www.compuware.com/products/optimalj/)

- Poseidon for UML (http://www.gentleware.com/products/index.php3)

- Rhapsody (http://www.ilogix.com)

- Rational Rose (http://www.rational.com/products/rose/index.jsp)

- Rational XDE (http://www.rational.com/products/xde/index.jsp)

- Simply Objects Modeller (http://www.adaptive-arts.com)

- Software through Pictures UML (http://www.aonix.com/content/products/stp/uml.html)

- System Architect (http://www.popkin.com/products/sa2001/product.htm)

- Visible Analyst (http://www.visible.com/Products/Analyst/vaooedition.html)

- WinA&D (http://www.excelsoftware.com/wina&dproducts.html)

- WithClass (http://www.microgold.com)

Bibliography

Adams, Scott. *The Dilbert Principle.* New York: HarperBusiness, 1997. ISBN: 0887308589. All the manager jokes you could ever need, coupled with Adams' vision of how to improve management.

Ambler, Scott W. *Agile Modeling: Effective Practices for eXtreme Programming and the Unified Process.* New York: John Wiley & Sons, Inc., 2002. ISBN: 0-471-20282-7. A great book to inspire a pragmatic approach to modeling.

Ambler, Scott W. *The Elements of UML Style.* New York: Cambridge University Press, 2003. ISBN: 0521525470. An even better pragmatic approach. Ambler provides 247 short, useful guidelines for better modeling with UML; and of those, I disagree with three (one rather strongly). The rest range from "OK, I guess" to "Right on!" to "Gee, I wish I'd thought of that!" After you read *UML Distilled* and *Applying Use Cases*, *The Elements of UML Style* should be next on your list.

Beck, Kent. *Extreme Programming Explained: Embrace Change.* Reading, Massachusetts: Addison Wesley Professional, 2000. ISBN: 0-201-61641-6. Ignore the hype. Ignore the cult-like fanaticism of the XP adherents. Just read the book. Beck makes none of the exaggerated claims that the fanatics make; rather, he simply presents his ideas and principles, along with reasons why they can work *and* reasons why they might not. I agree with more of his principles than I disagree with. Give him a chance, and you might, too.

Boehm, Barry W. "A Spiral Model of Software Development and Enhancement." *IEEE Computer* (May, 1998): pp. 61–72.

Booch, Grady. *Object-Oriented Analysis and Design with Applications, Second Edition.* Menlo Park, California: Addison Wesley Professional, 1994. ISBN: 0-8053-5340-2. This is the classic work on OOAD, and a must-read. Unfortunately, it predates UML, and is written entirely around one of the predecessors of UML, the Booch Notation. This will make a few of the examples confusing; but the book is well worth your attention (for the cat cartoons if for no other reason). The third edition— entirely rewritten in UML!—is due for publication in June 2004.

Booch, Grady, James Rumbaugh, and Ivar Jacobson. *The Unified Modeling Language User Guide*. Reading, Massachusetts: Addison-Wesley, 1999. ISBN: 0-201-57168-4. The originators of the UML explain the notation in exacting detail.

Cantor, Murray R. *Object-Oriented Project Management with UML*. New York: John Wiley & Sons, 1998. ISBN: 0-471-25303-0.

Cockburn, Alistair. *Writing Effective Use Cases*. Reading, Massachusetts: Addison-Wesley, 2000. ISBN: 0-201-70225-8.

Emerson, Ralph Waldo. *Self-Reliance and Other Essays*. New York: Dover Publications, 1994. ISBN: 0486277909.

Foo, Soo Mee, and Wei Meng Lee. *XML Programming Using the Microsoft XML Parser*. Berkeley, California: Apress, 2002. ISBN: 1-893115-42-9.

Fowler, Martin and Kendall Scott. *UML Distilled: A Brief Guide to the Standard Object Modeling Language, Second Edition*. Reading, Massachusetts: Addison-Wesley, 2000. ISBN: 0-201-65783-X. This is the first book that made sense out of UML for me: no high-minded philosophizing, just clear-cut explanations and an outline process. I have recommended this book to countless UML students. Now I'm recommending it to you.

Gough, John. *Compiling for the .NET Common Language Runtime (CLR)*. Upper Saddle River, New Jersey: Prentice Hall, 2002. ISBN: 0-13-062296-6. All you ever wanted to know about the internal mechanisms of .NET. Maybe more . . .

Gunnerson, Eric. *A Programmer's Introduction to C#, Second Edition*. Berkeley, California: Apress, 2001. ISBN: 1-893115-62-3. A nice introduction to the C# language.

Heinlein, Robert A. *Stranger in a Strange Land*. New York: Ace Books, 1991. ISBN: 0-441-78838-6.

Humphrey, Watts S. *Managing the Software Process*. Boston: Addison-Wesley, 1989. ISBN: 0-201-18095-2. This is the book that introduced the Capability Maturity Model, or CMM. That statement either impressed you or frightened you, depending on your view of formal processes and process improvement.

Jacobson, Ivar, Grady Booch, and James Rumbaugh. *The Unified Software Development Process*. Reading, Massachusetts: Addison-Wesley, 1999. ISBN: 0-201-57169-2. The originators of the UML explain their process for software development.

King, Stephen. *On Writing: a Memoir of the Craft*. New York: Scribner, 2000. ISBN: 0-684-85352-3. This is really two books: the first half is his life story told in vignettes, culminating in his struggles against addiction; and the last half is the story of his horrific traffic accident and his struggle to rebuild his life. Stuck in the middle is a large chunk of words on the craft of words. If you're a fan of King's fiction writing, this book will shed light on the brain behind the stories. If you're a writer, this book will reveal a few tricks of the trade from a man who believes he has no real right to give advice (million-seller novels notwithstanding), but believes he has something to say. As I write this book, I understand what he meant a little better. As he explains on p. 9, "What follows is an attempt to put down, briefly and simply, how I came to the craft, what I know about it now, and how it's done. It's about the day job; it's about the language."

Klutz Press Editors. *Draw the Marvel Comics™ Super Heroes™*. Palo Alto, California: Klutz Press, 1995. ISBN: 1-57054-000-4.

McCarthy, Jim. *Dynamics of Software Development: "Don't Flip the Bozo Bit" and 53 More Rules for Delivering Great Software on Time*. Redmond, Washington: Microsoft Press, 1995. ISBN: 1-55615-823-8. This book is the single most under-lined and dog-eared software engineering work in my collection. McCarthy really doesn't have as many facts as McConnell (*nobody* has as many well-researched facts as McConnell!); but what he has is *vision*, and it's infectious. He knows what's happening in your organization, and he knows how to fix it—if you dare.

McConnell, Steve. *After the Gold Rush: Creating a True Profession of Software Engineering*. Redmond, Washington: Microsoft Press, 1999. ISBN: 0-7356-9877-6. This book is disturbing—intentionally so. McConnell wants to persuade us that it's time for software engineering to grow up, *before* somebody gets killed. And that's *not* hyperbole.

McConnell, Steve. *Code Complete: A Practical Handbook of Software Construction*. Redmond, Washington: Microsoft Press, 1993. ISBN: 1-55615-484-4. This is a modern classic of software engineering. If you haven't read *Code Complete*, do so as soon as you're done with this book!

McConnell, Steve. *Rapid Development: Taming Wild Software Schedules*. Redmond, Washington: Microsoft Press, 1996. ISBN: 1-55615-900-5. In this book, McConnell does for software processes what he did for construction techniques in *Code Complete*. This is a comprehensive (650 pages!) tour of strategies and guidelines for speeding your development. It includes a survey of a wide range of rapid development best practices, including advice on how to tell whether each practice applies to your situation.

McConnell, Steve. *Software Project Survival Guide*. Redmond, Washington: Microsoft Press, 1998. ISBN: 1-57231-621-7. Pick up this book in the bookstore. Turn to page ii (facing the title page). If the "Winnie the Pooh" cartoon on that page reminds you of your software development environment, buy and read this book.

Microsoft. *The Microsoft .NET Framework*. Redmond, Washington: Microsoft Press, 2001. ISBN: 0-7356-1444-X.

Platt, David S. *Introducing Microsoft .NET, Second Edition*. Redmond, Washington: Microsoft Press, 2002. This is *the* book that really gets across what .NET is all about. ISBN: 0735615713.

Rumbaugh, James, Ivar Jacobson, and Grady Booch. *The Unified Modeling Language Reference Manual*. Reading, Massachusetts: Addison-Wesley, 1999. ISBN: 0-201-30998-X. The originators of the UML provide a handy encyclopedic reference to the notation.

Schneider, Geri, and Jason P. Winters. *Applying Use Cases: A Practical Guide, Second Edition*. Boston, Massachusetts: Addison-Wesley, 2001. ISBN: 0-201-70853-1. This book explores use case modeling in depth. The process it recommends is a little too document-centric for my tastes, but the authors nicely cover use cases as a mechanism for requirements gathering *and* for project planning. After *UML Distilled*, this is the UML book I recommend most often.

Spiegelman, Art. *Maus: A Survivor's Tale: My Father Bleeds History/Here My Troubles Began*. New York: Pantheon Books, 1993. ISBN: 0679748407. This is the biographical story of the Nazi Holocaust as told by a survivor to his cartoonist son (Mr. Spiegelman). The cartoonist finds the story too horrific to bear as history; so instead, he tells it as cartoon allegory, with the Nazis portrayed as cats and the Jews and other persecuted peoples portrayed as mice. *Do not* think that this Pulitzer Prize–winning graphic novel is even remotely funny as a result: it is a grim, personal reminder that evil exists, and will run rampant if we let it. It is also the inspiration for the title of my much less serious Chapter 5.

Spolsky, Joel. *User Interface Design for Programmers*. Berkeley, California: Apress, 2001. ISBN: 1-893115-94-1. A great book to get you thinking like the user of your application. Joel also produces the popular Joel on Software Web log (http://www.joelonsoftware.com).

Texel, Putnam P., and Charles B. Williams. *Use Cases Combined with Booch/ OMT/UML: Process and Products.* Upper Saddle River, New Jersey: Prentice Hall, 1997. ISBN: 0-13-727405-X. If you want a *very* formal OOAD process suitable for mission-critical and MILSPEC work, this is the book for you. Whereas most UML-based processes derive from the Staged Delivery lifecycle (or the Unified Process, which largely derives from Staged Delivery), this process derives from Boehm's spiral lifecycle.

Troelson, Andrew. *C# and the .NET Platform.* Berkeley, California: Apress, 2001. ISBN: 1-893115-59-3. This is a very nice exploration of C# and of .NET. C# programmers should have this book close at hand.

Troelson, Andrew. *Visual Basic .NET and the .NET Platform: An Advanced Guide.* Berkeley, California: Apress, 2001. ISBN: 1-893115-26-7. This book came after *C# and the .NET Platform,* and is much more than a VB .NET rehash of the earlier work.

Whitman, Walt. *Leaves of Grass.* New York: Bantam Classics, 1983. ISBN: 0553211161.

Wiegers, Karl E. *Software Requirements, Second Edition.* Redmond, Washington: Microsoft Press, 2003. ISBN: 0735618798. This is an excellent survey of the field of requirements management. Because requirements errors are so costly and so wide reaching in scope, the most effective improvement most organizations can make is to fix their requirements process. Wiegers can help you to do that.

APPENDIX D
Webliography

ALL URLS WERE ACTIVE AT the time of this writing. By the time you read this, of course, all that may have changed.

Beck, Kent, Mike Beedle, Arie van Bennekum, Alistair Cockburn, Ward Cunningham, Martin Fowler, James Grenning, Jim Highsmith, Andrew Hunt, Ron Jeffries, Jon Kern, Brian Marick, Robert C. Martin, Steve Mellor, Ken Schwaber, Jeff Sutherland, and Dave Thomas. "Manifesto for Agile Software Development" (http://www.agilemanifesto.org/). This manifesto, the consensus of the founders and signatories of the Agile Development movement, declares what these people think are the most important elements and practices in software development.

Boisjoly, Roger M. "Ethical Decisions—Morton Thiokol and the Space Shuttle Challenger Disaster." The Online Ethics Center for Engineering and Science Web site (http://onlineethics.org/essays/shuttle/bois.html). This is Boisjoly's personal account as a member of the Morton Thiokol engineering team that was overruled on a launch decision that contributed to the destruction of the Space Shuttle Challenger and the deaths of astronauts Jarvis, McAuliffe, McNair, Onizuka, Resnik, Scobee, and Smith. The next time you feel pressured to implement a wrong decision, read this essay, and ask yourself what the consequences of the wrong decision might be.

Construx Software Web site (http://www.construx.com). This is the Web site for Steve McConnell's company. Through this site, you can obtain the Construx Estimate software and a number of useful references for professional software developers.

Cutty Sark Trust Web site, The, (http://www.cuttysark.org.uk/). This is the official Web site for the clipper ship *Cutty Sark*, a model of which sits on my dresser as I write this book. One lesson from the history bears repeating: "The company had never built a ship of this size before and were keen to accommodate their client's every demand. Unfortunately for them, Willis [the owner], being so canny a Scot and wanting the best for the least, drove so hard a bargain that the builders, together with their brilliant young designer, sank without trace!" It sounds like they didn't have their design process under control.

Del Papa, Jeff, and the New England Rubbish Deconstruction Society. "The NERDS Tactical Rules for Scrapheap Challenges (Project Management for 10 Hour Projects)." The New England Rubbish Deconstruction Society Web site (`http://www.the-nerds.org/contestant-advice.html`). This essay appears on the Web site for a team of American software developers who went to the finals on The Learning Channel's *Junkyard Wars* series (known as *Scrapheap Challenge* on the BBC).

Gorilla Foundation, The. FAQ page, Koko.org Web site (`http://www.koko.org/faqsite/`). This site contains information on Koko, a gorilla who has learned to communicate through over 1,000 gestures of "a modified form of American Sign Language (ASL)."

Internet Assigned Names Authority Web site (`http://www.iana.org/numbers.html`). This is the organization responsible for registering IP ports.

Microsoft. *The .NET Show:* "What is .NET?" MSDN Web site (`http://msdn.microsoft.com/theshow/EPISODE011`). Hear Charles Fitzgerald talk about the .NET architecture, and hear Frystyk Nielsen talk about SOAP support in .NET.

Miller, George A., Ph.D. "The Magical Number Seven, Plus or Minus Two: Some Limits on Our Capacity for Processing Information," (`http://www.well.com/user/smalin/miller.html`). This article discusses the 7±2 limitation on short-term memory, and how similar limits apply across most of human cognition. Interestingly from a computer science perspective, much of the data in this 1956 psychology paper is expressed in terms of binary bits of discrimination.

Saxe, John Godfrey. "The Blind Men and the Elephant," quoted in `http://www.wordfocus.com/word-act-blindmen.html`.

Spolsky, Joel. "The Iceberg Secret, Revealed," Joel on Software Web log (`http://www.joelonsoftware.com/articles/fog0000000356.html`). Besides maintaining a popular Web log on software development issues, Joel is the author of *User Interface Design for Programmers,* a great book to get you thinking like the user of your application.

Wehr, Marcia, Ph.D. "THINKING AND LANGUAGE," (`http://inst.santafe.cc.fl.us/~mwehr/StudyGM/12Ove_Th.htm`).

Index

See also Appendix C, "Bibliography," and Appendix D, "Webliography" for lists of resources.

Symbols

(pound) sign, significance of, 167, 403

:: (double colon) format, significance of, 200

- (minus) sign, significance of, 166

~ (tilde), significance of, 167

+ (plus) sign, significance of, 166

----> (dependency arrow), significance of, 25

« » (guillemets), significance of, 68, 154

Numbers

0 (zero) in UML diagrams, significance of, 200

7 ± 2 Rule, explanation of, 144–146, 149

A

abstract use case, explanation of, 274

Acceptance Test object in XP UML model, explanation of, 463

Accountant actor, significance of, 45

Accountant Use Cases package, contents of, 242

Accounting Operations component, adding, 337

accounting operations in KMS, purpose of, 490

Accounting System node, purpose of, 420

Accounts package, contents of, 221

activities

dragging to swimlanes in Assign step, 78

examining in Assign step, 78

role in Refine step of UML, 56–57

Activity Diagrams. *See also* swimlanes

adding swimlanes to, 294–308

for Assign step, 78

branches in, 58

depicting Primary Scenario in, 63

description of, 15

evolution of, 57

example of, 18–19

for Find Owner, 125–126

forks in, 59

for Get Owner Name use case, 109

identifying dependencies from, 340–341

for Locate Pet use case, 94

merges in, 58

in Refine step, 55, 60–61

for Repeat step of UML, 105–106

subactivity states in, 61–63

threads in, 60

for threads writing to object flow state, 117–118

transitions in, 57–58

Actor Hierarchy Pattern in KMS, overview of, 195–197

Actor List, developing in Step 1 of UML, 52–53

actors

adding swimlanes for, 78

as constraints, 182

defining participating actors, 52

defining requirements for, 52

examples of, 45

generalization of, 170

identifying and organizing, 191–193

identifying in Define step of UML, 49–50

G

H

I

Objective Management activity in Spiral Process, description of, 444

objects

in Collaboration Diagrams, 473

relationship to OOP, 6

relationship to UML, 4–7

Objects element of Sequence Diagrams, purpose of, 470

ODBC (Open Database Connectivity) interface, relationship to Design step, 87

OOAD (Object-Oriented Analysis and Design), goals of using UML in, 8–9

OOA (Object-Oriented Analysis), purpose of, 7

OOD (Object-Oriented Design), significance of, 7. *See also* design

OO notations, origins of, 12

OO (Object Orientation), relationship to UML, 3

OOP (Object-Oriented Programming)

attributes in, 6

classes in, 5

components in, 6

inheritance in, 6

interfaces in, 7

objects in, 6

operations in, 6

operational constraints, description of, 182

operations

relationship to OOP, 6

role in UML notation, 47

OptimalJ, web address for, 501

Orders package, contents of, 222

The Outline Effect as benefit of modeling, explanation of, 11, 142, 234, 236

Owner Actors package, contents of, 199–200

Owner Info package, contents of, 222–223

Owner Info swimlane, description of, 68

P

Package Diagrams

description of, 15

example of, 26–27

package visibility, explanation of, 167

Pair Programming, role in XP, 464–466

patches, suggesting, 71–72

patterns, overview of, 195–196

pens, assigning to pets in Activity Diagram, 19

Pen Schedules package, contents of, 218

Pen use cases, example of, 54

performance comparison use cases, diagram of, 244

pessimistic estimating model, explanation of, 265

pet and owner features in KMS, overview of, 495–499

PetCam component, considering, 337

PetCam in KMS, purpose of, 490

Pet Handler Use Cases package, diagram of, 237–238

Pet Info interface, Component Use Case Diagram for, 104

Pet Info package, contents of, 223

Pet Information component, considering, 337

pet information in KMS, purpose of, 491

Pet Info swimlane, description of, 68

Pet Interfaces package, contents of, 315–316

Pet Location component, adding, 337

pet location in KMS, purpose of, 491

Pet Objects package, contents of, 215

Pet Owner actor, significance of, 45

Pet Owner Representative Use Cases package, contents of, 240

S

forums.apress.com

JOIN THE APRESS FORUMS AND BE PART OF OUR COMMUNITY. You'll find discussions that cover topics of interest to IT professionals, programmers, and enthusiasts just like you. If you post a query to one of our forums, you can expect that some of the best minds in the business—especially Apress authors, who all write with *The Expert's Voice*™—will chime in to help you. Why not aim to become one of our most valuable participants (MVPs) and win cool stuff? Here's a sampling of what you'll find:

DATABASES
Data drives everything.

Share information, exchange ideas, and discuss any database programming or administration issues.

PROGRAMMING/BUSINESS
Unfortunately, it is.

Talk about the Apress line of books that cover software methodology, best practices, and how programmers interact with the "suits."

INTERNET TECHNOLOGIES AND NETWORKING
Try living without plumbing (and eventually IPv6).

Talk about networking topics including protocols, design, administration, wireless, wired, storage, backup, certifications, trends, and new technologies.

WEB DEVELOPMENT/DESIGN
Ugly doesn't cut it anymore, and CGI is absurd.

Help is in sight for your site. Find design solutions for your projects and get ideas for building an interactive Web site.

JAVA
We've come a long way from the old Oak tree.

Hang out and discuss Java in whatever flavor you choose: J2SE, J2EE, J2ME, Jakarta, and so on.

SECURITY
Lots of bad guys out there—the good guys need help.

Discuss computer and network security issues here. Just don't let anyone else know the answers!

MAC OS X
All about the Zen of OS X.

OS X is both the present and the future for Mac apps. Make suggestions, offer up ideas, or boast about your new hardware.

TECHNOLOGY IN ACTION
Cool things. Fun things.

It's after hours. It's time to play. Whether you're into LEGO® MINDSTORMS™ or turning an old PC into a DVR, this is where technology turns into fun.

OPEN SOURCE
Source code is good; understanding (open) source is better.

Discuss open source technologies and related topics such as PHP, MySQL, Linux, Perl, Apache, Python, and more.

WINDOWS
No defenestration here.

Ask questions about all aspects of Windows programming, get help on Microsoft technologies covered in Apress books, or provide feedback on any Apress Windows book.

HOW TO PARTICIPATE:
Go to the Apress Forums site at **http://forums.apress.com/**.
Click the New User link.